Caged Heroes

Caged Heroes

American POW Experiences from the Revolutionary War to the Present

Jon Couch

authorHOUSE®

AuthorHouse™
1663 Liberty Drive
Bloomington, IN 47403
www.authorhouse.com
Phone: 1-800-839-8640

First published by AuthorHouse 11/18/2011

ISBN: 978-1-4670-6043-1 (sc)
ISBN: 978-1-4670-6042-4 (hc)
ISBN: 978-1-4670-6044-8 (ebk)

Library of Congress Control Number: 2011918106

Printed in the United States of America

This book is printed on acid-free paper.

Table of Contents

We asked for strength that we might achieve;
God made us weak that we might obey.

We asked for health that we might do great things;
He gave us infirmity that we might do greater things.

We asked for riches that we might be happy;
We were given poverty that we might be wise.

We asked for power that we might have the praise of men;
We were given weakness that we might feel the need of God.

We asked for all things that we might enjoy life;
We were given life that we might enjoy all things.

We received nothing that we asked for, but all that we hoped for.
And our prayers were answered. We were most blessed.

Found unsigned at Andersonville Prison compound following the American Civil War

Acknowledgments

The purpose of this book is to provide the reader a history of Americans held against their will while participating in major engagements, contingency operations, or in a few select cases, simply at the wrong place at the wrong time. This book contains a snapshot of experiences starting with the American Revolution and continuing through present day conflicts. Understanding a little of what these great Americans endured is to look into the American soul because these Americans endured horrors that only love of country and of fellow man could allow them to endure. This book is not intended to be the all encompassing source of POWs taken throughout history, rather the hope is for the reader to gain an appreciation of these POWs' experiences throughout our history and then for those that wish to conduct further research, an extensive bibliography is included.

I would be remiss if I did not express my profound thanks to all those that fought for American freedom, held as prisoners or hostages and were never able to return home to a land they so loved. We all owe this special category of Americans a debt of gratitude we can never repay. Moreover, although this book mentions a relatively small number of American prisoners of war, the thousands prisoners of war taken throughout our history and their contribution to our nations freedom is no less significant. All of these men and women are genuine heroes—in the fullest sense of the word.

I wish to thank my wife, Kristi for whom this book would not have been possible. Kristi long ago planted the seed of education in me and through our many years of marriage, has shown me that life is full of obstacles but with the right frame of reference and education, much is possible.

In addition to my wife, special thanks goes out to all that have endured the horrors of being taken prisoner. Although I cannot name all those by name that have contributed in some way, I want to specifically thank some very special people that helped make this idea of a credible POW history into a reality. Many of these are former prisoners of war (or their spouse) that contributed their time and thoughts and in no small measure made this book possible. These include Colonel Fred V. Cherry, Sr. USAF (Ret), Commander Everett Alvarez, Jr. USN (Ret.), Colonel Clifford Acree, USMC (Ret.) (and his wife, Mrs. Cindy Acree), LtCol Tom Hanton, USAF (Ret.), Mr. William (Bill) Wilson, and Colonel Bill Andrews, USAF (Ret). Likewise, I want to thank a retired Special Forces Sergeant Major and currently an American Military University professor, Dr. Steven Greer for his insight, mentorship, and friendship. Lastly, I also want to thank my graphic artist, Ms. Shannon Faulconer who made possible the quality graphics throughout.

Numerous first person accounts are used in the chapters that follow. Great care was taken to ensure clarity and accuracy of the information in this book; however any omissions, errors, or mistakes in the pages that follow are mine alone.

Jon C. Couch
Stafford, Virginia
August, 2011

Diagrams

Chapter 1

Introduction to Prisoners of War (POWs)

In some cases, the taking of prisoners of war occurs without deliberation or active planning on anyone's part. In other cases, prisoners are taken in a very deliberate manner, sometimes to provide manpower for one side's war efforts, while at other times they may have been taken for intelligence or propaganda purposes. Whatever the reason, the taking of prisoners of war (POWs) is a topic commonly misunderstood and wrongly glamorized. Prisoner and hostage events bring out the very best and worst mankind has to offer. Prisoners, governmental detainees, and hostages, as well as their counterparts—guards or captors—are the focal point of this book. Moreover, as the reader will discover, most of these Americans' strength, courage, honor, and commitment to something larger than themselves displays the American soul is at its very best.

Three terms are used to describe captives. These are prisoners [of war], governmental detainees, and hostages. In today's environment, persons may be held in a number of environments and may be held captive by different groups of people, each meaning different things to the person being held. We most often see the term prisoners of war used when someone is held by an opposing military force such as that seen in World War II, Korea or Vietnam. On these occasions, the POWs are often held in prisoner compounds. If the term governmental detainee is used, this most often describes persons being held by a hostile government such as China. As the 2001 Navy EP-3 aircraft incident showed, our men and women can be held by hostile governments during periods of heightened tensions but a time where formal war does not exist between the two countries. In governmental detentions, those held could be held in jails, prison facilities, or in some cases that nation's intelligence apparatus holding areas. Lastly, the term hostage. This term is often used when persons are being held against their will by terrorists or criminals. The term hostage is most often used when the captors want something in return for the captives' release. Hostage and ransom scenarios may be the result of criminal groups, while on other cases, the hostages may be held by rogue governments.

The phrase "American soul" is an important term to understand. What is this "American soul," and why is this important to understand? The term "American soul" best describes the core of American ideals. Some call this a core tenet of American greatness. It is this greatness which is often displayed in the worst imaginable conditions, unspeakable pain and terror, and at the hands of captors—that truly displays the American soul at its best.

A few other questions should be kept in mind as the reader journeys through the American POW experiences spread throughout these pages. First, as former President Ronald Reagan said in 1983 when talking about Beirut bombing: "Where do we get such men [and women]?" Are these POWs who give so much from a different stock than most Americans? What is their source of strength under such trying conditions? And, although many other questions might come into the reader's mind, perhaps one of the most important questions is: "Who are these men and women, and how can the American people possibly repay them for their sacrifices?" The pages that follow describe horror, humor, and everything in between. Although the term "American soul" may seem unclear to some readers, by the end of the book you will have peered into this elusive and nebulous term and possibly begin to understand it.

In order for this story to be told but more importantly for this story to be understood, the reader must be familiar with what occurs in prisoner (detention or hostage-taking) events. The perspective of both captors and captives are provided so the reader can develop a certain understanding as to what unfolds and some of the contributing factors which led to the prisoner's experiences. In many cases, the reader will see what the captives did to prepare for the events, physically and mentally. It is this preparation for captivity environments that often has a profound effect upon what happens next—whether it is being rescued, rejoining American forces, or becoming a captive. Moreover, the prisoners' experiences are often impacted by political, military, economic, and social factors in the location where captured. The political climate within the United States may also affect the prisoner's plight, since governments have on occasion used prisoners as political pawns.

PREPARATION FOR ISOLATION

Currently, the American military has no shortage of guidance for the training of its soldiers for isolation or detention environments.[3] Today's military personnel, government civilians, and in some cases, contractors go through extensive training to prepare them to survive, evade, resist, and escape operations and interrogations on the modern battlefield. Moreover, the personnel deemed most at risk of becoming isolated or being taken prisoner undergo extensive training to prepare them for the conditions they might experience if captured (or taken hostage).[4] It was not always this way, however.

During the American Revolution, such a system did not exist to prepare forces for captivity environments. Likewise, from the American Civil War through World War II, very little specialized training, equipment, or rules existed for those at high risk of being taken prisoner or having to evade capture. Moreover, laws or rules for how American military forces should treat potential captured forces were scant when they existed at all. The Law of Land Warfare was not developed at the turn of the nineteenth century. What was used for guidance in the conduct of warfare was known as the Lieber Code, sometimes referred to as General Order 100.[5] The Lieber Code, officially known as the Instructions for the Government of Armies of the United States in the Field, General Order № 100 provided guidance to US military forces in their conduct of warfare. In the case of POWs, section III the Lieber Code talked to US forces taking prisoners of war but gave no guidance on how US personnel were to act should they become prisoners of war. World War II saw slight increases in guidance for US personnel should they become POWs but the War Department (now called the US Department of Defense or DOD) did not enjoy a significant amount of attention paid to US prisoners of war until after the Korean War when US personnel, formerly prisoners of war of the North Koreans and Chinese, were charged as being collaborators. The result during the immediate post-Korean War period was the issuance of the DOD's Code of Conduct; a moral guide for US servicemen should they become prisoners of war. Formal guidance for potential prisoners of war saw small increases following the Vietnam War and into the later years of the Cold war but did not enjoy any levels of maturity until American and other allied personnel were taken prisoners and hostage during the war in Iraq in 2003.

STAGES OF CAPTIVITY

Being taken prisoner is a horrifying experience and one that no amount of training can fully prepare a person to endure. Nevertheless, certain events typically occur over the course of the captivity. If these stages were better understood the captive's stresses may be lessened. The stages of capture are most easily described as initial capture, movement, detention, and release.

The initial capture phase is the period of time where the prisoner is (visually or verbally) told: "Put your hands up—you are my prisoner." History has shown that this phase may be the most dangerous. During the initial capture phase, the prisoner must make split-second decisions about whether to flee and avoid capture, or to allow himself (and perhaps those with him) to be taken prisoner. Often times, when this initial capture takes place, both sides are involved in combat operations and, as such, emotions are very high. The enemy soldiers may have just witnessed their fellow soldiers being killed by American forces. Aside from conditions on the battlefield at the moment of capture, those taking prisoners are often untrained in prisoner handling. This can be an important factor for several reasons. First, since these personnel may be untrained, their understanding of the value of prisoners of war may be limited. Likewise, these soldiers' lack of training may also provide opportunities for escape that might not have been otherwise possible.

After taking (prisoners, hostages, or governmental detainees), the captors may be hailed as heroes in their hometown newspapers. Conversely, if the captors commit crimes while handling prisoners, they could be tried before military tribunals for committing war crimes, or in cases where the prisoners are released, might deal with guilt for not doing what their society demands of its soldiers. The initial duties of captors typically include searching and disarming prisoners, segregating the prisoners by rank, and in more developed countries, filling out reports of the circumstances under which the prisoners were captured.

In some armies, new prisoners may face rudimentary questioning by the detaining parties. If this occurs on the battlefield, the initial questioning is typically conducted by untrained combat soldiers. If the captors are untrained, it is also possible that captives receive very rough and brutal treatment. Both captors and captives may have gone long hours without adequate sleep, food, water, nutrition, and may have experienced recent psychological trauma, which greatly adds to the stresses felt. On both sides, fellow soldiers may have just been killed, and either party may have sustained injuries as the result of combat.

The classic capture scenario can take the prisoner through a wide range of emotions, including feelings of extreme isolation, self-pity, anger, and guilt for being captured. At the time captured, the prisoner is often the closest to friendly forces that he will be from that point forward. Decisions made at this point include whether or not to fight his captors, to run, or to surrender.

Following the initial capture phase is the movement phase. The movement phase is where the prisoners are searched, segregated and transported to more secure areas and eventually to some sort of permanent detention facility. This movement may occur by train, by truck, boat, or even on foot. Like the initial capture phase, decisions made during the movement phase are critical to the captive's long-term survival. Those guarding the prisoners may be untrained in prisoner handling. The guards may be wounded soldiers conducting this duty until they are healed and fit to resume combat duty, or in other cases, the guards may be older military personnel who were recalled to active duty and assigned this task. The capturing units' guards may view these duties with disdain, or in some cases may relish these duties since guard duties are often away from the sights and sounds of combat.

And, since the guards may be untrained, the captives may have more than ample opportunity to overpower, trick, or deceive their guards in order to escape. Conversely, the moment captives are placed in a transportation network—be it by foot, truck, or train—the prisoners begin to move farther and farther from friendly forces, thus lessening their chance of assistance from members of the local populace should they escape. Likewise, while the prisoners are being transported, they could be detained in such a manner as to lose any sense of direction. For instance, they could be held in closed transportation or might be blindfolded, both of which serve to disorient the captives as to both their own movement and that of friendly forces.

Under some circumstances, such as those experienced in the American Civil War, the movement phase may last for weeks.[1] In other cases, such as DESERT STORM, the movement phase may last only a few days. In either case, the end of the movement phase marks the beginning of the permanent detention phase. Many things change for the captives once they reach the detention facility. They are often introduced to professional guards, trained interrogators, and intelligence professionals. Moreover, captives are often times held in facilities designed to hold others against their will. Sometimes these facilities may be temporary, such as the open fields and abandoned buildings used in the American Civil War, and other times the detainees may be held in structures built to hold prisoners, such as civil prisons or jails. No matter the exact venue, several things change when these facilities are entered—most importantly, the prisoner's chances of successful escape and the increased distance to friendly lines.

POW interrogations may be conducted by professional interrogators. Interrogators are trained in extracting information from captives. These interrogators may be military personnel, or in some cases, they may be police or intelligence agency interrogators on loan to the military in support of the war effort. These interrogators could also be from military units allied to the cause of the capturing forces as was seen in the Vietnam War where Cuban interrogators were used to extract information from US POWs.

In order to move prisoners about in the detention facilities, or to prevent their escape, the enemy uses guards. When untrained, guards may be more ruthless or in other cases, more humane, but in either case the captives will often experience heightened levels of security in the detention phase. Security at the detention facilities is often sufficient to discourage most escape attempts, but in some cases, prolonged efforts by escape-minded prisoners may prove successful. If unable to escape, prisoners must endure loneliness, despair, torture, and food and sleep deprivation before they regain their freedom.

An American prisoner of war's release and eventual repatriation to his home country may happen in one of several ways. The prisoner might escape, the United States government may make a deal for his release, or the war may end with a negotiated settlement for the treatment and repatriation of prisoners held on both sides. Furthermore, when a prisoner is released (or escapes) and rejoins his nation's forces, the returnees will often participate in a reintegration process; now known to be beneficial for the returnee's long-term physical and psychological well-being.

This repatriation (currently known as reintegration[2]) was non-existent in most wars prior to Vietnam. During the war in Southeast Asia, Americans were held by the North Vietnamese, Laotians, and Chinese. Following the negotiated peace settlement, the United States devised a plan for the repatriation of the hundreds of American POWs returning from Southeast Asia. The result was called OPERATION HOME COMING.

Phase	Description	Advantages (for the POW)	Disadvanatages (for the POW)
Initial Capture	• Often within sights and sounds of combat • Often very close to own unit	• Less distance to travel if escape • May be well nourished, hydrated, and clothed	• Captors often front the units–untrained in prisoner handling • Captor's emotions very high
Movement	• Cursory searches conducted • Transportation to rear areas	• Guards often untrained in prisoner handling • Opportunities for escape may be easily exploited	• From the moment this phase begins–the POWs are moving AWAY from friendly units
Detention	• Camps may be temporary or permanent • Trained personnel often located at these facilities	• Food/shelter often better in movement • Strength in numbers (fellow prisoners)	• Profession guards and interrogates–less chance of escape • If escape, much further away from friendly units
Release/ Escape	• May be negotiated release at war's end • May be POW hostage rescue • May end with prisoner's escape	• Freedom (or re-capture in the case of unsuccessful escapes)	• Heightened tension by the captors for negotiated releases or escape (may result in injury to the prisoners

Diagram 1.

Phases of Capture

The chapters that follow contain a small glimpse of American prisoner of war experiences; often taken from diaries, published sources, and in some cases, personal interviews and correspondence with former POWs and their family members. In each of these chapters, the reader will get a small glimpse of the prisoners' experiences from the initial capture, movement, permanent detention, and eventually release phases. In the case of the American Civil War, the reader will be exposed to the experiences of Union and Confederate prisoners' wartime experiences. Likewise, in the chapter detailing World War II POW experiences, parallels will emerge between American prisoner experiences in the Pacific and European theaters of war. In the latter chapters detailing operations in Afghanistan and Iraq, as well as the broader War on Terror, the changes in prisoner environments will be noted for the reader.

The final chapter serves as a review, a look at American POWs' achievements under such trying conditions throughout our history, what the future holds for POWs, detainees, and hostages, and a list of sources to assist the reader in further study. Perhaps most importantly, the reader will hopefully gain an appreciation of how much was sacrificed by these great Americans. By the end of the book, the reader should have a better understanding of the horrors our prisoners have endured and, at the end of the day, realize that heroes live amongst us, many of their experiences unknown even to their own families.

Chapter 2

Prisoners of War during the American Revolution

When thinking of the American Revolution, many recall the oft-spoken phrase "one if by land and two if by sea." However, much more needs to be to understood about this war fought long ago by those aspiring to break out of colonial bondage from their British masters. These young Americans endured unspeakable miseries, and in many cases died, in the name of freedom while fighting their former colonial masters. Perhaps most spectacular, but assuredly the least well-known, is the plight of those held prisoner by the British during this conflict. This is a story of great sorrow. It is also a story that inspires pride in all of us because of how these early Americans conducted themselves under the worst of conditions. Yet, this is also a story that clearly demonstrates the harm one man can inflict upon another.

The genesis for America's struggle for independence occurred decades prior to those famous shots heard "round the world." The American Revolution was slow in coming, owing to many events and circumstances—some of which would later have an impact on those unlucky enough to become captives of the British. During the early to mid-eighteenth century, the British Empire experienced severe economic woes due to an ongoing struggle for global dominance with Spain and France. To raise money, the British levied additional taxes on its North American colonies. In addition to the taxes levied upon its subjects, the British soldiers were quartered in the homes of the colonists. Both of these actions contributed to the American Revolution.[1] Moreover, the British saw the colonists as ruffians and, in many cases, persons who did not deserve the honorable treatment afforded to combatants due to what it viewed as treasonous acts against the crown.

Due to the Crown's thirst for more territory, additional soldiers were required to take, hold, and often protect these newly acquired lands. For these security tasks, the British used its own citizens, mercenaries (the Hessians), as well as the colonists. When colonists were recruited for the King, one of the first consequences was these subjects-turned-soldiers being sent to serve in locations great distances from their homes—often for extended periods of time. This method of recruitment caused friction because the recruited soldiers, often far from their homes, could not protect their families or tend to their crops. Perhaps most importantly, they could not conduct their merchant business, which often caused severe economic hardships. A system was eventually developed under which the colonists could hire replacements to serve on their behalf, but this did not entirely remove the colonists' stress.

Colonists were, by and large, a very hardy stock: self-reliant, excellent outdoorsmen, and accustomed to the "Spartan" way of life in the Americas. This combination of outdoor acumen and self-reliance often served as an excellent foundation for top-notch soldiers. Those chosen to serve in the colonists' place did not always meet this same standard, and resentment soon developed.

The British generally believed the colonial militia were unfit as soldiers after witnessing the colonists sometimes deserting their ranks. Often, these desertions were often not out of fear, but from the need to help their families. This resentment and lack of respect likely manifested itself through harsher treatment of the colonists when they were captured in the coming revolution.[2] By this time, George Washington secured a fine reputation as a leader of men on the battlefield. In fact, as "hostilities approached, he was chosen by the independent companies, formed through the northern parts of Virginia, to command them; and was elected a member of the first congress which met at Philadelphia."[3]

To understand the plight of the Revolutionary War POWs, the entire war's history will not be told, nor will all of George Washington's exploits be detailed. Instead, the conditions and circumstances of prisoners of war taken by the British are highlighted. These include enlisted prisoners, officers taken prisoner, as well as accounts of their varying conditions by geographic location, e.g. in New York City as opposed to prison ships, or in other cases, southern Colonist vessels captured at sea with those prisoners taken to New York, Great Britain, France, and in some cases, various Caribbean islands.[4]

Many of those Americans taken prisoner in the late fall of 1776 included members of the "Flying Camp". These soldiers, called the "Flying Camp" of Pennsylvania, and were one hundred and thirty strong. These men served under Captain Michael Cresap. Captain Cresap and his men bore the brunt of British resentment not only because of their outdoors skills but also due to their fighting abilities. Many of Cresap's men had proven themselves in battle against the Indians.[5]

These soldiers' marksmanship was highlighted in several pieces of literature of the time. According to these pieces of literature, the men held informal shooting contests in which someone (often a brother or close friend) held a piece of wood in his hand with a small target attached while his comrade shot the target, often from incredible ranges considering the accuracy of the firearms of the day. Moreover, the leadership shown by the men earned respect that would be envied by even the most elite modern day units. In part, it "seems that all [who went] out to war under [Cresap] not only [paid] the most willing obedience to him as their commander, but in every instance of distress look[ed] up to him as their friend and father."[6] By any measure, respect by subordinates like this is earned by true leaders of men while on the field of battle.

The Flying Camp was not the only force to meet the British on the battlefield during the summer and fall of 1776. General Washington called up other units as well, including two independent companies that served in the siege of Boston.[7] Captains Stephenson from Frederick, Virginia and Morgan from Winchester, Virginia commanded the first two companies to be raised in the state for continental service.[8] When news of these companies being raised surfaced, a great race ensued to see which company would be manned the quickest, since both companies wanted to be the first active units in Virginia.

Both companies were raised to full strength in less than a week but the records do not reflect who won the honor of being the first company raised in support of the revolution. June 14, 1775 marked the day that George Washington became "General, and Commander-in-chief of the armies of the United Colonies, and all the forces now raised, or to be raised by them."[9] From this date forward, the officers and men of the Colonial armies and state militias captured in battle should have been afforded the same rights as other combatants of the day—but they were not.

By July 16, 1776, two companies were suitably armed and equipped for service against the British. By early September, following their initial training, the companies marched into the area south of New York and Fort Washington to assist in the fort's defense. The 15th of November saw the British and Americans pitched in battle. The British commander General Pattison appeared demanding that the Americans surrender in light of the British preparations for storming of the American defensive positions. The Americans declined the offer of surrender and on the next morning the battle intensified.[10]

The British used their artillery to clear the hill ahead of their advancing ground forces. The British eventually took the hill, and with it, two thousand American prisoners. But this was not done free of costs to the British. Before winning the battle, the British were partly repulsed and suffered numerous casualties. The American forces were tired and dehydrated; their ranks included many wounded (including numerous in command positions). Finally, by about two o'clock in the afternoon, the British took possession of the hill. By sundown, the British were within 100 yards of the fort. Finding themselves in a no-win situation, the American leadership "dispatched a flag to Gen. How [Howe] who commanded in person, proposing to surrender on conditions . . ."[11]

CAPTURE AND MOVEMENT

At the time of its capture, the American garrison occupying Fort Washington numbered 2,673 enlisted men and 210 officers.[12] When captured, the men's' weapons were taken and they were moved to the "White House" (no relation to the present building in Washington, DC). Instead of being treated as previously agreed to in the terms of surrender, the men's baggage, clothing (including hats viewed as valuable), and other prized possessions were taken from them. They were subjected to foul language and physical abuse. Unfortunately, this would not be the last time their British captors treated their prisoners poorly.

By November 18, 1776, the third day following their capture, the American prisoners marched from Fort Washington to New York City—a distance of 14 miles.[13] Upon their arrival in New York City, the prisoners were fed raw pork and spoiled biscuits. It was at this point that the treatment of the officers and enlisted men took a marked and terrible turn. The officers were paroled, which meant that they were confined to a certain area of New York City. These officers were forced to beg for food and stay in quarters without heat or proper beds. Moreover the men were forced to sleep on straw laid out on the ground.

The enlisted men, on the other hand, were given little food and forced to live in buildings without heat. In many instances, the prisoners were confined to such cramped quarters that no more than a few of the prisoners could sleep at any one time. It was said that these conditions were so appalling than in just over two months, 1,900 of the 2,673 original enlisted who were captured at Fort Washington perished.[14]

During these times of great stress, one would expect to see the worst come out in the prisoners—but in most cases, the officers and enlisted soldiers alike went to extraordinary lengths to assist fellow Americans in need—a feature they held in common with Americans to the present day. One demonstration of this selflessness was seen through the actions of an American officer held prisoner in New York City. In part, while "in New York Major Williams received from a friend about forty silver dollars. He was still down with his wound, but requested Captain Shepherd, your Father and myself to come to his room, and there lent each of us ten Dollars, which enabled each of us to purchase a pair shoes, a shirt, and some other small matters: this liberality however, gave some offence. Major Williams was a Marylander, and to assist a Virginian, in preference to a Marylander, was a Crime almost unpardonable. It however passed off, as it so happened there were some refugees in New York from Maryland who had generosity enough to relieve the pressing wants of a few of their former acquaintances."[15]

Likewise, and as would be seen in latter wars, efforts to rescue captive American prisoners were considered and many times planned for, but unfortunately such plans were generally discovered by the British before they could be executed. In part, during

> *"the fall of 1777 the British Commander was informed a plan was forming by a party of Americans to pass over to Long Island and sweep us off, release us from captivity. There were then on the Island about three hundred American officers prisoners. We were of course ordered off immediately, and placed on board of two large transports in the North River, as prison ships, where we*

> *remained but about 18 days, but it being Very Cold, and we Confined between decks, the Steam and breath of 150 men soon gave us Coughs, then fevers, and had we not been removed back to our billets I believe One half would have died in six weeks." . . . .*[16]

Like prisoners that would follow, attempts were made to maintain morale while being detained in such hellish conditions. In this case, some prisoners engaged in limited forms of physical and mental activity that undoubtedly staved off some of the effects of their brutal confinement. Among these activities were playing cards, running, jumping, wrestling, and throwing heavy objects.[17]

The numbers of prisoners detained by the British in New York City (and harbor) eventually rose to four thousand. In many cases, the exact places of confinement and specific details of the deaths of many Americans will never be known. However, known holding locations included former jails, three sugar houses, churches, the Columbia College, and the New York hospital. All were used to detain and starve American prisoners of war. Of the three sugar houses used, the Rhinelander's Sugar House, located at the corner of William and Duane streets, was considered the most heinous.[18] Another detention location was the North Dutch Church. All of these locations had several things in common: no heat, little to no food, and cruelty demonstrated by the guards (British soldiers, Hessians mercenaries, and Loyalists). Loyalists were colonists who sided with the British cause and in some cases aided the British during the Revolution. American prisoners of war were not destined for these New York City locations alone, however. The British also used ships to house their prisoners. These ships would turn out to be floating hell for the men held in them.

PRISON SHIPS

One of the harshest of environments for man to serve in is the sea. In the case of prison conditions during the Revolutionary War, the sea proved doubly harsh for the men confined to British ships. The events leading up to the taking of these maritime soldiers are often predictable. The ships would be trapped in coves or other disadvantageous positions, leading to the crew's surrender followed by the ship's sinking or in some cases, the captured ships were taken back to New York harbor and thereafter used in the service of the crown. Unlike their counterparts taken prisoner on land, those captured at sea were not separated by rank during confinement. The prisoners were kept together below deck with no more than twenty minutes of sunlight per day. In some cases, the prisoners were not allowed above deck at all. The conditions below deck were similar to those suffered in ground prison locations: cold, damp, despairing, and disease-ridden.

Diagram 2.

Revolutionary War Prison Ship

(Courtesy of US National Archives)

In one Revolutionary era periodical (*Southern Literary Messenger) American* naval prisoners' experiences were described. In part,

> *"But of all the sufferings in these troublous times none endured such horrors as did those Americans who were so unfortunate as to become prisoners of war to the British. They were treated more as felons than as honorable enemies. It can scarcely be credited that an enlightened people would thus have been so lost to the common instincts of humanity, as were they in their conduct towards men of the same blood, and speaking the same language with themselves. True it is they sometimes excused the cruelty of their procedures by avowing in many instances their prisoners were deserters from the English flag, and were*

> *to be dealt with accordingly. Be this as it may, no instance is on record where a Tory whom the Americans had good cause to regard as a traitor, was visited with the severities which characterized the treatment of the ordinary military captives, on the part of the English authorities. * * * The patriotic seamen of the Virginia navy were no exceptions to the rule when they fell into the hands of the more powerful lords of the ocean. They were carried in numbers to Bermuda, and to the West Indies, and cast into loathsome and pestilential prisons, from which a few sometimes managed to escape, at the peril of their lives. Respect of position and rank found no favor in the eyes of their ungenerous captors, and no appeal could reach their hearts except through the promises of bribes. Many languished and died in those places, away from country and friends, whose fate was not known until long after they had passed away. But it was not altogether abroad that they were so cruelly maltreated. The record of their sufferings in the prisons of the enemy, in our own country, is left to testify against these relentless persecutors."*[19]

In a separate periodical, The *Connecticut Journal* of January 30, 1777, recorded the sufferings of these men. In part,

> *"As soon as they were taken they were robbed of all their baggage; of whatever money they had, though it were of paper; of their silver shoe buckles and knee buckles, etc.; and many were stripped almost of their clothes. Especially*

those who had good clothes were stripped at once, being told that such were 'too good for rebels.'

Thus deprived of their clothes and baggage, they were unable to shift even their linen, and were obliged to wear the same shirts for even three or four months together, whereby they became extremely nasty; and this of itself was sufficient to bring on them many mortal diseases.

After they were taken they were in the first place put on board the ships, and thrust down into the hold, where not a breath of fresh air could be obtained, and they were nearly suffocated for want of air.

Some who were taken at Fort Washington were first in this manner thrust down into the holds of vessels in such numbers that even in the cold season of November they could scarcely bear any clothes on them, being kept in a constant sweat. Yet these same persons, after lying in this situation awhile, till the pores of their bodies were as perfectly open as possible, were of a sudden taken out and put into some of the churches of New York, without covering, or a spark of fire, where they suffered as much by the cold as they did by the sweating stagnation of the air in the other situation; and the consequence was that they took such colds as brought on the most fatal diseases, and swept them off almost beyond conception."[20]

Food, in the best of circumstances, allowed prisoners to maintain a natural weight in periods of moderate work or extremes of temperatures. The British were infamous for the substandard food and horrid conditions that their American prisoners were forced to endure. Once healthy men, these prisoners were reduced to emaciated hulks of their former selves; more dead than alive. In part,

> *" . . . both the bread and pork which they did allow them was extremely bad. For the bread, some of it was made out of the bran which they brought over to feed their light horse, and the rest of it was so muddy, and the pork so damnified, being so soaked in bilge water during the transportation from Europe, that they were not fit to be eaten by human creatures, and when they were eaten were very unwholesome. Such bread and pork as they would not pretend to give to their own countrymen they gave to our poor sick dying prisoners.*
>
> *Nor were they in this doleful condition allowed a sufficiency of water. One would have thought that water was so cheap and plentiful an element, that they would not have grudged them that. But there are, it seems, no bounds to their cruelty. The water allowed them was so brackish, and withal nasty, that they could not drink it until reduced to extremity. Nor did they let them have a sufficiency of even such water as this."*

If these human indignities experienced were not enough, on top of the starvation and cold, the Americans faced unrelenting psychological torment from their captors. In part,

> *"Nor ought we to omit the insults which the humane Britons offered to our people, nor the artifices which they used to enlist them in their service to fight against their country. It seems that one end of their starving our people was to bring them, by dint of necessity, to turn rebels to their own country, their own consciences, and their God. For while thus famishing they would come and say to them: 'This is the just punishment of your rebellion. Nay, you are treated too well for rebels; you have not received half you deserve or half you shall receive. But if you will enlist into his Majesty's service, you shall have victuals and clothes enough.'*
>
> *As to insults, the British officers, besides continually cursing and swearing at them as rebels, often threatened to hang them all; and, on a particular time, ordered a number, each man to choose his halter out of a parcel offered, wherewith to be hanged; and even went so far as to cause a gallows to be erected before the prison, as if they were to be immediately executed. They further threatened to send them all into the East Indies, and sell them there for slaves."*[21]

CHRISTOPHER HAWKINS

The plight of those taken while on the high seas offers one look at prisoners' treatment and opportunities for escape, which as already stated was often different from those of Americans captured during land battles. The example that follows is of a thirteen-year-old boy, Christopher Hawkins, first captured by the British while at sea, later escaped, was recaptured, and escaped a second time, evaded by swimming then over land to reach his home—all before his eighteenth birthday![22] Originally from Providence, Rhode Island and following his harrowing sea tales of escape and recapture followed by more escapes, young Hawkins eventually grew old with a wife and seven children.

Hawkins was employed as an apprentice to learn the tanner's trade when news of the coming revolution reached him. Like many others before him, the young lad had visions of fortune and thoughts of the glory of battle. Hawkins signed up to be a privateer so he could seek adventure while seeing the world. During May of 1777, Hawkins set sail in the privateer *Eagle*, whose job it was to seek out British ships and seize their cargo. The *Eagle* was a small schooner bearing twelve guns, six per side. Those that have experienced life at sea will appreciate that young Hawkins never stepped foot onboard a seagoing vessel prior to his enlistment. After being at sea for a short time, the *Eagle* saw her first vessel, a French schooner. When this French ship was hailed and finally caught it was nearly dark, and the decision was made to follow the schooner for the remainder of evening and then take possession of it at first light the next morning. Although there was much disagreement among the crew about the timing of the operation, the captain of the *Eagle* made the decision to follow and monitor the French ship throughout the evening. When the sun finally rose the next morning, the French vessel was nowhere to be seen—it outran the *Eagle*.

Later, following a squall which disabled and nearly capsized the *Eagle*, the ship and crew was seized by a British man-o-war. The *Eagle's* crew were hauled onboard the British war ship *Sphynx*, some prisoners receiving comments such as "put it [a rope] round your damned neck you damned Yankee . . ."[23] Once onboard, and with the exception of three of the crew—Hawkins among them—the crew of the *Eagle* was confined below deck. The *Eagle* was scuttled at sea, meaning its valuables were removed and the ship was sunk. Being one of the three persons kept above deck, the young Hawkins enjoyed limited freedoms when compared to those confined below deck.

As the *Sphynx* continued her journey, Hawkins was questioned by the ship's captain. Among the information sought by the captain were details of the *Eagle's* previous activities. Hawkins relayed to the ship's captain information about the French vessel that escaped the *Eagle's* earlier chase. The questioning of Hawkins, as well as the other ship's steward from the *Eagle*, was done while the two were tied to the ship's cannon, and sometimes while being beat with a cat-o-nine tails.[24] After three or four additional days at sea, the *Sphynx* made a port call in New York Harbor. Once the *Sphynx* reached port, its crew observed the French vessel earlier seen and chased by the American ship, the *Eagle*. After learning that the crew of the small schooner that chased her was captured, the crew of this warship cried out in joy.[25] The crew of the *Eagle* was transferred to a British prison ship, the *Asia*.

In similar fashion to those prisoners taken on land, those taken prisoner at sea were immediately stripped of their clothing, particularly if their clothing was deemed a better quality than the British soldiers. Moreover, anything else of value the Americans had in their possession was taken: buttons, hats, shoes, and money. Like their ground counterparts, after being stripped, the soldiers were commonly marched at least some distance from their place of capture by foot. Of course, this whole time the prisoners were moved away from friendly lines, and like their ground counterparts, without needed water. Once the prisoners reached the shoreline, they boarded via docks and wooden planks used as gangways, or in some unlucky cases, the prisoners were forced to wade through cold waters to get to their prison ship.

After being onboard the prison ship *Asia* for three weeks, Hawkins was chosen to be moved onboard the British man-o-war, the *Maidstone*. Once onboard the *Maidstone*, Hawkins was made part of the indentured crew as the ship prepared for a cruise. Although he was still a prisoner, as a deck aid and part of the indentured crew, Hawkins enjoyed more freedoms than the other prisoners. Hawkins was assigned as a captain's aid and given the chores of maintaining the captain's quarters. Due to this status, Hawkins was provided food that allowed him to remain in better health than those held below decks.[26] Likewise, due to the amount of freedom he experienced, Hawkins did not suffer the sicknesses other shipboard prisoners experienced, since he got fresh air on a regular basis. Hawkins' health and diet were to play a large part in Hawkins being able to later escape and evade.

As time went on, Hawkins witnessed the taking of several vessels by the British warship, among them several smaller tobacco-laden vessels from Virginia.[27] Later, while at sea, the *Sphynx* again took prize ships and cargo, and Hawkins was asked by his master, Mr. Richards, if he would escape if given the chance. Hawkins replied that he would indeed escape if provided the opportunity. Mr. Richards reportedly said "he would or could retake me [Hawkins] 99 times in 100 escapes by me."[28] Hawkins was one of the few crew members who was neither sick nor invalid. Upon reaching the harbor, Hawkins was allowed a greater amount of freedom than expected—he was allowed to come and go as he pleased while on shore.

While moored in New York's East River, opposite Governor's Island, Hawkins and a young British boy, William Rock, were tasked with going ashore to wash Master Richards' laundry. While on shore, Hawkins and Rock developed an escape plan. Although rudimentary by most standards, the two youth decided this was be their best opportunity for escape. Leaving the ship at about one o'clock in the afternoon, the young lads were directed to go to a named woman in the city and return no later than five o'clock that evening. After dropping off the laundry for cleaning, the two youth engaged in a conversation about escaping. Hawkins attempted to dissuade the young English youth from coming with him since Rock, an Englishman, would face harsh treatment if recaptured. Additionally, Hawkins told Rock that he had family members in the vicinity that would, in fact, support him in case of escape.[29]

Rock and Hawkins then entered into a discussion of the terrain they needed to traverse prior to reaching Hawkins's home state of Rhode Island. The young British boy was wholly ignorant of America's wilderness. In their conversation about escape, Rock mentioned the "wild beasts and savages"[30] that he believed to be on the immediate outskirts of New York City. Although the two youths' planning at this point relied more on hope and less on valid escape planning, young Hawkins left valuables onboard the ship to disguise his true intentions. Items Hawkins left on ship included some of his better clothing and a small amount of money. In doing this, Hawkins believed Mr. Richards would believe that the two youth would actually return from their daytime errands. The two did not return that evening as promised.

The next morning, Mr. Richards went ashore to search for the two escaped youth. Starting first at the city's shopping areas and then he then searched the nearby wharfs, all without success. The two youth seemingly left the city. While traveling, the English youth soon grew weary, tired, and hungry, and suggested they stop to get some food and rest. Hawkins thought this would be an unwise idea, and gave reasons for not stopping or not contacting others at this point. Nevertheless, the two escapees designed a story which would hopefully serve as an explanation for their presence in the event they ran into loyalists or Tories. The story devised by the two youth was that they were able-bodied seamen who recently returned from sea after capturing rebel schooners and were going home for a short visit before returning to sea.

Nine miles outside of Long Island, the two escapees took the opportunity to get a health-sustaining breakfast at a small tavern. After eating and not getting stopped, the two continued on their way. While proceeding for several more days and being questioned several times, their story seemed to hold up under scrutiny. At one point, the two were stopped and questioned, and nearly taken back to New York as a result. But after Hawkins mentioned his relative in Sag Harbor, the two were released to continue on their journey.[31]

The two escapees finally reached Captain Havens' house, where they enjoyed food and drink. Havens told the two boys that there were British loyalists and soldiers walking around in the nearby town, and if the two hoped to travel on to Connecticut without being captured they must remain unseen and wary of strangers they might encounter along the way. After enjoying another day and night with friends and telling their story of escape from the British, the two finally got a good night's sleep in beds.

The next morning, Hawkins woke to find his English escape partner gone. Believing Rock simply took the opportunity for an early morning walk; Hawkins went outside and, to his amazement, saw Rock marching at the head of a recruitment formation of soldiers marching down the street. Rock enlisted in the service of the Queen! Hawkins was forced to continue his escape alone. The next day, Hawkins was placed upon a small sailing craft and finally reached his home in Providence.[32]

Back with his family, in late November 1778, Hawkins contacted his former employer and graciously declined their offer to return to sea. Hawkins insisted that his eighteen months of seafaring days quenched his desire for adventure, and that he instead wanted to return to a slower-paced and less exciting life of farming. After farming and laboring for between two and three years (by mid-1780), Hawkins agreed to return to sea after being propositioned by two men while he was cutting grass.

After packing his belongings and bidding farewell, Hawkins made his way back to Providence and signed onto the crew of a schooner as a privateer. After only four days, the vessel Hawkins and the rest of the crew were on was captured by a British man-o-war ship. Hawkins was again a prisoner of war. Hawkins and much of the rest of the brig's crew were immediately taken to New York City. It was here the fate of the crew turned decidedly worse; much of the crew was then taken to the infamous prison ship the *Jersey*, while a select few were allowed to be confined in the city, the sugar mill, and a few of the city's churches which were used to confine prisoners. Hawkins was among those selected to be imprisoned on the *Jersey*.

For three days, the crew was confined below deck with other colonists previously taken prisoner. The new prisoners were in high spirits for the first two days with much singing of patriotic tunes, but upon the third day, when two fellow prisoners evidently died during the night, their high spirits and singing abated. Upon reaching New York harbor and the prison ship *Jersey*, Hawkins observed conditions that were worse than anything he previously endured.

> *"The ship had mounted 74 guns in the british navy, but was old and out of commission and kept in the port of New York for the purpose of confining captured seamen—had been dismantled of her sails and rigging and moored in the East river, but a short distance from the Long Island shore. When our crew were put on board her, the number of prisoners amounted to about 800 . . . . Our rations were not sufficient to satisfy the calls of hunger. Although the british had a hospital ship near us for the accommodation of the sick yet we had a great deal of sickness on board the Jersey, and many died on board her."*[33]

After being onboard for a very short while, Hawkins learned of the great misery onboard this vessel. Many prisoners were forced to sleep while standing or, in many cases, tried to rest in shifts since the numbers in the ship's compartments greatly outnumbered the ship's design and capability to house prisoners. Due to his small size, Hawkins was able to secure a small cubby at one end of the prisoners' compartment in which he could adequately rest. Although Hawkins and two other smaller prisoners were able to secure this location for rest, this location had its detractors. The British allowed only a few prisoners at a time above deck to relieve themselves. This "relieving themselves" was quite horrid since the result was the urine or defecation often leaking to the lower decks—right into the prisoners' already cramped and filthy quarters. During the night, dead prisoners were discovered in the areas below deck. The unsanitary conditions in the prisoners' quarters certainly contributed to the high death rates.

Hawkins witnessed numerous cruelties; among them one of the prisoners received 36 strikes across his bare backside as punishment for pilfering food. When the prisoner fainted from the strikes to his body, water was thrown upon him to revive him, and the beating continued. Hawkins was later informed that the sufferer died two or three days after this beating.[34] At this point, Hawkins started considered options for ways of escaping from this vessel. Before escaping, however, Hawkins observed and participated in a conversation that shook him to the core and likely played a large part in his final decision to escape.

> *"I will mention another thing which added to the horror of this prison ship—this was filth. It was permitted to such an extent that ev'ry prisoner was infested with vermin on his body and wearing apparel. I one day observed a*

> *prisoner on the fore-castle [upper deck of sailing vessels forward of the foremast] of the ship, with his shirt in his hands, having stripped it from his body and deliberately picking the vermin from the plaits of said shirt, and putting them into his mouth . . . . I stepped very near the man . . . and inquired for his name which he gave me . . . . To my question, 'How long have you been a prisoner on this ship?', he answered after some hesitation, 'two years and a half or eighteen months."*[35]

Although Hawkins' memory and even state of mind may have been off as to the actual time confined to the prison ship, when combined with the cruelties and conditions endured; he knew that if he was to live, he must escape. About a week later, Hawkins and a fellow prisoner, Waterman decided they would escape, slipping over the side of the ship, swimming nearly a half mile to shore in the frigid waters.

Now October 1781—summer turned to fall and the prisoners made several observations and calculations to support their escape successful. The holes and cannon ports were covered since these ships were used as prison ships. If they were going to escape, escapes routes through the ship's hull would have to be made and the work hidden from view until the prisoners were ready to make good their escapes. Once in the cold New York harbor waters, the two escapees had to swim ashore, then they had to dry themselves. Following this, the two escapees had to remain undetected by British or Tories long enough so that they might re-join American forces or reach colonist-controlled territory. In their escape, Hawkins and his cohort, Waterman devised and then used thunder during an evening storm to mask their strikes at one of the planked-up cannon covers. Using crude tools, the two prisoners removed bolts and rivets that secured planks of wood. They then carefully replaced the bolts and rivets so that in the event guards came down to observe, the loosened wood looked normal and would not be discovered. Moreover, the two hung clothes to dry over the area being worked, creating the appearance that the area was used for a clothesline. Later, when continuing preparation for their escape the two estimated the distance to shore a mile and a half in frigid waters. These were all obstacles but the two were determined not to die in this floating hell.

To keep their escape quiet, the two secured a piece of rope with which they would use to silently slide down the side of the ship into the New York harbor's chilly waters. They also made haversacks to carry dry cloths so that once they reached the shore they could get in warm clothes. Finally, both knew friendly Americans that would assist them once contacted—they had only to get ashore undetected. One of the big dilemmas the two faced, however, was how to identify friendly forces. How would they differentiate those persons that would assist them or those that would not turn them over to British forces as opposed to hostile forces? This was an issue these two escapees dealt with, no different from present day escapes or evasion episodes. To assist in this return to friendly lines, Hawkins packed a pack with supplies to help him in this journey. In this pack, Hawkins's escape items included a woolen sweater, socks (stockings), shoes, rum, and two silver dollars.[36]

On the evening designated for their escape, the weather was as pleasant as could have been expected. It was cool but hazy with low lunar illumination meaning the two would have a better chance of remaining undetected during their escape. These two (and a few other prisoners that escaped this same night) soon slipped down the ropes. Waterman and Hawkins put their plan into motion. They used the onshore sentinels' lights, as well as sentinel lights from the *Jersey* and other ships in the harbor, to guide them in their swim to freedom. Although the two were almost immediately separated while swimming to shore, Hawkins later learned that Waterman also completed his long trek to freedom.

During the swim ashore, Hawkins lost his haversack. The cold waters drained some of Hawkins strength as well as limited the dexterity in his fingers—thereby causing a loss of ability to hold onto his pack. Hawkins was in the chilly water for nearly two hours at that point. Once ashore, Hawkins was nearly naked.[37] The original plan was to meet up with Waterman in an old barn, but due to Hawkins's swimming off course, their meeting did not occur as planned. After finally reaching shore, Hawkins, now clothed only in a hat from the *Jersey*, evaded capture and survived the cool fall temperatures while making his way back home to Providence.

During one of his first evenings ashore, Hawkins found a barn to hide in. He believed it was the very one he and Waterman planned on meeting in following their escape. He slept in hay, and after making several attempts to milk some cows, using his hat as a container, he was forced to move on or face possible detection. While evading the next day, a hard rain started, stinging his back with each drop. Hawkins found two melons but, lacking the correct tools, he was unable to open the fruit. Later, hearing approaching horses, Hawkins sought cover to prevent his detection. Hawkins was still on Long Island and, as such, was worried about being spotted and recaptured by Hessian soldiers.[38] When morning grew near, Hawkins again took refuge in a barn and rested during the daylight hours.[39]

As he continued his southerly trek from New York City, Hawkins hid in barns and, on one occasion, eavesdropped as two farmers talked about having to bury a member of their family who died during the previous evening. On one occasion, Hawkins discovered three overly ripe pears and made a very welcome meal out of them. As he continued his southeasterly movement, Hawkins saw a field of potatoes and took a few, but was immediately seen by a young woman gathering potatoes in the same field. Running in a southerly direction, and the whole time being worried about being chased or spotted by Tories, Hawkins picked up a large stick for protection. Hawkins later found field corn and, although not tasty, the corn provided him with much-needed energy.[40] Like many evaders to present day, the young Hawkins learned two very important evasion techniques: unless absolutely necessary, move only during hours of limited visibility and remain undetected by all since he could not tell friend from foe.

Some time later, Hawkins saw two men and solicited their assistance. In this case, the two men appeared to be brothers and said they would have to ask their mother before they provided any assistance. Hawkins asked them for food and clothing. The mother later came back with the men and provided bread with butter and clothing. Additionally, the woman instructed Hawkins that she would lay clothing across a clothes line and, once she was out of sight, he could then retrieve the clothes.[41] Moreover, she also warned Hawkins to not let her slave see him, since in her estimation this slave would raise the alarm. After departing this area, he later received assistance from others who provided him directions to a small boat and oars with which he crossed the channel.

Now four days into his escape, Hawkins came upon another barn. This barn (and nearby house) appeared to be occupied, so in this instance, Hawkins hid until after dark. After dark, Hawkins found a way into the barn, but his presence was later detected by some of the house's occupants. In an attempt to deceive those who discovered his presence, Hawkins snored while the occupants went to the main residence to get the aid of others. By the time the occupants came back, Hawkins slid out through the orchard area. Although movement along commonly used routes or areas frequented by locals is discouraged for evaders, Hawkins generally stayed close to roads so that he would maintain his southward movement.[42]

At one point along his journey, Hawkins was surprised and taken into custody by a Tory, partially dressed in British military attire.[43] When questioned, Hawkins disclosed the truth, fearing that lies and falsehoods at this point might further endanger him and diminish his chances of release or escape. He told the Tory that he was an escaped prisoner and told them of the *Jersey* prison ship. Hawkins was then told that he would be hung by the neck the following morning. A local inhabitant—a doctor—was also present. Unbeknownst to the British, the doctor supported the Americans' cause. The doctor asked the Tory contingent to at least allow the prisoner a decent meal before he was returned to the prison ship or hung. The doctor was allowed to take the prisoner along with a guard to get food and dry clothing.

While accompanying the doctor and Hawkins, the guard stopped and remained at the front entrance of the house. The doctor then explained that if Hawkins were able to get six miles south of their current location, his chances of evading capture would have increased threefold. Hawkins was then taken to a sentry holding area about two miles away. Still later, Hawkins was taken before a British Colonel and repeated his story of escape and survival. After being fed, and more mistreatment at the hands of his captors, he made another plan for escape. Later, Hawkins left his shoes partially tied so that he could quietly and quickly remove them. When the opportunity presented itself, Hawkins quietly escaped out the back of the building and made his way through a cornfield.

Once more, following his established pattern of following roads while trying to avoid contact and sleeping in barns during hours of darkness, Hawkins continued his trek southward. Hawkins came upon a mansion with few occupants and employed deception to secure his freedom. In this case, the lady of the house asked Hawkins about his loyalty to the King. Realizing the lady's Tory tendencies, Hawkins told her he supported the King and their cause but was simply traveling to get back for some rest after fighting the rebels. This deception and ploy did the trick—the lady gave Hawkins additional food and wished him well as they parted ways.

Later, Hawkins met up with a Captain Daniel Havens. After recognizing Hawkins from their previous dealings, Captain Havens told Hawkins to go to his house for two day's safe haven until Captain Havens returned from his business and further assist Hawkins in his escape. After receiving instructions and names of where and from whom to receive assistance, Hawkins departed on his journey. While continuing on towards Providence, Hawkins again met colonists who were willing to help—this time a young lady whose husband was away on business. Later, after receiving word of a southbound vessel, Hawkins secured permission to board and sailed towards Providence.

After numerous encounters with British loyalists, friendly Americans, and many near captures, Hawkins reached Providence, where he was able to reach others that knew of his escape partner, Waterman. They informed Hawkins of his friend's death. Christopher Hawkins enjoyed a long life: raising a family, enjoying grandchildren, and finally publishing his exploits as a book.

SOUTHERN COLONIST NAVAL PRISONERS

Although unknown to many, each of the colonies' states maintained their own navies. The ships' names and locations where they were built are interesting in themselves, but in this case, simply the experiences of prisoners within these navies will be described. Details are scarce for many of these ships, the crews, and their time spent as prisoners, but fortunately the facts are not altogether absent. In one case,

> *"The Hermit was early captured by the British. The gallant little Mosquito [ship] was taken by the Ariadne [a British man-o-war]. Her crew was confined in a loathsome jail at Barbadoes. But her officers were sent to England, and confined in Fortune jail at Gosport. They succeeded in escaping and made their way to France. The names of these officers were Captain John Harris; Lieutenant Chamberlayne; Midshipman Alexander Moore; Alexander Dock, Captain of Marines; and George Catlett, Lieutenant of Marines."*[48]

In a separate portion of his book, Danske Dandridge goes on to provide more details of the treatment Americans were forced to endure by their British captors.

> *"But of all the sufferings in these troublous times none endured such horrors as did those Americans who were so unfortunate as to become prisoners of war to the British. They were treated more as felons than as honorable enemies. It can scarcely be credited that an enlightened people would thus have been so lost to the common instincts of humanity, as were they in their conduct towards men of the same blood, and speaking the same language with themselves. True it is they sometimes excused the cruelty of their procedures by avowing in many instances their prisoners were deserters from the English flag, and were to be dealt with accordingly. Be this as it may, no instance is on record where a Tory whom the Americans had good cause to regard as a traitor, was visited with the severities which characterized the treatment of the ordinary military captives, on the part of the English authorities. * * *. . . Respect of position and rank found no favor in the eyes of their ungenerous captors, and no appeal could reach their hearts except through the promises of bribes. Many languished and died in those places, away from country and friends, whose fate was not known until long after they had passed away. But it was not altogether abroad that they were so cruelly maltreated . . ."*[49]

Aside from the conditions described concerning New York detentions and prison ships, it is also interesting to note that some Colonists endured similar conditions while held in the Mid-Atlantic states, specifically Virginia. In part,

> *"It will be remembered that, in another part of this narrative, mention was made of the loss in Lynhaven Bay of the galley Dasher, and the capture of the officers and the crew. Captain Willis Wilson was her unfortunate commander on that occasion. He and his men were confined in the Provost Jail at Portsmouth, Virginia, and after his release he made public the 'secrets' of that 'Prison House,' by the following deposition, which is copied from the original document . . .*
>
> *Some of the prisoners soon caught the disorder, others were down with the flux, and some from fevers. From such a complication of disorders 'twas thought expedient to petition General O'Hara who was then commanding officer, for a removal of the sick, or those who were not, as yet, infected with the smallpox. Accordingly a petition was sent by Dr. Smith who shortly returned with a verbal answer, as he said, from the General. He said the General desired him to inform the prisoners that the law of nations was annihilated, that he had nothing then to bind them but bolts and bars, and they were to continue where they were, but that they were free agents to inoculate if they chose . . ."*[50]

CORRESPONDENCE BY AND FOR PRISONERS

Although correspondence about the well-being of prisoners is a subject often only thought of by prisoners' relatives and loved ones, correspondence about prisoners started with General George Washington. On June 14, 1775, General Washington was appointed as Commander-in-Chief. During mid-April of 1775, American forces were engaged in the Battle of Boston.

The British leadership viewed the Americans as criminals, thugs, and ruffians. [44] In their view, this seemed to back up the British forces' claim that the two belligerents were not at war at all, but that the Americans were committing acts of treason. General Washington, on the other hand, viewed the war against the British as a war for independence.

> *"On the 10th of June, 1777, Washington, in a long letter to General Howe, states that he gave clothing to the British prisoners in his care. He also declares that he was not informed of the sufferings of the Americans in New York until too late, and that he was refused permission to establish an agency in that city to purchase what was necessary to supply the wants of the prisoners.*
>
> *It was not until after the battle of Trenton that anything could be done to relieve these poor men. Washington, by his heroism, when he led his little band across the half frozen Delaware, saved the lives of the small remnant of prisoners in New York. After the battle he had so many*

> *British and Hessian prisoners in his power, that he was able to impress upon the British general the fact that American prisoners were too valuable to be murdered outright, and that it was more expedient to keep them alive for purposes of exchange."*[45]

Furthermore, the sufferings and ailments of the prisoners did not go unnoticed, and were written about in the official records of that time. In part: "After the sufferings of the prisoners in New York had been extreme, and great numbers had perished in confinement, the survivors were liberated for the purpose of being exchanged; but so miserable was their condition, that many of them died on their way home. For the dead as well as the living, General Howe claimed a return of prisoners, while General Washington contended that reasonable deductions should be made for those who were actually dead, of diseases under which they laboured when permitted to leave the British prisons."[46]

"Until this claim [of prisoner mistreatment] should be admitted, General Howe rejected any partial exchange. General Washington was immoveable in his determination to repel it; and thus all hope of being relieved in the ordinary mode appeared to be taken from those whom the fortune of war had placed in the power of the enemy."[47]

ESCAPE, RELEASE, OR REPATRIATION OF PRISONERS

The methods by which Revolutionary War POWs rejoined their forces varied greatly. Some escaped by sliding down ropes or over the side of the vessels holding them. Other POWs escaped their prison compounds on land by slipping through windows or holes in fences, while still others were only released by their departure to the hereafter. One factor greatly limiting the success of some escapes was the availability of outside assistance once the prisoner escaped the confines of the detention area, be it a ship, jail, stockade, or other building.

If the prisoners escaped while held in areas where a high percentage of the population supported the Americans' revolutionary cause, support or aid for escapees increased. On the other hand, if the prisoners escaped while being held in New York or New Jersey, there was a much higher rate of support for the British viewpoint and therefore much less support for escapees. In some cases, a lack of support for American prisoners was prompted by British promises of services or goods.[51]

In some cases, the British released their prisoners. The Freeman's Journal dated January 1777 details one such instance.

> *"General Howe has discharged all the privates who were prisoners in New York. Half he sent to the world of spirits for want of food: the others he hath sent to warn their countrymen of the danger of falling into his hands, and to convince them by ocular demonstration, that it is infinitely better to be slain in battle, than to be taken prisoner by British brutes, whose tender mercies are cruelties."*[52]

The conditions, treatment, or exchange of American prisoners was one of the many factors dealt with by General George Washington. In part,

> *"It was on the 20th of January, 1777, that Washington proposed to Mr. Lewis Pintard, a merchant of New York, that he should accept the position as resident agent for American prisoners. In May of that year General Parsons sent to Washington a plan for making a raid upon Long Island, and bringing off the American officers, prisoners of war on parole. Washington, however, disapproved of the plan, and it was not executed.*
>
> *No one sympathized with the unfortunate victims of British cruelty more deeply than the Commander-in-chief. But he keenly felt the injustice of exchanging sound, healthy, British soldiers, for starved and dying wretches, for the most part unable even to reach their homes. In a letter written by him on the 28th of May, 1777, to General Howe, he declared that a great proportion of prisoners sent out by the British were not fit subjects for exchange, and that, being made so unfit by the severity of their treatment, a deduction should be made. It is needless to say that the British General refused this proposition."*[53]

In the final years of the Revolution (1781-1783), the British started recognizing colonists as prisoners of war. "American prisoners captured before 1778 were not legally 'prisoners of war'. Not until March 25, 1782, (six months after Yorktown) did Parliament pass a law designating Americans as prisoners of war, allowing them to be detained, released or exchanged."[54] Even prior to the war's end, prominent Americans were involved in trying to secure better treatment and release for Americans held by the British. Benjamin

Franklin, working in France, attempted to secure more favorable conditions and release for his fellow Americans.

Most historians cite the mortality rate of American POWs held by the British as rather high; two out of every three. Most believe this number to be astoundingly high, yet in later wars; American prisoner deaths would reach these same percentages again, such as with Americans held by the Japanese in World War II. In parallel to many other conflicts to follow, a very large percentage of these Americans held true to their morals and refused to capitulate in the face of the enemy.

Chapter 3

Civil War Prisoners of War

Few periods in American history evoke as much emotion as the American Civil War. No matter what the reader's views are on the history of slavery, the Northern War of Aggression, the cotton industry, or any other such phrase referring to this war, one cannot help but marvel at the conditions under which the Americans on both sides fought and died, and all while on American soil.

The Civil War nearly ripped the young country apart at the seams and yet, the Civil War is one of the most interesting periods of American history to study. This interest is heightened by the amount of firsthand accounts of the war's events such as published diaries or memoirs. Moreover, many battlefields were preserved along with the memories that are brought to life through numerous re-enactments. This is all in addition to the many Civil War artifacts readily available in museums and antique shops across the country. In the writing of this chapter, several first-person accounts of Civil War POW experiences were used.

As with the chapter detailing the plight of Revolutionary War POWs, this chapter discusses the initial capture, movement, detention, and finally escape, release, or repatriation phases. Unlike the previous chapter, however, the reader will see the POWs' experiences from two opposing perspectives: those of Union soldier John Worrell

Northrop and Confederate soldier John Wesley Minnich. Before detailing Northrop or Minnich's prisoner of war experiences, it is helpful to understand the political climate of the times so that their stories will be viewed within the social and political environment each soldier was forced to endure.

Many views of the Civil War's causes exist; a few of which will be restated here. The Union view opined the cause of the Civil War to be slavery. Additionally, the North viewed the Confederate States of America's acts of secession as treasonous and one of the war's main causes. The southern view held that the Civil War was necessary since the Confederate States' of America secession was necessary in order to preserve their heritage. Either view is inflammatory but when mixed with wartime emotions and events such as starvation, depravation, and the acts of violence commonly seen in war, a truly caustic situation soon developed. This point is crucial to understand because, although states fought states, and in some cases family members fought fellow family members, when prisoners were guarded, chased, interrogated, or released, it was often this raw emotion that culminated in excess violence towards the prisoners.

The foul language and utterances of violence were not restricted to common soldiers or ordinary citizens fighting or witnessing the war, however. The floor of the United States Senate was the location for one particularly savage incident regarding the issue of slavery. The event, partly recorded here, attests to violence committed even by those in senior leadership positions within the United States' national government. In part,

> *"On May 22, 1856, the 'world's greatest deliberative body' became a combat zone. In one of the most dramatic*

and deeply ominous moments in the Senate's entire history, a member of the House of Representatives entered the Senate chamber and savagely beat a senator into unconsciousness.

The inspiration for this clash came three days earlier when Senator Charles Sumner, a Massachusetts antislavery Republican, addressed the Senate on the explosive issue of whether Kansas should be admitted to the Union as a slave state or a free state. In his 'Crime Against Kansas' speech, Sumner identified two Democratic senators as the principal culprits in this crime—Stephen Douglas of Illinois and Andrew Butler of South Carolina. He characterized Douglas to his face as a 'noise-some, squat, and nameless animal . . . not a proper model for an American senator.' Andrew Butler, who was not present, received more elaborate treatment. Mocking the South Carolina senator's stance as a man of chivalry, the Massachusetts senator charged him with taking 'a mistress . . . who, though ugly to others, is always lovely to him; though polluted in the sight of the world, is chaste in his sight—I mean,' added Sumner, 'the harlot, Slavery.'

Representative Preston Brooks was Butler's South Carolina kinsman. If he had believed Sumner to be a gentleman, he might have challenged him to a duel. Instead, he chose a light cane of the type used to discipline unruly dogs. Shortly after the Senate had adjourned for the day, Brooks entered the old chamber, where he found Sumner busily attaching his postal frank to copies of his 'Crime Against Kansas' speech.

Moving quickly, Brooks slammed his metal-topped cane onto the unsuspecting Sumner's head. As Brooks struck again and again, Sumner rose and lurched blindly about the chamber, futilely attempting to protect himself. After a very long minute, it ended.

Bleeding profusely, Sumner was carried away. Brooks walked calmly out of the chamber without being detained by the stunned onlookers. Overnight, both men became heroes in their respective regions."[1]

The cast was set; violence between members of this nation pitted against one another in the name of slavery, for southern values and tradition, but perhaps mostly to preserve the union.

JOHN WORRELL NORTHROP

John W. Northrop, a Union soldier, was captured in Fredericksburg, Virginia and eventually spent time in the infamous Andersonville Prison in southwest Georgia before being released at the war's end. On May 3rd, 1864, while near Culpepper, Virginia, Northrop's unit moved towards what they believed would be a very large and bloody battle for the Confederate's capital, Richmond, Virginia. Northrop was in an established evening camp, handing out rations for the next day's movement. By eight o'clock that evening, rumors of pending unit movements were being widely circulated among the soldiers. Spirits were high as the men readied themselves for action and contact with the enemy forces.

By the time the sun was high in the sky, the day was hot and humid—to the point that uniforms, clothing, and other gear was strewn along their route of march as soldiers discarded what they deemed useless in the hot and humid conditions. By about 11 A.M., Northrop's unit—part of the Fifth corps—crossed the Rapidan River.

That evening, Northrop's unit—the 76th New York Brigade—moved through the Wilderness area, and finally into Chancellorsville, Virginia where they started breaking off into successively smaller-sized elements in preparation for making contact with the enemy. On Thursday, May 5, Northrop's unit got up and moving before dawn—bugles sounding all around. Finally, Northrop's unit reached Plank Road, which took them into Orange Courthouse where the unit made final battle preparations. The brigade's leadership deployed skirmishers and soon contact with the enemy was constant. Firing was soon heard, both sides engaged in advances and countermoves. Fighting would abate, then later pick up again. Northrop said it was "3 o'clock and quiet all around. We were perplexed, tired, hungry and hot, besmeared with powder and dust, clothing torn, and faces and arms scratched with brush."[2] Northrop's company avoided capture in this initial engagement. Soon their advanced guard spotted numerous enemy units in the woods. While advancing and trying to capture Confederate soldiers, and before having gone barely half a mile, Northrop's unit again made contact with the enemy.

This time, however, Northrop observed events unfold that spelled doom for his unit. Northrop saw his company's leadership,

"Captains Swain and Clyde in the midst of the Rebels waving their hats not to fire.' Then Northrop "saw the two captains throwing off their belts and swords, holding their swords up by their points. The rebels rushed at us screaming 'surrender you Yanks', 'throw down them guns."[3] Northrop and many of his comrades in arms were now prisoners of war.

By 5 or 6 o'clock that evening, Northrop and others in his unit were standing before the enemy where they were asked all sorts of questions, as well as being the subject of much ridicule and insults. Some of the questions asked were about their unit's senior leadership, while other questions were about who they believed might be the next president. By this time, Northrop was very thirsty, as were many others captured with him. Likewise, Northrop and his comrades were being marched further to the enemy unit's rear, cannon and artillery fire was still heard.

Shortly after limited tactical questioning by their captors, the prisoners were ordered into a formation and to prepare for continued movement. Soon orders were given to move out. These new prisoners continued their march to the rear, soon reaching wooded areas where they were handed over to other Confederate units. Throughout the prisoners' movement to the rear, rifle and cannon fire was heard; sometimes close by, at other times more distant. Eventually the prisoners reached a location where they were instructed to bed down for the evening, of course under the watchful eyes of the guards. They had not yet been treated harshly. Was this indicative of what was to come? Northrop and his comrades would soon find out.

When they woke up the next morning, Friday, May 6, 1864, the ground was replete with implements of war, as well as the dead, whom the new prisoners were forced to bury. These prisoners were a mere 100 yards from General Lee's field headquarters, where General Longstreet and his staff arrived for a meeting. While observing the two senior officers talking on horseback, Northrop was awestruck at their demeanor and bearing. In part, Northrop said of these officers, "Magnificent men: but I felt oppressed with the fact of their attitude toward their country, fighting to disrupt it, to maintain a claim of right to perpetuate slavery by unlimited extension . . .".[4] Northrop and those with him would not be able to enjoy this scene for long. They were prisoners of war and things got much worse for them.

These Union prisoners continued their march towards rebel rear area units. The roads around Fredericksburg were congested with wagons—civilians trying to avoid the fighting, military units moving, as well as limping soldiers. The prisoners were told that if they lagged behind or attempted to escape, bayonets awaited them. As the sun drew straight overhead, the men were allowed to rest in a wooded area. Northrop was able to wash his head in a nearby stream and even engage in light conversation with an enemy soldier. Continuing their movement, the prisoners arrived at Orange Courthouse at about 8 o'clock that evening. The prisoners were instructed to lie down in an area of cobblestone surrounded by an iron fence. The area so small they rested in shifts. Early the next morning, the prisoners awoke to yelling as they were herded to train cars for their continued southward movement. The prisoners were ordered to discard excess gear and make room for the prisoners that were to be crammed onto these box cars. Prisoner of war trains such as these carried many times the normal number of passengers—this ride was not designed with the prisoners' comfort in mind.

The train eventually moved out, clanking as it made their southward trek. At one point, the train passed Gordonsville,

Virginia. Northrop witnessed some very beautiful scenery along the way. Once in Gordonsville, Virginia the prisoners were taken off the train, moved to an open area, and searched and formally registered as prisoners of war. Northrop sold his blanket to a rebel soldier and later cut up his tent into strips so that the rebs could not make further use of it. With the five dollars he made from selling his blanket, Northrop was able to buy some biscuits.

By the next day, the prisoners were again put on the train and continued southward towards Lynchburg and Charlottesville, Virginia. Once in Lynchburg, the prisoners were guarded by a combination of older soldiers and ordinary citizens armed with an assorted lot of weapons provided by the local provosts. On Tuesday, May 10th, the prisoners received their first rations since being captured. By that Friday, their prisoner train reached Burkville, Virginia, a train junction for the south side of the Richmond and Danville railroads—not far from Farmville. For the previous three days it rained and many of the prisoners experienced deep chills.

By May 19th, the prisoners left Danville, Virginia and began a southward trek on rail towards Columbia, South Carolina. While passing through Greensboro, North Carolina, and other points south, Northrop was able to strike up conversations with a rebel guard. This guard indicated that he believed the south made a mistake in going to war; agreeing that no one forced the Confederacy into the war but that they brought the war on themselves.[5] On Friday, May 20th, their train reached Greensboro, South Carolina. Although the south was getting progressively hotter, Northrop observed the beauty of this southern town—forgetting for a moment that he was not on a pleasure trip. That weekend, their train entered Columbia, South Carolina and moved on to Augusta, Georgia. After very little food for the previous several days, the men started trading or selling anything they had of value for food. The things sold included their pocket knives, brass buttons, coats, and the like. By Tuesday, May 24th, the prisoner transport train passed beyond Macon, Georgia and arrived at their final destination, Andersonville, Georgia.

After two weeks cramped on trains, with the incessant movement side to side and the clanking of the tracks, little sleep, smoke-induced coughing, chilly rain, and very little rations, the men arrived at what they hoped would be a relief. What they saw at the gates of Andersonville was thousands of prisoners strewn about on the ground; blankets and shirts strung up on small bushes and branches which served as makeshift shelters from the sun and heat. The new prisoners were marched through the southern gate of Andersonville Prison and, after stopping near the middle, they looked around and very quickly realized they arrived at hell on earth, not something better than the cramped train rides, as they once imagined.

Diagram 3

Main gate of Andersonville Prison during the Civil War

Courtesy of the US National Archives

Andersonville was initially established as a stockade and then later converted to be a prisoner of war compound. It is best described as sixteen acres of sparse land (only two trees in it) with a small stream separating the northern and southern halves of the POW's grounds. It was surrounded by eighteen-foot pine trees vertically driven into the ground so close together that they formed an impassable barrier. Sixteen feet in from the pine tree barrier was a "dead line," a point at which the Confederate guards were ordered to shoot anyone that passed. The soil was sandy but interspersed with clay. The land was nearly worthless. Atop the pine-tree outer perimeter were guard positions with ladders which allowed the guards to oversee the prison grounds and its unfortunate inhabitants.

Upon first entering the prison grounds, Northrop and his comrades were shocked and dismayed at the tragic sight. Fellow Americans were walking around, looking more as emaciated skeletons rather than human beings. This was indeed a hell on earth.[6] Northrop, as well as his newly arrived comrades were not yet aware of the prison's deadly rules. Northrop approached a stream to get water and wash himself; having no idea of the danger he was in. After walking to and bending down next to the stream, Northrop was pulled back by a fellow prisoner, and then realized two Rebel guards had their weapons trained on him; ready to kill him in the very next moment.

Later, after getting settled, Northrop and a comrade walked around in the large field-turned-prison to see their new home. What they saw were other prisoners milling about while others laid down or sat to pass the time. Some prisoners read books while others just sat and talked. Favorite topics of discussion included life before the war, their favorite food dishes, their families, and, of course, what they expected to do following their release and the eventual end of the war.

The next morning, their prison routine commenced. Roll call at 8 o'clock—occasionally followed by feeding. On the morning following their arrival, Northrop received a "lump of bread and a lump of bacon"[7] for breakfast. During the night, Northrop often heard cries and was later told these cries were the result of men known as raiders. The raiders were bands of prisoner-turned-criminal opportunists who used force to get anything they saw as valuable, often clubbing or striking fellow prisoners who were unable to defend themselves or those who were alone and susceptible to the violence of these roaming gangs.

Some time later, Northrop heard of a plan to conduct a mass escape from the prison. This plan was discovered and the Camp Commandant, Captain Wirz, posted a sign proclaiming that if any indications of an escape attempt were made, the compound grounds would be swept with grapeshot fire from cannons. Grapeshot fire is multiple rounds steel or lead balls placed in the cannons (instead of the single cannon balls)—then upon firing having a shotgun like effect—especially deadly for anyone caught in their line of fire. All the men knew the devastation that would be caused under such crowded conditions.[8] Evidently, some of the other prisoners planned on tunneling in locations where the soil was such that it might support this escape idea.

At this time Andersonville was nearly filled beyond capacity; some of those imprisoned were captured during Virginia or Tennessee campaigns, while others were captured in Georgia and some as far south as Florida. White as well as black soldiers were confined at Andersonville, including some officers who commanded black units. The Rebels did not believe these white officers (commanding blacks in battle) deserved the recognition or consideration normally given to such prisoners and were thus imprisoned and treated the same as white or black enlisted prisoners.

Towards the end of May 1864, conditions in Andersonville worsened. Water in the stream separating the northern and southern halves of the compound became contaminated; lice were found floating in the water in addition to the refuse and other matter which made anyone using the water sick. At the same time, Northrop fell ill, developing a bad cough, fever, and chills. The weather in southern Georgia, Andersonville was such that when combined with the lack of food or adequate shelter, many saw their health decline rapidly. On a few occasions, the prisoners dug wells in attempts to get sanitary water. But on most occasions, however the prisoners' requests for tools such as spades were refused since their captors believed that the prisoners would attempt to dig escape tunnels. Although the prisoners' food was scarce, they were able to trade or barter for some foodstuffs. Onions, apples, and dried hog peas were available on limited occasions, but the prices were greatly inflated, making such goods out of the reach of most.

By early June 1864, Andersonville was so overcrowded that the prison holding area needed to be enlarged. Moreover, the prisoners were provided some tools to slightly better their conditions by burying their filth. However, the realities of prison life remained—everyday "men die, every morning [the dead] are carried out. The average number of deaths now is said to be 40, although 70 [men] have died some days."[9] The main contributors to these deaths included starvation, diarrhea, scurvy, malaria, and of course, a loss of hope. The POWs simply lived out in the open. By June, heavy showers were common. The prisoners endured heavy rains, sweltering heat, and the combination of humidity and sun, which all greatly contributed to deaths from heat stroke.

On some occasions, Andersonville's Commandant was seen in the ranks of the prisoners listening to their complaints. The prisoners' complaints and comments received did no good, however. Death and misery continued. During mid-June 1864, a Union soldier's head was shaved by an unknown group for swearing the allegiance to the Confederate States of America. Likewise, the raiders' actions during the hours of darkness continued. On July 11th, six raiders were hung by the rebels for their actions against fellow prisoners.[10] Even the rebels running the camp had their limits. Although the spectacle lasted for a few hours, this event was overshadowed by the misery endured by all—day by day, hour by hour, and minute by minute. Only death it seemed could remove the misery created by Andersonville.

By August 1st, Northrop recorded that he was "faint and weak."[11] Throughout August, high heat and constant humidity, starvation, and disease were on the rise. All of these factors were compounded by the prisoners' increasing loss of hope and contributed greatly to the high death rate of the prisoners. By mid-September, rumors circulated about the fall of Atlanta and the Confederacy being in its death throes. These rumors finally turned to fact as the prisoners were assembled for their release from Andersonville. By September 12th, Northrop stated "Our detachment (36th) expects orders [for early release/parole]; twelve of fifteen thousand have gone out."[12] During this time frame morale increased with many of the prisoners while others just lost hope of ever seeing their loved ones again.

On September 13, 1864, Northrop was among those on a train car leaving Andersonville.[13] Traveling by train once more; their trek north carried them through Kingsville, Augusta, and Florence, South Carolina. Although they did not know it at the time, they were bound to remain in Florence for the next three months. While in Florence, the prisoners experienced better rations, but still endured the constant guard and now increasingly cold temperatures of the south's early winter months. At the end of the first week of December, Northrop and others finally left Florence and boarded Confederate transports at the rate of 1,100 prisoners per ship. The ships, bound for Baltimore, Maryland, transported the prisoners under conditions similar to their previous trains: poor security and few rations.

On December 17th, Northrop reached Baltimore Harbor and spent the next two months in the hospital regaining his strength and ridding himself of the many illnesses he contracted while a prisoner of war. Finally, on February 9th, 1865, Northrop was put on 30 days' furlough but due to his health, remained under the care of doctors in his native New York for the next fifty days. Northrop survived the war; many did not.

JOHN WESLEY MINNICH

John W. Minnich, a Confederate soldier from Louisiana, was captured by Union forces and eventually interned at the Rock Island, Illinois prisoner facility until his release at the end of the war. Minnich was originally from Pennsylvania but moved to Louisiana when he was 12 years old. Minnich moved back to Pennsylvania in 1865 following his release from prison, but later moved back to Louisiana to live out the remainder of his life. In 1861, many men, including Minnich, felt the desire to assist in the Confederate cause of secession. Soon, Minnich found himself in an artillery unit.

Minnich was serving in the Sixth Georgia Calvary during January 1864 while conducting military operations in eastern Tennessee when his unit engaged in combat and he was eventually made a prisoner of war—but not without experiencing a small piece of warfare through the captors' eyes first. Minnich's horse was lame and he was separated from his unit, making him vulnerable to capture. On this cold January day, however, luck was on his side. Minnich rejoined his unit, and to make matters even better, members of his unit found him a steed grazing in a nearby field. Minnich finished securing the saddle on his new horse and rode hard to rejoin his unit.

Along the way, Minnich encountered a group of about two hundred Union forces. Minnich was a decent horseman and although his horse made spectacular six-foot leaps over fences and brush, Minnich managed to stay atop his horse long enough to successfully evade capture.[14] After meeting up with a fellow Sixth Calvary member, Minnich and his comrade decided the best thing to do would be to find and rejoin their unit. Along the way, Minnich and his comrade came under Union small arms fire and fled on horses, but not without firing a few shots at the Union forces. When he fired, this new horse was not accustomed to hearing weapons and reared up, ejecting Minnich from the saddle.

Minnich was slightly injured when he was thrown from his horse, and limped along in the direction of travel he believed would lead to a reunion with his unit. After meeting back up with his unit, Minnich slept through the night, and the next day was a little sore from the previous day's adventures. That morning, the decision was made that someone needed to reconnoiter outlying areas for Union forces that might be lurking about. Minnich was chosen for the task. While slowly and quietly advancing through the woods, Minnich surprised a Union soldier by sneaking up on him while on horseback. Although the Union soldier swung his weapon about, he was too slow. Minnich had his weapon pointed at the soldier's chest. This soldier was now a Confederate prisoner of war. After taking him back to their unit, as well as receiving praise from a general for the capture of the Union soldier, the prisoner was eventually processed and sent to the infamous Andersonville prison in southern Georgia.

On January 27, 1864, less than two weeks following Minnich's capture of the Union soldier, Minnich himself was to become what soldiers fear more than anything else on the battlefield—become a prisoner of war. Minnich was captured in an engagement at Hamburg located near Sevierville, Tennessee. Loaded onto a boxcar, Minnich was sent to the Rock Island prison facility in Illinois. Rock Island is a rocky outcropping of land on the Mississippi adjacent to three towns, the largest of which is Davenport, Iowa. Originally the government occupied this site in 1804; the United States government's tenants improved the site's buildings, including the prisoner facility present when Minnich arrived.

Like Andersonville, which was used to house Confederate prisoners, Rock Island was chosen for a similar reason—it was relatively isolated. Rock Island also offered the advantage of being surrounded by water and had only one land connection—a bridge connecting the island to the mainland. In short, if prisoners here escaped, their immediate concern would have been "how do I cross these waters?"—waters that are frigid and dangerous in the winter months. Only completed in the weeks prior to Minnich being taken prisoner, Rock Island boasted eighty-four barracks, each being one hundred feet long, twenty two feet wide, and twelve feet high. Each building had its own kitchen, doors, and windows, and was designed to house 120 inmates. The facility also contained two hospitals: one for prisoners and one for the staff.[15]

While in the confines of the facility, the prisoners were allowed free movement, with the exception of the dead line, similar to the one at Andersonville where, if prisoners moved beyond the line, they were subject to being shot by the guards atop the watchtowers. Like their counterparts in some Confederate prison camps, the prisoners arrived by train. Many of the same comments were received concerning Union movement of prisoners to Rock Island: that they did not get enough rations or water during the journey, they were cold, and they could not get adequate rest due to the close confines of the train cars.

In stark contrast to southern camps, however, Rock Island was notably colder in the winter months. When captured, Minnich was only wearing a light shirt, a thin sweater, pants, and shoes. Minnich was lucky in some ways; some prisoners showing up at Rock Island did not have shoes, which automatically made frostbite and hypothermia immediate concerns. While being transported north to Rock Island, some of the prisoners asked the guards to open the train car doors as the boxcars sped along Lake Michigan, so they could marvel at the beautiful scenery. This enjoyable two-minute view was sometimes used by sadistic guards as a cruel punishment because once opened, the doors were sometimes left open much longer than a minute or two, exposing the prisoners to harsh cold winds and forcing them to huddle together to maintain body heat.[16]

Daily routine for John Minnich was in many ways like that of other prisoners of war, north or south. Morning musters to account for the prisoners, the passing out of rations, over-crowding, disease, loss of hope, infighting between prisoners, cruelty by the guards, and, of course, the elements—be it heat, cold, rain, or sun. In the case of Rock Island, many of these factors were present but, as in every prison, it had a unique flavor based on the politics, geographic location, prison staff, and economics of that location.

One of the conditions unique to Rock Island seemed to be the indiscriminate acts of violence, acts that were often deadly in their outcome, although the intent may have been less severe. The 133rd Illinois Regiment guarded Rock Island and those imprisoned within its walls. As was commonly seen in prison compounds during this time, and to some extent a practice that carries forth to the present day, those left to guard the prisoners are often the very young, very old, or in some cases, those not physically capable of the rigors of regular combat duty. To make matters worse, the training of these soldiers was often less than adequate. In the case of Rock Island, the result was indiscriminate shootings into the prisoners' often overcrowded barracks, so that the result was almost always someone being injured.[17] To make matters worse, since the prisoners' numbers far exceeded the camp's design, the prisoner's hospital was ill-equipped and understaffed to handle the high numbers of sick and wounded prisoners. As a result, many of those shot by the guards received substandard medical treatment in the prison hospitals.

One example of the guards' cruelty was the result of a baseball that accidentally struck one of the camp's guards. In this instance, the ball struck a guard known for his cruelty towards prisoners. As luck would have it on at least one occasion, this violence was directed towards John Minnich. The guard came over to Minnich and aside from cussing at him, seemingly using every foul word known to man, the guard struck Minnich in the face. Minnich hunched over to try to reduce the injuries and this seemed to only infuriate the guard further, unable to strike in the manner he desired. At one point, the guard drew out his pistol and threatened to shoot Minnich. Although Minnich also lost his temper, screaming back at the guard to just shoot him and get it over with, Minnich was further punished by having to wear a ball and chain fastened to his ankle for thirty days.[18]

Another type of violence towards the prisoners often occurred when they were going to the restrooms, or "outdoor sinks, "as they were known. The prisoners' quarters had bathrooms, but these small outhouses were built on the exterior of the barracks and aligned with the dead line. Often, when prisoners relieved themselves at night, they would be made to drop their trousers, and, if they were wearing any, their undergarments, which seemingly pleased the guards while further tormenting the prisoners.[19] One of the more sinister aspects of the Rock Island prison was the unprovoked shooting of prisoners, with no consequences for the guards. One such instance was the shooting of three prisoners while they were getting fresh drinking water from the well. In this case, the hundreds of prisoners lined up to draw fresh water with their buckets grew impatient. To maker matters worse, the water pump malfunctioned. When the pump quit working, the prisoners got impatient—shoving and pushing each other. The guards fired several shots, striking three prisoners; one of whom later died, with the remaining two going to the prisoners' hospital for care. No charges were ever brought against the guards, which is not surprising in this case, because there was much dispute over who fired the three shots.[20]

An interesting and unique aspect of life in Rock Island Prison was the prisoner organization called 7 C K (which stood for Seven Confederate Knights). The organization was started in apparent reaction to a Union official offering Confederate prisoners immediate parole if they swore allegiance to the Union cause, thereby joining the United States Government forces and turning their backs on the Confederate States of America. This offer was made in January 1864, when a Union naval officer came to Rock Island. When the offer was made, more than 660 Confederate soldiers accepted and took this oath of allegiance to the Union's cause. This number far exceeded the forecasted numbers, so new and separate barracks were required to house these men. Understandably, those Confederate prisoners that did not pledge their allegiance to the Union cause felt betrayed by those who switched their allegiances. In the eyes of the loyal Confederate prisoners, those taking this allegiance committed treason to the south's ideals and forever gave up any rights to return to the south.

Thus, the 7 C K was formed—an organization whose goal it was to provide moral support for the remaining Confederate prisoners. The intent was to provide hope to those remaining prisoners, as well as a method to provide plans for escape and continued resistance to the Union propaganda and offers of early release.[21] Interestingly, this organization, and captors' use of amnesty or release offers, is a facet of prisoner life that would be seen again. As in future wars, it is noted that without training in enemy interrogation, propaganda, or offer of early release schemes, prisoners are much more susceptible to such offers.

Similarly, escapes were often discussed within Rock Island's walls, sometimes planned, but rarely executed in a fashion favorable for the escapee. In one such instance, a Confederate prisoner in Rock Island observed the changing guard's routine. This prisoner then acquired pieces of Union guard uniforms through bartering or purchasing them. It was believed that he then carved a pistol from wood, and then on the decided day, mingled in with the changing guard while they marched out of the prison compound.

Likewise, tunneling was also a method of escape planned and sometimes carried out at Rock Island. On at least one occasion, Minnich was known to have participated in escape planning. During the summer of 1864, Minnich learned of the tunneling operations through whispers amongst the prisoners, although he was not able to actually carry out this escape.[22] As was seen in other captivity environments, the tunneling itself was not the most difficult part of the operation. The real challenge started once the outside was reached. Factors to be considered and therefore planned for included escape maps, road maps, populated areas (or areas that should be avoided), waters to be crossed, and of course, people who might offer assistance to escaping prisoners.

Rock Island's winter temperatures made water crossing especially perilous because swims in frigid waters are extremely dangerous due to hypothermia. Other factors that contributed to the dangers were the fast currents and ice. If the current was too strong, the difficulty of swimming increased threefold. When swimming in such cool waters, the core body temperature cools much faster than in warmer waters. In addition to the currents, ice in the river increased the dangers, because if trapped under the ice, one could drown in seconds. Lastly, but certainly not least, extremely cold water robs the human mind of its sound decision-making abilities—abilities that are critical in such conditions.

As in other prisons, one of the first conditions that affected any prisoner at Rock Island was hunger. Moreover, clothing for the winter months was also required if the prisoners were to survive. In the case of Rock Island, many civilians living in nearby local towns offered foodstuffs as well as clothing for the prisoners. When Minnich arrived at Rock Island in February 1864, hunger was the first thing he noticed, as made obvious by the emaciated condition of some of the prisoners. Although each of the barracks was equipped with a kitchen, that alone does not tell the complete story. In one case involving clothing, a nearby citizen who had roots in Kentucky wrote to those she knew from this southern state. After some time, boxes of clothing started coming in for the prisoners. There is no doubt that some of the prisoners at Rock Island owed their survival to the common people's good will as evidenced by their donations of clothing.

With regard to the prisoners' lack of food, diseases such as scurvy were common at both Rock Island, as well as southern prisons like Andersonville. Scurvy is a disease resulting from a deficiency of vitamin C, required for the synthesis of collagen in humans. The chemical name for vitamin C, ascorbic acid, is derived from the Latin name of scurvy, scorbutus. Scurvy often led to the formation of spots on the skin, spongy gums, and bleeding from the mucous membranes. The spots are normally most abundant on the thighs and legs, and a person with the ailment looks pale, feels depressed, and is partially immobilized. In advanced scurvy there are open, suppurating wounds, and loss of teeth. In small towns across America at this time, outside contact by the inhabitants was rare, given the communication and transportation limitations. When these children grew up and went to war, they mingled with persons from other cities, states, regions, and in some cases, even different countries. The immune systems of these young soldiers were often lacking due to their lack of exposure to other populations. This same circumstance was magnified when these soldiers-turned-prisoners were forced to eat less food, thereby decreasing their vitamin intake and further reducing their bodies' immunities to disease, such as the all-too-common smallpox. All of the aforementioned sicknesses were further complicated by being exposed to the cold without proper clothing, having to wear damp clothing, and finally being forced to drink and bathe in polluted water.[23]

Smallpox claimed the largest number of deaths among any of the illnesses reported. Statistics showed that by the time the prison closed at the end of the war, 1,960 prisoners and 171 Union guards died of smallpox.[24] Smallpox is highly contagious and due to its transfer rate, as well as the virus's ability to live outside the human body for long periods of time, the disease's progress was all but impossible to stop at Rock Island.

Looking past diseases, significant change took place at Rock Island during September 1864. The 133rd Illinois unit responsible for the guard duties was replaced by the 68th Illinois. The all-white 133rd was replaced with an all-black unit to guard the prisoners. Now the Confederate prisoners experienced what they most feared; the blacks they once enslaved (and many in this unit were former slaves) would rise up against them. "To look up on the walls and see armed black men was almost more than the Confederates could bear."[25]

In at least one instance, the reversal of fortune was more than anyone could have dreamed. "David Sears, a local mill owner, was delivering flour to the camp one day when a prisoner told him that he recognized a few of his former slaves patrolling the wall. Sears noted the inmates' frustration because 'it was more than he could stand to be guarded by his own niggers.'" Like the white counterparts they replaced, some of the 108th Regiment guards showed hostility, but unlike their white counterparts, it was seen that many of the black guards in the 68th simply exercised their duties as instructed.[26]

From the time Minnich was imprisoned at Rock Island in February 1864, the fortunes of war changed both for the failing Confederacy and for the prisoners held by Union forces. As the spring of 1865 came and went, many changes affected the Rock Island prisoners. Minnich would sometimes catch a glimpse of a newspaper; on occasion, he would read about events such as the fall of Richmond, the burning of Atlanta, the imprisonment of Capt.

Mirz, or Lee and Johnston having surrendered. These pieces of news crushed this southern spirits; the south he loved was no more. As these bits of news reached the prisoners, the banter between the loyalists—those Confederates who did not swear their allegiance to the Union—and the "newly made Union men" increased. On at least one occasion, this banter led to guards shooting some of the Confederate loyalists.[27]

On June 18, 1865, Minnich took the oath of allegiance and was released and put on a train to his mother's house in Pennsylvania. John Minnich later noted that his signing the oath of allegiance was the only manner in which he could obtain release from prison, although for all practical purposes the war was over. Moreover, Minnich noted in his book that he believed, contrary to popular belief of the day, that prisons of the Confederacy and Union were deadly and the prisoners were always one step away from death, no matter which facility they were in.

ANDERSONVILLE VS. ROCK ISLAND PRISON

The prisoners at Rock Island, Illinois were allowed to play baseball, which implies they had the space but most importantly, the prisoners' rations were such that any of the prisoners possessed the strength to undertake such an activity. Second, and although the source did not record the exact details, in Andersonville the prisoners did not have wood for shelter, much less a baseball for recreation. The climates of the two prisons were starkly different; southern Georgia had cool winters but very hot and humid summers. Rock Island, conversely, had bitterly cold winters and relatively mild summers. Heat and cold both kill; be it hypothermia or heat stroke, the prisoners had to have clothing, shelter, food, and water to allow them to survive in climates which were often alien to them.

Some of the diseases the prisoners were exposed to were the same in Union and Confederate POW compounds. Scurvy, the result of a nutritional deficiency is one such example. In other cases, smallpox was seen. The biggest differences in diseases on a large scale were malaria due to mosquitoes, which was much more common in Georgia. In either prison, however, the inmates' general decline due to poor diet and lack of shelter or clothing were perhaps the largest factors in the prisoners' waning health.

The records reflect the true differences between Andersonville and Rock Island. In part, Rock Island was in operation as a prisoner holding location for twenty months. During that time, approximately 12,409 were held. Of this number, "730 were transferred to other prisons, 3,876 were exchanged, 41 successfully escaped, approximately 4,000 enlisted in the U.S. Army after swearing an oath of allegiance, and 1,960 men died. This translates into a mortality rate of about 16 percent for Rock Island compared to 35 percent [mortality] rate for the Andersonville Stockade."[28] The one factor which remained constant in both of the two main prisons was the prisoners' belief in their cause.

DIX—HILL CARTEL AND ITS EFFECTS ON POWS

Most people agree that the lack of formal POW compounds in the United States, Confederate or Union, was justified, because most believed POWs would not be captured in numbers requiring such facilities or material commitment.[29] Moreover, since the start of the war, Abraham Lincoln was in an extremely difficult position because of the Confederate states' secession from the Union. This meant that Lincoln could legally have Confederate soldiers shot as traitors. Moreover, all understood the cascading effect this could have, since the Confederate forces could do the same in retribution. This put the federal government in an awkward position, since if the Union recognized the Confederate soldiers as prisoners of war, this might have the effect of legitimizing the south's position of secession from the Union. Lincoln and the national government had to carefully consider their actions, as well as closely weighing any intended (or unintended) consequences. At first, the Union held the upper hand in POW exchange negotiations since they held most of the prisoners, but as the war progressed, the numbers shifted. Later, on July 22nd, 1862, Union General John A. Dix and Confederate General D. H. Hill signed what became known as the Dix-Hill Cartel, a loose set of agreements on how exchanges between the two warring parties would be conducted.

Essentially, the cartel called for the exchanges of prisoners at specified locations, as well as citing who would negotiate for each side and the conditions of prisoner exchange. The cartel broke down for a number of reasons, however. Among these were 1) disagreements over the parole conditions—that the soldiers, when released, could not fight, which in itself caused many administrative and logistical burdens on both sides. Following the Vicksburg Campaign of 1863, a Confederate negotiator attempted to get paroled prisoners of war that would greatly help the Confederates. The Union forces then slowed paroles of Confederate forces down to a trickle, followed by 2) the second and perhaps the major issue that led to the collapse of the Dix-Hill Cartel, the issue of blacks or slaves within prisoner exchanges. The north wanted blacks included in the exchanges of prisoners at the same rate as the white prisoners. The Confederate government refused blacks being included in the exchanges, believing that if the CSA accepted this term, the CSA would have been admitting the wrongs of slavery and perhaps opening the door to the question of black citizenship. By the end of 1863, the Dix-Hill Cartel broke down—never to be revived.[30]

Chapter 4

World War II Prisoners of War

Readers may recall seeing war movies in which President Roosevelt was shown condemning the Japanese military's cowardly attack on the U.S. 7th Fleet moored in Pearl Harbor, Hawaii. War finally came to America but the Europeans had known war for some time by December 7, 1941. In the late thirties, Hitler's Third Reich annexed Austria and later Poland as the Nazis fought and nearly conquered all of Europe. Much of Europe stood by as this occurred. Germany and Japan's actions engulfed the world in a Second World War for the next half-decade. The reasons the Japanese and German militaries waged such wars were different in their origins but similar in the desired ends: control and influence over large portions of the globe. Once the United States entered the conflict, prisoners of war were taken—and Americans soon discovered that the Axis powers' treatment of American POWs were markedly different.

Prior to the Japanese surprise attack on Pearl Harbor, the Japanese conquered much of the Pacific realm: parts of China, Korea, Hong Kong, and the Philippines. Likewise, the Japanese showed their propensity for violence and cruelty towards prisoner or captives as displayed by their treatment of civilians and military taken in Nanking, China.[1] The word was slow to get out at first but the Japanese eventually became well known for raping, torturing, and mutilating their prisoners—men, women, and children—purely for entertainment purposes. American military and civilian personnel who were held by the Japanese in the Pacific theater soon experienced many of these same cruelties.

Conversely, Hitler's military forces more closely followed the commonly accepted standards of treatment towards Allied POWs. One example of this treatment was the Luft Stalags (or German Air Force Prisoner of War Camps), where Allied prisoners generally received rations and care packages from home. This chapter details the experiences of American prisoners at the hands of the Japanese in the Pacific, as well as those held by the Germans in wartime Europe.

Many readers may have heard of the Japanese Bushido code, a warrior ethos reflecting the best of the martial spirit, espousing civil and humane attitudes about life, death, and conduct as a member of the warrior class. Unfortunately for those captured in World War II's Pacific theater, the Bushido Code was not an attribute the Japanese military displayed. The behavior exhibited by many of the Japanese Empire's soldiers included savagery, brutality, and racism. To make matters worse, the Japanese military experienced very little contact with the United States prior to the war. Most members therefore accepted what the Japanese war machine's propaganda messages told them about Americans. Likewise, most Americans had not experienced any previous contact with Asians. The two cultures 'clash in the coming war caused a very caustic situation often resulting in harsh treatment.

HARRY JEFFERIES AND OKLAHOMA ATKINSON

Before the Japanese attacked Pearl Harbor, Marines and civilian contract workers were stationed on a small, sleepy island in the south Pacific called Wake Island. The Marines on Wake served as protective garrisons against possible Japanese aggression (since Washington saw the coming war with the Japanese as inevitable[2]). The contract personnel (or government contractors) were responsible for the heavy construction, welding, ironwork, and construction of facilities on this island. Among the contract workers on Wake Island were two steel workers, Harry Jeffries and his good buddy Oklahoma Atkinson, previously employed as ironworkers on California's Golden Gate Bridge. Due to varying experiences and circumstances, the two decided to sign contracts for work on this faraway island with hopes of amassing fortunes and then later return to the United States to live the good life.[3]

To get to Wake Island, Harry and Oklahoma—along with hundreds of others seeking their fortunes endured a two-week-long journey by transport ship, stopping in Hawaii to refuel and receive additional stores, then spending additional days at sea before finally reaching Wake Island. Once on Wake, many contractors took advantage of the opportunity offered by Marines of receiving free marksmanship training with the Marines' weapons.

Still war seemed a remote possibility. After working for several months, the airfield was completed and the island was designated as a naval air base. With this new designation as an airfield came a new Commanding Officer—U.S. Navy Commander Cunningham. Prior to the attack on Pearl Harbor, mock attacks and drills were conducted on Wake Island to simulate Japanese aggression and practice their defensive plans. Since Wake Island is due west of Hawaii and across the International Date Line, news of the attack on Pearl Harbor did not reach the garrison until December 8th (Wake Island time). The message simply read "SOS. ISLAND OF OAHU ATTACKED BY JAPANESE DIVE BOMBERS. THIS IS THE REAL THING."[4]

The war in the Pacific started for those on Wake as Japanese planes appeared over Wake on December 8th to drop their deadly bombs, catching some of the American Navy's fighter aircrafts by surprise, destroying them before they had a chance to get airborne and defend the island's garrison. The attacks began at midday on the 8th and continued through the 10th of December. Finally, in the early morning hours of December 23rd, after several long weeks of incessant attacks and the stressing of the defenders' nerves, a message was sent notifying the United States' military command on Hawaii that Wake was besieged and about to be overrun. The message simply read: "ENEMY ON ISLAND. ISSUE IN DOUBT".

Harry and Oklahoma did not know the commander ordered the island's garrison to surrender to the Japanese forces. Along with other island defenders, Harry and Oklahoma continued fighting until they observed Americans waiving white flags.[5] By about noon on December 23rd, the Japanese naval infantry gathered their prisoners up at a central point on the island. The Japanese forces marshaled their prisoners at this airfield—more than 1600 prisoners, Harry and Oklahoma among them. The prisoners were stripped of all gear and clothing and then "hog-tied" with ropes and wires in such a fashion that if they moved the wrong way, they would strangle themselves. By mid afternoon the sun was blazing hot—the men were sunburned. They remained at this location; barbed wire strung around the makeshift prisoner holding areas, the Japanese ominously peering down their machine gun sights at their American prisoners.

As hours turned to days, given little water, having been forced to endure horrid sanitary conditions, and little to no food, the prisoners started getting diseases common to the tropics, including dysentery and cholera. Moreover, the sun's rays caused severe sunburns, while the cooler evening hours brought chills that forced the men to huddle together for warmth. Food they ate, when they were able to get it, included moldy bread with a smear of jelly from their former kitchen area.[6]

The prisoners endured these conditions until January 11, 1942, when the prisoners were herded to the shore where and then ferried onto the Japanese cargo ship *Nitta Maru.* Once onboard the ship, the men were forced into the holes of the ship, where the hygienic conditions worsened significantly. The rumor—or scuttlebutt as it was called—was that all except three hundred of the prisoners were going to be taken to Japan to perform slave labor. Since the Americans neither spoke nor understood Japanese, the prisoners had nobody to tell them what was occurring. Rumors such as this were inevitable. The language barrier also made the internment under the Japanese even harsher since not understanding what their Japanese captors demanded often resulted in punishment for disobeying or not reacting fast enough to their captors' commands.

Oftentimes, the commands although given in Japanese were clarified through Japanese soldiers' use of bayonets or rifle butts. As soon as their movement started, the prisoners soon came to understand, it would invariably mean a greater distance from home. To the prisoners, this also meant an alien culture to deal with, as well as a much greater distance to travel if an escape was to be planned or executed. Many, including Harry and Oklahoma, knew that movement onto a Japanese ship was the start of a very bad turn of events for them—greatly decreasing their chances of surviving and returning home to their loved ones.

Once onboard the transport, the prisoners experienced horrid conditions. "The air was foul, the heat was fierce. The Japanese refused them drinking water, and men went so crazy for moisture they were down to licking like dogs at the condensation of sweat and breath vapor on the steel bulkheads. Twice every twenty-four hours, buckets of miserable thin rice gruel came down on ropes, one time out of two with a few slivers of some sort of smelly pickled radish."[7] As the trip progressed, the men received ominous signs of their eventual fate—since after some days at sea, the bulkheads of the ship turned from warm to ice cold as the ship transited into northern Pacific waters. After pulling into a port and getting more coal and food stores for the Japanese, the ship again set sail. It was at this time that the men started experiencing their captors' extreme cruelty and sadistic tendencies at unprecedented levels.

Many of the Americans were six foot or more in height—much taller than the average Japanese soldier. This height difference was compensated for by cruelty and murder, and initially manifested itself in two forms while on ship. First, the Japanese would take the taller prisoners above deck for judo practice. They would practice kicking and flipping their much larger opponents, who were obviously not allowed to do anything to defend themselves. The next, much more sadistic, form of cruelty was one the Japanese previously conducted in other locations such as Nanking China. On the *Nitta Maru*, prisoners were taken topside in groups of five. "When they were taken on deck, there were Japanese everywhere, a crowd of well over a hundred . . . The five were blindfolded, and one after the other they had their heads chopped off. For each one a different guard stepped up and forced the prisoner to his knees, and swung his long sword. The blade swished through the air. When it bit into the neck, it made noise like a wet towel being cracked. The Japanese applauded . . ."[8] After taking one, two, or even three chops to completely sever the heads of the prisoners, the Japanese would then use the torsos for bayonet practice, finally throwing the bodies overboard when they were content with their deadly games.

Although the atrocities of the Japanese are now well known, most Americans at this time had only heard scant rumors of what had occurred in other countries in the late thirties. Most notable were the Japanese atrocities occurring in Nanking China. As Iris Chang tells us in her book *Rape of Nanking*, there "seemed to be no limit to the Japanese capacity for human degradation and sexual perversion in Nanking [China]. Just as some soldiers invented killing contests to break the monotony of murder, so did some invent games of recreational rape and torture when wearied by the glut of sex . . . Perhaps one of the most brutal forms of Japanese entertainment was the impalement of vaginas. In the streets of Nanking, women lay with their legs splayed open, their orifices pierced by wooden rods, twigs, and weeds."[9] Some of these women lived, but most died and were relieved of the pains and sufferings endured at the hands of their tormentors.

In addition to the cruelty and sadism carried out on women, men did not escape the cruelty in Nanking. Some of the Japanese conducted contests to test the sharpness of their swords by seeing how many heads their swords could cut off before having to be re-sharpened. Chang further describes the cruelties. In part, the "Japanese media avidly covered the Army's killing contests near Nanking. In one of the most notorious, two Japanese sublieutenants, Mukai Toshiaki and Noda Takeshi, went on separate beheading sprees near Nanking to see who could kill one hundred men first."[10]

As the American prisoners onboard the *Nitta Maru* soon found out, the cruelty of their captors knew no bounds. During the last week of January 1942, the *Nitta Maru* made port in Shanghai, China, where the prisoners experienced their first prisoner of war compound and long-term confinement under the Japanese. Once at this prison, known as Woosung, these men were in the company of Allied personnel captured during the fall of Bataan in the Philippines. Allied POWs also included British and Australians captured by the Japanese in China. Like prisoners in other wars; these prisoners had their obstacles. First were the frigid nighttime temperatures. The cold was numbing, even in the best of times with proper clothing. In this case, the fortunate ones had a Japanese blanket left over from the ship. Some of the luckier Americans had shoes and in a few cases, boots to protect their feet.

In this case, Harry and Oklahoma were both strong enough to fight off fellow prisoners looking to take advantage of weaker ones, and industrious enough that they survived thus far with their boots, pants, and shirts. Another potential threat was the sickness brought on by lack of proper nutrients, compounded by the extremely hard labor the prisoners were forced to perform. To make matters worse, the Japanese rationed food; those working got more rations than those confined to the barracks or a medical facility.

Rules issued by the Japanese government on prisoners' diets were not immediately established and, even when these rules were developed and put in place, those responsible for the care of the

POWs often fed them far less that the designated amounts. When rations were distributed, "they fixed the basic daily ration for a prisoner of enlisted-man rank at 570 grams (1 pound 4 ounces), plus 220 grams (7 ounces) for working . . . . The Japanese scale for a prisoner doing hard labor—790 grams—was about 60 percent less than the American peacetime ration. And that was only the numbers on paper. Food actually delivered to the camps was less again."[11] Aside from limited rations and clothing, there were other crucial factors in these men's struggle for survival in Japanese prisoner of war camps.

One factor was what kind of job the prisoner was able to secure. This was true in the cold of northern Japan as it was in the Union POW compounds in the American Civil War. If a prisoner worked in coal mines, digging rock, or doing other work outside, he was exposed to the elements, thereby increasing the required caloric intake to maintain strength. Likewise, the continued exposure to cold conditions without proper nutrition increased the chances of catching diseases or sicknesses that could not be defeated without proper medications—medications that were impossible for these prisoners of war to obtain. This meant that those prisoners able to secure one of several positions were better off: cooking, which meant access to increased calories, inside work, which meant fewer calories had to be burnt in order to stay warm, and finally, jobs that kept the prisoners out of the constant sight of their captors, and therefore less likely to receive constant beatings and other mistreatments that reduced their immune system's ability to fight colds and diseases. Other forms of labor that provided advantages to prisoners included truck driving, working bulk foods jobs along the piers, and other jobs with access to food. Since the prisoners were denied sufficient caloric intake, diseases associated with vitamin deficiencies were common. Among these were scurvy, pellagra, protein edema, and beriberi. Although many nations defeated beriberi by this time, the American prisoners were forced to endure a diet consisting mostly of rice. This diet of rice made beriberi a prime issue for the Pacific prisoners of war. Aside from their meager diet, the prisoners had to deal with not understanding the Japanese language or culture.

To start the day, the Japanese required the men to be able to respond to their commands in Japanese. The fact that the prisoners did not speak the language thus made matters much worse for the Americans. The first commands of the day to which the prisoners had to respond were initial roll calls. The prisoners also maintained wooden identification tags and a system for keeping track of the men inside the compound, and of course, the numbers were written in Japanese. Punishments for disobedience would range in severity, but ranged from routine beatings for minor slights to death for more severe infractions of the established camp rules.

The men participated in several activities to keep them occupied while not at work. They gambled, although the Japanese placed restrictions on gambling for profit or gain. The men also talked and engaged in an all-time favorite pastime of prisoners—thinking and dreaming about their return home, and about food. For example, prisoners from Texas talked of their relatives' pecan pie and fried chicken, while men from the northern parts of the United States spoke of their favorite Italian or German dishes. Smokers who experienced nicotine cravings traded food for tobacco products. These tobacco products were used, in turn, in exchange for other goods—shoes and clothing among them. On very rare occasions, the prisoners received mail or news of how the war's progress.

As in other wars, when news came from the guards, it was generally bad whether or not the accounts provided to the prisoners held an ounce of truth. One method of defeating this false word of the war's progress was through the use of secret radios. Prisoners caught with radios would have certainly have faced a death sentence by their captors—but the risk was worth the risk since information was and has always been vital to prisoners' survival. Various radio parts were smuggled into camp inside pieces of fruit as well as secret compartments in the prisoners' hats, clothing, or shoes.[12]

Once the radio parts were smuggled inside the camp, the prisoners devised hiding places for the radio parts, and of course, the guards were always trying to locate these secret hiding places. Although discovery by the Japanese of such devices had severe consequences, the alternatives were just as likely to cause problems due to misinformation and rumors in the camps. So, the hiding and risk-taking continued in camps—a contest of wills. Whenever American prisoners built something or hid something from the Japanese, a victory was enjoyed. Though small, these triumphs supported the prisoners' ability to fight propaganda and interrogations in such a hostile environment.

Harry and Oklahoma's barracks had electricity, but the lighting fixtures were low-wattage. The heat to be gained from them was therefore minimal—the men stood around the bulbs cupping their hands close to the bulbs to get some heat. With an ambient air temperature of 15 degrees Fahrenheit, the 25-watt light bulbs did not produce nearly enough heat—but under these conditions, any heat was better than none. Aside from light, the men needed to eat.

To cook or heat their food, the prisoners made stoves, which were also forbidden by the Japanese, and had to be hidden. The

Japanese fed the prisoners three small scoops of rice per day, and on the very rare occasion that they made it through, the prisoners also received Red Cross packages—which were of course pilfered by the guards, with one exception. This one exception was cheese, which the guards found distasteful.[13] At one point during their internment, Harry and Oklahoma were caught stealing food and were severely punished, as the rest of the prisoners resorted to coercion to force Harry and Oklahoma into admitting their thievery. Harry and Oklahoma were put in the brig, and after a series of events, the two contracted dysentery and malaria. The continued punishment for the two included brig time, forced standing for hours, days spent without talking to anyone, and reduced rations.

So, Harry and Oklahoma, along with hundreds of other POWs, did what was required to survive their imprisonment—one minute, one hour, and one day at a time. Although, as already mentioned, there were Red Cross packages, International Red Cross members were wary of being too loose-lipped about what they observed, and were never permitted to visit the prisoners. In fact, on a few occasions, Red Cross members were imprisoned by the Japanese after being accused of being spies for the Americans. But the Americans held at Woosung were not the only prisoners the Japanese held—far from it. Allied prisoners numbered in the thousands.

Other prisoner camps existed, as did those in China, and, of course, the Philippines following the mass surrender of MacArthur's forces in 1942. The death rate of POWs in the camps were appalling, but the deaths of the prisoners in Burma that built the railroad were a staggering twelve thousand men, and for some years of its operation, the prisoner death rate was as high as seventy five percent (as compared to roughly 1:3 in the camps on the Japanese mainland).

As the war progressed, the death rates climbed as the food allotted to the prisoners decreased. "In 1942 the official daily rice ration of a Japanese soldier was 850 grams; by late 1944 it was 400 grams."[14]

By early 1942, the war favored the Japanese. The Japanese military conquered parts of China, Burma, India, and the Philippines while those defending Corregidor were just hanging on. Then the Doolittle raid occurred. American B-25 bombers struck the Japanese homeland. And although the raid did not decapitate the Japanese leadership or hamper the Japanese industrial might, it did strike a chord with the Japanese. The Japanese came to understand that they could be struck with American military might. The Japanese Empire was not invincible.

By 1944, food was scarce in Japan. As such, normal Japanese civilians resorted to other sources of food. There was a hierarchy in Japan. At the top was the royalty and military—since they defended the country. In the middle were ordinary civilians, and at the bottom were the POWs. For Harry and Oklahoma, this meant continued bartering. They had to maintain their diets and health until they could regain their freedom. At the same time, the American military tightened its grip on the Pacific, surrounding the Japanese islands one at a time and retaking formerly Japanese-held territories. In some cases, the Japanese made plans to kill all of their prisoners before withdrawing from POW compounds. This was the case in the Philippines, where Americans there had to carefully time their escape according to the advancing Americans—if they left too early, they would starve in the jungles, and if they were too late, they would be mowed down by the Japanese machine guns prior to their captors' withdrawal.

At this point in the war, it was a game of pure survival for Harry and Oklahoma. They had to remain healthy enough for liberation or release. Being on Japan's mainland, even if their escape from imprisonment was successful, the likelihood of escapees receiving aid from Japanese civilians was highly doubtful. At this point in their confinements, they were in differing degrees of health. Harry had amoebic dysentery with recurring bouts of malaria, while Oklahoma's health was still surprisingly good. The camp Harry and Oklahoma were in was known as Kawasaki 5, "known as Dispatch Camp, on Honshu between Tokyo and Yokohama. This camp supplied workers for steel and iron works and, being so large, Oklahoma drew the task of doing very hard labor lumping steel billets."[15]

Oklahoma and Harry made arrangements to work alternating shifts, which allowed one of the two of them to keep an eye on their belongings. Oklahoma gambled and ran his racket to win more rations, Red Cross packages, and other items. As the war progressed, Harry, Oklahoma, and others were moved away from Kawasaki to more rural areas, since the more industrialized areas were being constantly bombed by America's B-29 Super Fortresses. They were sent to an area of northern Honshu, north of their previous camp. This new location was known as Sendai 7B, and appeared to be an abandoned mine of some sort.

Once there, Harry and Oklahoma recognized the camp's remoteness and the slim chance for escape. Harry was still having trouble with his mobility due to the malaria and amoebic dysentery. Oklahoma and a cast of others decided they continue planning for their escape. Their plan was to get across the water to what they believed was Russia. The POW compound's fences were fifteen feet tall with barb wire on top. The plan was for all of the prisoners to make their way over the fence and then meet up on the outside. On the designated night, several of the prisoners climbed over the fence, although a few evidently changed their minds at the last moment. Once over, Oklahoma and, eventually, all the others were caught and severely punished by the Japanese.[16]

The war continued. During July 1945, Japan was given an ultimatum to surrender or face utter destruction. Japan did not capitulate. In mid-August, the prisoners' hidden radios, as well as rumors in camp brought word of the Americans having dropped some new type of super bombs: one on Nagasaki on August 6th, the second on Hiroshima on August 9th. After the atomic bombs were dropped, the prisoners saw B-29s overhead along with many other types of American planes, some of which dropped supplies and leaflets. Some of these leaflets talked of Japanese surrender while others instructed the POWs to paint "POW" on the roofs of their compounds.

Finally, on August 15th, the Japanese received instructions to listen to their radios for news of great importance. In this announcement, the Emperor of Japan announced that Japan surrendered and the war was over. The Japanese sent out word to their field commands to destroy evidence of their wartime atrocities. At about the same time, the American POWs saw leaflets that instructed them to remain in their compounds—that this was safer than venturing out into town. Many of the Americans did as they were instructed. This was good for the POWs, because some of the townspeople took their anger out on Americans during this period. American planes continued to fly over and drop more bundles with food, clothing, chocolate bars, and similar items; many donated by the pilots or other crew members. Some of the leaflets that were dropped said "*DO NOT OVEREAT.*"[17]

Some of the leaflets indicated liberation was coming. Eventually small water craft such as PT (or Patrol Boat, Torpedo) boats started arrived in Tokyo Harbor. Some prisoners were so jubilant to see liberating American forces they jumped in the water and attempted to swim to the craft, not realizing they were not yet strong enough to take on physical activity such as ocean swimming. Eventually, troops, medical personnel, and food started appearing on the Japanese mainland in great numbers. The severely injured were carried on stretchers to hospital trains. Hospital ships started arriving. Once onboard the ships, the order of the day was the removal of the filthy POW clothing, followed by hot showers, delousing, shots, and continued medical care.[18]

These scenes took place against the backdrop of American personnel, big strapping men, and Red Cross girls and women who were clean and full of energy. The POWs were overwhelmed and did not know how to take this. They were weak, scrawny, mere skeletons of the Americans captured three or more years prior. In the hospitals ships' mess lines, the prisoners ate what they wanted, twenty-four hours a day. It was obvious to all except the former POWs that they were not yet adjusted to freedom. The former prisoners hid food in their new hospital-provided pajamas, concealing the ship's electronic devices—all without realizing that they were again free men and did not have to be packrats. In WWII, returned POWs were called RAMPs or Returned Allied Military Personnel. Initial forecasts predicted that it would take months to get all the former POWs out of Japan—Americans, Australians, Brits, Koreans. In reality, six weeks after the atomic bombs were dropped; all the POWs had been extracted. In total, more than 32,624 POWs were repatriated.[19]

The former prisoners faced a huge challenge. First, they needed to go through a process that few understood—decompression. In short, decompression is the psychological readjustment to freedom, the process of gaining a true understanding and internalizing what occurred to them during their time as POWs. These were normal men who had gone through an abnormal situation and then, three and a half years later, were once again free Americans, full of hope and excitement about their future. But these men were still regaining their strength, most of them hating the sight of Japanese people because of what they endured for so long. Although it was unplanned, the long ship rides on hospital ships facilitated this decompression, since it gave the prisoners the opportunity to talk with their fellow prisoners, retelling horrors and recalling events. Unbeknownst to the returnees, this retelling of their experiences as POWs greatly aided in their decompression.

Years later, Oklahoma and Harry both died before reaching their seventieth birthdays. Oklahoma keeled over one day with a stroke and died. Harry's health, on the other hand, gradually deteriorated as he continued to petition the Veteran's Administration (VA) for disability support. His heart, brain, kidney and other major organs were all starting to have problems, and in the end, he was taking thirteen different medications a day. Finally, after fighting with the VA long enough, Harry took sleeping pills and died in his sleep.

JAPAN'S SURRENDER AND AFTERMATH

This chapter in history is not complete without answering a few questions about the Japanese military's actions before and during World War II. A few of these questions include:

Did the Japanese military conduct atrocities against military and civilian personnel, men, women, and children with full knowledge that their actions were war crimes?

Were the Japanese held accountable for their actions?

Why did the Japanese military commit these acts, given what most have heard about *Japanese honor* and the *Bushido* or *honor codes*?

Some of the answers may never be fully explained to our satisfaction, given the thousands that suffered so terribly at the hands of the Japanese; however, those who suffered deserve a response to this question. The National Archives and Records Administration (NARA), working in support of the Nazi War Crimes and Japanese Imperial Government Records Interagency Working Group, sponsored research and the resultant 2006 issuance of "*Researching Japanese War Crimes Records: Introductory Essays*" (by Edward Drea and others), under the Nazi War Crimes and Japanese Imperial Government Records, Interagency Working Group in Washington, DC.[20]

All evidence supports the belief that the Japanese conducted these atrocities with the knowledge that they were crimes. This answer is consistently found throughout the thousands of documents obtained in the waning months of World War II by American, Russian, and other nations' military forces, as well as through wartime signals intelligence (or SIGINT) collections. Americans collected data on the Japanese through a variety of means, as well as employed specialized military forces to do so—the fathers of today's Army

Special forces in the China-Burma-India Theater called OSS or Office of Strategic Services. These forces conducted unconventional warfare operations behind enemy lines, but also collected data on the Japanese. Among the data collected was information on POW sightings and their treatment by the Japanese. The Americans also covertly collected SIGINT through intercepting and deciphering Japanese communications between senior headquarters and field units. Finally, conventional military units from America, Holland, Russia, China, and other countries also helped collect data on the Japanese.

At the end of the war, the Japanese sent communications to their field units, instructing them to destroy all evidence of their activities in POW camps. Some of this evidence was captured by advancing Allied units before the Japanese could do so. Although vast amounts were destroyed, the Japanese left thousands of pages of evidence of their effort to systematically torture and kill any people—military or civilians, men, women, and children—in their possession.

Many are aware that German war criminals were tried in Nuremberg, Germany following World War II, and that many of those convicted of crimes against humanity were either imprisoned or found justice at the end of a rope or facing a firing squad. The trials of Japanese war criminals, however, are not as well known. While some escaped justice, many were found guilty in post-war criminal proceedings and punished for their crimes. In part,

> *"Twenty-eight Class A war criminals accused of crimes against peace, conventional war crimes, and crimes against humanity included many of Japan's wartime leaders, such as Prime Minister Gen. Tojo Hideki. The*

Tokyo War Crimes Tribunal, the counterpart of Nuremberg, began in May 1946 and ended in November 1948 with the conviction of twenty-five of these defendants. Seven, including Tojo, were hanged, sixteen were sentenced to life imprisonment (of whom four died in prison), and two received lesser terms. Of the three remaining, two died during the proceedings, and one was declared unfit for trial. The Japanese government paroled all those imprisoned by 1956 and the Foreign Ministry released them unconditionally in April 1958. Allied nations also held war crimes trials throughout Asia and the Pacific. Americans, British, Australians, Dutch, French, Filipinos, and Chinese held trials at forty-nine locations between October 1945 and April 1956. The British prosecuted numerous Japanese for war crimes in Southeast Asia, including those involved in the construction of the Thai-Burma railway of death, immortalized as the Bridge over the River Kwai. Australian prosecutors worked in conjunction with British and American courts to bring Japanese to justice and tried large numbers of Japanese at Amboina, Dutch East Indies, and at Rabaul, New Britain. China tried at least 800 defendants, including some involved in the Nanjing massacre. France and the Netherlands tried several hundred more. The French brought to justice a Japanese civilian on Java who forced dozens of women into prostitution for the military authorities, and the Dutch condemned Japanese to death for the murder of indigenous people and Dutch prisoners. In late 1949 at Khabarovsk, the Soviet Union

> *also put twelve Japanese on trial for biological warfare crimes—six were members of Unit 731, two of Unit 100, an independent biological warfare entity, and four from elsewhere—and later transferred several hundred Japanese ex-servicemen suspected of war crimes to the People's Republic of China, where Chinese authorities judged them in the mid-1950s. Of 5,379 Japanese, 173 Taiwanese, and 148 Koreans tried as class B and C war criminals for conventional crimes, violations of the laws of war, rape, murder, maltreatment of prisoners of war, about 4,300 were convicted, almost 1,000 sentenced to death, and hundreds given life imprisonment."*[21]

At the end of the day, some Japanese war criminals escaped justice, but many did not. It is not the purpose of this book to discuss or cite political responsibility or culpability in allowing any war criminals go unpunished. Instead, the focus will remain on illuminating what happened to our brave prisoners of war and providing some background on the captors that inflicted so much upon our prisoners.

The final question posed with regard to the Japanese atrocities was: why did the Japanese commit these crimes, given the Bushido code of ethics? First, the Japanese were signatory parties to the Geneva Convention established at the turn of the twentieth century. It is also known that the Japanese did an admirable job of following the tenants of this agreement in the Russian-Sino conflict prior to World War II. So what changed—the people, the conditions, or maybe both? As Daqing Yang tells us, with "some exceptions during the Sino-Japanese War of 1894-95, Japanese armed forces at war seemed to abide by international standards. Japan signed *The Hague Conventions* and the *1929 Geneva Convention*, but the Imperial leadership failed to approve the latter. When Japan invaded China in the 1930s and launched a full-scale war in 1937, neither country formally declared war, thus raising the question of whether they were obliged to abide by the international conventions of war."[22] Whether or not war was declared, and whether or not both sides recognized the conflict as a war, the Geneva Convention applied, and was required to be followed in the mid-thirties when Japan attacked mainland China and conducted its atrocities in Nanking China. Those horrific events are brought out in Iris Chang's seminal work, *The Rape of Nanking: The Forgotten Holocaust of World War II.* Japan was also obliged to follow the Geneva Convention in World War II.

EUROPEAN THEATER PRISONERS OF WAR

Two sources are used throughout this portion on POW camp experiences in the European theater of war. The first source depicts 1st Lt. Stanley Edwards wartime experiences; a crewmember of a C-47 shot down in the opening hours of the D-Day invasion over France. After multiple escapes and recapture, Edwards finished the war in a German Luft Stalag.[23] The second account details the wartime experiences of George Watt, a B-17 crewmember forced to bail out over occupied Belgium, who evaded capture and later received the assistance of a secret organization known as The Comet Connection, a secret underground mechanism used to covertly move downed fliers through occupied Belgium back to England.[24]

STANLEY EDWARDS

On June 4, 1944, Stanley Edwards and thousands of other military personnel stationed in England attended long briefings to prepare for the long anticipated invasion of occupied Europe. The invasion was postponed due to weather until June 6, 1944. Early on the 6th of June, Edwards and the rest of his C-47 crew readied their aircraft, picked up their 18 paratroopers, and took off at the appointed time for occupied Europe. The mission of Edwards' C-47 was to drop paratroopers in northwest France and then return to England for follow-on missions. The C-47s, as well as the thousands of other assault and support aircraft joined up and then headed to Europe for their assigned missions. Once they were over their assigned areas, the paratroopers would wait for the signal of an internal green light near the aircraft's door and then jump out of the aircraft in one-second intervals. Once the paratroopers exited the aircraft, a static line would pull their parachutes from the packs on their backs and then the lines would break free, allowing the paratroopers to float to the earth in what would turn out to be a 3-10 second descent (based on their aircraft's altitude). The paratroopers' hopes at that point were to have a safe landing and join up in the assigned areas once on the ground.

Diagram 4

C-47 Aircraft at a European airfield during World War II

Courtesy of the National Archives

Once over France, Stanley Edwards' C-47 came under fire, and after some casualties the paratroopers exited the airplane at 600 feet over occupied France. Shortly thereafter, the aircraft came under very intense German anti-aircraft fire, forcing the remainder of the crew to bailout over France. Edwards sustained only a slight ankle sprain in the parachute landing and initially evaded capture alone, later linking up with members of the U.S. Army's 82nd Airborne Division early the next morning. Following this meeting, Edwards was given a Thompson machine gun by one of the infantrymen. This patrol of slightly less than a dozen Americans continued moving and avoided being spotted by German patrols, who were by this time very active due to the ongoing invasion. Eventually the patrol spotted a farmhouse and, after consulting with the farmhouse's owner, they went inside, rested, and enjoyed fresh steaks and coffee.

After seeing and then firing on a small German patrol, the American patrol fled the French farmhouse due to the overwhelming German presence. The American patrol was chased into a nearby field where they were eventually surrounded, and after weighing their options, wove a white handkerchief[25] to signal their surrender, believing it better to live to fight another day. One of the hardest decisions military personnel in combat have to make is when to stop fighting and surrender themselves, and sometimes fellow members of their units. In the Philippines, for example, an American Army officer had to make the decision to surrender an entire division to the Japanese in 1942. At other times, commanders of small teams have to make similar decisions—fight or surrender. Although many find it easy to second-guess these decisions made in war time, it must be kept in mind that the decision to fight or flee are made to ensure the best chances of survival for their men.

After raising their arms to surrender, the Americans were disarmed and searched. Edwards and his companions were put in the back of a German transport truck. They were taken to nearby Valognes, France, where they were transferred to a temporary holding area with other Allied forces also taken prisoner during these opening hours of the D-Day invasion.[26] Although this was a temporary compound, essentially made up of temporary buildings and barbed wire, locations such as these were commonly used as initial holding places for prisoners of war. At these temporary locations, the captors started their process of cataloging the prisoners, making records of who was captured, when, and under what conditions.

In their first prison compound, Edwards spotted Stan, one of the other members of his crippled C-47. After talking with Stan, Edwards learned that they were the only two surviving members of that airplane's crew. That evening, the POWs in this compound were given hardtack, a type of simple bread made of flour, water, and sometimes salt baked into a rough cracker-like substance. Hardtack was common on ships, but also used in field conditions where formal kitchens and associated baking devices were not available.

The next morning, the Germans moved these prisoners to another temporary holding location in Cherbourg, France. Once there, the prisoners found beds and furniture. A couple of days later, the Germans decided to move the prisoners further away from the advancing Allied forces. At this point, the prisoners discussed the idea of escaping their captors during movement—perhaps by jumping from the moving trucks into nearby hedgerows, using the heavy brush for cover and concealment as they pursued further escape. They soon had the opportunity to test their plan.

The trucks soon got underway. And, as they got under way, American planes flew overhead and distracted the German guards. Edwards and his companions again made their move. They jumped from the truck at just the right moment. Their escape was successful—and they were uninjured. After walking all night, the Americans walked into what they believed was simply a meadow with horses—but realized only too late that had come too close to a sleeping contingent of German soldiers, and were again captured.

Once captured, the Americans were taken to an old three-story French castle where they enjoyed more freedom, although the Germans had guards and placed limits on the prisoners' movements. The prisoners quickly discovered that the Germans were very detailed in accounting for American officers, but were much less concerned about keeping track of junior American personnel—privates and the like. Moreover, Edwards discovered that this old castle had a secret attic and secret door, through which they could access areas outside the castle. Their plan was set—they would switch hats and uniforms with three junior officers, and those junior enlisted men would wear hats with officers' insignia for remaining roll calls. It was hoped that this ruse would allow the three officers enough time to escape while the German guards searched inside the castle grounds for them.

Their escape plan worked. They escaped through the trap door and made their way out through an adjoining field unnoticed. After escaping this time, the three men became aware of several things. First, the area was swarming with Germans. They would have to limit their movement to hours of darkness and would have to be cautious in the hedgerows. The hedgerows provided concealment from enemy observation but whose lack of visibility meant that they could walk up on enemy patrols without realizing it.

After a few close calls, the Americans continued their movement through the French countryside, finally deciding to hide under a large shrub-like lilac tree whose leaves and flowers offered good concealment. For a few hours, this location seemed good—until a German soldier came by and started cutting branches for camouflaging their vehicle and discovered the Americans. Due to the proximity of many German soldiers, there was no escaping. The Americans were simply outnumbered, and any resistance would have meant death. Once more, they became POWs.[27]

This time, about ten days into their European adventure, the prisoners were taken to a nearby farmhouse that served as a command post for SS troops in the area. After interrogations, the prisoners were put in a farmhouse set up as a temporary holding compound. After a few days, and after discovering that the bars on the prisoners' compound could be defeated, the prisoners developed a plan. While some kept watch for approaching guards, others started weakening the bars for a nighttime escape through the rear of the farmhouse, where they discovered were no guards. As they were working on loosening the bars, they were surprised by a German guard, who entered the cell and clearly saw the ongoing escape activities. They had to kill this guard, stuff him in a closet inside their prison room, and hastily complete their escape before the dead guard's absence was noticed. After moving away from this location, the Americans received some food and water from nearby farmers and continued their southeasterly trek. The Americans stayed in a farmhouse with a French family whose house was occupied by Germans, whom the family was forced to serve cheese and bread (while, of course, secretly siphoning off some of this food for the Americans).[28]

On the run again, following his third escape, Edwards and his companions moved carefully through the hedgerows, trying to avoid detection. Later, moving through a field, the night pitch black, the escapees stumbled upon a German contingent bedded down in the middle of a horse field. They were able to escape this near-capture incident, but later they saw a light on in a house and thought it might again be signs of a French family willing to assist Americans. After knocking on the door, however, the Germans occupants of this building quickly surrounded the Americans—they were prisoners again!

Taken in a 1935 Ford truck, the prisoners found themselves in the company of SS officers. The SS were the German secret police, which in this case interrogated the prisoners of war and took them to Rennes, France. Once there, it became quickly and painfully apparent what was in store for these prisoners, because Rennes was a prisoner rail (train) trans-shipment point. The Germans used rail lines to move prisoners all over Germany, and now moved their newest prisoners away from the French countryside into the German heartland. This movement signaled to them that escapes had to be executed quickly because their movements were quickly taking them farther away from friendly forces.

Edwards and hundreds of other POWs were put on trains—fifty to a boxcar. They spent the next twenty-three days inside these train cars. These were not the train cars some of these men were accustomed to. In America, train cars contained seats, windows, and bathroom accommodations. These German boxcars had wooden slats for floors, there was no furniture or windows, and a large drum in the middle of the car served as the lavatory. The train kept moving, which created horrid conditions for the men—very similar to the train cars that had taken Americans to Andersonville seventy-five years earlier. The stench and the lack of proper food, water, and clean air was almost unbearable. Except for one case where a dozen ingenious soldiers pried their way out of moving boxcars, the next three or more weeks were a true misery. The prisoners all had to sleep on their sides, and a command was given when all prisoners in a car were to turn over at the same time.[29] At one point in their journey, the train was attacked by French Resistance fighters—but to no avail. The train continued on towards central Germany.

Once the prison trains arrived in Luft Stalag III in Trier, Germany, the prisoners were registered with the Red Cross. Although this might have seemed an ominous confirmation that they were indeed prisoners, it was important for the prisoners since it ensured others back home knew they were alive and accounted for. Edwards was now introduced to POW camp life, which included playing hours of cribbage and cards, talking of events in the war, and of course more escape planning.

After the prisoners completed their POW registration, they were grilled by Americans in the camp to ensure that they were not plants sent by the Germans to infiltrate their POW organizations and thereby gain information on escape plans. Upon acceptance by their fellow Americans, the POW leadership in the camps looked at a man's background—his language skills and his ability to forge documents, make maps, sew clothes, and other things the escape committees required. From August 1944 through January 1945, Edwards remained in this camp.

On January 27, 1945, the Russian military forces were getting closer to central Germany. To prevent the prisoners from being liberated by the advancing Russians, the prisoners were forced to conduct a grueling march to Moosburg prison compound, west and south of Luft Stalag III. Edwards and the remaining 127,000 Allied prisoners remained at Moosburg until they were liberated on April 29, 1945 by Allied forces. The Army did not know what to do with this number of prisoners. After some scouting of the local area, the men discovered there were no areas large enough for C-47s to start shuttling prisoners home. At this point, former prisoners started hitching rides on trains, trucks, and just about anything moving away from the camps.

Edwards and a friend somehow made it to Paris, where Edwards met up with a former squadron-mate. After listening to Edwards' tales of escape, this officer got them on a general's plane to the airfield in northern France, where Edwards re-joined his former squadron. After asking if he and his fellow former prisoner friend could accompany the squadron back to the United States, they were told that no, former prisoners of war had to be processed through Camp Lucky Strike.[30] At Camp Lucky Strike, the former prisoners were issued new clothing, given $200 in cash, and put onboard ships bound for the United States.

The ship Edwards boarded reached New York in 10 days. Edwards enjoyed a private stateroom, hot showers, and food any time he wanted. Once in New York, the prisoners were taken to Camp Kilmer where the men were put on trains home and given 90-day passes (for time off). Upon reaching his hometown, Edwards married his childhood sweetheart, and they remained married for the remainder of their lives.

GEORGE WATT

Now, the story of American B-17 crewmember George Watt's wartime experiences in occupied Belgium, located on the northern European coastline. The date was November 5, 1943, and Watt was assigned to fly as part of a B-17 bombing mission over wartime Europe. As the B-17 crews moved into the briefing tents, what they dreaded most was the unveiling of the maps which detailed their bombing routes. Some routes were known to be far more perilous than others. In a few seconds, their fate would be known—their targets.

As luck would have it, Watt's crew was part of a raid package flying to the Ruhr, the central industrial region of wartime Germany. This area was heavily protected by flak (88 and 107mm anti-aircraft guns), as well as the feared German Focke-Wolfe-190 fighter aircraft.

Their assigned target was a railway station. Their plane, a B-17, was a ten-man heavy bomber, at that time being used for light daytime bombing raids. This was the crew's seventeenth mission together. As tradition had it, once the crew reached 25 missions they would be allowed to go home. The question was whether or not they would live long enough to see that golden number.

Once airborne, the planes rose to altitude and, eventually, when they drew sufficiently close to their targets the planes started drawing flak. With one engine hit, the crew decided to turn back—and after being escorted part of the way back, the American P-47 escorts eventually had to assist other aircrafts in trouble. Almost immediately, a German FW-190 descended upon the stricken B-17, which was easy prey for this nimble war bird. After taking fire, the order was given to bail out. Unlike modern planes with ejection seats or capsules, the method for emergency egresses from these planes was simply opening the doors of the plane and jumping out. On some occasions, if after the aircraft was hit by antiaircraft fire and the pilot could not retain control of the airplane, the force of gravity could force the planes' crew to the walls or seats—making them unable to bail out. This time, they crew was lucky.

Watt obeyed, and after deploying his parachute he saw six others, meaning that seven of the ten in the crew made it out before the giant war bird impacted in the countryside.[31] As Watt descended in his parachute, he began his mental preparation for what was to follow. First, he would have to land safely—if he was injured, it would greatly decrease his chances of a successful evasion. Second, he had to start considering his gear. He would have to hide that gear deemed non-essential. Finally, what would his location on the ground be? What direction must he go? Who would he turn to for assistance?

Lastly who would he be able to link up with? Fellow Americans? Would the locals be willing to help him? All these are necessary and critical things to consider for someone in Watt's situation.

Watt hit the ground hard, but after a quick self-assessment, aside from a sore ankle he realized he was uninjured. His immediate concerns returned to his location and equipment. He was in occupied Belgium, and from what he could observe during his parachute descent, he was in between three towns, recalling from earlier Intelligence briefings—all three of them German-occupied! He landed just south of a river and right in the middle of several open areas of plowed farmland. People started approached him at an alarming rate. Although he had only been evading capture for a very few minutes, his intuition immediately told him that a large crowd of people—old, young, kids, dogs—surrounding an aviator who just bailed out of a distressed aircraft while flying over an occupied country was not a good thing. Watt did not know which, if any, of these people were friendly, or which ones might be German collaborators. Watt had heard of the French resistance, an organization that assisted isolated flyers by providing them shelter, food, clothes, transportation. But how could he contact such a group, with no ability to look them up or ask for them by name?[32]

Soon, people were talking to Watt, but unfortunately in languages he could not understand. Eventually, Watt received direction to move to a ditch and out of the open. When he did this, a man named Eduard Lauwaert approached him and instructed him to get in a ditch at a nearby location, and that he would come back to get him later that evening. Not long afterwards, two men approached Watt's hiding place. Watts earlier saw one of the two men talking to the German security personnel immediately after Watt's initial landing.

Now Watt had to make a decision. Was this man approaching him a pro-Nazi, or someone that would assist his escape and possibly help him reach freedom through the underground apparatus?

This man's name was Raymond, who Watts later learned was a local, and assisted Watt in joining two other downed allied aviators, as well as provided them with food. Moreover, Raymond told Watt that he would help him later that evening. Soon, the men scurried from the ditch where Watt originally hid. A pair of people approached Watt, but his gut instinct said not to go with them, even though they offered to help. Watt declined and stayed where he was at. Soon afterwards, another man approached Watt and offered him a coat to keep him warm, as well as the advice that he must go with them at once.[33] As they were walking away, yet another man whistled, and the three broke into a slow jog which they maintained for two kilometers (or about 1.5 miles), during which they crossed fields, ditches, and country roads. It was dark by the time the three approached a village. Watt and his guide went through a small gate and into a structure (which, given the odor, was obviously an outhouse), where Watt was instructed to wait silently inside and told that someone would come and get him. Eventually, a young woman came and retrieved Watt and took him into the house. After staying at this house for some time, Watt moved on. Watt's had seen quite a few people since he started evading German capture. How would he truly know who was friendly and who would turn him over to the Germans? One person took him, hid him, later retrieved him and then passed him to someone else and this cycle seemed to continue. Was this how these evasion networks worked? How long would this go on?

He changed clothes and, except for a single dog tag which he kept in a shoe, was now completely in civilian clothing. Watt had originally given up the dog tags, but feared that if he were captured, he would be shot as a spy without some proof that he was an American serviceman. Unless he opened his mouth, it was entirely possible for Watt to pass as a local—except for the fact that no one would recognize him. Watt and his host now walked to a different house, and while passing by Germans, Watt was terrified but walked right past them with no problems. His clothes fit the environment perfectly.

Asking about his route to freedom, Watt soon learned that it would require a train (or tram) ride into Brussels—a trip that included sitting among German military personnel. Raymond was true to his word, sticking with Watt even though his wife believed this was too great a risk to take for an unknown foreigner. Raymond then offered to take Watt on to the next phase of his journey—to see Raymond's cousin, who could arrange transportation across the French border.

After arriving in Brussels, about an hour's train ride away, the two made their way to the house of Raymond's cousin, who was a doctor—but he was not home. His wife Hedwige Proost, however, gladly showed the two in. After she cooked some food for Watt, Dr. Jena Proost came home and also greeted the two visitors. After a few more hours of waiting, a young man came to the doctor's house, and Watt was asked a series of very specific questions about his mother, father, date of birth, and military rank. Watt provided responses to the questions asked.

The man who demanded this information said he would return to them at eight o'clock that evening if everything was OK. At precisely eight o'clock, the young man was back. He confirmed that everything was OK and that he had some instructions for Watt to follow. He would buy two train tickets and Watt would follow close behind him—but Watt would not under any circumstances speak, and if anything happened, he would not in any way indicate that he knew the man. Watt agreed. Watt bid farewell to the doctor, his wife, and Raymond.

What Watt did not know was that the earlier questions he was asked about his mother, father, date of birth, and military rank were all question intended to allow confirmation of who Watts was—friend or foe. Had the answers to these questions not been answered correctly, Watt would have been taken out back and shot. Moreover, Watt likely did not realize these personnel who were passing these questions by secret radio to London and eventually to American headquarters. These communications were part of a techniques used to confirm Watt's bona fides or true identity.

Moreover, each time Watt was handed from one person to another, the handlers from the two cells were not allowed to see each other. This ensured that if one cell of the escape mechanism was compromised, they could not identify other members. This is called compartmentalization. Likewise, Watt was periodically left alone and later, someone else retrieved him. What Watt did not know, is that throughout the entire duration of his escape, members of the Belgium Underground were moving alongside him and protecting him. In underground movements such as these, the security of the elements is the primary factor when conducting covert operations. This was not a game, and the security of this escape mechanism depended on absolute certainty.

After some anxious waiting, Watt was finally taken to the train station where they made their way to the French border. They were handed over to a woman named Madame De Bruyn, at which time Watt was delighted to discover the presence of someone he knew—H.C. Johnson, one of his crippled plane's crewmembers. They were then told, "Welcome to Free France!"[34] The next day, the group was split up; Johnson and Watt were taken to a new hideout in a suburb of Paris. This safe house was a family's house—Johnson and Watt slept in one half, while the family remained in the other. When the time came for their next movement, since Watt could not speak passable French, a plan was hatched where a letter was prepared stating that Watt (using a fictitious name) was a mute and thus unable to speak. The plan worked. When an SS Officer asked Watt for his papers on the train, the letter was presented and, after it letter was read, Watts was ignored. The next leg of the journey took place on bicycle, and eventually the perilous portion of the journey ended when they reached the Spanish frontier and the British embassy compound. Watt was home at last.

JAPANESE VS. GERMAN CAPTIVITY ENVIRONMENTS

The conditions of prisoners of war in the European theater of war were very different from those suffered by those held by the Japanese. Although both were caged and denied freedom, cruelties towards American POWs on the scale we know were committed by the Japanese were rare in the European context. Moreover, if American POWs escaped or were fortunate enough to evade capture initially, their chances of assisted evasion, or receiving outside help in their attempts to escape, were much higher in Europe than in Japan or Asia.[35]

As compared to the mindset in the Pacific theater, the typical European had a different cultural outlook on Americans and on the war in general. Americans looked like Europeans, many (Europeans and Americans) spoke the same languages, and in many cases, the two groups were linked by family bonds—in fact, the national lineage of most Americans had been linked to Europeans up to the point when they broke away from Great Britain in the American Revolution.

EPILOGUE ON WORLD WAR II PRISONERS

Millions of men, women and children died in World War II. That being said, it is useful to put the numbers into perspective, examining the plight of POWs versus all deaths in the war, and of course, considering how the POW experiences of the Germans compared to those held in the Pacific (or Japanese) theater. Some final questions should be answered before moving onto the years following World War II and the Cold War.

How many Americans (or others) were held prisoner by the Japanese—and how does this compare to the German (or European) theater of war?

How were both of these Axis powers, the Japanese and Germans, held accountable? Were they held accountable?

The "judgment at the Tokyo Trial noted that, whereas four percent of some 235,000 American and British POWs in German and Italian captivity died, almost a third of the 132,000 American and British POWs lost their lives while in Japanese captivity. Some put it in a starker way: one percent of American POWs died at German hands; thus, 9 out of 10 American POWs who died in captivity during

World War II did so under the Japanese."[36] The European theater also produced war crimes trials.

By 1944, American political and military personnel were discussing post-war tribunals for war crimes for the European theater; mainly the German military and political leadership. "The indictment of the German war criminals was served on October 6, 1945, and the Nuremberg trial began on November 20, 1945." The charges were drafted and finally approved so that by August 1945 formal charges, including crimes against humanity, were raised. "This position became the basis of the formal declaration of an international tribunal at the London Conference in late June and early August of 1945. The indictment of the German war criminals was served on October 6, 1945, and the Nuremberg trial began on November 20, 1945."[37]

Americans experienced captivity at the hands of the Japanese and Germans and while the severity of the treatment varied in lengths and intensity, atrocities committed by the Japanese were generally more brutal. World War II would not be the last war where Americans would be held against their will. Within five years, Americans would again be at war; this time on the Korean peninsula.

Chapter 5

Korean War Prisoners of War

On June 25, 1950, the North Koreans started the Korean War by attacking into South Korea. This war had three dimensions. One was the internal war between the two Koreas. Second was the conflict involving the UN, and finally, third, the United States'—standoff with the Communists in what was known as the Cold War. Although the fighting stopped a few years later, the war had far-reaching effects on those who fought in it, including the 4,428 men who became prisoners of war. Of these nearly forty-five hundred men, slightly more than one-third died in captivity. Moreover, as a direct result of the Korean War POWs, on August 17, 1955, President Dwight D. Eisenhower signed Executive Order 10631, which contained the findings of a committee charged to study the war's effect on POWs, and ultimately led to the writing and issuance the Code of Conduct of the Armed Forces of the United States.[1] This chapter's goals are to look at a few examples of who was taken prisoner, their POW experiences, what the North Koreans and Chinese did to them, and finally, the war's legacy and aftermath.

When World War II ended, millions of American military men hung up their uniforms and resumed civilian life. Five years later, when the Korean Peninsula became engulfed in conflict, the draft was resumed to fill the skeleton of the American military's uniformed services. Following their victory in World War II, America's armed services drew down; with that, a lot of combat experience born on the fields of Europe was gone. Now the United States, as well as the United Nations, faced its first major test—communist North Korea, with the aid of communist China, wanted to conquer South Korea and push the United States and United Nations' forces back into the sea from which they came. Eventually, there were twenty prisoner of war compounds in North Korea. It is impossible to detail them all; rather, we will examine wartime experiences from several POWs'. The Korean War POW stories of Robert Maclean, Robert Coury, and Akira Chikami will be described.[2]

ROBERT MACLEAN

Maclean enlisted in the Army in 1948 and, after a couple of previous duty assignments, decided to reenlist and go to Japan followed by a posting in Korea. Arriving with the forces of the famous Inchon landing, Maclean served in the northern portions of North Korean border when his unit was told to retrograde south. The day after Thanksgiving in 1950, Maclean was captured and thus became a prisoner of the communists. As the American units evacuated south, they were overwhelmed by a communist unit—besieged north of Hamhung—and Maclean and others were captured the next morning. Once captured, Maclean was one of several American POWs instructed by the Chinese to go back and recover wounded North Korean soldiers strewn across the battlefield.[3] Before the American prisoners were moved to the North Korean rear areas, they were disarmed and had much of their cold-weather gear taken from them. In many cases, the POWs were left without proper footwear.

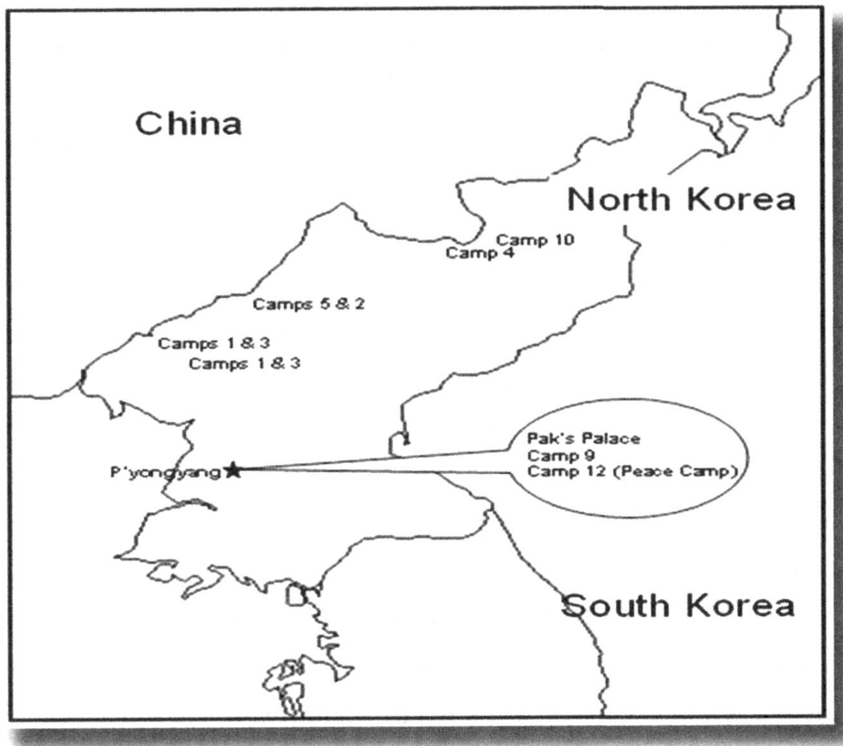

Diagram 5

North Korean / Chinese POW Camps

Courtesy geography.about.com/library

Maclean and his fellow POWs marched from Hamhung, located on the eastern coast of North Korea near the Sea of Japan, through central North Korea to a POW camp near the North Korean-Chinese border near Changsong. Due to the freezing temperatures, many POWs experienced cold-weather injuries during this movement. The POWs experienced frostbite, a freezing of the skin and, in bad cases, and the freezing of the underlying tissue. In other cases, the POWs got trench foot—a swelling of the feet, many times followed by gangrene and often resulting in forced amputation of the affected limbs. Maclean was fortunate when compared to many of the POWs captured on that fateful day. He packed his Alaskan cold weather gear in his duffel bag before shipping out to Japan—he was previously stationed in Alaska and was accustomed to conditions that required cold-weather gear.[4]

The march to POW Camp One along the northern North Korean border was a long and arduous one. The prisoners were allowed little food, some days none, and minimal rest. In fact, the marches were so tiring that the prisoners often found themselves walking in their sleep. To keep from walking off cliffs while asleep and during these long marches, many men used shoestrings or other materials to stay tied to the man in front of them.[5]

POWs' best opportunities for escape are often during periods of transport or movement. However, in this instance, by the time the prisoners' initial capture shock wore off, they were so deep in hostile territory, sleep-deprived and weak from lack of food or water, that merely staying alive was hard enough. To make matters worse, due to the conditions of the war-ravaged countryside, often devoid of any plants or wildlife, the men likely surmised that their prospects of survival would be better if they stayed the course and tried to sit the war out in a POW compound.

Many of these POWs were inexperienced in outdoors life—most having been just drafted. Many of these men likely asked themselves, how bad could life be in a POW compound? They had memories about the POW compounds during World War II, when American prisoners received relatively good treatment under their Germans. Arrival at their permanent camps would take care of this illusion—they would soon experience life in POW camps under the

Communists. This was no Luft Stalag and these were not Germans. Once again, Americans were held by Asians—whose outlooks were much different from their own.

Maclean was one of the first prisoners to reach Camp One. In part, Maclean said the "Chinese started their so-called brainwashing very shortly after we got into Camp One. In those indoctrination sessions, some individuals would keep their mouths shut and some would speak up. I happened to be one who spoke up, and there were a few others . . . . The Chinese would rip Mellon, Rockefeller, and guys like that . . . . They never made any sense. After a few hours you got so numb, it just went in one ear and out the other."[6] Aside from the indoctrination, the poor food, and the horrid living conditions, some Americans were introduced to marijuana by Turkish prisoners. The prisoners went to nearby fields and picked the plants, drying the leaves on stoves within the kitchens. As bad as it might seem to some, the getting high or intoxicated from marijuana must have presented some relief from the hellish conditions in the camps.[7]

In his book, detailing his experiences as a POW, Maclean offered insights into daily life under the Communists at this POW camp. In part, "if they wanted to kick your ass, they could, and I really got in trouble this one time. We were up in the mountains, and I was very weak. I was trying to get a log up on my shoulders [the prisoners were collecting wood for their stoves], and this Chinese guard kicked me and shoved me down. This was in 1953, just before the armistice."[8] At this point, rather than strike their guards, which would surely have resulted in severe punishment, Maclean and a fellow prisoner decided that they would escape for a short while and just get drunk. The two prisoners did just that, and later walked back to camp. After seeing the guard that had tormented him earlier, Maclean assaulted the guard—which of course resulted in numerous Chinese guards hitting them with the butts of their weapons, as well as threatening to keep Maclean in a Chinese jail for a "long time".[9]

Some of the attributes Maclean recalls as particularly helpful during his captivity included not dwelling on the low amounts of food the prisoners received, not thinking constantly of home, and generally not falling into a state of self-pity. In total, Maclean endured three-plus years as a prisoner under the Chinese. His captors eventually emptied out Camp One for the long trek south to Freedom Village and repatriation. Maclean commented that as "for the twenty-one American prisoners who remained behind [at the end of the war], I thought they were looking for more adventure than anything else . . . . The Rats were the guys you had to worry about, not the guys who were going to stay behind or who even seemed to swallow the Communist line. The Rats wanted that extra bowl of rice and that favoritism from the Chinese cadre. And all of them came home."[10]

ROBERT COURY

Ground personnel were by no means the only prisoners. Robert "Bob" Coury was a pilot who was shot down and captured on June 10, 1953. Coury flew a bomber aircraft that was dispatched to attack a target north of the 38th parallel. On the ingress to his target, all seemed normal, but when exiting the target area, Coury noted lights on his aircraft's dashboard lighting up to indicate very well-placed anti-aircraft artillery (AAA) fire. Coury tried to keep his distressed aircraft airborne and flying south long enough so that if he had to bail out of the aircraft, he would be over friendly territory or at least over water so the naval search and rescue forces could pick him up. After trying to go south for a brief period, Coury realized that his crippled aircraft had seen its last flight. He was forced to eject. Due to his low altitude, Coury hit the ground after only a few seconds' parachute ride and landed uninjured except for a small abrasion on his head from the canopy being blown off the aircraft's fuselage.[11]

During his descent, Coury realized he was near friendly lines. He hoped that once he reached the ground, he could land within, or conduct a short escape to, friendly lines and call it a day. Once he had landed, he was crawling along the ground when he felt sharp objects being stuck in his back. He rolled over and saw two Chinese soldiers armed with rifles, stabbing him with their bayonets. At first, Coury was unsure where he was, but the two soldiers took him to a nearby bunker; Coury saw a red star and immediately realized this wasn't South Korea and that he was a prisoner of war.

After remaining in this bunker for a few hours, Coury was moved by foot for several miles. He was escorted by two soldiers for a mile or so, and then two other soldiers came out to turn him over to his new guards, where the walk continued—carrying him further from friendly lines. Coury walked for most of the night of June 10, 1953. The next morning, they arrived at a prisoner collection point—a cave dug into the side of a hill. Coury stayed at this location for about eight days. During this time, he started escape planning after realizing that the timbers being used as bars over one of the windows could be loosened. At one point, on about the seventh day, Coury tried to escape, but his attempt was unsuccessful. On the eighth day, he was blindfolded and put on the back of a truck along with a few other prisoners for continued movement north.[12]

Along the journey, the trucks made intermediate stops. The prisoners were sometimes transferred to new trucks while at other stops the prisoners were fed. At one point, the prisoners were placed in an old Korean family's house and fed rice. After another truck ride, Coury arrived at what he believed to be a command post, where was interrogated. Coury provided the interrogators with his "name, rank, and serial number, and he [the interrogator] instructed the guards to take me away." Later, Coury was moved and once again placed in a civilian's home. This time, the house was still being occupied by a family. The Chinese guards moved the family out of one of the rooms, which was used as Coury's prison cell for the night. Initially, he was instructed to remain lying in his cell and was interrogated a couple of times a day, but eventually the number of interrogations were reduced to one a day. During the last days of his captivity, Coury was allowed one bowl of rice and one can of water per day.[13]

After an undetermined period of time, Coury noted with some concern the lack of aerial activity over their camp—where he previously observed aircrafts from both sides engaged in aerial combat. He was taken blindfolded in a truck to a new location, where he was again interrogated. This time, however, he was told by his captors that they were disappointed in his responses and he might as well be taken out back and shot in the head for his lack of cooperation. After a few days at this new location, Coury walked outside and immediately realized where he was. He was near the city of Sinuiju at the mouth of the Yalu River along the North Korean-Chinese border (the far western portion near the Korea Bay). Coury described the interrogations as relatively routine. During one of the interrogations, a Korean, tried to befriend Coury, claiming that he was a former

South Korean soldier forced to do this because his family was being held by the Chinese. The other interrogators attempted to use more straightforward techniques—direct questioning with no false pretenses of who they were or what they wanted.[14]

While at this same POW compound, Coury easily discerned the war was still on by the air activity he observed in the skies above. At one point, Coury was told, "We expect a cease-fire momentarily. You should be going home soon."[15] A few days later, Coury and two other prisoners were again blindfolded, placed on a truck, and instructed not to talk. After stopping at a few POW camps—some vacated, others not—Coury and the other prisoners were finally put on a southbound train for Freedom Village. Freedom Village was the point along the DMZ (or demilitarized zone) where the POWs were exchanged.

According to Coury, the "folks running the place questioned us a bit, fed us, and let us make phone calls home." Following this initial transfer of former POWs, they were all moved south. Coury went on to say, "I was put on a hospital ship to come home. I weighed 145 pounds when I was shot down and about 105 before repatriation." During one of their first evenings on ship, an Air Force Colonel advised the former POWs to forget about good guys and bad guys and have a good trip home. A former Marine POW explained to Coury that he, a Marine Colonel, had signed a document confessing to war crimes, but did this because the Colonel was told by the Chinese that they knew who his family members were, citing their names and where they lived. This Colonel was willing to say anything they wanted to prevent harm to his family. All of the returnees experienced counter-intelligence interrogations, and most including Coury went through at least three separate interrogation sessions after being repatriated. Later, Coury received a letter stating that he conducted himself admirably while in captivity and wishing him a successful Air Force career.[16]

AKIRA CHIKAMI

A third Korean War POW's story contains some of the same basic events, but reveals some distinctly different interrogation and propaganda techniques. This prisoner, a resident of Reno, Nevada with Japanese ancestry, Akira Chikami, joined the Army after seeing newsreels that depicted the glory of battle. Chikami was a World War II veteran, who signed up for duty in Korea. After a short stint in orientation training, Sgt. Chikami was assigned to the 2nd Army Division. He was in Korea by December 1950, and by August of 1951, Chikami and his unit were engaged in combat operations with the enemy.[17]

Chikami's unit was supposed to have been in a short-term position known as a blocking position for a few days. His unit experienced nightly probing attacks, meaning that the enemy was testing them by advancing in small numbers, firing some rifle and even machine gun shots, and then withdrawing. The intent during these probing actions was to test the American's strength, as well as to judge the character of the unit. Additionally, these probing attacks were used to see how easily the unit could be lulled into firing key weapons such as machine guns, thereby allowing the North Koreans to discern the Americans' key weapons emplacements.

Finally, after a number of probing attacks, the enemy launched their main offensive, inflicting 50 percent casualties on Chikami's company. Chikami was woubnded in the leg but, fortunately, his wound was simply a flesh wound—meaning that no bones or major internal organs were hit. When Chikami's unit was overrun, his company commander came by and, seeing that Chikami was injured, said he was going to have to leave him behind as they retreated. Two other soldiers, however, did come to Chikami's aid. The three of them were hobbling back towards friendly lines as best they could when a machine gun fired and killed the two soldiers with Chikami, who was almost immediately taken prisoner by a young Chinese soldier.[18]

Initially, the North Koreans herded the Americans towards their own lines; Chikami and others believed they were simply being forced to march into the American artillery and mortar fire to commit suicide. What they later found out was that the prisoners were being positioned so that they could help move injured North Korean soldiers off the battlefield. Including Chikami, there were thirty-five American prisoners total in his group. The Americans initially stopped firing at them, but later recommenced. By the time the Americans' artillery had stopped, all but five of these original thirty-five were wounded. The prisoners were moved on foot, crossing a river the next day and finally stopping at a cave command post. Here, Chikami underwent some grueling interrogations. The initial questioner used the Direct Approach, using threats and inducing fear. The Direct Approach is described as:

> *. . ." the questioning of a source without having to use any type of approach. The direct approach is often called no approach at all, but it is the most effective of all the approaches. Statistics tell us that in World War II, it was 85 percent to 95 percent effective. In Vietnam, it was 90*

> *percent to 95 percent effective. The direct approach works best on lower enlisted personnel as they have little or no resistance training and have had minimal security training. Due to its effectiveness, the direct approach is always to be tried first. The direct approach usually achieves the maximum cooperation in the minimum amount of time and enables the interrogator to quickly and completely exploit the source for the information he possesses. The advantages of this technique are its simplicity and the fact that it takes little time. For this reason, it is frequently used at the tactical echelons where time is limited."*[19]

Follow-up interrogators were friendly, sometimes offering the prisoners cigarettes and trying to convince the prisoners that they, too, were simply soldiers who wanted to go home. As the guards and interrogators learned the prisoners' backgrounds and weaknesses, the approaches used by the guards varied. The Incentive Approach was used on some of the prisoners. In part, "The incentive approach is a method of rewarding the source for his cooperation, but it must reinforce positive behavior. This is done by satisfying the source's needs. Granting incentives to an uncooperative source leads him to believe that rewards can be gained whether he cooperates or not."[20] A specific example might be as simple as offering the prisoner of war a cigarette or water.

About ten days following their capture, the prisoners were asked who the ranking officer was among them. Sgt. Chikami was the most senior man and told his captors this. At this point, Chikami and one other prisoner were moved to a POW camp just outside North Korea's capital, Pyongyang. This camp was known as Camp

Twelve, and upon their arrival, Chikami and his companion received a less than open-arms welcome by their fellow prisoners. Years later, Chikami found out that this was because, prior to their arrival, the North Koreans told the other prisoners at this location that two new prisoners were coming in who had voluntarily surrendered. Although they did not know it at the time, this camp was chosen for these two enlisted men because they were viewed as hard cases. Since this camp's purpose was propaganda, it was hoped that varied approaches on these two prisoners might prove more successful.

The North Koreans actively sought prisoners who would make propaganda recordings for them. At one point, Chikami was told that the North Koreans were getting ready to march a bunch of them to the propaganda center. Chikami used the ploy that his previous injury, a leg wound, made the march to the propaganda center too painful. He was moved to the North Koreans' field hospital, where he received adequate medical care and food—medical care comparable to the battle-injured Chinese and North Korean soldiers at this same hospital.[21]

At one point in 1951, the prisoners were told that they were going to be freed and that a negotiated peace was close at hand. The prisoners were moved, but the war was not over and they were not being freed. Later, in Camp Five, Chikami decided to annoy the guards. One night, the guards peered in at him and realized he was not sleeping. They came in and ordered him to sleep. He replied that he could not. The guard asked him why he could not sleep, and reiterated that the "camp regulations required him to sleep". Chikami replied that he had lost his dog. The guard said, "You don't have a dog," and Chikami replied, "No, it's gone." This went on for a few more minutes until the guard again, "You don't have a dog," and Chikami responded, "The Turks gave me a dog." The guard had finally had enough, fetched his Sergeant of the Guard, and told him of Chikami's insolence. The prisoner repeated the same story to the Chinese Sergeant, who spoke a little English and said "OK, let's call a spade a spade." Chikami then said, "Oh, you want to play cards?" At this point, the guards put Chikami in solitary confinement for several days.[22]

Later during his imprisonment, another comical incident occurred. The Chinese told their personnel that their senior leadership wanted them to rid China of flies. Therefore, the guards would get points based on the amount of flies they killed. As ridiculous as it sounds, this offer was soon discovered by the prisoners. When Chinese leadership at the camp discovered that prisoners were now pitching into this ridding-China-of-flies game, they offered a Chinese cigarette for every two hundred flies the prisoners killed. This caught on like wildfire, not because the prisoners wanted to help the Chinese in their fly-ridding exercise, but this gave the prisoners something to do—and for those that smoked, a chance to get a cigarette or two while they were at it.

Soon, prisoners were catching flies by the hundreds. Industrious prisoners made fly traps that bewildered the Chinese by how many hundreds of flies they were killing and turning in. Soon the Chinese raised the ante and had to start weighing the flies, since counting that many soon became unrealistic. The Chinese then started cheating, adjusting the scale, and the Americans reciprocated. Ingenious prisoners used discarded toothpaste tubes, which were cut into small slivers and inserted into the flies' bodies, thus greatly adding to their overall weight. Soon, the flies turned in by the American prisoners weighed more than anyone else's and their captors could not figure out why. The Chinese never discovered how the Americans caught such heavy flies.[23] To some these two incidents with their captors might seem a small matter, but in this case, Chikami won victories over his captors. In situations such as these, small victories can make huge differences on the prisoners' attitude and therefore improve their psychological well-being. A prisoner's psychological well-being can make the difference between surviving the captivity or dying and never returning home.

Chikami was eventually released and continued serving his nation. After retirement, under the Freedom of Information Act, he requested copies of his files containing the statements and charges made against him following the Korean War. Chikami was astounded at the amount of unsubstantiated and completely false charges in the files—some by people who did not even know him but had only seen him in the camp.[24]

These are synopses of three soldiers' stories as POWs in the Korean War. But, what is to be made of these propaganda and exploitation methods? As the reader has already surmised, there were many allegations of misconduct by US POWs while held captive by the Chinese and North Koreans following repatriation to the United States. Sometimes, these former POWs were known as the Bad Guys, Progressives, Reds, or on occasion, outright collaborators. Interrogation and indoctrination were the main methods of the Americans' captors during the Korean War. Many have heard that the Korean War POWs were collaborators and signed onto this communist brainwashing. But what is this "brainwashing", and how did it affect the former POWs? And, how did the U.S. government respond to these allegations?

During the period 1954 to 1956, a U.S. government-sponsored investigation sought information on communist interrogations and indoctrination.[25] During this investigation, the government collected information on communist techniques used in this war as well as past eras. Part of this study compared communist techniques of the 19th and 20th century to Chinese techniques.[26] The formal indoctrination of prisoners of war was originally developed by the Germans in World War II, and generally followed the overall propaganda methods developed by Joseph Goebbels, the Nazi Propaganda Minister. Later, the Japanese, Russians, and even the Chinese used some of these same techniques, but these were greatly refined following the maturation of the Chinese Communist state following World War II.

Time Period	Applied Techniques
19th Century	Most highly organized and effective of any European state. • Sudden arrest. • Dossier • Repetitive Interrogation • Isolation of the prisoner
20th Century (Russian)	• Highly organizes and refined method • Communist ideology and logic • Abandonment of direct brutality • Development of persuasion techniques; exploitation of the captive-captor relationship.
20th Century (Chinese)	• Group pressures • Self and group criticisms applied • Prisoner indoctrination • Rote learning • Autobiography and diary writing

Diagram 6

Communist Exploitation Methods

Many of the techniques discussed here were developed by the Russians but later refined as the Chinese Communist state developed its own propaganda techniques. In part,

> *"The most important of these is the use of group pressures, generated among prisoners who are confined together in cells, each of whom is required to demonstrate his own reform by tearing down the statements and deriding the past behavior of his fellow prisoners. The routine of "self-criticism", self-abasement, punishment, recantation, and ultimate rehabilitation, which was developed by the*

> *pre-war Russian Bolshevik Party as a means of insuring discipline among party members, has been extended to the civilian and prison populations by the Chinese, who use these procedures very effectively within cell groups to produce pressure on individual prisoners. In addition, the Chinese have introduced into the prison system pedagogical methods based upon rote learning, recitation, and the repetition of long, hand-written, essay-like "confessions", as a means of indoctrinating the prisoner with Communist concepts of economics, politics and current events. These teaching methods have been drawn directly from those which had been in use in China for many centuries."*[27]

After seeing some of these techniques, it is also helpful to note the effects of these pressures experienced by the untrained and often uneducated soldier.

> *"The essential features of it [confinement and solitary] are uncertainty, anxiety, complete isolation from the social environment, and an overwhelming awareness of the control exercised by the jailers. This, added to the physiological effects of lack of sleep, alterations in diet, the temperature in the cell, and the pain and circulatory disturbances produced by unusual postures long maintained, leads to a steady disorganization of the prisoner which, in the case of new prisoners unfamiliar with the routine, is usually well advanced within three to six weeks. The characteristics of this disorganization are*

> *mental dulling, loss of ability to make discriminations, feelings of helplessness, depression and despair, associated with inactivity, filth, self-soiling, and an active fantasy life of a fearful nature. The reaction may go on to frank delirium. The lack of discriminatory capacity makes it difficult for the prisoner to differentiate what actually has happened from what might have happened, or to understand the fine distinctions contained in the legal documents which he may be called upon to sign. Sometimes prisoners actually confabulate. Accompanying all of this is an intense need for companionship and an intense desire to talk to someone, which is utilized effectively by tile interrogator."*[28]

Many of these soldiers did not have high school educations, and therefore did not even understand basic government functions, ours or theirs. Likewise, many young soldiers did not understand economic systems such as capitalism and socialism. Therefore many of the soldiers who had these exploitation techniques applied to them were wholly unprepared for and, in reality, unarmed for such wartime confinement, isolation, and exploitation. The logical question, and the last question for this chapter, is what the government then did with this information. How did we ensure that our men and women would be prepared for future conflicts?

The Department of Defense, as part of the Secretary of Defense Advisory Committee on Prisoners of War, issued several documents to better prepare the military fighting man, as well as lay a foundation for future training and regulations. First, the committee issued a report on July 29, 1955 that contained the findings of the committee, as well as recommending a way forward for the Department of Defense. Second, an Executive Order directing the establishment and issuance of the "Code of Conduct for the Armed Forces of the United States" was drafted, accepted, and signed by President Eisenhower on August 17, 1955. The Code of Conduct was then made mandatory for all members of the Armed Forces of the United States.

This precedent is carried forth to the present day and includes regulations for the training and guidance of US government civilian employees, as well as US government contractors. The current Code of Conduct is seen in the pages that follow. The original Code of Conduct was changed in 1983 to be more gender-neutral, since women's roles were changing in the Department of Defense, and therefore, women were much more likely to be taken prisoner of war, as seen in Desert Storm in 1991. For instance, the new code reads, "I am an American, fighting in the Armed Forces . . . .", whereas the older version read "I am an American fighting man . . . ." The six portions of the Code of Conduct follow.

I. I am an American fighting in the forces which guard my country and our way of life. I am prepared to give my life in their defense.

II. I will never surrender of my own free will. If in command, I will never surrender the members of my command while they still have the means to resist.

III. If I am captured I will continue to resist by all means available. I will make every effort to escape and aid others to escape. I will accept neither parole nor special favors from the enemy.

IV. *If I become a prisoner of war, I will keep faith with my fellow prisoners. I will give no information or take part in any action which might be harmful to my comrades. If I am senior, I will take command. If not, I will obey the lawful orders of those appointed over me and will back them up in every way.*

V. *When questioned, should I become a prisoner of war, I am required to give name, rank, service number, and date of birth. I will evade answering further questions to the utmost of my ability. I will make no oral or written statements disloyal to my country and its allies or harmful to their cause.*

VI. *I will never forget that I am an American, fighting for freedom, responsible for my actions, and dedicated to the principles which made my country free. I will trust in my God and in the United States of America.*

The logical question, after seeing these six points, involves their spirit and intent. We will start by understanding some of what was learned through thousands of interviews, scientific studies, and previous knowledge about the endurance of the human mind and body. First, it was discovered that "the big four and nothing more" that was taught in previous wars was unrealistic. Every man has his breaking point; therefore, to believe a man should not give anything more—or be held accountable should he break under interrogation—is expecting our men to be supermen. We now know that a more realistic approach is to withhold information for as long as possible and then, if you have broken, to bounce back—assuming the psychological stance of, "OK, they beat me in this round, but I'll come back in the next round even stronger."

Man's limitations and the instruction for him/her to hold out as long as possible is reflected in the fifth point of the code: "When questioned, should I become a prisoner of war, I am required to give name, rank, service number, and date of birth. I will evade answering further questions to the utmost of my ability." With regard to the many POWs who were alleged to have aided the enemy through making statements of their own free will, the fourth code reads: "If I become a prisoner of war, I will keep faith with my fellow prisoners. I will give no information or take part in any action which might be harmful to my comrades." When we consider the psychological pressures put on the Korean War POWs, we see a war in which the enemy captors had an end state in mind—they were looking for propaganda to further the spread of communism. The reality was that the tactics used were communist techniques that evolved at the highest levels of government in China and the former United Soviet Socialist Republic.

Diagram 7

Korean War POW being welcomed back

Courtesy of the National Archives

The Code of Conduct is not a legal code but a moral guide, although one could argue that if one does not follow the code, he/she might be in violation of part of the Uniformed Code of Military Justice. For example, the fourth point reads, in part, "I will give no information or take part in any action which might be harmful to my comrades." This sentence seems clear enough. Given the following sentence, however—"Do not take part in actions which might be harmful"—the question may then be what actions are deemed harmful to our nation. If a prisoner is made to sign for blankets, for example, this is clearly not a harmful action. Yet, if the prisoner were tricked into signing a receipt which he believed was for blankets and his signature was then used to forge a document stating that he/she believes the "US war effort was criminal," did criminal conduct then take place? Most would say, NO.

For this reason, many months of careful deliberation went into the wording the code, so that it would provide our fighting men with what they needed—a simple, easily understood code that guided then in their conduct before the enemy. Simply stated, the Code of Conduct is a moral code with guidelines that, if followed, gives prisoners, detainees, and hostages advice without the often confusing legal language commonly found in US codes or laws.

Many former POWs from the Korean War went to their deathbeds with hatred and bewilderment at the treatment they received, both at the hands of their captors and, perhaps worse, from their fellow Americans who blamed them for a conduct they did not understand because they were not trained or prepared to do so. In short, the United States government sent men into the POW environment unprepared for this new battlefield. Worse, many were charged or blamed for crimes when they did nothing wrong. But what is the rate of POWs returned who actually did commit crimes, thus warranting further action on the part of the US government? One study reports that "only 192 of the 4,428 repatriated prisoners (1 in 23) were found to be chargeable with serious misconduct. To demonstrate that the scale of disaffections had been distorted, the committee compared this actionable misconduct rate with the one in fifteen of Americans who, according to Federal Bureau of Investigation reports, have records of alleged misconduct of sufficient gravity to have occasioned fingerprinting."[29] Said another way, there was more crime on the US streets than was ever substantiated in the POW compounds during the Korean War.

In 1955, the US government had a long way to go in terms of the training provided to and expectations placed on the military forces it put in harm's way. As was once said, all gave some but some gave all. Nowhere is this truer than with respect to the brave Americans who fight in wars. It especially holds true for those that were held against their will and then treated poorly upon their return home.

Chapter 6

Southeast Asia Prisoners of War

Many Americans experienced or were witness to the race riots and protests of the late 1960s. Likewise many Americans felt the effects of racial inequality, even though the Civil Rights Act and Voting Rights Acts were signed into law in 1964. As seen from the perspectives of a different and very select group of people, the memories of this period of American History are vastly different, however. To this select group of Americans—former prisoners of war—the Vietnam War era brings up memories of depravities and suffering, as well as their unending love and sacrifices for their fellow man.

In telling this story of Americans held POW during the War in Southeast Asia, eight prisoners of war stories are summarized. The personal experiences that follow are included because each of these prisoners' experiences offers unique insights into this war's conditions. That is not to say that those POWs' stories not recounted here are less significant—it is simply a matter of limited time and space. All POWs' stories need to be told and heard by all Americans. All of these men, to use a common phrase, stand out in the crowd. They are all heroes.

The first POW's story cited is of the first naval officer shot down and captured in North Vietnam and subsequently held for the duration of the war. This pilot was US Navy Lieutenant-Junior Grade Everett Alvarez, Jr. Following Alvarez's story is another first, then USAF Major Fred V. Cherry, Sr. Cherry was one of the first black officers held during the war and a POW whom the V (short for the North Vietnamese) saw as a propaganda prize due to the color of his skin. Others that follow include US Army Special Forces 1st Lieutenant James N. Rowe who was captured and held in a southern jungle camp until his escape five years later.

Still others include a junior Navy-enlisted man, Seaman Douglas Hegdahl, who while a POW at the Hanoi Hilton, pretended as if he was mentally disturbed and, during an SRO (Senior Ranking officer)—approved early release, Hegdahl took back vital information back about Americans held at the Hanoi Hilton. Other POW stories include USAF 1st Lt Tom Hanton, a crewman on board an Air Force F-4 Phantom flyer shot down in June 1972 and, Bill Wilson, an Air Force F-111 flyer shot down in December 1972 who evaded capture for seven days before being captured and was a POW for the remainder of the war.

The United States committed ground combat forces during July 1965 when President Lyndon Baines Johnson ordered Marines ashore in Da Nang, South Vietnam. By this time during the war, the insurgency in this Southeast Asian nation was mature. Nguyen Ai Quoc (known to the west as Ho Chi Minh)[1] and his small circle of devoted followers organized their nationalist struggle for a forced re-unification of the two Vietnams. During WWII, the North Vietnamese fought the Japanese and later the French in what they viewed as the First Indochina War. To the North Vietnamese, this was a nationalist war of independence—a war of liberation. Ho Chi Minh's strategy was a unique blend of North Vietnamese and Chinese (Maoist) philosophies.[2] The coming war was to be a war of attrition, a war that America's military forces neither fully understood nor were equipped to fight. Today we call this tactic "unconventional warfare" and it is adopted as a part of the larger counterinsurgency strategy. We must step back to earlier times to understand the escalation of America's military might in this war, however.

In 1962, President John F. Kennedy, and later Lyndon Baines Johnson set in motion a series of events that eventually led to our nation's full military engagement in this war in Southeast Asia. Among the first of these events was the issuance of National Security Action Memorandum 124 (NSAM-124) dated January 18, 1962. This NSAM directed counterinsurgency be elevated to equal standing alongside other forms of warfare.[3]

At this same time, the US was becoming increasingly involved in the Cold War. Earlier the US watched as the French were defeated in the battle of Dien Bien Phu in the central highlands of North Vietnam. A sizable French force was besieged and finally surrendered to the fledging Democratic Republic of Vietnam forces. The French were done, and bearing in mind the Domino Theory, the United States did not stand idly by and become another nation to fall to communism, having already watched several European nations suffer that fate.

As time went on, American support for the conflict in Southeast Asia increased. Likewise, America's military activity increased—secretly in Laos and Cambodia, and quietly in South Vietnam. In the early sixties, the American Department of Defense developed Operation Plan 34A (or OpLan 34A), a classified war plan that directed actions intended to convince the North Vietnamese to stop their attempts at unifying the two Vietnams. Early in 1963, the US Navy deployed its new special operations forces to South Vietnam—US Navy SEALs (which stands for "Sea Air Land" teams). Until 1963, these operations remained under the control of the Central Intelligence Agency (CIA) but the military, under the newly established Military Advisory Group, Vietnam (MAC-V), took control of operations in Vietnam in early 1964.

By mid-summer 1964, the North Vietnamese increased their naval defenses in the areas patrolled by the Americans and South Vietnamese commandoes. Moreover, the Americans greatly increased their presence in the Gulf of Tonkin and surrounding waters. Just after midnight on the evening of July 31, 1964, four Nastie patrol craft (operated by US Navy SEALS) and carrying South Vietnamese commandoes approached targets off the North Vietnamese coast. After receiving word that the North Vietnamese knew of the presence of US personnel (operating the craft) and South Vietnamese commandoes, the Nasties decided to use some of their deck-mounted guns to fire on the North Vietnamese coastal gun emplacements. After the Nasties completed their firing, they departed the area and returned to their bases in South Vietnam. At about the same time, the *USS Maddox* was involved in offshore signal collection activities known as Desoto Patrols. The *USS Maddox* was not aware of the SEALs operating along the North Vietnamese coast. American history then records during the period from July 31 through August 4, 1964, North Vietnamese surface combat vessels conducted unprovoked attacks on two American war ships in international waters—the *USS Maddox* and the *USS Turner Joy*. President Johnson consulted the US Congress and, through the Gulf of Tonkin Resolution, received permission to commit US combat power to assist the South Vietnamese in their battle against Communism.

This "US combat power" included US aircraft carriers, one of which was near Hong Kong and was told to immediately redeploy to the Vietnamese coast. The two carriers soon moved into the area for retaliatory raids on North Vietnamese military targets—and thus provided ample opportunities for American servicemen to be taken prisoner by our new foe in Southeast Asia. But were the Americans ready for such an environment? Not entirely, at least not according to Alvarez and many others shot down early in the war.

> *"It was during the latter part of 1964 and early 1965 that the needs were fully recognized for a specialized jungle survival, evasion, and escape course to cover those aspects of SEA that could not be fully treated at a generalized school, such as that at Fairchild AFB. As USAF combat involvement increased, starting with the Rolling Thunder campaign over North Vietnam in February 1965, the need became more and more apparent. Aircrews survival-trained in January, sloshing through the snow of northeast Washington State, were not being really prepared for what awaited them if they had to eject over a monsoonal forest of Vietnam four months later. Headquarters USAF directed PACAF to establish a school to "provide SEA bound aircrews with Jungle Survival techniques and procedures, Southeast Asia indoctrination, practical application of evasion and escape techniques peculiar to SEA, and rescue procedures." The PACAF Jungle Survival School was officially designated*

at Clark AB, P.I., on 12 April 1965, in compliance with Hq USAF requirements for USAF aircrews being assigned to Southeast Asia."[4]

Nevertheless, President Johnson appeared on national television on August 5th and told the American people that the United States had conducted air operations against the boats and facilities that were responsible for the earlier Gulf of Tonkin incidents. Ironically, some of the forces that were assigned to fly these missions heard President Johnson's declaration of these attacks before they launched into North Vietnamese airspace for the attacks being talked about on television. The President did not make allowances for the time differences (between East Coast Time—Washington, DC and Vietnam) before making these televised statements about military operations being launched. Hanoi/Saigon are eleven hours ahead of Washington DC time. The North Vietnamese knew the American planes were coming before they even took off. The story of American naval POWs in Southeast Asia started here.

EVERETT ALVAREZ

The first naval prisoner of war in North Vietnam was U.S. Navy Lieutenant-Junior Grade Everett Alvarez, Jr., who flew one of two aircrafts mentioned earlier by President Johnson's televised announcement as having been shot down. On the evening of August 4th, Alvarez's ship, the aircraft carrier *USS Constellation* moved into the Tonkin Gulf to support the retaliatory strikes in Haiphong Harbor and other selected targets in North Vietnam.

LTJG Alvarez flew a single-seat attack aircraft called the A-4 Skyhawk. The *USS Constellation* (or the Connie) was previously in Hong Kong on a port call, but her stay was shortened due to brewing hostilities in the Tonkin Gulf. In the dark of the night, a flight of A-4 Skyhawks soon launched and headed for its target area, 450 miles away, in the dead of night and with very low visibility. After flying a few frustrating hours in dismal conditions, the flight of A-4s returned to the mother ship, none of the pilots having seen any ships, vessels, or anything else. Frustration was high among the aircrew.

Diagram 8

Everett Alvarez, Jr. present day

Author's Personal Collection

By 08:30 that morning, the United States Department of Defense and national intelligence agencies started receiving North Vietnamese military communications that had been intercepted during the previous two days. By noon on August 5th, the US military and political leadership ordered retaliatory strikes, amidst controversy surrounding exactly what had occurred. Soon the pilots were woken up on the Connie and told that they would be taking in part in raids into North Vietnam for the next several days.

On August 5th, 1964 two ships launched aircraft—the *USS Constellation* as well as the *USS Ticonderoga.* Launching in mid-afternoon, the Connie's crew had already received word that the Ticonderoga's flight of twenty-two aircraft were returning from their strikes—and with only one aircraft hit—and had been able to divert to Danang and land safely. After going through his normal pre-flights, Alvarez rendered a salute from the cockpit of his aircraft, signaling to the carrier's launch crew that he was prepared to launch. Seconds later, Alvarez's plane was airborne and headed for targets in North Vietnam.

Although Alvarez was airborne and on the way to his assigned targets, did an apparatus or system exist to ensure his speedy recovery should he be shot down? One government report speaks to this issue. In part, the

> *". . . Joint Personnel Recovery Center (JPRC), activated on 17 September 1966 served as the coordinating agency for the recovery of US military and civilian personnel, as well as those of other Free World Military Assistance Forces (FWMAF), who managed to evade capture, to escape, or to benefit from the occasional and unexpected*

> *hostile forces' generosity in releasing certain American or allied personnel. As the parameters of the war were extended, the JPRC's operations expanded to include North Vietnam, Laos, the Khmer Republic, and Thailand."*[5]

Alvarez was shot down prior to the formal establishment of the JPRC's support of operations in Southeast Asia. Still, a limited rescue capability existed at this time. In part, in

> *"1964 when the first units of the Air Rescue Service reached Southeast Asia with Kaman HH-43B helicopters, they were not prepared for the unique challenges of combat aircrew recovery in the jungles and mountains of Vietnam and Laos . . . . Accordingly, Air Rescue Service doctrine focused on providing peacetime search and rescue (SAR) for the continental United States, coverage along the overseas' air and sea lanes, and recovery of astronauts and space equipment . . . .*
>
> *In October 1961, the Air Rescue Service integrated 70 local base rescue units into its structure, acquiring 69 H-43Bs, 17 older, piston-driven H-43As, 58 obsolete Sikorsky H-19Bs, and four even less useful Piasecki SH-21 Bs. The Kaman H-43s, meant to augment the base fire and crash rescue capability, had no armor, no weapons, and a mere 75-mile radius of action. Still, they were destined to form the nucleus of the early aircrew recovery force in Southeast Asia."*[6]

Once Alvarez reached his target area, he started his ingress to the assigned targets—patrol craft in a North Vietnamese harbor. Alvarez did not immediately see the target ships, but at the last moment, he spotted them and tried to readjust his aircraft into firing position for his rocket pods. Alvarez was forced come around a second time. Alvarez went in for a second attempt at the enemy ships, some of them already hit and on fire. During this second run, he was behind his wingman.[7] As Alvarez conducted his gun run, he saw his 20mm rounds hit the enemy vessel. Pulling off target but remaining behind his wingman, Alvarez noticed a lot of tracer rounds, followed by a bright yellow flash on the left side of his aircraft. Alvarez was hit, and a few seconds later he communicated over his radio that he was in trouble. He pulled the eject handle and soon descended in a parachute to North Vietnamese waters.[8]

Alvarez knew his best chances of remaining free would mean going farther out to sea where friendly search and rescue (SAR) forces could reach him. Failing this, if he got far enough out to sea, at least friendly naval vessels such as cruisers or frigates could recover him. In this instance, the targets his plane had struck were too far inside enemy territory for this to be a realistic option. Alvarez realized he was in the water being pursued by North Vietnamese craft. At about this same time, he recalled once being told that a some enemy forces in Southeast Asia "would shoot if we were armed," so he took his pistol out of its sheath and let it go. It instantly sunk in the ocean.[9]

After orally inflating his life preserver, Alvarez realized this made him an easier mark for capture. He attempted to release some of the air so he would not simply bob in the water like a cork. Unfortunately for Alvarez, it was already too late—he had been spotted, and the enemy was bearing down on him fast. Rounds splashed around him in the water. Very shortly thereafter, Alvarez was pulled inside a fishing boat along with some of his gear. The enemy craft "pulled alongside, looped my hands and neck with ropes and yanked" him aboard.[10]

Once on dragged onboard the North Vietnamese vessel, Alvarez was searched and his knife and pistol were confiscated. Anything else of value was taken from him, including his boots, socks and G-suit. G-suits, or gravity suits, are vests pilots wear around their torso and legs to prevent blood from rushing to their legs during high speed turns. During high speed maneuvers, pilots not wearing G-suits would lose consciousness due to the loss of blood in their upper extremities. Alvarez lay on the Vietnamese boat, not knowing what would happen next. Alvarez recalled stories of the horrible treatment he would likely receive as a POW.

During his initial capture, Alvarez experienced a certain level of capture shock. This capture shock is the physical effect brought on by traumatic events such as battle, capture, or car wrecks. For POWs, however, this part of capture is quite important because when men are first captured, understanding this "capture shock" can mean the difference between life and death due to the decisions that must be made. For example, the "fight or flight" decisions are made at the time of capture. The person being captured must calculate the situation correctly. In this case, Alvarez attempting to overpower the guards might have seemed heroic, but in reality, an attempt to escape would have, in all likelihood, ended in his death.

Alvarez was transferred to a larger vessel and eventually to shore—to the small coastal port village of Hon Gai. Ominously, Hon Gai was the very port he had just strafed with his A-4 aircraft's 20mm guns. Alvarez was taken from the boat, blindfolded and barefoot. He was led to a small room where he remained for several hours, at which time his picture was taken. Alvarez was later questioned and fed. When questioned, he gave his name, rank, serial number, and date of birth, as required by the Geneva Conventions.

Although slightly injured, Alvarez was in relatively good shape given that he had undergone an uncontrolled ejection from an aircraft going in excess of 500 miles per hour. Alvarez ached—he had suffered a flesh wound as the result of being struck by a bullet. Later, his flight suit was removed and he was forced to wear blue and white-striped prison garb. Shortly after changing his clothes, Alvarez was placed in a jeep and again blindfolded.

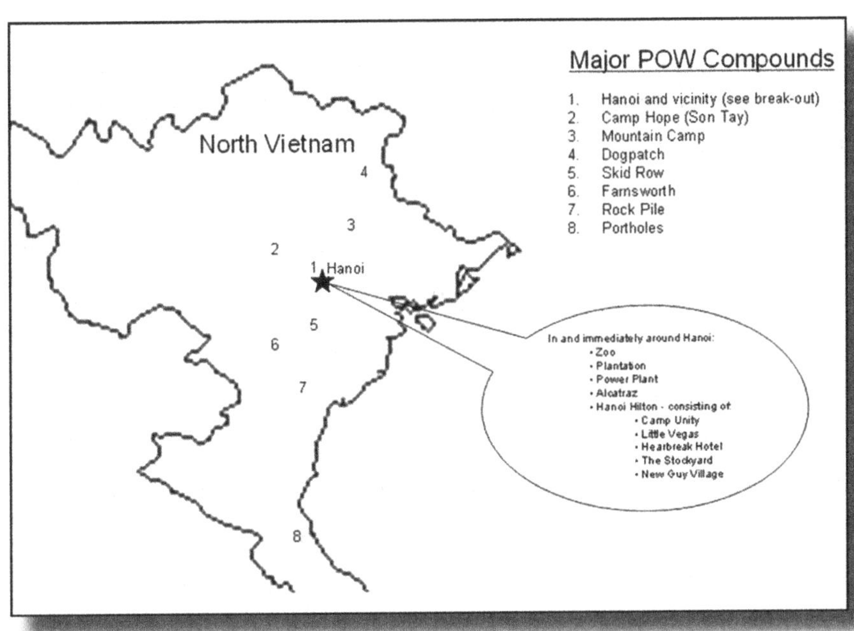

Diagram 9

POW Compounds in / around Hanoi during the war in Southeast Asia

After arriving at an interim movement location, the Hon Gay jail, Alvarez was interrogated by North Vietnamese military officers.[11] Following two days of interrogations, the two North Vietnamese officers conducting these interrogations became frustrated, telling Alvarez that he was being deceived by his own government and that the Gulf of Tonkin incident had never occurred, unlike what the American and Western press professed.

Later, Alvarez's interrogator, Owl, asked him about his family. When Alvarez refused to give any information regarding his family, Owl parroted information about Alvarez's wife, children, and hometown. Although startled that Owl knew this information, Alvarez surmised that the North Vietnamese obtained this information from newspaper stories detailing Alvarez's shoot-down. On August 11, 1964, nearly a week after his shoot down, Alvarez was taken to the Hanoi Hilton.[12]

Hoa Lo—or the Hanoi Hilton, as it was known—lies in the center of Hanoi, North Vietnam. Hanoi (named 'the City in a Bend of a River') sits primarily along the western banks of the Red River which runs southeast to northwest through the city. Besides being a formidable prison, the Hanoi Hilton served as the headquarters of North Vietnam's prison system. The compound took up several city blocks. The walls are said to have been 4-6 feet thick and, to discourage those that would consider an escape attempt, the walls were adorned with broken bottles, barbed wire and an electrical wire. Once outside the compound, any American escapees would also have had to blend in with the city's population, a near impossible task given the height of most Americans when compared to the height of the average Vietnamese citizen. This is, of course, in addition to the color of most Americans' skin. In short, escaping over these walls of from within this city would be no easy matter.

Upon his initial entry into the Hanoi Hilton, Alvarez was issued prison garb. At first, he found the food revolting: pieces of animal, dead birds, and other foul objects were served to him at various times in his bowl. A short time later, Alvarez was taken to an exhibition of American aircraft previously shot down, his aircraft among those being displayed. Then, one day, an officer Alvarez had not previously seen came in flanked by Owl and the guard from the Hon Gay jail. This officer was obviously important, and to make matters worse, he spoke impeccable English. This introduction was the start of six weeks of interrogations that took place nearly 12 hours a day, six days a week. Before Alvarez knew what was occurring, the officer started talking about soccer, and soon had Alvarez freely talking about American soccer. Alvarez was tricked by his interrogator into talking about presumably innocent topics. Throughout these seemingly harmless discussions, Alvarez was reminded that his cause was useless and that he was a war criminal since the United States had never made a formal declaration of war. These discussions were not so innocent after all; the V had distinct motives in their conversations with Alvarez—and they were good at extracting information as Alvarez would come to know all too well.

As the interrogations continued, late summer turned into early winter and Alvarez was eventually allowed to send and receive mail, albeit when his captors decided that he deserved such a privilege. As was expected, the V read his outgoing and incoming mail first—but at least his wife, Tangee, knew that he was alive. It also became apparent to Alvarez that his captors did not wish to kill or shoot him, but wanted to keep him alive and exploit him for propaganda.

Later, Alvarez met another interrogator—one that many American POWs came to know and come to loathe. He was known as "Rabbit" because of the size of his ears in relation to the rest of his head.

As 1964 turned to 1965, the war intensified in the south with the Marines having gone ashore in Da Nang, South Vietnam in July. Alvarez was not the sole American prisoner of war for long. As America's war in Southeast Asia intensified, another flyer, Shumaker, joined Alvarez at the Hanoi Hilton. Later, more Americans joined those already at the Hanoi Hilton. The war was on and the Hanoi Hilton was filling up with prisoners. By mid-1965, the prisoners communicated using the POW TAP Code (see Figure 10, below). Although normally used to pass along information vital to the POWs such as what had been communicated to the interrogators, comical messages were sometimes sent as well. In one instance, the message "JOAN BAEZ SUCCS"[13] was sent, indicating that the popular folk singer was very unpopular in the Hanoi Hilton because of her anti-war views—much to the temporary enjoyment of its recipients.

A	B	C/K	D	E
F	G	H	I	J
L	M	N	O	P
Q	R	S	T	U
V	W	X	Y	Z

Diagram 10

The POW TAP Code

It was these early prisoners in the "Heartbreak Hotel" who refined the use of the POW TAP Code. The prisoners needed a way to covertly communicate to each other due to the guards' ability to hear the prisoners' voices. More importantly, confining the prisoners in different locations with only a gap high up in the cells through which they could communicate made communications more difficult. By the end of his first year in Hanoi, Alvarez was one of more than a dozen American prisoners. The prisoners included notables such as Guarino, Purcell, and Denton among others. Although these POWs didn't know it at the time, movies and books would later be written about the exploits of these pioneering POWs of the war in Southeast Asia.

A prisoner of slightly more than a year by the fall of 1965, Alvarez's food was cut in half. Time allowed outside of his prison cell was cut down to ten minutes, just enough time to empty and clean his waste bucket, wash his clothes, and wash himself. The remaining time of each 24 hour period was spent in his cell. While in his cell, he communicated with others using the POW TAP Code. He would daydream about his wife, Tangee—thinking about romantic times they spent together. When able, Alvarez and many of the other prisoners did push-ups, take long walks in their cells, and anything else they could do to keep their minds and bodies occupied. Not long after this, on September 12, 1965, Commander James Stockdale joined the more than a dozen Air Force and Navy fliers. By the time Stockdale reached the Hanoi Hilton, and having been shot down three days prior, Stockdale was wearing a cast on his leg and had a broken back. This POW was the Commander Air Group 16 from a naval carrier positioned in the Tonkin Gulf.

One Sunday, in fact, the first Sunday after being moved to another part of the North Vietnamese prison system—the Briar Patch, and although the guards forbade the prisoners to talk, Alvarez prayed in their ritual Sunday services—loud enough for him to hear the others, and for them to hear him. At the end of the prayer, the Star Spangled Banner was sung. Tears ran down Alvarez's face—not from self-pity or despair but from pride that he was in the company of such men.

Many of the prisoners closer to the main Hanoi Hilton compound were moved to compounds outside of the capital city due to the constant air raids. The V needed the prisoners alive if they were to get propaganda from them. The prisoners' new home was the "Zoo", a compound so named because the prisoners were able to watch those outside their prison cells. The Zoo, adjacent to a North Vietnamese airfield was a couple of miles southwest of the Hanoi complex. The senior prisoner, Colonel Robbie Risner, soon passed along guidance to the other prisoners on how to conduct themselves.

The SRO told the other prisoners to collect everything: nails, information on the camps, rooms where they were held, information on the guards. This information would be passed to the other prisoners, using letter dead-drops and the POW TAP Code. Risner also told the other prisoners, Alvarez included, not to antagonize the guards—but not to give in to them either. Risner was the SRO, or senior ranking officer. These prisoners' battlefield was the prison—they did not think of themselves as discharged as a result of their capture. They simply were in a different area of the country in which to fight the enemy—and different means at their disposal.[14]

On July 6, 1966, many of the prisoners at the Zoo and Briar Patch were placed in trucks and transported into Hanoi. They did not know why they were taken, but they soon found out. The prisoners were taken into Hanoi for a parade of prisoners; displayed on camera so the world could see the American war criminals. The prisoners were shackled to each other as they marched along the crowded streets. The parade did not turn out as the North Vietnamese planned, however. As the prisoners walked along the parade route, North Vietnamese citizens struck the prisoners with their fists, rocks, and bottles—so much so that the guards instructed the captives to stay together and run back to the safety of their compound. The senior prisoners ordered the men to keep their heads high while being pelted, which they did. The North Vietnamese propaganda plan failed in front of the world, their propaganda ploy turned public relations nightmare. The world got a glimpse of the supposedly "fair and lenient" nature of the North Vietnamese government. In addition to the world witnessing the march, many previously unconfirmed prisoners of war—until then declared Missing in Action—were seen on television; therefore their condition and presence confirmed. By all accounts, the parade was a strategic failure for the North Vietnamese.

That summer, and for some time thereafter, the interrogations got progressively longer and harsher. The V wanted signed confessions, and they wanted the POWs to believe that they were war criminals. In one interrogation, Alvarez was tortured until he wrote a confession which, due to the wording and content, also revealed that he had produced the statement while being coerced. Later, he was forced to read a statement which would be later played over the radio. When Alvarez and others kept misspeaking and pronouncing words incorrectly, the V complained that for a group of people who were supposed to be so well educated, the Americans could not read very well. This was not the case at all. Most of the American officers were college educated, some with advanced degrees. The Americans could read very well indeed but this appearance of poor grammar and reading skills was part of their resistance posture, and it worked.[15]

During December 1966, Alvarez was again asked to write a letter stating how good his Christmases had been since he was taken prisoner. Although he did not write this letter as requested, the Christmas season brought on a slight but brief relaxation of camp rules and regulations. The prisoners were allowed to make a few crude decorations and even receive mail from home. Alvarez got a letter from Tangee from the previous August. The prisoners even received a turkey dinner and were permitted to watch a Christmas "movie". In this film, Vietnamese girls were seen frolicking about until they all of a sudden were killed by American bombs. The prisoners were in individual cubicles, and although the guards hung blankets in the hopes that they could not see each other, the POWs were soon chatting in TAP Code. The POWs received updates on who was at which compound, who the new guys were, and new guidance from the SRO, etc. This was all done to maintain their spirits and follow SRO regulations.[16] In the words of several POWs all the tapping made the Hanoi Hilton sound like a place infested with woodpeckers.

Following the Hanoi parade, Alvarez and others felt the wrath of their guards in the form of torture and interrogations. In one particularly brutal session:

> *"They held my hands behind my back and closed the ratchet cuffs around my wrists, squeezing the metal to the last notch. But my wrists are smallish and they could see they were not biting in hard enough. They opened them up, bent my arms as close together as they could and fastened*

the cuff tightly a few inches below my elbows. The pain was excruciating. It felt like a hacksaw had stuck deep in my flesh. The cuffs seemed to cut through to the bone. My head was pushed far forward and all I could do was yell and scream to ride with the pain . . . . The worse it got, the louder I shrieked. The more I howled the more they slapped and punched. J.C. [his interrogator] preferred to strike from behind but when he came from in front it was always with the underside of his closed fist. My eyes felt like popping . . . . Write, they shouted . . . . By mid-day I knew I had reached the end of my tether. There was no fight left in me . . ."[17]

When they took the cuffs off Alvarez, his hands were numb and he temporally lost the use of them. It took several hours before Alvarez regained the use of his hands. Finally, he penned a "confession" for his captors. Later, Alvarez found out that his cellmate had also been tortured to gain a confession of their "war crimes". Alvarez felt he had betrayed his country, but like many other POWs who were coerced into confessing, they bounced back—making the V work harder for the information next time. To cite a phrase often used, broken POWs "bounce back", becoming stronger for the next time and holding out for as long as they can. The prisoners' strategy was that when the V tortured you and got certain information, you recovered and then made them torture you again for the same information—never allowing them free information.

In fact, while they were in Camp Unity, the cell next to Alvarez's was a torture cell. Alvarez and his cellmate, Tom, heard the screams of pain and agony being inflicted on fellow Americans just feet away from them and were powerless to do anything about it. In one case, Ed Davis, a Navy Lieutenant, Junior Grade, was brought in and interrogated and tortured for a week. During the times when Alvarez believed the guards had left the room, the POWs would send TAP Code messages of encouragement to Davis. One such message was "Hang in there buddy. We're with you all the way. And Good night, Ed. God Bless."[18] Later the POWs used phrases like "GBU" for "God Bless You" to shorten their coded messages. In time, the POWs came to understand the vital importance of these covert communications. When new POWs arrived, following the confirmation of their bona fides to ensure that they were not plants from the V, the new prisoners were trained in these communications techniques.

Later, in 1967, the prisoners learned a Cuban interrogator—a guest of the North Vietnamese—was brought in to the Hanoi Hilton. The interrogator, whom the Americans eventually named Fidel, was ruthless and sadistic. Although the Cuban interrogated and tortured many of the POWs, Alvarez was left alone after the first couple of sessions. When the Cubans took over part of the Zoo, they "were mean, they killed people . . . . they were pretty hard. He's the one that when I was being screened . . . he played the race card with me [Alvarez] about how both of these two were Hispanics and the neo-colonialist powers were exploiting them . . . how the [Americans] would give the Cubans sugar and they'd give us Coca-Cola . . . but it didn't seem to be an issue of race for assigning his cell-mate." It seemed to be more an issue of rank—when Alvarez had cellmates, it seemed to be more a matter of equivalent rank and whether or not they would sign the North Vietnamese' confessions and propaganda documents.[19]

Maybe it was because Alvarez was the longest held POW in the Hanoi Hilton that the V felt he was their special one, or for other reasons? In any case, the Cubans tortured and inflicted pain for information that at times seemed meaningless, such as questions regarding the planes they flew. Two Air Force officers were once beat unmercifully with rubber hoses and received electric shocks. After one of these two prisoners evidently died, the V became disenchanted with Fidel and the other Cuban guests—and after that, their ruthless torture was curtailed. The Cubans' actions were then monitored much more closely and they were no longer free to roam about the camp, causing pain at will.

The V understood that if the POWs remained alive, they could be exploited for valuable intelligence and propaganda.[20] Their attempts to separate Alvarez from the other POWs due to his "Mexican background" continued, but Alvarez believes that the attempts to separate people by races were much more extensive for the African American prisoners than for him as a Hispanic. Notably, however, Alvarez did not discover that he was Hispanic until after being released: "I [Alvarez] didn't know I was Hispanic until I got back". The term had not been in use when he was shot down in 1964, but he was called Hispanic upon his return from captivity, as "a term that was coined during the Nixon Administration . . . . I thought Hispanic was some sort of sewing circle [when I saw it on the banners when I returned]."[21]

Because of such torture and interrogations, communications remained the lifeblood of the POWs. Alvarez believes that contact "with one another was essential as a deep sea diver drawing on a reserve tank of oxygen. Without it, we were doomed. We could not allow our coded links to be silenced nor our invisible bonds to be sabotaged . . . . This commitment to unity saw many a lame and hobbled individual through the darkest days and the most perilous moments."[22] Alvarez used two main forms of communication, aside from talking with fellow prisoners when the opportunity presented itself. These two methods were the POW TAP Code and the Mute Code. Alvarez wasn't formally taught the Mute Code. One of Alvarez's cellmates, Kile Dag Berg—nicknamed "Red"—had a relative who was mute and therefore taught Alvarez and many of the other prisoners at the Hanoi Hilton how to communicate using this method. Alvarez and the other prisoners would stand on each other's shoulders and sign to each other, using the small hole provided for ventilation near the tops of their cells.[23]

On January 17, 1969, Alvarez received a care package from home. This care package contained powdered milk, a plastic comb, vitamins, and aspirin. One of the other POWs received instant coffee in his care package. This was a real treat for the POWs, but unfortunately these did not come without a cost. The V continued with their requests for the POWs' written statements of "fair and lenient treatment" by the Democratic Republic of Vietnam. The spring of 1969 marked a frenzied increase in torture by the North Vietnamese. One of the believed causes of this worsening in treatment was an escape attempt by two officers; Dramesi and Atterberry. The two successfully broke out of the Hanoi Hilton and made it to the Red River but were soon caught by North Vietnamese soldiers. They were interrogated and tortured—Atterberry later died. Likewise, many of the Hanoi Hilton's POWs were also interrogated and tortured for their apparent part of knowledge of this failed escape attempt. The SRO's reasons for not approving of the escape attempt were sound. He believed that their likelihood of a successful attempt was so low that it made the attempt not worth the likely outcome. Moreover, the Paris Peace Talks were occurring in France and the SRO did not want to derail those negotiations. Following the escape attempt, the guards beat the POWs, moved prisoners to different cells, and broke small portions of their code—but they were unable to stop their resistance and covert communications.[24]

In coming weeks, the V continued their pressuring of Alvarez for a recorded message containing contritions' for his acts as a "war criminal." In one such torture session, Alvarez received communications with words of encouragement from Fred Cherry, the senior ranking officer of another cell. In part, Fred's TAP Coded message read "Just do your best."[25] Eventually, Alvarez was beaten enough to get him to submit to making the recording. For the V, however, this was a failed attempt because many of Alvarez's words were so slurred and the grammar so poor that the V could not use the recordings. They never came to Alvarez again for a recording.[26] Alvarez won this round, although he may not have felt like it at the time.

On September 3, 1969, the guards approached the prisoners wearing black armbands. Their leader, Ho Chi Minh, died and the country was in national mourning. Aside from September 1969 being when the V's leader died, something more important for the POWs also occurred that month—their treatment improved significantly. They started receiving more food and less brutality. Although Ho Chi Minh's death contributed to this better treatment, the realization that for the Paris Peace Talks to succeed, the bargaining chips had to be worth the effort—and the prisoners were those bargaining chips also had its effects. The POWs had to survive. Ho Chi Minh's death was a turning point and marked the convergence of several periods of captivity for Alvarez.

Although conditions slowly improved, news from home was still vital for the POWs' morale. In Alvarez's case, communications with his wife and parents critical. Over the next few years Alvarez noted a decrease of letters, as well as a noted change in the tone of his letters from Tangee. Although she eventually told Alvarez's parents that she had moved on. Tangee went to Mexico to get a divorce and marry another man. Alvarez himself first learned this news from his interrogator before finally seeing it in writing. His wife left him.[27]

In the final months and weeks of 1970, the POWs' treatment continued to improve.[28] Given more time outside their cells, some sports equipment, and a lessening of torture, the prisoners' health got markedly better—some POWs even gained weight. When this period of increased food and improving health began, Alvarez could only do five push-ups. Later, he was doing ten times that amount. But these were not the only changes that occurred.

The POWs, almost 400 in total, were brought together in a central location: the Hanoi Hilton in central Hanoi.[29] Why? Because the Americans had conducted a raid on a small POW camp northwest of Hanoi called Son Tay. Although no POWs were rescued in this action, the North Vietnamese were shaken in their belief that the prisoners were in secure locations and could not be rescued. Once together, the POWs could talk and confirm who was being held, and who had died in captivity. The SRO rules, called "plums" to disguise them in case the V intercepted coded messages, had been in place since 1967 or 1968. These plums matured through time and were communicated to POWs.

In September 1971, Alvarez and a fellow POW named Jerry Coffee briefed two new prisoners on the POWs' rules, as well as on the history and intensity of interrogations. For three days, Coffee and Alvarez recounted all the details to the two new arrivals: the hoses, the manacles, the beatings, the forced confessions, etc. The two new POWs seemed to take the information almost with indifference. It was later discovered that these two new prisoners were collaborators who passed information along to the V. They made deals with the guards for better treatment and more food. In addition, the two even went as far as informing on fellow prisoners when they were communicating covertly. The two also helped the V lock up prisoners—fellow Americans. The remainder of the POWs in Hanoi continued to live up to the code, however.

On Christmas Day, 1971, Alvarez was finally told that his wife had left him. This also happened to others while being held POW in Vietnam. "Rabbit was heartlessly forthright. 'Alvarez, here is a letter from your mother. Your wife has left you for another man.'" Alvarez was floored by such news, after all those years of not receiving much information. He had considered possibilities like his wife being in bad health or suffering a car wreck, but never thought she would leave him for another man. Still, Alvarez loved Tangee and hoped she was happy. During the spring of 1972, while out among the new flowers and nice clean air, Alvarez finally made peace about his wife leaving him. He then considered what he would do once freed—after all he'd be a single man again.[30] Time went on—the war went on. The nightly air raids continued. The POWs regularly saw B-52s in the skies over Hanoi. The year 1972 slowly turned into 1973, and a few days prior to the end of January, the guards came into the cells with news.

The guards ordered everyone on Alvarez's room into a central room filled with official-looking Vietnamese people. They started reading translations of what they claimed were agreements from the Paris Peace Talks for the end of the war and the release of all POWs. The prisoners had heard such talk before. Later, the guards paid the Americans a tribute by saying "You Americans, you're not like the French," meaning that the V had not been able to make us break rank. A few days later, on February 11, 1973, the POWs were given new clothes and shoes to wear. The next day, they were given a bus ride, but unlike on the previous one, the prisoners were not handcuffed or otherwise restrained. Then, while at Gia Lam Airport, they saw big planes, American C-141s, coming in to land—their rides to freedom. The Americans had their names called out and were put in groups on the airplanes headed for the Philippines and then Hawaii before finally reaching the continental United States. While in the Philippines, the returnees received medical checks, showers, uniforms, and, of course, intelligence debriefings.

The entire war—the eight and a half years Alvarez spent as a prisoner of the North Vietnamese—can be divided into three general periods. First was the period from 1964 through January 1966. During this time frame, the North Vietnamese did not know exactly what to do with Alvarez. At first, the V had believed that Alvarez might be from Algeria—due to the color of his skin—and possibly believed that he was a French Legionnaire. Attempts to extract information and exploit Alvarez for propaganda purposes were common throughout this and all the periods.

The next period of time was roughly from January 1966 to September 1969—the end of this period marked by Ho Chi Minh's death and the commencement of the Paris Peace Talks. This second period was characterized as particularly brutal as evidenced by frequent North Vietnamese torture. During this time, Alvarez recalls many grueling and painful torture sessions that on some occasions seemed more sadistic in nature than having any military purpose. By the July 6, 1966 Hanoi parade, Alvarez writes, "they were already harsh . . . and I think what happened was after that, they had free reign . . . they themselves [had been] treated this way by the French" in these same buildings built at the turn of the nineteenth century. "The same people that were our interrogators had been in these prisons themselves built by the French."[31]

Finally, the third period lasted from September 1969 through OPERATION HOME COMING in February and March of 1973. Following the death of Ho Chi Minh on September 2, 1969, the conditions slowly improved. The prisoners started receiving better food, got more frequent mail and care packages, and were allowed more outside activities within the prison yard. At latter points during their captivity, Alvarez and his fellow inmates were allowed to play basketball within the prison walls.[32]

Today, only the front portion of the Hanoi Hilton remains. The remainder of this complex was torn down due to postwar concerns over the negative international image created by the prison's notoriety. The small section still standing—and the Hanoi Hilton complex once spanned several city blocks—was turned into a museum. Alvarez visited Hanoi in 1999, and has taken other trips since then. On his 1999 visit, he enjoyed a drink and a Casadia in a restaurant known as the Purple Onion and a corresponding bar, Fat Jax, atop one of Hanoi's five-star hotels. He enjoyed the nice view of the city, but soon noticed something much more ironic. His seat in this fine restaurant-bar was directly above what used to be his prison cell in the Hanoi Hilton—known as Little Vegas.[33] Alvarez had spent six months in solitary confinement in Little Vegas before being released and joining the other prisoners.[34]

In total, Everett Alvarez was held by the North Vietnamese from August 5, 1964 until his release in OPERATION HOME COMING. He retired from the United States Navy as a Commander (O-5). Afterwards, Alvarez continued to serve his country, first as the Deputy Director of the Peace Corps, then later as Deputy Director of the Veterans Administration. Alvarez is now the Chief Executive Officer of a successful business in Silver Spring, Maryland, and lives with his wife, Tammy, in the Washington, DC area.

FRED V. CHERRY, SR.

Being the first or one of the early pioneers in a sport or any other activity can be challenging. This statement is even truer when the event being discussed deals with prisoners of war. Cherry's story is one of an officer and a gentleman in the United States Air Force; an officer who served his country with distinction as a combat pilot during the Korean War, a Vietnam-era combat pilot turned prisoner of war who performed above and beyond the call of duty as a prisoner of war. This is the story of one of the few black pilots during the early 1950s who endured racism on and off base, and finally, because of his race, it is the story of a prisoner singled out by the North Vietnamese in their attempts to use him as an integral part of their propaganda program at a time when America was being torn apart at the seams over racism.

Fred Cherry was one of eight children reared in Suffolk, Virginia. Fred was the youngest of eight; four boys and four girls, whose father was a farmer. His family was very close-knit, morals and integrity being the family's foundation. From an early age, Cherry figured out that honesty was far more important than money and other physical possessions. What his family had was minimal, but whatever they had, they learned to take care of. While a youngster, Cherry heard tales of the Tuskegee Airmen and associated programs designed to give blacks more opportunities such as flying. At the time, many whites believed that blacks simply did not have the aptitude for such complicated tasks as flying. Until the First Lady, Eleanor Roosevelt, was flown by a black pilot while on a visit to Alabama, many did not believe blacks should be given such opportunities.[35] The Tuskegee Airman program was successful, and this did not pass young Cherry by. Flying was what he wanted to do.

When Cherry was eleven years old, he got sick with an acute appendicitis and moved in with his sister shortly thereafter. Although he moved in with his sister, he kept in close contact with his mother. Due to his sister's affluence, he was afforded the opportunity to gain good medical care and later attend college. Although his sister and brother-in-law wanted him to be a doctor, the young Cherry had other plans. When Cherry was sixteen, he got a summer job in the Norfolk shipyards, where he learned lessons that would serve him well later in life. After high school, he went on to college and eventually was far enough along in his studies to contact the military and sign up for a pilot cadet program. When contacted by Cherry, the US Navy recruiting personnel continually gave Cherry one excuse after another to explain the constant delayed responses. Finally, after figuring out that the true reason the Navy kept stalling was racism, Cherry went and talked to the Air Force recruiting office.

When Cherry received his initial correspondence from the Air Force and was directed to report to Langley Air Force Base to take a battery of tests to ensure he met the requirements to commence Air Force flight training. After these tests, Cherry was notified that he was accepted into the Air Forces' pilot cadet training program and was put on a waiting list to start pilot cadet training. When Cherry's initial training started in late June 1951, Cherry had the highest score of the eighteen aviation cadet program applicants and was congratulated on having the highest entrance exam scores. Cherry had been the only black among these eighteen applicants.[36]

Soon thereafter, Cherry was sent to basic training. The military was also full of racism, but this training was the closest thing to equal treatment Cherry had known up to that point. By July, 1951 Cherry was on active duty. By October of that same year, he commenced his aviation cadet training in Craig, Alabama. At this time in Alabama, there were still parts of town where black men simply did not go. On base it seemed like a "totally different country or environment."[37] The senior pilot instructor in Malden, Missouri, Jon Thorne was the only member of the all-white cadre of instructors, who unbeknownst to Cherry at that time and not discovered until years later, was the only white who agreed to teach or fly with Cherry, of course due to the color of his skin. [38] Proudly, Cherry stated that he was the first in this group to solo—a true indicator of both the his skill and the instructor's confidence in the trainee.

After going through the different phases of flight training, and following a close call for a violation of pilot trainee protocols, Cherry was awarded his wings and new Second Lieutenant bars. All was not redeemed, however, because when he later graduated from the final phase of training in Texas, Cherry could not have any relatives come to his graduation or pin his bars on. This was because at that time in Big Springs, Texas—in fact, anywhere in the state[39]—blacks were not allowed to rent hotel rooms. In the spring of 1952, the Commanding Officer of his flight training regiment ended up pinning the newly promoted Lieutenant.

Others saw something special in this young pilot that he did not yet see. Although foreign to many now, this racism-provoked inability of his family to attend such important occasions was part of the world young Cherry lived (and millions of other blacks) lived in at the time. Interestingly, Cherry was the first black aviation cadet to attend the training in Malden, Missouri, although a small number of black officers followed in his footsteps—some successfully, others not. After Cherry graduated, he was assigned to combat crew training. While flying in Korea, Cherry flew "just over fifty one or two"[40] missions in the F-84 Thunderjet, a ground support aircraft. "The Thunderjet became the Air Force's primary strike aircraft during the Korean War, flying 86,408 missions and destroying 60% of all ground targets in the war as well as eight Soviet-built MiG fighters."[41] The mission of Cherry's aircraft was frontline support for infantry units and interdiction (on enemy troop resupply capabilities such as truck convoys and supply trains).

Cherry's many combat missions carried him deep into North Korea. He was the single black pilot in his squadron. Cherry and a close African-American friend were the only two black pilots in this entire group (several squadrons are organized into groups). Following the Korean War, Cherry went to Tinker Air Force Base, where he was again one of only two blacks in his squadron. Throughout the 1950s, he remained one of the few; if not the only black pilot in the units he was assigned. Cherry, however, transcended the labels of black or white and simply excelled at being an officer in the United States Air Force, one who was privileged to do something he dearly loved—flying.

On one occasion, Cherry's commanding officer, Colonel Schultz, told him that he did not allow his duty officers to fly combat missions. Cherry immediately replied that he was there to fly combat missions. There was so much racism and bigotry in the United States that at this point, blacks really had to learn to either allow such comments to roll off or ignore them, because if every such comment was rebutted, they would have faced nothing but conflict and, more than likely, would have been much less successful in the long run. Cherry knew which guys in the squadrons were good people and who sympathized with the plight of the blacks. There were also, of course, those who resented blacks. Even during their off hours, the squadron officers periodically went into town to relax and have a beer. On at least two separate occasions, one of them in Reno, Nevada, the officers walked into a bar and the whites in their group were served beer, but the bartenders refused to serve Cherry because he was black. He was also refused admittance and permission to gamble in Reno casinos. For some of the officers in this squadron, this was a completely new and bewildering experience, but Cherry had seen this treatment before. It was racism, pure and simple.[42]

During the mid-fifties, Cherry was part of Strategic Air Command (or SAC—pronounced "sack") under General Curtis Lemay. General Lemay believed in realism in everything the pilots or crews did in preparation for combat—bearing in mind that this was at the height of the Cold War. Part of the training these pilots received was survival, evasion, resistance, and escape (or SERE) school. This instruction prepared pilots and other crew members for survival in the event that they were shot down, and taught them how to evade capture by the enemy, how to resist interrogation, and finally, if possible, how to escape their captors. Cherry stated "that was a very very realistic, physically . . . mental . . . physical . . . school out in Reno . . . it was 9 days long . . . and I spent 16 hours in a small box" where he could not completely stand up, nor could he sit or squat. In this school, they gave each student a few vegetables and a live rabbit, and that was all they had to live on for 9 days.

Cherry attended this escape and evasion training seven times before being shot down in Vietnam. Like many of his fellow air crew, he knew a little about what to expect if shot down over enemy territory. This school woke a lot of the students up to the realities of an isolating event.[43] "Because I was in SAC, we went once a year—every year." It was very realistic, he wrote: "They beat the hell out of you." Cherry recalled escaping from the mock POW compound, which really infuriated the SERE staff. This "ticked them off, there was nothing they could do." This training was post-Korean War—and since President Eisenhower had already signed the Executive Order for the Code of Conduct, Cherry and his fellow fliers were taught the Code as part of their training. In fact, Cherry later stated, "when we went down we knew and went by the Code of Conduct religiously."[44]

In 1960, Cherry was given an accompanied tour of duty in Japan, meaning that his family went with him, and although he would periodically deploy from Japan, they saw him much more often than they would have had they been left in the United States. Later, in October 1965, still stationed in Japan with his family and in receipt of orders to go stateside to become a pilot instructor, Cherry asked his commanding officer for just one more rotation to Vietnam for combat missions. The reply was that Cherry had done his share of combat and was going home.[45] Cherry was persistent in this request to his commanding officer, who finally agreed to let Cherry remain in Japan and do just one more combat rotation.

Taking off from Yakota, Japan at 06:52 AM with 2 X F-105's, he flew through Kadina Air Force Base in Okinawa, Japan and finally to Tok Li, Vietnam following a few aerial re-fuelings. One hundred miles out of Vietnam, Cherry experienced unknown aircraft problems and jettisoned his spare fuel tanks, safely landing in Danang, South Vietnam. The next day—after his aircraft's maintenance issues were fixed, he switched missions with another pilot for an earlier mission that same day. After averting a near disaster when another plane had collapsed its landing gear in the middle of the runway, Cherry was off for, unbeknownst to him, his last aerial combat mission in Vietnam.[46]

The weather in the target area provided a 200-300 foot ceiling since Cherry's F-105 was armed with Snake Eyes[47] and CBUs[48], he knew he would have to fly 50-100 feet above the ground to have a good effect with the ordnance he was assigned to drop. "So I was below the clouds," he stated, "with the people armed with rifles and rocks." Cherry had to slow his aircraft to 500 knots in order to drop his weapons. "When I ejected from the aircraft at about 400 feet and doing 600 knots—plus, I knew I was hit prior to the target . . . was egressing from the target . . . . told the remainder of my flight I'd been hit." He was now in a slight climb and accelerating, attempting to turn off a switch while his aircraft started to exhibit signs of catastrophic system and engine failure. Cherry knew he had to bail out. Since he had to use his left arm to steady the aircraft's controls as he ejected, Cherry tore his "left shoulder up, broke my wrist, broke my left ankle." These injuries were the direct result of having to have his left arm secured while holding the stick of his aircraft, so that the crippled plane would remain in somewhat level flight.[49]

When he ejected, Cherry's lap belt was supposed to open but, he writes, "it didn't work for me" and he had to manually free this belt. This malfunction actually saved his life due to the speed and altitude at which he ejected. Cherry looked up after ejecting, saw he had a good canopy, saw his wingman, and a few seconds later, hit the ground. "So I was captured". He landed right in the middle of the North Vietnamese. Cherry was sitting on the ground and was told to raise his arms, but Cherry couldn't move his left arm and had to point with his other arm to the pistol so that they would remove it from its holster. The North Vietnamese "crept in real slow" and took his pistol and survival knife. They did not know what to do with Cherry's G-suit, and almost stabbed him with his own knife. He showed them how to work the zippers, and they removed his suit. Once they had his gun, knife, and G-suit, they tied his arms around his waist and marched him to a nearby village.[50]

Once at the village, they allowed Cherry to rest on a bunk where a medic treated his face wounds and other injuries. At this point, his ankle, wrist, and shoulder were really starting to hurt. He had not yet been interrogated, and recalls wondering "when they going to do something?" Later, Cherry was put on a jeep for continued movement. His ankle was swollen, and after he pitched a fit, they finally let him keep his boots. Cherry had been shot down at 11:44 AM, and it was now late in the afternoon. The jeep went through many checkpoints and finally stopped at a high school for his first interrogation, making Cherry promises and attempting propaganda. Cherry's SERE school training started kicking in. Up to this point, the V had not showed any racism or hinted at his race in any way other than by touching his darker skin.[51]

At one point, the North Vietnamese villagers crowded around Cherry and the guards actually had to protect Cherry. It wasn't until they reached the Hanoi Hilton that they started interrogating him. A North Vietnamese officer nick-named "Rabbit" was Cherry's first interrogator. Many of these interrogations showed similarities to other prisoners held at the Hanoi Hilton. About six weeks after he was shot down, Cherry was introduced to his new cellmate, Navy Flier Halyburton, whom he thought was "a plant". The two did not initially trust each other. Halyburton, being a Navy flier—a service that did not allow blacks to fly—also believed that Cherry was a plant. Halyburton was a young white officer from Texas, who had never spent much time around blacks.

The V thought that Cherry and Halyburton sharing a cell would be a propaganda coup for the North Vietnamese. They did not realize that US military personnel had the Code of Conduct, as well as a legal code that required officers in the uniformed services to conduct themselves in a certain way. Cherry later reflected that the Vietnamese had to take everything they got from him through interrogation or torture; he did not give them anything willingly, which they strongly disliked. Neither Cherry nor Halyburton gave the V what they wanted in terms of sympathies towards their communist cause. In short, Cherry stated, "I am your prisoner but I am still a United States military officer." In fact, when he was first captured, the V had made their opinions about the Geneva Conventions were made abundantly clear. When Cherry showed the V his Geneva Conventions card, "they tore that thing up right in from of me". The

V tried to convince the Americans that they were war criminals and therefore the Geneva Conventions did not apply to them.

The V were "shrewd and masters at propaganda" and they "were good at it." The Americans had put so many restrictions on the targets that could be struck, under the military's "Rules of Engagement," that it was "unbelievable". In Korea, the pilots had been allowed to strike dikes and dams, but this was not so in Vietnam. In the war in Southeast Asia, the accidental striking of dams or dikes would feed the V's propaganda. This information could then be later used against prisoners as "evidence" of their war crimes.[52]

Before the younger Halyburton was introduced to Cherry, he had already taken a shower and been allowed to clean up. Cherry had been a prisoner for about six weeks at this point, while Halyburton had been there for seven weeks. When introduced, Halyburton was clean, looked youthful, and did not fit Cherry's idea of a fellow prisoner of war. And, because Cherry did not fully trust Halyburton yet, he provided no information on his family in Japan since, if the V knew this, they could have used it against Cherry. He had not been taught the TAP Code in SERE school, since it was a code developed by the Americans while in the Hanoi Hilton. Cherry therefore did not know how to use this code until Halyburton showed him. Halyburton had previously scratched this code in the Heartbreak Hotel, and after he had taught it to Cherry, the barriers were let down. At this point, Cherry was sure that Halyburton was a genuine fellow prisoner. At this point, the two learned to trust each other with their lives. In retrospect, the survival schools helped Cherry—especially with regard to not trusting others immediately.

The TAP Code uses the alphabet, in rows of five with the letters C and K interchangeable. Prisoners can tap, sniff, blink, or make noises to indicate the letter being sent. As an example, if a prisoner wanted to send the word "CAT", the following would be tapped out 1-3, 1-1, and 4-4. The first number in a set stands for the row, the second number stands for the column.

Over the years, Cherry noted changes in their treatment by the North Vietnamese. President Johnson issued his "14 Points" in January 1966, which was his plan for ending the war. Up to that point, quite a few of the POWs requiring surgeries were able to receive them. On February 13, 1966, Cherry received surgery on his left shoulder, but later that year, after Ho Chi Minh denied President Johnson's proposals for ending the war. Likewise, medical care Cherry and the other prisoners who had previously received surgeries came to an abrupt end when the hopes for peace failed. Later that year, Cherry developed an infection. He received no medications or bandage changes—and between March and June, Cherry got real "close to dying". The V did not want Cherry to die, but they allowed him to suffer. In July of 1966, there were 3-4 inches of bedsores over his backbone where his body cast had rubbed his back raw to the bone. It was not healing properly, and the V gave Cherry a small inner tube to keep his back off the bunk. After fixing the tube a few times the V gave up on repairing it, so Halyburton used his own sweatshirt as a pad for Cherry's back.

Halyburton was taken from Cherry's cell not longer after that. On July 6, 1966, the V took some of the POWs out and others requiring medical care, like Cherry, were brought to the hospital to scrape the infected decay out—using no anesthesia. This was the same time that the Hanoi march occurred. Upon arrival back at his cell, Cherry was still bleeding, and his cellmate attempted to help. On the 10th of July, Halyburton was removed from Cherry's cell—and the two would not be reunited until OPERATION HOME COMING in 1973. Following the Son Tay raid in November 1970, the V moved all of the POWs to one location. The prisoners were then free to communicate and get organized. Starting the day after Christmas in 1970, the prisoners were reunited. Following this, some of the more senior POWs got complacent, believing that the worst of the interrogations were over. The prisoners had started communicating via signing when the V reacted, and reacted harshly. They were not out of the jungle yet.

Once the POWs came together, all learned the POW TAP Code, as well as other methods, such as the Mute Code. The prisoners remained in constant contact, and this was their strength. They could communicate using one or both hands, by sneezing, by using the Mute Code, and on some occasions, could send communications throughout the complex by using openings in the top of the cells (prisoners standing on one another's shoulders). The prisoners did not need to see each other in order to communicate to all their fellow Americans—allowing others to learn what had been revealed in interrogations so that future POWs being interrogated did not have to suffer for information the V already had.

Prior to their release in Vietnam, those POWs who had collaborated with the V[53] were told that they would be the last to get on the buses and planes, and last to exit the aircrafts. Two weeks prior to the release of the POWs, they were given more food, allowed more open communications, and even gained a few pounds. A few days prior to their release, the POWs received clothes and shoes. On the appointed day, the buses drove up. The prisoners had discussed their own "Go Home Plan" and envisioned waving flags and such. They did not expect the level of support that was actually provided when they were repatriated. The progressives (or collaborators) were not allowed to march with the other prisoners to the buses. Those with medical problems left first, followed by date of shoot down. These POWs are now known as the 4rd Allied POW Wing.

Diagram 11

Colonel Fred V. Cherry, Sr.

Author's Personal Collection

During his repatriation, the result of the successful Paris Peace Talks and the POWs' release, Cherry noticed positive developments in his nation that may have seemed sub-standard to others, but to Cherry, these transformations were profound. He had not seen positive changes like these changes in race relations and attitudes towards blacks "since I don't know when" . . . ."I had been out of the country since 1960 . . . . so when I came back . . . . through the Philippines, it was Black History Month . . . I didn't have a clue what was going on back here" and "I just saw just a huge change . . . . a big positive change" in this country and how they treated blacks.

Some of the blacks Cherry encountered in this process saw his actions and demeanor as "Uncle Tomish".[54] The reality was that, while they witnessed incremental changes in the country's treatment of blacks and other minorities, Cherry was experiencing a range of huge changes all at once.[55] There were differences in opinion between Cherry and his friends about the tremendous changes that had occurred in the United States, not to mention the changes experienced by Cherry and his immediate family. Some of the specific changes that had occurred since Cherry and his family went to Japan in 1960 included blacks being able to check into a hotel, being able to ride on a bus and not be told "blacks to the back", being able to attend desegregated schools, and experiencing vast improvement in how blacks were treated by whites in public.

When Cherry left for Japan in 1960, there were very few TV shows depicting blacks in leading roles, such as the popular entertainer Nat King Cole, who was on television for a very short time. When Cherry returned to the States in 1973, the amount of shows with black in prominent roles had significantly increased. Popular shows with blacks in leading roles then included *The Bill Cosby Show, Good Times, Grady, The Jeffersons* (the longest-running black sitcom ever, with 253 episodes), *Sanford and Son, That's My Mama,* and *What's Happening!!*[56]

After being freed, Cherry went on to complete a successful USAF career, retiring from the US Air Force in 1981 at the rank of Colonel, and now works in the Washington, DC area.

JAMES N. ROWE

James, or "Nick," Rowe was a Special Forces officer in central South Vietnam who worked in a camp built to train indigenous personnel how to fight, as well as ran projects to better the lives of the locals. An artillery officer turned Special Forces officer, Rowe who eventually deployed as part of a Special Forces A-Team. Rowe had eleven other men assigned to work with him. Special Forces A-Teams were groups of twelve personnel comprised of two officers and ten enlisted men, typically mid-level to senior noncommissioned officers. This story of imprisonment is special because its setting is different from many of the others discussed in this chapter. Rowe and those captured with him were held in jungle camps, often held in bamboo cages and exposed to the elements 24 hours a day—in Rowe's case, for over five years.

On the morning of October 29, 1963, Rowe and other Special Forces personnel, along with their South Vietnamese counterparts, went out early in the morning to set up an ambush and, using a trap, hoped to catch the same VC who had been conducting probing attacks at their camp for weeks. The Special Forces A-Team departed the camp at 04:30 and by 05:30, the sun started breaking on the horizon. The A-Team was nearing their location by the canal designated for the ambush. At 05:57, the first rifle fire was sounded. A firefight ensued.[57]

The VC fled and soon, Rowe, the other members of his A-team, as well as their strikers entered the deserted village nearby. When the remaining company came up, the combined forces made the decision to search for the elusive VC, whose presence in the village was obvious. While searching, Rowe and those with him later suddenly started receiving fire. With wounded men all around them, and the assisting company ambushed and dead, this group of Special Forces soldiers were on their own. As the battle turned towards the enemy's favor, Nick Rowe, his team medic Staff Sergeant Dan Pitzer, and Rocky, a fellow Special Forces officer were on their own. Throughout the day, the three men and their Vietnamese and Cambodian counterparts continued their battle with the VC from one canal to another until, finally, it was the three Americans against an overwhelming number of VC. The fight ended, and they were captured by the VC that afternoon.[58]

Immediately, Rowe was tied up—his hands behind his back, tied at the wrists and elbows, which made it almost impossible for the young officer to keep his balance as he and his captors trotted down a muddy and slippery path. Rowe had been fighting for hours and he was thirsty, his lips parched from lack of water. After moving back to where they had fought earlier, Rowe spotted many enemy personnel and quickly surmised that these were not simply VC, these were hard corps North Vietnamese Regulars. No wonder they had fought so well and their methods conventional military small unit tactics. After moving quickly through various trails, Rowe sat down and, after requesting water, was given a small full tin to drink. Later, Rowe passed out from exhaustion. When he awoke, he was in a small canoe-like boat. Still later, he was fed and eventually linked up with Pitzer, who seemed to be OK.[59]

Finally, after more walking along slippery paths, more temporary overnight stops in small huts, and a few more dug-out canoe rides, Rowe arrived at the first jungle camp. He was definitely pleased to see that the two Americans he was captured with. The first task before the three POWs was to tend to the medical needs of Pitzer and Versace. Pitzer had a broken ankle and (Rocky) Versace had a flesh wound in his back and a more serious knee injury that, without medical care, could get much worse. From this point forward, the camps and routines took on a monotony that could only be described as misery, prolonged by not knowing if they were going to die.

In one such instance, Pitzer and Rowe were waiting for their evening rice when the guards became very excited, put the two back into their bamboo cages and reattached their leg irons. The two had no idea what was occurring and tried to ask questions—they later found out that Versace had attempted to escape but was recaptured. Later, when Rowe had a chance to talk to Versace, he found out that his fellow prisoner was caught while dragging himself through mud, trying to reach a canal where he hoped to swim to freedom. This was a heroic attempt, but not one that had much chance of success given Versace's physical condition.

During the 1965-66 time frame, the three Americans' main propagandist was Mr. Ba. Ba spent hours trying to "enlighten" the Americans, explaining the intent of the National Liberation Front (NLF), their lenient treatment, and how the North Vietnamese had been tricked and betrayed in the 1954 Geneva Accords. As Ba talked to Pitzer and Rowe for hours, Versace could be heard yelling and arguing with his captors—refusing to give in, and moreover, continuing to tangle their words and frustrating those who tried to twist his words. In the V's eyes, Versace was a troubled case. Periodically, the NLF would send requirements to the camp—usually in the way of forms to be filled out with information about the prisoners. One example was a form that the NLF said must be filled out with details required by the Geneva Conventions. When the form asked for name, rank, social security number, and date of birth, Rowe did not question it. But the same forms also contained detailed questions about his military background, family, and locations where he had been stationed in South Vietnam.

Rowe refused to answer in these cases and Ba became upset, saying the front required this information, and by that providing it would prove his repentance so that he could be pardoned by Ho Chi Minh and allowed to go home.[60] Eventually, Versace came to be considered a corrupt prisoner who would not be pardoned by the NLF—his escape attempt, they claimed, further proved him to be a troublemaker, as did his unwillingness to provide statements of repentance for his "war criminal" actions.

Periodically throughout their imprisonment, the prisoners were moved, sometimes to old camps that had been fixed up, and at other times to new locations built for them. Rowe's health continued to decline, mainly from a lack of nutrition which caused dysentery and beri-beri (a vitamin deficiency). As they had been taught in survival training, the POWs also knew that their best hopes for a successful escape had been in the earlier stages of captivity, such as while they were initially being moved. In Rowe's case, he was concerned about his teammates, Pitzer and Versace. Pitzer, who had originally been physically able, had become incapable by the time conditions had improved enough for him to consider escape. All the while, their main propagandist Mr. Ba continued with his attempts to obtain written confessions and statements concerning the war. Rowe's health waned—when captured, Rowe had weighed 165 pounds, and at this point—mid-1965 or so—he weighed around 140 pounds.[61]

Unlike POWs held in formal compounds in Hanoi, the TAP Code did little good for prisoners in the jungle camps because their jungle bamboo cages were separated by other structures. Still, Rowe, Pitzer, and Versace were able to communicate on occasion. They sometimes snuck in a word or two while cooking their rice, cleaning their cages, or bathing. Moreover, Rowe and Pitzer established dead-drops[62] for written communications—locations where one person leaves a note or other signal for later recovery by the other party. The key to dead-drops is that they must be either hidden from plain view but retrievable without attracting attention, or the messages left in plain sight close by something that belongs at a particular site, such as a water faucet.

In this case, Rowe and Pitzer used blood for ink, wrote on small slips of paper or tree bark, and left the messages throughout the camp at pre-designated spots. Another way of communicating was by singing. The prisoners would insert innocuous words into songs the guards may have heard, but since their captors were not astute in the use of the English language, slipping in odd phrases or words throughout the songs was done without needing to compromise.

Rowe's plan was to attempt to hold out for six months without telling Mr. Ba anything about their unit or its location. After that point, they agreed, the units would have rotated and the base camp they operated from would have changed its defenses, so what they knew about the base camp's tactical defenses would be outdated.[63] Another method Rowe used to deceive the enemy was to hide the fact that he was a Special Forces officer. The VC knowing Rowe was a Special Forces officer would have put the others in grave danger.

The NLF knew the Special Forces to be elite soldiers responsible for many of their countrymen's deaths. Rowe claimed to be a West Point graduate trained in engineering, and since engineers were used throughout South Vietnam in civil projects such as well-digging and civic improvement, he was thus perceived to be much less of a threat. This ruse worked for a number of years.

From 1964 through 1966, Rowe signed various forms, giving the VC small tidbits of information, always interspersed with incorrect words or phrases that made his statements useless to the NLF and their propaganda strategy. Mr. Ba and others would always re-approach Rowe and tell him he still needed to correct this paperwork to prove his repentance. Towards mid-March 1965, the prisoners were moved again. The conditions were the same; mosquitoes, too little of the boiled rice, no rest to be had on the bamboo shelves in their cages, a *lac* fungus infection on Rowe's skin, and incessant diarrhea. His health continued to decline. During the third week of August 1965, Rowe and another POW decided that they would attempt an escape.

Their plan was to sneak out of camp by night. They had planned to bring extra clothing, which would be used for flotation devices once they were in the water. They had hopes of being long gone before the guards discovered their escape attempt. They had also been hiding extra food parcels for the trek to freedom. Since all were locked up in separate cages, the plan was to link up during the hours of darkness. On the afternoon prior to their escape, they sung various tunes indicating to the other whether to go or not. Rowe hummed the tune "Old Man River" to indicate that the escape was a go. That evening, the two joined up, with Dave coming to Rowe's cage. Once in the woods, they found the going much rougher than anticipated.

They found themselves traveling in circles. Finally, however, the two were caught and severely punished for their attempt.

In January 1968, Rowe was moved again. Before this move, however, his teammate Pitzer was released. Rowe now faced his most daunting situation yet—he would be facing his tormentors alone. There were no others to encourage him through the rough times. His last several months in the camp were particularly trying, since he was now faced the VC alone.

Finally, in October of 1968, Rowe was summoned in for what he was told a very serious accusation by the NLF. Evidently, someone from the United States had told the NLF (on a fact-finding mission in North Vietnam) that Rowe was not an engineer officer but was, in fact, a Special Forces operative. When placed in front of the NLF spokesman, Rowe was told, "According to what we know, you are not an Engineer. You are not assigned to the many universities which you have listed for us. You have much military training which you deny. The location of your family is known. You were an officer of the American Special Forces . . ."[64]

At this point, Rowe's heart sank. He knew he was done for. They would kill him for embarrassing and stalling the NLF and the guards for this many years. In late December 1968, Rowe was scheduled for execution by the VC due to his constant unwillingness to give into their demands. The VC were moving Rowe to his execution site when, suddenly, a flight of American helicopters appeared overhead. Rowe seized the opportunity and, killing his guard, Rowe ran into a clearing waving. Rowe was rescued.

Later, to teach others how to survive the terrible conditions he had faced, Rowe set up a SERE training program at Fort Bragg, North Carolina's Special Forces school. He was then a Lieutenant

Colonel. Dan Pitzer also taught at this school at Fort Bragg's Camp McCall in Southern Pines, NC.

During the spring of 1987, Lieutenant Colonel Rowe was stationed in the Philippines as part of the US Military Advisory Group, whose job it was to help the Philippine armed forces in their ongoing insurgency problems. Rowe was killed in an ambush in April 1987. Today, he rests peacefully in Section 48 of Arlington National Cemetery. Dan Pitzer, who is now also deceased, wrote on the author's diploma from Fort Bragg's SERE School, "Freedom is our greatest gift."

DOUG HEGDAHL

Doug Hegdahl's story is very different from that of the other POWs discussed so far. Hegdahl was not an officer—he was an enlisted man. Hegdahl was not a pilot or air crew member; he was stationed onboard a naval vessel serving in North Vietnamese waters during the war in Southeast Asia. And unlike all the others discussed so far, Hegdahl did not escape or come back as part of OPERATION HOME COMING. Hegdahl was an (SRO authorized) early release by the North Vietnamese.

> *"Seaman Apprentice (E-2) Doug Hegdahl, USN who fell overboard from the USS Canberra during ship maneuvers [in April 1967] in the Gulf of Tonkin. He swam for his life until picked up the next day by fishermen. Although captured in international waters, he was taken to NVN and held there until his release. Doug was ship's crew. The American POWs agreed that they would not accept*

> *early release without all the prisoners being released, but in early August 1969, the POWs decided it was time the story of their torture was known. Allowing someone in their midst to accept an early release would also provide the U.S. with a more complete list of Americans being held captive. A young seaman, Doug Hegdahl, together with Bob Frishman and Wesley Rumble were released from Hanoi as a propaganda move for the Vietnamese, but only Hegdahl went with the blessings of the POWs. When they were about to be released, Stratton told Hegdahl, "Go ahead, blow the whistle. If it means more torture for me, at least I'll know why, and will feel it's worth the sacrifice." Eventually, after world pressure ensued, torture of American POWs ceased. Douglas Hegdahl brought back a list of over 200 POWs names which he memorized to the tone of a nursery rythme 'Old McDonald Had a Farm'."*[65]

When captured and dragged aboard a small VC canoe, Hegdahl was first believed to be a spy. After all, Hegdahl's claims that he went out topside at night to watch his ship fire their guns seemed incredible to the VC—who would be so foolish? After continued questioning, the VC realized that, in their minds, they had captured a very insignificant prisoner of the war, a simple-minded naval boy from the American Midwest. One POW, Jerry Coffee, later wrote: "Dough Hegdahl was dumb like a fox." Moreover, because the VC viewed Hegdahl as no threat, they allowed him more freedoms, like sweeping and cleaning his area with little supervision, which in turn allowed Hegdahl to collect information and become a real communications asset for the other American prisoners.[66]

Although a few POWs signed confession of war crimes in order to obtain early releases without the permission of the senior ranking officer,[67]Hegdahl was ordered to continue his ploy—acting like a mentally challenged person, and therefore received an early release in August 1969 through the NLF. Hegdahl's cellmate for a short period was Dick Stratton, a seasoned, Harvard-educated naval officer. Stratton realized that this POW's orders were distasteful since he was overtly receiving an early release. The true purpose of Hegdahl's release, however, was a ruse on the NLF is a legend still discussed throughout the military. Most importantly, in addition to committing a successful ruse on the NLF and the V at the Hanoi Hilton, Hegdahl's ability to recall names allowed some POWs to be confirmed alive—and in many cases, this allowed the United States to tell the NLF that they knew they were holding those POWs at that particular location. Hegdahl's recollection of POWs' names went beyond prisoners of the North Vietnamese. He remembered not just the POWs' names and service numbers, but also the prisoners' family names and their home towns.

The V were unsure about Hegdahl. After all, he was a lowly seaman who had been in the navy only a short time and, in their eyes, most likely knew no military secrets at all. When released, Hegdahl also confirmed "the existence of transferred Laotian POWs in Hanoi's prisons"[68] as part of the 200 total POWs he confirmed for US authorities over the course of his debriefings. The intelligence debriefers, however, were not prepared for Hegdahl's quick recollection of the names. When Hegdahl started singing his tune and reciting the names of the POWs, the debriefers could not keep up. He told them that he could only recite the information while singing the tune. The debriefers stopped Hegdahl, got recording devices, and later transcribed the names and information into written records.

These 200 names impacted the Paris Peace talks, since we now had information to bring more POWs home than they realized we knew about. Hegdahl's actions thus saved lives. After being discharged from the Navy, he worked for (and continues currently) as a government civilian employee of the Navy's SERE School outside of San Diego, California. As late as 1989, Hegdahl still recalled the names of these 200 POWs.

TOM HANTON

Captain Thomas J. Hanton, an Air Force F-4 Weapon System Officer (WSO), was shot down over North Vietnam on June 27, 1972 and released on March 28, 1973. Hanton graduated from Long Beach State College in June 1967. Following college, and with a draft still in effect, Hanton decided if he had to go to war he wanted to fly. After looking into all the services, Hanton chose the Air Force. After passing the required physical, officer, and aviation qualification tests, Hanton went to Officer Training School followed by flight and electronic warfare officer (EWO) training. Following this training, Hanton was assigned to EB-66 training, an electronic warfare version of the Navy's A-3D Skywarrior, with an assignment to Tahkli Air Force Base (AFB), Thailand. While checking into Shaw Air Force Base in October, 1969, Hanton was informed his assignment was changed to F-4 Phantom training at George AFB, CA.[69] Following his training for the F-4 back-seat mission, Hanton served in a stateside fighter wing (9th Tactical Fighter Squadron (TFS) of the 49 Tactical Fighter Wing (TFW)) where he received a significant amount of combat training and experience from others within his unit that had already served several tours in Southeast Asia and Europe.

On 31 January 1972, with two years and 500 hours in the F-4, Hanton was assigned to the 366 TFW at Da Nang Air Base, Republic of Vietnam in the 4th Tactical Fighter Squadron. After five months and 135 combat missions, on 27 June 1972, Hanton was downed over North Vietnam while on a search and rescue (SAR) mission following an escort mission over Hanoi. Although 135 combat missions in that short period of time might seem high, this was a combat tour where if you were not flying, there were few other ways to spend your free time. Some rested; others wrote letters, some enjoyed physical activity, some spent time at the officers club—but Hanton came to fly and requested the scheduling officers to "keep me on the flying schedule until I cry uncle." Some of the sorties were less than an hour but many of the sorties were longer, especially when flying into North Vietnam. "There were so many targets to bomb, you couldn't fly enough sorties . . . . so for weeks some of us were flying up to three sorties a day within 50-100 miles of our base."[70]

With the drawdown of forces in Vietnam, then know as Vietnamization of the war, Hanton's squadron was moved to Tahkli Royal Thai Air Force Base. On 27 June 1972 Hanton was flying his first mission from Tahkli in a large 100 plane strike force going into Route Package 6 of North Vietnam and was in a flight where he "knew absolutely no one in the flight . . . . I had not even met any of them.". All these crew members had been transferred into the 4 TFS when it moved to Thailand. As a last minute addition to the mission, Hanton was not involved in the mission planning; only the flight planning for his aircraft. Mission planning for the large mission was typically done by the mission commander and flight lead crews. Operational level planning conducted at the Tactical Air Operations Center would determine the targets, major routes into and out of North Vietnam, areas to conduct air-to-air refueling, and how to coordinate between the assortment of aircraft flights; many having different roles in the mission. For example, Hanton's flight was assigned strike escort with a secondary mission of rescue combat air patrol (RESCAP). In RESCAP missions, it was the flight's job to protect the H-3 rescue helicopters and the slower A-1 Sky Raider aircraft (flying rescue missions for those shot down) from North Vietnamese fighter aircraft. In short, it was their mission to protect the rescue forces from enemy aircraft such as MiG fighters.

Following mass and individual crew briefings, Hanton and his pilot walked out to their aircraft to discover the rear ejection seat resting on the ramp and fuel leaking from the wing tips. The ejection seat was removed for maintenance access. The maintenance crew assured Hanton and his pilot that the aircraft would be ready for their mission. Hanton asked about the spare aircraft but the maintenance crew was able to fix the aircraft. After inspecting the aircraft, Hanton was able to finally get airborne around 9:00 AM, catch up with the flight, and re-fuel. Hanton's primary mission was to escort the three F-4 flights dropping chaff to lay a chaff "corridor." Cruising at about 20,000 feet, the F-4s dropped this chaff—small metallic pieces of tinfoil like material meant to confuse enemy radar systems by reflecting the radar's energy and hopefully making radar signatures of aircraft harder to distinguish. The chaff corridor was to "hide" the follow-on F-4 flights attacking a military complex on the edge of Hanoi.

Once in the target area, enemy MiG fighters (enemy fighter aircraft made by the former Soviet aircraft company, Mikoyan and Gurevich) were up and engaging the American aircraft. The flight jettisoned their centerline fuel tanks to engage the enemy MiGs. This centerline fuel tank was a spare gas tank that, if the pilot desired could eject this tank and thereby give the aircraft more maneuverability and speed. Soon thereafter Hanton's aircraft had to re-fuel from an aerial tanker. Very shortly after the re-fueling, noon quickly approaching, the airborne command and control aircraft (ABCCC) directed Valent Flight (their flight's call sign) back into North Vietnam to execute their secondary mission—supporting a search and rescue mission already in progress.

Over the course of that day, five American aircraft were shot down—among them two F-4s over Hanoi on the earlier mission. Having both AIM-7 Radar Guided and AIM-9 Heat Seeking air-to-air missiles and an internal 20MM Gun, Valent Flight was a very good aircraft for protecting the slower moving search and rescue force—the Sky Raiders, known by their call sign "SANDYs", the H-3 Jolly Greens, called "JOLLYs". The Jollys had specially trained aircrew; among their crews were Paraescuemen (PJs). PJs are specially trained to go into hostile territory as part of these rescue crews, if necessary are lowered to the ground to locate, provide medical care for the rescued personnel, and then recover isolated personnel—most often downed air crew members. This mission was called combat search and rescue (CSAR); a very specialized and dangerous mission which, when successful, prevents the loss of a valuable US combat member and denies the enemy prisoners—and in this war that meant fewer sources of potential propaganda and intelligence sources (since many of the aircrew knew sensitive information about our military's capabilities and in some case war plans).

This CSAR mission went smoothly and the flight cycled to and from the tanker a second time. Following this second refueling, they were vectored toward MiGs closing in on the CSAR forces. The flight jettisoned their external wing tanks, further limiting the range of the F-4, a gas "hog," already deep inside North Vietnam's airspace. This follow-on mission was going as planned but soon Hanton's F-4, being number four in the flight was the lowest on fuel and they had to slow its airspeed and maneuver lower to conserve fuel, unable to maintain the combat lookout formation, in order to reach the closest divert airfield in Thailand—Nankom Phanom if they were unable to re-fuel again. Finally, Hanton's aircraft was so low on fuel they were unable to maintain speed with the remainder of the flight. At this point Hanton asked his pilot to kick-turn the aircraft so he could see behind and below the aircraft as they egressed from North Vietnam trying to reach safe airspace in nearby Thailand.

When he looked back and below their aircraft, they were struck without warning by an enemy MiG-21's heat-seeking air-to-air missile (code name ATOLL). Their aircraft went out of control because the hydraulic systems for the flight controls were cut by the engine fires. Hanton was bounced around violently. The aircraft was initially at about 20,000 feet over a valley; but Hanton knew that 5,000 foot mountains were below. In reality, Hanton and his pilot had less than 10,000 feet to decide when to eject from their crippled, out of control, F-4E. Hanton was unable to reach the ejection handles above his head but he was able to reach the lower handle located between his legs.

The next thing Hanton recalled was floating quietly and peacefully but with some injuries. With the aircraft tumbling to the ground, Hanton ejected at 10,000 feet between 400 to 500 knots. He focused on the altimeter not the airspeed indicator before ejecting.

The ejection was so violent that Hanton's watch, gloves, and helmet were stripped off—a real surprise as the helmet was tightly secured with the visor down. While in the chute he could hear communications on his survival radio, a PRC-90—pronounced "Prick—90". As he descended, Hanton attempted to steer clear to a karst[71] beyond a village and three peasants firing at him from a rice paddy. Hanton did not have much luck avoiding the peasants and the village because of his low altitude and wind direction so now he tried to reach a stand of bamboo trees away from the village. Hanton's chute was caught by the tall bamboo which softened his landing, much softer than a parachute landing on open terrain.

Once on the ground, Hanton hid under a reasonably thick bamboo thicket. He could hear rescue force radio transmissions but was unable to get a reply from several radio calls. After hiding for about an hour, Hanton was discovered by the three peasants from the nearby village. One of them hit him in the head while another pushed his rifle's muzzle into Hanton's face. The third one joined in as the three of them began to beat Hanton with their rifle butts. After this beating, Hanton was disarmed, his hands tied behind his back, and then marched towards the village.[72] Approaching the village, Hanton saw burning huts but no people. Hanton knew the source of these fires. He could hear sounds of aircraft and helicopter flying in and around the area, the Sandys' bombing and strafing, and the Jollys' mini guns firing—presumably to recover his pilot (who was later rescued at great costs to the rescue forces)—but Hanton did not know this at the time. Hanton was taken a short distance up the karst until twilight, well after the CSAR mission had ended.

The peasants and Hanton remained in this village until after dark, likely around 9:00 PM or so, and then took him to a second, larger village. Once at this village, they tied Hanton's hands to the bamboo floor in a raised hut and conducted a more thorough search of his gear. There was a can of water in Hanton's survival kit and after saying "water" in French then making a drinking motion to his captors, they finally allowed him to open the can of water and drink it. Although Hanton spoke some French, it was hand motioning that convinced the guards that he was not a threat and finally convince his captors he wasn't a threat and to let him have some water. The guards also brought Hanton rice to eat and then the next morning they took Hanton's flight suit and gear from him. Then "we walked all day blind folded with my hands tied behind my back." Periodically, they gave Hanton water and short rest. Then by dark, they arrived at another village where he was placed in a four by six foot bamboo cage in an open courtyard with a single guard at the door. He had been turned over to the North Vietnamese Army (NVA).

This was the second of three times that Hanton feared for his life (the first at capture and later while in solitary confinement) because during the night a crowd of locals constantly shouted and prodded with long sharp sticks. Additional NVA soldiers arrived and the agitated Vietnamese citizens left. The next day "we walked another half a day." On an open dirt road he was transferred to a Russian "Jeep-like" vehicle. Hanton sensed an American on the other side of the guard but was unable to see or communicate with him. Hanton assumed it was his pilot. They rode the remainder of the day to Hanoi. The next thing he recognized was city noises and he knew we were on the outskirts of a large city—Hanoi. From photographs seen while attending SERE training, Hanton realized he'd arrived at the Ministry of National Defense—to most this place was known as the Hanoi Hilton.[73]

Initially, Hanton was placed in a dimly lit 15 X 15 foot cell. There was a small wooden table, chair, and short stool in the center of the room below a single bare light bulb that burned 24 hours a day, a boarded up window, wood pallet bed on the floor in one corner, and a honey bucket in another. After several hours, in the middle of the night, Hanton received his first interrogation. Initially, based on the Geneva Convention rules, Hanton gave them his name, rank, serial number, and service branch. After that, and for the first few days, Hanton was given water and meager food several times during the day. The North Vietnamese (nicknamed "the V") interrogators, of course, wanted more than that basic information. They soon started asking very specific questions about his unit, aircraft, capabilities, etc. Although he didn't realize it until about ten days in his captivity, he had more than just superficial injuries. When he was allowed to wash—Hanton discovered the nature of the injuries from his ejection and beating by the peasants. The injuries to his right eye and right ear had affected his ability to judge distances or hear well. His face was unnaturally bruised and purple in color.

Hanton used these injuries to keep the V at bay by appearing to not be able to hear or understand their demands and questions. Moreover, Hanton told his interrogators he didn't know who he flew with—which as is recalled—he knew no one in Valent flight as they were all new to his squadron and assigned to D Flight; while Hanton was in B Flight. In this case, Hanton's playing dumb about mission specifics was no act, but the interrogators didn't believe this at first.

Finally, however, the interrogators decided Hanton was a junior officer with little information they wanted. After about three weeks into captivity—mid-late July 1972, they finally eased off Hanton's interrogations.

Up to this point, Hanton had not been tortured but was for the third and last time he feared for his life when one of the interrogators lifted a pistol from the table, holding it to Hanton's temple while being told by the sitting interrogators—no one knows where you are. This occurred about ten days into his captivity after not answering the interrogator's questions. Hanton decided at that point he'd better get a story and stick to it. His story was that he was a navigator instructor, didn't know much about F-4 aircraft or tactics and was at the end of the formation when shot down because they put the least intelligent pilots there, knowing they'd be the ones to get shot down. The interrogators believed this since it coincided with what Hanton would later learn—that Valent 3 and 4 were also shot down in this manner.

The V finally lost interest in Hanton and in mid-July he was moved. Guards came in the middle of the night and told him to grab his gear and come with them. He rolled up his clothes; two pairs of shorts, long pants, tooth brushes, sleeping mat, and one towel—all wrapped in his sleeping mat. Hanton was initially moved in with two other flyers, Chuck Jackson and Rick McDowell into a large room of Little Vegas area of the Hilton. Hanton learned from one of these two cell-mates, McDowell, that he—McDowell—was in Valent 3 and shot down in the same Mig attack that downed Hanton's aircraft (Valent 4). The North Vietnamese tactic had been to vector two MiG 21 fighter aircraft, flying at 5,000 feet above the valley floor in trail formation at very high speed, toward Valent Flight's four aircraft egressing North Vietnam. When the lead MiG saw an F-4 lagging behind the flight, he popped up and got the tail shot from the F-4's blind spot—below and behind. The MiG in trail also popped up and downed Valent 3, seconds later. Hanton later found out their two planes were reported to have collided in mid-air as opposed to having been shot down. At this point Hanton realized that none of the crews in the other three aircraft were keeping track of Valent 4's predicament in spite of numerous radio calls announcing their fuel state, with the obvious ramifications. One night the guards came into their cell, blindfolded them and placed them in a truck and took the three of them to a prison located a few miles from the Hanoi Hilton in the southwest of Hanoi called the Zoo.

Now in the Zoo, Hanton was with Jackson and McDowell along with other downed F-4 crewmembers added over a period of weeks. This group eventually grew to twelve. The North Vietnamese did not interrogate Hanton once out of solitary and while at the Zoo. Hanton's prior survival training—SERE School at Fairchild Air Force Base in Spokane, Washington and jungle survival training at Clark Air Base in the Philippines prepared him well for this eventuality. The Air Force's SERE training was very realistic, covering the basics of survival as well as resisting interrogation. Moreover, Hanton was accustomed to being in the woods from his childhood years in the Boy Scouts. In all, the worst physical treatment Hanton received was during capture and his initial movement by civilians. Of the different phases of capture, the initial and movement phases are typically where the captives would face harsh treatment at the hands of their captors due to the captors being angry and untrained in handling prisoners. This held true for Hanton, as well as other cases cited through out this book, citing specifically Stanly Edwards escape from the German transport train.

Throughout Hanton's first five months of captivity, he did not receive any mail. It is not known if this was retribution for Hanton's lack of cooperation in the interrogations, his outspoken nature, or his resistance posture. In any case, Hanton knew how to antagonize his captors—and did so—on a somewhat regular basis. Throughout these first five months, Hanton's wife sent a letter and a package every month, as allowed by the Geneva Convention. Hanton started receiving letters toward the end of November; but never a package. Hanton was listed as Missing in Action (MIA) until he became a confirmed POW in late October 1972. It was through a news release that Hanton was confirmed a POW. For those five months, Hanton's wife and family did not knowing his actual situation. This was undoubtedly the worst period for his wife. However, after Hanton started receiving mail, in November, he learned his wife gave birth to their son on October 19,1972. He later received pictures of his new son. That was "almost torture"—waiting to see his newborn son.

When Linebacker II started in December, Hanton was still at the Zoo. Across the river, to the Zoo's west was North Vietnam Air Force Base, Bac Mai, which was the V's primary command and command center. One day, Hanton saw two U.S. Marine F-4s come streaking through and drop bombs on the airfield. After the airfield started getting attacked by B-52 strikes, they moved the prisoners back to the Hanoi Hilton—about two miles to their northeast. The V did not like placing all the prisoners in a central location because the V knew that in order to break the Americans; they had to keep them from communicating—but they failed to prevent it. However, to keep the Americans alive during the bombings and as a result of the Son Tay raid two years prior, the V had to co-locate the prisoners.

Once together, the prisoners did not have to use covert communications methods; they could freely talk. One of the earlier codes used by Hanton was the TAP CODE while in the Hanoi Hilton. He used this code while in solitary confinement on the walls of the adjoining rooms but never got responses from his code. Hanton later used the Mute Code used when prisoners were in other areas or rooms of the prison. The first time Hanton saw the Hand Code—he didn't recognize it as such. He saw another prisoner across the courtyard in the Zoo flashing his fingers in different shapes, three in a row, over and over. Hanton showed his cell-mates and together they figured out it was some sort of signaling code, similar to both deaf signing and the communication-out signals used in formation flying when the radio failed. After that fact, he repeated the hand signals, going through the entire alphabet and numbers one through 10. Hanton was only caught once while communicating early in captivity; in this case, the V did not severely punish him—but they undoubtedly added this infraction as a reason for withholding letters and packages from him.

As January 1973 turned into February—now in New Guy Village, following the Paris Peace Agreement, the POWs were informed by the V of their release conditions and were provided copies of the agreement. The prisoners received this news with a lack of outward emotion—but were happy inside and would only believe it when the time came. They were then moved back to the Zoo, and in early February the V started consolidating late shoot down prisoners at the Zoo and aligned in rooms by release date.

From the Zoo they were able to see the C-141s, with the Red Crosses painted on the tail, arrive for the first two release dates approaching Gia Lam Airport. The POWs were measured and fitted for release clothing and received Red Cross packages. Once the actual repatriation day arrived, the prisoners were given their release clothing, turned in their POW possessions but allowed to choose one pair of prisoner clothing item and either their cup or spoon to keep, and all the letters and package items. They were loaded on a small bus and taken to Gia Lam airfield, to the north and east of Hanoi—across the river.

Hanton was in the third group of POW releases; released on 28 March 1973. Since January, the prisoners had received better food, allowed out of their cells for half of the day. Towards the very end of their captivity, the guards were noticeably irritated; perhaps because their jobs were going away as the war ended, or perhaps that the truth of their scandalous, cruel, and barbaric treatment they had given American Prisoners of War would be soon revealed. Treatment that fell far short of what the North Vietnamese had agreed to when signing the Geneva Conventions.[74]

When the freedom flights during Operation Homecoming began, those with medical issues flew out first followed then by date of shoot down—the longest held POWs flown out first. Once at Gia Lam airfield, the prisoners approached the release area in military formation. When called forward by name, the individual POW would approach the V and US Military Officers sitting at tables. The senior American was a US Air Force Colonel. Each prisoner would report to the American Colonel with a hand salute stating their rank and name and "reporting as ordered, sir." Junior ranking officers from each side would check the POW's name on the release roster, and then the POW would be escorted to the parked C-141 by one of the release crew. The POWs then knew they were free but real celebration was withheld until the aircraft was airborne and the

Aircraft Commander announced they were out of North Vietnamese air space.[75]

Once airborne, the C-141 proceeded to Clark Air Base, Philippines where Hanton only stayed two days due to his relatively good health. From Clark, he was flown on to Travis AFB, California where he met his wife and five-month old son. Hanton stayed at the Travis Air Force Regional Hospital for a couple of days where he was the released on convalescent leave. Initially, Hanton was granted convalescent leave, but after a few days he became overwhelmed by many requests for activities and being treated a hero that he felt undeserving. Hanton felt the longer held prisoners, such as Everett Alvarez who was held eight and one half years, were the real heroes. Hanton felt he had not endured anything by comparison, being held only nine months. However, the reality of the POWs' true experiences came out in a later conversation with [now Senator] John McCain's brother when talking about his short incarceration when compared to POWS held much longer than he; like McCain, Alvarez, Cherry or others. When McCain's brother Joe heard of Hanton's comparison in captivity lengths, he remarked to Hanton "Did anyone give you a card with your release date on it when you checked in?" When Hanton said well, NO—Joe McCain then said, "well then you could still be there."[76]

Even after surviving the POW ordeal, with the day to day hardships endured throughout, Hanton believes there are more important lessons learned. Top among those is how those experiences fit into the bigger scheme of life. To him the real lessons are: how did faith help—faith in yourself that you can, your fellow prisoners that they will resist with you, and your government that they will get you home? Other important elements involve organizing, communicating, endurance, the will to survive, to the point where you can still function and stay true to your convictions and beliefs. Hanton says these can be taken to any level one desires, personal life, family live, and work environment. The POWs learned to communicate which was important to survival, as was remaining organized in a military manner. For example, as one might have observed that frequently people are talking to each other, but they're not communicating. To Hanton, those are the important things that came out of his POW experience.

Hanton returned to flying and completed a 26-year Air Force career, retiring in 1993. After completing as post-masters degree program he spent 15 years as a Department of Defense contractor. He and his wife currently live in Alexandria, VA.

BILL WILSON

First Lieutenant William [Bill] W. Wilson, call sign Jackal 33B, originally from Mt. Pleasant, Iowa,[77] was one of two crew members of an Air Force F111-A aircraft shot down on December 22, 1972 while flying a combat mission over North Vietnam. Wilson "was shot down at approximately 9:45 pm on the 22nd of December 1972 as a Pilot/weapons officer . . . in the F-111A."[78] Wilson and his aircraft commander, Robert (Bob) Sponeybarger, call sign Jackal 33A,[79] "were each held in solitary confinement [separate, non-adjacent cells] in the Heartbreak section of the Hilton until the end of January, when they were taken to the Zoo and allowed to rejoin the general population. During their time in Heartbreak, Wilson and Sponeybarger underwent interrogations once or twice a day that primarily focused on the aircraft, "since we were the only crew captured flying that aircraft—it was also the most modern of any aircraft flying in SEA . . . neither of us was tortured."[80]

Wilson's "main goal was simply to keep critical information that could result in other F-111s being shot down by sticking to the same story time after time . . . . No 'requests' for political statements were made and none were given."[81] By the end of January 1973, Wilson and Sponeybarger were moved to the Zoo, where they were allowed to mingle with the other POWs. The two men were leery of other POWs at first, well aware that the two known collaborators "had been in that building before they were released."[82] During OPERATION HOME COMING, Wilson "was on the last airplane out of Hanoi . . .".[83]

As seen earlier in the book, training, the survivor's presence of mind and sometimes simple acts performed while under great duress have profound impacts on a prisoner's future. There is much more to this story than Wilson simply being captured and held by the North Vietnamese for three months. He successfully evaded capture for a week after he and his pilot ejected from their crippled aircraft over North Vietnam on December 22, 1972.[84] Wilson was prepared for this eventuality. He attended the Air Force's SERE School in Spokane, Washington, water survival training and the immensely successful jungle survival school at Clark Airbase in the Philippines.[85]

For their mission on December 22, Jackal 33's route called for them to ingress (or proceed) to their target at 300 feet above ground level while flying at 552 miles per hour and drop their ordnance. At this speed and altitude, there was very little time for course adjustments—even with the F-111's excellent terrain following radar. That day, Jackal 33 was armed with 12 Mk-82 Snake-Eye (500 pound high drag) bombs. Their airplane was one of the first that night to strike their targets, which meant that the enemy would have less warning of their approach than the aircraft that followed them.

For their missions, Wilson and Sponeybarger typically conducted their planning solo because their aircraft went in alone, without other aircraft such as electronic warfare planes to escort and protect it. They generally did their own mission planning once they were provided with their assigned target location, time to strike the target, and refueling data (where to meet their aerial refuelers). Then on

> *"the evening of the 22 December, Bob and I did our final pre-mission brief. In the unlikely event that we had to eject, Bob would give the command, and I would pull the handle. The F-111 was the only operational aircraft to eject the entire cockpit and the crew would, according to theory, float down with no wind-blast effects. In three months of combat, we had lost five crews with no survivors, so I didn't expect to survive if we got hit. But being a young Lt., I knew that nothing would happen, even when I added up the number of SAM rings and the AAA we would be facing. After all, they had shot at us before and missed. As a result, I had two one-pint water flasks, no food, two spare SAR radio batteries and two SAR radios plus the other standard issue survival items and, of course, my trusty 38 cal pistol."* [86]

At first, the mission was fairly routine. Jackal 33 drew flak—anti-aircraft fire—from Soviet-supplied towed 23 and 37 mm guns. These guns could operate independently with the use of optical sights, since the F-111 could literally fly "under the radar." Their targets were struck at or about 9:40 PM. When Jackal 33 released its bombs, it made a hard bank to the left to get away from the center of the city. When it turned hard left,

> *"a utility hydraulic light illuminated. Since we had two hydraulic systems, that did not seem like a big deal. Neither Bob nor I felt any impact. However, shortly thereafter, the right engine fire light came on, so we went through the Bold Face procedures. Bob fired both fire bottles through the engine with no luck. We couldn't climb unless we wanted to give the NVN another "great victory," so we stayed low until we approached the foothills west of Hanoi. As we went through some low scud, I could see the reflection of the fire in the clouds. About that time, Bob muttered something and stirred the stick, there was no response. We were heading for the first mountain, and still weren't clear of it. He ordered "eject, eject"! I looked at him and he wasn't kidding so I pulled the handle. We ejected at 1000 feet AGL and at 300 knots; 17 miles from Hanoi."*[87]

In a conventional aircraft, the air crew would each ride through the ejection system in their independently fired ejection seats, but in the case of the F-111, the pilot and weapons systems officer both are ejected from the aircraft in a single pod designed to protect them in such ejections while on high speed attacks, which was exactly what this aircraft was designed to do. Wilson and his pilot watched the huge fireball as the 16,000 pounds of jet fuel and the tons of aircraft hit the ground. "*We hit the ground (in the capsule) on the side of the mountain over which, seconds earlier we planned to climb. The capsule rolled to my side so I had to follow Bob out his side. We split-up, as we were trained to do for E&E (escape and evasion) . . .*"[88]

Diagram 12

First Lieutenant William [Bill] W. Wilson

Author's Personal Collection

Wilson had to do what he was taught in SERE school at Spokane Air Force Base and at Jungle Survival School in the Philippines. He would have to evade capture, survive, get water and food, and successfully make contact with and be recovered by friendly forces. While still in training many considered the evasion portion of SERE School fun, but now Wilson was fighting to retain his freedom. During evasion operations, the escapee is most susceptible to detection by enemy forces since it is movement that most easily catches the eye's attention and, in most cases, leads to the evader's capture. Some very specific things Wilson had to worry about at this point were: the enemy who could capture him, the terrain which could assist or hinder his evasion by allowing him to remain undetected, and the weather—rain might both provide needed water and reduce the enemy's visibility.

> *Wilson was able to make contact with his pilot the next day. In Wilson's own words, "The day after the ejection, we each were able to establish radio contact with a plane overhead. Shortly after that, I heard gunfire and that was the last I heard from Bob until I saw him in the Hanoi Hilton. On the 24th, I was again contacted by a flight in the area. They verified who I was. However, there were low clouds in the area, so I didn't think much more would happen. I was mistaken. A SAR (Search and Rescue) operation was launched. However, things soon went wrong. Jolly 02 experienced a primary hydraulic failure. If that wasn't enough, a fire started in the helicopter's left forward electronics bay. Jolly 02 aborted and was escorted home by a OV-10 Nail FAC. The remainder of the SAR force pressed on. The weather was bad in my location and the SAR was aborted."*[89]

Many in the United States were getting ready for Christmas and watching new movies such as "The Getaway" (Warner Bros.). A solid action hit that Christmas, the film came from action director extraordinaire Sam Peckinpah and starred Steve McQueen as a recent parolee forced into action after a daring robbery. Other popular movies about outdoorsmen such as Jeremiah Johnson were also released.[90] But there would be no Steve McQueen action movies in Wilson's immediate future. This was North Vietnam where the good guy didn't always win.

> *"Christmas day came and went with neither friendly nor enemy activity. I didn't really expect any friendly activity. Apparently Dodge Flight did attempt to contact me. I didn't hear any aircraft that day so I didn't turn on my radio. My water was now gone and so were any hunger pains. On the 26th, things began to look promising. I got in contact with a couple of A-7 Sandys91 who were able to generally fix my location. I had found a good hiding spot in the tall grass that covered the mountain, though I wasn't about to stand up and wave at them. One of my radios quit working, and I used one battery up in the other radio while the Sandys were in the area."*[92]

While this was occurring, rescue helicopters called Jolly Greens (or HH-53s) launched from their bases in Thailand to hopefully recover Wilson. The Sandys departed the area in search of more fuel from an aerial tanker aircraft. When the A-7s returned, the weather had deteriorated and cloud cover precluded further search air rescue (SAR) support for the remainder of this day. On the following day, December 27th, the weather improved. As told by Wilson,

> *"A new rescue package was put together consisting of four HH-53s, three HC-130s and nine SAR A-7 Sandys plus*

three A-7s configured to lay down smoke. The primary rescue helio was to be Jolly 01. On board were Capt Rick Shapiro, pilot, flying one of his first SAR missions, co-pilot Captain Miguel Pereira, Flight engineer Sgt Chuck Rouhier, two Pararescue specialists, Sgt John Carlson and A1C Robert Jones, and a combat photographer, Sgt Jim Cockerill. Jolly 01 suspected that they might be flying into a trap but as long as I was on the ground and free, they were willing to give it a go. The plan was to make the attempt at the same time as a Linebacker93 mission over Hanoi.

The launch of the SAR went smoothly enough, except Jolly 01, after passing into Laos, discovered that the window mini-gun would not work. Sgt Rouhier found that there was a loose wire in the Cannon plug that supplied electrical power to the mini-gun. Sgt Rouhier proceeded to fix the gun by replacing the Cannon plug from the gun on the hoist side of the aircraft. By the time that Jolly 01 reached the NVN boarder, the gun was fixed and tested. Unfortunately the Linebacker strike was late and the entire SAR was held up for two hours forcing several refuelings.

On the ground, the weather was sunny and I watched what looked like A-7s heading home after the strike mission. They were high and in a perfect V formation. I thought that was strange given that they weren't out of SAM country yet.

Sometime after the strike, Sandy 01 and 02 came in to locate me while Sandy 03 and 04 went higher. After multiple passes, they seemed to find my general location. On the ground, I heard no firing of any sort and only the noise of the A-7s as they flew very low overhead. The A-7s then left to refuel.

Sandy 04 had been sent back to lead Jolly 01 to where I was. As Jolly 01 approached the Black River, two of the "Smoke" A-7s laid a 300-foot wide corridor of smoke. Jolly 01 flew between the smoke columns picking up only a single clip of 57mm fire. They then proceeded towards my location. Sandys 01 and 02 were now back, had verified my identity, and again checked the area. Things were looking up from my viewpoint.

Jolly 01 was coming in very fast and completely overshot my position. They began to pick up some 51 cal fire. Jolly 01 was apparently hit at that time as one of the Sandys reported fuel streaming from the right side of the helo. I neither saw nor heard the chopper. Sandy 01 then directed Jolly 01 to execute a right turn to return to my location. During the turn-back, Jolly 01 flew into the Red River Valley where the crew could see Hanoi in the distance. Jolly 01 flew down the far side of a ridgeline and then came over the top of the mountain towards my location. Jolly 01 again came under the 51 cal fire. A1C Jones on the aft ramp returned fire into the gun position, silencing it.

Sandy 01 directed me to pop my red smoke. However, I was facing the wrong way and my first sight of Jolly 01 was again flying past me heading for the Red River Valley. To me, he was moving very fast and very low. He quickly turned around and began to go into the hover about 100 yards uphill from me. I was directed to vector him to my position. I did, but to this day, I believe that I did not do a very good job and wasted precious time. Instead of telling him to turn right or left and the distance as I was trained, I told him to slide down the hill (his right), to watch out for some trees I was afraid he was going to hit, and then to proceed straight forward. I could see the ramp gunner firing at something and I thought that was strange since things had seemed quiet until then. I could see Sgt Rouhier standing in the doorway like it was another SAR exercise states side. Sgt Rouhier later reported he was anything up calm, because he was "more like scared and frantic" because he couldn't immediately locate me and they were taking fire. (I had not yet broken my cover and was pretty dirty by this time.) I couldn't hear any ground gunfire because of the noise from the Jolly.

Inside the Jolly, Capt Shapiro couldn't hear my vectors because of static from my set and the firing of the helo's weapons. Sgt Rouhier did locate me and was giving vectors to the pilot via the interphone. The Jolly went into a 30 foot hover and was apparently responding to my vectors, or so I thought. The window mini-gun that Sgt Rouhier had fixed, failed when Jolly 01 went into the hover. TSgt

Carlson who was manning the gun, grabbed his AR-15 and began firing out the left window at the NVN running toward the helo, as was the ramp gunner. AK-47 rounds were flying into the cockpit. The copilot, Capt Pereira, was hit in the right elbow and multiple other rounds were coming through the plexi-glass leaving little trails behind them as they flew past the pilot's head. But still, Capt Shapiro continued the hover. The combat photographer went back to get his camera. Not finding it, he began to fire his AR-15.

I could see the penetrator start to come down. Even though the penetrator wasn't directly over me as we were taught in survival school, I broke cover and headed for the penetrator, still holding my radio. I was reaching up to grab the penetrator when something hit me from in front of both shoulders, which was either from static electricity or the helo's downwash. I did a back flip down the steep slope, When I got up, the helio was leaving. Later, Capt Shapiro estimated that they were in the hover from 60 to 90 seconds. In any case, from both perspectives, the hover seemed to go on forever.

At the time I did my back flip, the co-pilot reported that he had been hit and it appeared that the situation was hopeless. Capt Shapiro decided enough was enough and that it was time to leave. The co-pilot had now been hit twice and need to get medical help. They were still taking fire from all sides except from the side where I was.

Bullets were flying through the cockpit leaving plexi-glass trails. Capt Shapiro was also covered with blood from his wounded co-pilot. As Capt Shapiro pulled on the collective, the helio went into a nearly uncontrollable oscillation that required him to use full right rudder. He accelerated the aircraft to 150-170 knots. He was experiencing frequent rudder kicks as he headed out of the area.

Meanwhile, I had picked myself up and still not understanding how "hot" the area was, I transmitted that I was ready for the other helio to come. About that time, someone transmitted, "Why didn't you get on that penetrator?" I replied that I got knocked down the hill. Sandy 01 then told me that Jolly 01 had been hit and that it was standard procedure for 02 to stay with 01 (a very wise decision). Things got very quiet around my location and I was certain that I would soon be captured. I asked for vectors to any streams in the area. The Sandys couldn't see any."[94]

The Jolly that was hit by ground fire later made its way to Laos to make an emergency landing. The crew was recovered and the aircraft was destroyed on the spot with the use of bombs so the enemy would not be able to exploit any of the equipment of systems on the crippled helicopter.

Wilson writes: "As for me, I waited until dark then left the area. The next day I was nearly caught when a NVN search party passed close enough to me to move the grass

> *over my head. On my last day of freedom, the 29th, the Sandy A-7s came in and dropped a package with water and radios near me. Despite hearing AK-47 fire directed toward the A-7s, I went for the package. I hit a trip wire and was soon captured. The first thing the NVN took was my Seiko watch not my pistol."*[95]

After the V took his watch, they then took Wilson's complete flight ensemble, his weapon, and his flight suit. He was left in his underwear, green t-shirt, socks, and flight boots. He and his captors then made several stops while en route to Hanoi's POW facilities. While moving down the trail, Wilson was blindfolded and had a stick stuck in the crooks of his arms behind his back, with his wrists secured in front of him at about waist level. Being tied in this manner made for very rough going down the mountains and over the trails to reach the various stopping points. After stumbling along for hours, likely nearing collapse from dehydration and sleep deprivation, Wilson was untied and assisted by a North Vietnamese under each arm. Once down on level ground, they retied him and repositioned the pole. The movement continued into a village, where the prisoner was struck by locals with sticks and fists. "Apparently the militia had instructions because at one point"[96] the escorts formed closely around Wilson to protect him.

Wilson was placed in a jeep-like vehicle and given water. After a while, a larger canvas-covered truck arrived and Wilson was taken to the infamous Hanoi Hilton. For the first thirty days, he was interrogated once or twice a day. Since he did not fully cooperate, his captors accused him of having a bad attitude. Wilson was nearing collapse from lack of water, food, and sleep, and finally told them what aircraft he was flying. At that point, the V did not continue to interrogate him. His first night was spent in a "big room—just by myself and a honey bucket and some water but no food."

Diagram 13

Prisoner Cell in the Hanoi Hilton

Author's Personal Collection

The next day, Wilson spent hours listening to the Political Officer, whose rantings sounded "almost verbatim like the words I heard at Fairchild. I could not believe that. I thought they would come up with something new." Wilson did not respond during these lectures; he just drank more tea and listened: " . . . he kept rattling on and I just kept drinking the tea." Wilson was then moved into a cell in the Heartbreak section of the Hilton. The cell had two concrete beds with rusty shackles at the end of the beds. Fortunately for Wilson, the shackles had not been used in a long time. The cell where Wilson was placed was in a block of eight cells. The only other person in the cell block was Sponeybarger who, after a few days, Wilson contacted. "He was two cells down from me on the same side of the cell block." For about the next month, the interrogators continued questioning both of the prisoners, although Wilson did not know this at the time. The questions were solely related to the F111. "They had a lot of interest in the aircraft," which meant that the NVN had been told to obtain very specific information about the F111. "They took a nap every afternoon," during which time Wilson and Sponeybarger passed information to each other by whispering about what the V had so that their stories would be consistent.

At one point, Wilson gave the V interrogator an inaccurate account of a missile (the F111 did not carry any air-to-air missiles) and was closely questioned by the interrogator. During the nap time, Sponeybarger and Wilson talked and aligned their stories. Then, at the next session, Wilson told the interrogator he realized he had made a mistake and corrected the story to match Sponeybarger's. The Vietnamese were quite pleased, because they believed the story was collaborated since the two pilots had shared the same story.

Later, the two also told the Vietnamese that they only knew their side of the aircraft's cockpit consoles (left or right) so that they would not have to worry about collaborating stories with their captors. Still later, the Vietnamese showed Sponeybarger pictures of their capsule. From these pictures, the two captives were able to determine the exact speed, altitude, and time of their ejection since the dials were frozen in place. This made resisting interrogation on the F111 even more difficult.

At one point, the Vietnamese interrogator asked Wilson about the angle of the variable swept wing of the F111. Wilson replied with "70.0 degrees" and this interrogator, who seemed more intelligent than the others, corrected Wilson, saying "you are wrong . . . the angle of your wing is 72.5 degrees—I know all about your airplane." The interrogator told Wilson that he had read about the F111 in *Aviation Week* magazine. From then on, this interrogator got a lot of "play back," meaning that Wilson simply confirmed data that was in the aforementioned magazine.

This was a very valuable advantage over his interrogators—Wilson knew the V read the magazine article, so he could now waste their time talking about information he knew they already had. Some time later, the Vietnamese brought in two MiG pilots to talk to Wilson. Their translator was so inept that their questions, and Wilson's convoluted replies, were all confused in translation.

Wilson was fortunate in that he did not have to endure torture sessions like the older POWs at the Hanoi Hilton. At one point near the end of his stay in the Hilton, Wilson and Sponeybarger and were reunited. The Vietnamese then tried to take photographs of the two together, but these pictures were not of much use for propaganda since Wilson continually gave the finger in various poses—while wiping his eyes, etc. About thirty days into his captivity, when he had still had no contact with other Americans, the guards came in the middle of the night and instructed Wilson and Sponeybarger to gather their belongings. The guards did not say where the two were being taken. Wilson figured that they were either shipping Sponeybarger and him to Russia or going out to a ditch to be shot and buried. They were neither shot nor moved to Russia. Instead, they were taken to the Zoo, which was about two miles from the Hanoi Hilton and was the holding area for captives from the 1972 shoot-downs.

Once in the Zoo, Wilson was reunited with other American POWs. Moreover, while in the general population, and after hearing about the two collaborators, Sponeybarger and Wilson only revealed to other POWs that they were F111 crew members and nothing more—simply that "we flew the F111". On 29 March 1973, Wilson was on the last C-141 to fly out of North Vietnam as part of Operation Homecoming.[97]

After a two-week hospital stay in the United States, Wilson was released from the hospital and placed on three months' convalescent leave. Like Tom Hanton, Wilson soon felt overwhelmed by everyone's requests for speeches and being treated as a hero. Wilson then stopped talking publicly about his time in Hanoi, and did not speak to a civilian audience again until 1991. Wilson did a few more years of active Air Force duty, followed by a short time in the National Guard before leaving the military altogether and working for Boeing until his retirement. Bill is currently enjoying a well-deserved retirement in Seattle, Washington.

POW WIVES AND THE WAR

Of all the wars Americans have participated in, there are likely none where the positive impact on the wives was felt at such high levels as during the conflict in Southeast Asia. POW wives were received by heads of state and other American and North Vietnamese officials, which had not been envisioned by anyone prior to this conflict. This is perhaps best illustrated in the case of Sybil Stockdale, wife of then Commander (and later Vice Admiral) James Stockdale, a prisoner in the Hanoi Hilton whose story is told in their book, *In Love and War*.[98] In 1965, the war in Vietnam reached its height in popularity, and by 1968 it was quickly becoming a quagmire that forced Secretary of Defense (Robert McNamara) from office and supported the presidential election of Richard Nixon, whose promise was to get America out of this war—or in vernacular of the Nixon Administration, effect the "Vietnamization of the war." This moniker "Vietnamazation of the war" really stood for U.S. forces pulling out of the region, operated under the illusion that, as a nation, we were withdrawing forces not due to defeat, but because we were allowing the South Vietnamese to take charge of their own future.

Commander Stockdale became a POW on September 9, 1965, and spent 2,713 days as a POW in the Hanoi Hilton. During the period from October 1965 through May 1968, Sybil had not done a lot in terms of going public and talking to the press, reporters, or politicians about the plight of her and many other wives' husbands who were POWs in Southeast Asia (Laos, North or South Vietnam). This all changed in May 1968, when Sybil talked to a POW who received early parole from the North Vietnamese and had been allowed to come home and recount stories of the lenient treatment of POWs in the war. Sybil received word from her husband in letters that his treatment had been anything but lenient.[99]

Later, Sybil received a letter from Felix Greene, a liberal and anti-western British-American journalist who chronicled several Communist countries over the course of the 1960s and 1970s. In this letter, Greene said that he had just returned from North Vietnam and doubted her husband's claims of mistreatment by the North Vietnamese. Greene wrote that from "what I have seen and from what most other reporters from Europe have observed . . . . their treatment has been good . . ."[100] As can be imagined, Sybil was incensed, and started a letter-writing campaign to the other POW wives across the country to get them involved. What she very quickly discovered was that these other wives yearned for more information on their husbands, and that they, too, desperately wanted their government to do more to ensure their husbands' safe and speedy return.

Later that summer, Sybil sent a telegram to Clark Clifford, the new Secretary of Defense, replacing Robert McNamara. In this telegram Sybil asked very specifically what was being done about the North Vietnamese people's treatment of the POWs. In response, Sybil received a telegram from U.S. Ambassador-at-Large Averell Harriman essentially saying that he had no such information about POW exploitation. The Ambassador went on to say that he had had very recent communication with North Vietnamese counterparts confirming that three POWs were released as a gesture of good will. Sybil then went into a period of uncertainty of whether or not to write letters to the press, not knowing whether the letters would do any good. More importantly, she wondered, would any harm come to the POWs as a result of such letters?

Finally her mind was made up, and one of her letters was published on October 28, 1968. The letter spoke to the North Vietnamese military breaches of the Geneva Conventions, and announced the formation of a new organization, the League of Wives of American Prisoners in Vietnam.[101] Following the publication of her letter in the San Diego Union Tribune, things started happening. First, Sybil received a phone call which she at first believed to be a joke, but soon realized was from the then 33rd governor of California, Ronald Reagan. Reagan promised to pass her letter on to the White House, as well as ensuring her that she could talk to the President whenever she wanted to.

From that moment, Sybil and the League of Wives of American Prisoners in Vietnam's national message began to be heard, and soon Sybil, as its national founder, was received by the President of the United States, Richard M. Nixon. Prior to that meeting, Sybil and other POW wives flew to Paris to meet with officials form the North Vietnamese government, who were at the time also participating in the Paris Peace Talks.

In the introduction, the reader was introduced to the idea of the American Soul. In this case, the American Souls of the POW wives, most of whose names are unspoken in these pages, also deserve our unending support and admiration. Like POW spouses of current day, these wives did not forsake their husbands in their loved ones' greatest hours of need—much like the POWs did not forget their commitment to our great nation during its hour of greatest need.

THE GENEVA CONVENTIONS

The Geneva Conventions, signed on August 12, 1949, provided the POWs of the War in Southeast Asia additional guidance for their conduct as POWs. This is the third of a triad of regulations controlling POWs' as well as their captors' actions. For the POWs, they had to abide by the Uniformed Code of Military Justice (based on US Law), the Code of Conduct, and finally, the Geneva Conventions.[102] The detaining powers also had two sets of rules guiding their conduct: the Geneva Conventions and their own internal laws. During the diplomatic conferences held for the establishment of the development of international laws that protected victims of war, from April 21 to August 12, 1949, four separate points were agreed to. These are:

1.) Geneva Conventions as applied to the Wounded and sick on the field of Battle.
2.) Geneva Conventions as applied to the Wounded, sick and shipwrecked.
3.) Geneva Conventions as applied to the Treatment of POWs.
4.) Geneva Conventions as applied to the Treatment of Civilian Persons in Time of War.

Of these four, the third convention (Relative to the Treatment of POWs) is the one most relevant to the situation of the American POWs in the War in Southeast Asia. Space does not permit the complete reproduction of all of the articles, but many of the more important articles are listed below.[103] Notably, although the Democratic Republic of Vietnam signed the conventions in 1957, they did so with numerous exceptions, for example with regard to war crimes.[104]

Article	Synopsis
Article 4	Military member of the armed forces of the warring parties enjoy the protections granted by the conventions.
Article 13	"Prisoners of war must at all times be humanely treated."
Article 17	Every prisoner of war, when questioned on the subject is bound only to give his surname, first names and rank, date of birth, and army, regimental, personal or serial number, or failing this, equivilant information."
Article 18	Personal effects such as clothing, uniform, shoes, identification should be left with the prisoners.
Article 26	Food rations shall in quantity, quality and variety for the prisoners to retain good health.
Article 29	Sanitary measures shall be afforded so that the prisoners will maintain a reasonable level of health.
Article 30	The prisoners will have an infirmary where the prisoners' health will be monitored and maintained.

Diagram 14

Extracts of Geneva Conventions (as applied to POWs)

REFLECTIONS ON THE WAR'S IMPACT ON POWS

The war officially ended with the signing of the Paris Peace Accords during the January, 1973. For the POWs, their struggle in the camps and prisons ended with OPERATION HOME COMING, which started with the first flight of POWs coming home on February 12 and ended on April 1, 1973. During this operation, 591 POWs were brought home. The trip home for these POWs was done on C-141 Starlifter or C-9 aircraft operated by the United States Air Force. The C-141s were specially configured for the transport of former POWs. Some of the aircraft were configured to accommodate stretchers, but all were designed with the POW's comfort and medical care in mind. The POWs requiring medical care were brought out first, followed by the remaining POWs in order of capture—the longest held coming out first. The C-141s were all configured to carry 40 POWs each; the C-9s carried less.

The breakdown of the POWs coming out during Operation HOME COMING is shown below. These 591 POWs were not all released or repatriated from North Vietnam. Of the totals already stated, thirteen were captured in Laos but released in North Vietnam, 122 were captured in South Vietnam and taken to North Vietnam, 28 were released in South Vietnam, 94 in North Vietnam, and finally, three were released from within China. The number of 591 POWs does not, however, account for all releases over the course of the war. There were 76 early releases from captivity—some authorized by the Senior Ranking Officer, some brokered politically, and a few arranged through unauthorized deals with the VC by individual POWs for their own releases.

Service	Number of POWs
United Stated Air Force	325
United States navy	138
United States Army	77
United States Marine Corps	26
Civilians	25
Total Military	**566**
Total Civilians	**25**
Grand Total	**591**

Diagram 15

Total released Southeast Asian POWs

The C-141s operated by the Air Force were each manned by two flight nurses and three aero-medical evacuation technicians, along with a couple of flight surgeons. Most of the aircraft and medical evacuation crews originated out of Clark Air Force Base in the Philippines. In addition to the medical and support staff already discussed, each returning POW was assigned two escorts, also on the aircraft. Finally, Air Force news media teams were also assigned to various aircraft. When the operation began on February 12, the C-141s spaced themselves out with thirty-minute lags between the aircraft. This space between aircraft was because of the potentiality that, if North Vietnam tried anything, such as taking more hostages (the aircrafts' crews), then less aircraft would be in danger at one time, and therefore, fewer additional prisoners would be taken. The first C-141's special passengers included POWs who had averaged "6-8 years" as POWs.

In total, there were fourteen POW camps (or locations) in North Vietnam. Of these fourteen camps, all but five (Portholes, Rockpile, and Farnsworth to the south and Mountain Camp and Dog Patch to the north) were in fairly close proximity to Hanoi. Of the other nine, three (Hanoi Hilton[105], Alcatraz, and the Plantation) were in Hanoi proper.

The POWs who came home from the war in Southeast Asia will not be at complete peace until all POWs and MIAs are brought home or accounted for. As in previous wars, these special Americans truly embody the maxim that "all gave some, but some gave all."

Chapter 7

First Gulf War Prisoners of War (Desert Shield And Desert Storm)

During the early morning hours of August 2, 1990, Iraqi infantry, special operations, and aviation units invaded and occupied their small northern Persian Gulf neighbor, Kuwait. World opinion was almost unanimous in condemning Saddam Hussein's actions. As Iraqi forces occupied key objectives in and around Kuwait, US military forces were put on alert for possible deployment into the region. It was feared that Saudi Arabia's oil fields would be the next to fall to the Iraqi dictator. Within days, U.S. Army, Navy, Air Force, Marine Corps, and special operations units were deployed to Saudi Arabia. Over the next several months, American and British forces formed the nucleus of what would become the coalition, which grew to consist of dozens of western and Arab nations who eventually ejected Hussein from Kuwait.

Not since the war in Southeast Asia had the United States forces deployed in such numbers. Moreover, much of the equipment and most of the men and women who fought in the coming war were not battle-tested. This buildup of forces for the protection of Saudi Arabia was known as Operation DESERT SHIELD, while the offensive operation to eject Hussein's forces from Kuwait was known as Operation DESERT STORM. Within weeks, orders were signed that sent nearly a half a million American men and women to the region.

At the direction of the President, and with the consent of the US Congress, the Secretary of Defense ordered forces deployed into the region to protect "U.S. interests in the Gulf and, in response to the King of Saudi Arabia and the Emir of Kuwait, I have ordered U.S. military forces deployed to the region."[1] These military forces were deployed for two purposes: first, to protect Saudi Arabia and their oil fields, and second, to enforce UN Security Council Resolutions 660 and 661.

Throughout the fall of 1990, American and coalition forces built up on the Arabian Peninsula, in the surrounding waters, and on the lands of many of the nations in the region. American military forces deploying for DESERT SHIELD included active, reserve, and National Guard forces from the Marines, Army, Navy, and Air Force. The deployments consisted of entire units, individual augments, and a large contingent of government contract personnel. The training of these forces exceeded that of previous wars, especially with regard to survival, evasion, resistance, and escape (SERE)-related training.

At this time, the Army, Navy and Air Force all ran SERE schools and training programs. Those who attended this specialized training were mostly aviation and special operations personnel, from air crew to US Army Special Forces, US Navy SEALS, US Marine Corps Reconnaissance, and USAF Special Operations personnel. Those trained, including the author, were selected because they were deemed to be at highest risk of capture. Only those personnel operating in billets that put them at a greater than average chance of being isolated and captured received this training.[2]

Following a six-week air campaign, American and coalition forces commenced offensive operations to re-take Kuwait from Saddam's military. The start of this air campaign marked the first of many cases during the war in which American and coalition personnel became prisoners of war or otherwise unaccounted for. The first missing U.S. service member was Navy Commander Michael Scott Speicher. On the first day of the air war, Speicher's plane was discovered missing when the remainder of his squadron landed back on their aircraft carrier operating in the Red Sea.

During this war, 47 U.S. service members reported unaccounted for or missing. All but a few were aviators; those few being personnel engaged in ground combat operations as well as a few specialized ground personnel part of rescue operations onboard aircraft. Moreover, of those 47 unaccounted for or missing personnel, 25 were declared killed in action—body recovered (KIA-BR) or killed in action—body not recovered (KIA-BNR). Of the remaining 22 personnel, the status of one—Commander Scott Speicher—changed numerous times from KIA-BNR, or KIA, to missing in action (MIA) until his body was finally recovered eighteen and a half years later.[3] That leaves 21 personnel who were taken prisoner and released on one of two release dates following the end of the war: March 6 and 9, 1991 respectively.[4]

The 21 personnel taken prisoner and released in March 1991 are the subject of the remainder of this chapter. What follows are two accounts of POWs in Operation DESERT STORM. The first is the story of a U.S. Marine Corps OV-10 (observation aircraft) shot down over Kuwaiti airspace on January 18, 1991. The crew of this airplane consisted of the commander of VMO-2, then Lieutenant Colonel Clifford Acree, and Chief Warrant Officer Guy Hunter.

Aside from the Marine Corps' OV-10 shoot-down, this chapter details the experiences of then US Air Force Captain William (Bill) N. Andrews, an F-16 pilot shot down two days prior to the cessation of hostilities.

Following Hussein's invasion of Kuwait, major military bases across the globe, including United States Marine Bases at Camp Lejeune, North Carolina; Cherry Point, North Carolina; and Camp Pendleton, California were all bustling with young Marines full of naive hope that this war would not pass them by. Lieutenant Colonel Acree's OV-10 squadron located in southern California's Camp Pendleton was no different. These Marines were alive with naive hopes of glory they believed would be gained in war. Many of the Marines had never experienced the horrors of war. Very few Vietnam War veterans were still on active duty; those remaining were mainly senior officers or senior enlisted personnel. It was Acree's job to take his unit to war and, with the grace of God, bring them all back home again.

Throughout the summer and fall, CNN and the other news networks were alive with talk of the building of the coalition. Questions abounded surrounding how the American or British forces would do once they arrived in the theater of war. Likewise, there was speculation on what Israel might do, since their actions could have proved crucial to the fragile coalition remaining intact long enough to eject Hussein from Kuwait. And, perhaps more than anything else, the news networks spoke of Hussein having the fourth largest land army in the world as well as his possession of weapons of mass destruction. The US military personnel deploying for this war were told to pack and plan for a year or longer, and that they did not know when they would return. To use a phrase common in the Marine Corps, this was going to be a real shooting war.

The President of the United States eventually issued an ultimatum to Saddam Hussein. Essentially, he stated: "By 15 January 1991—withdraw Iraqi forces from Kuwait or face annihilation by coalition ground, air and sea forces." At the time of the deadline, the coalition consisted of military forces form the countries of the United States, Great Britain, France, Saudi Arabia, Kuwait, and numerous other Western and Arab nations. The risks were high, however. Israel had been the target of Hussein's SCUD missiles—intercontinental missiles designed to carry conventional (high explosive), chemical (such as saran gas), or biological toxins.

Hussein previously displayed his propensity for using such weapons by ordering their use on his own people, as well as on Iranian forces in the recent Iran-Iraq war. Nevertheless, Hussein fired missiles at Israel with hopes that Israel would strike back at Iraq, which would certainly have caused the fragile coalition to fall apart. In any case, Israel refrained, and with the help of American Patriot missile batteries, the coalition held and the January 15th deadline came and passed without Hussein's forces withdrawing from Kuwait.

CLIFFORD ACREE

On January 18, 1991, Acree's squadron readied themselves and their aircraft for a second day of combat sorties. For Acree and his spotter, Hunter, this war marked their first combat mission. Finally, "after five months of living in 'tent city', five months of grueling day-and-night training, insufficient sleep, and way too much to do"[5],

Acree and his Marines were at war. The two aviators got up well before sunrise, received their intelligence and operations briefings, and reviewed their maps and assigned areas so that their support to the Marines or other forces on the grounds would be the very best available. These missions were flown very low and slow, which made them prime targets for any tactical SAMs (surface-to-air missiles), AAA (anti-aircraft artillery), or anyone else that wanted to shoot at their slow, twin-engine turbo prop aircraft. Their mission on this date was to "scan for targets, locate them on the map, and coordinate air or artillery strikes."[6]

Diagram 16

Lt. Colonel Clifford Acree during DESERT SHIELD

Author's Personal Collection

By 05:45, Acree and Hunter were in their OV-10 Bronco ready to launch. Both aviators were buckled into their ejection seats, ready to fly into the morning Kuwaiti skies. By 06:00, the small aircraft was airborne. Before long the two Marines heard what nobody wanted to hear. Marines were in trouble and they needed assistance. Acree knew that if they were going to assist these Marines in distress, they would have to be able to see the targets, which meant flying below the cloud deck. Once they made it below the clouds, Acree and Hunter scanned the ground for signs of enemy activity, and saw what they believed to be a FROG (or Free Rocket Over Ground) ballistic missile system. FROGs are truck-transportable missile systems that can fire high-explosive or chemical weapons out to a range of about 250 miles. This was a huge find, and the FROG was a priority for their Marine headquarters. They had to get the radio report sent in as soon as humanly possible.

At about this same time, Acree saw something every aviator fears—a shoulder-fired surface-to-air missile. Within a second or two, the missile impacted the OV-10's left engine and the aircraft began to disintegrate. In the seconds that followed, Acree decided they had to get out of this airplane. This airplane had flown its last mission. Acree's command ejected the two men from the crippled plane. In this aircraft, and many others with more than one ejection seat, all except the pilot can elect to individually eject when in peril, or, as was the case here, the pilot can make the decision to eject all crewmembers at once. In most aircraft, there is an ejection sequence so that the crewmembers do not eject at the exact same time and cause them to collide in mid-air. Before ejecting, Acree was able to transmit SOS calls notifying Marine headquarters that their aircraft had been hit and they were going down in occupied Kuwait. Due to the adrenalin involved with their aircraft being shot down, neither Acree nor Hunter were aware that they were injured.

Once on the ground, Acree and Hunter linked up and assessed their medical and tactical situation. They addressed their immediate medical needs and got a few more radio calls out. These pilots were well-trained, and knew that there were specific issues that must be addressed if they were to survive and possibly get rescued. First, their medical concerns had to be addressed. "The whole left side of his [Hunter's] face was bloody from a gash over his eye," and when asked how well he could see, Guy answered "Not very well".[7]

A few moments later the two aviators saw Toyota trucks with soldiers in the back bearing down on them. The two aviators attempted to get a few more radio calls out in hopes of providing others with their exact location, condition, and circumstances. The speed with which they were overtaken, however, and the obvious signals for them to quit using their radios, signaled the start of a very bad chapter in their life. Although they did not know it then, Acree and Hunter were among the earliest prisoners of war taken during Operation DESERT STORM.

Four Iraqi soldiers surrounded the two Americans. The Iraqis disarmed the aviators and confiscated their flight ensemble, pistols, knives, survival radios, and blood chits. Blood chits are small (roughly 6 X 9) pieces of waterproof material called Tyvek. On these pieces of Tyvek was printed an American flag, and text (in multiple languages) offering compensation for anyone assisting the bearers. The only problem for these two Americans was that Hussein offered a reward for the capture of aviators—and even if he had not done so, the Iraqi soldiers would have been shot if their leadership ever learned of its own citizens assisting American military personnel.

After stripping the Americans of their survival gear and weapons, Hunter was given first aid by the Iraqis. This surprised Acree, because the soldiers treated them professionally and compassionately.[8] The two Americans' hands were tied behind their backs and they were taken to a small cinder block-type building, in fact, the one Acree thought he might hit on his parachute decent. The four soldiers each had tasks. One guarded their truck and kept a lookout for other Americans who might come to rescue the two downed aviators. Two others guarded the prisoners, and the fourth man searched to identify an unknown beeping noise. This noise that the Iraqi soldier heard was the signaling beacon located on Acree's ejection seat, which automatically came on after separation from the aircraft. In this case, the ejection sequence activated the emergency beacon. Eventually, the Iraqis located the beacon and smashed it, discovering that it was part of the aircraft's seat and fearing the beacons would lead to a rescue attempt. Hunter and Acree were told not to speak, but they still talked in an effort to make noise that would distract the guards and mask the sound of the seat beacon. Aside from the initial warning not to speak, the two were not bothered much at this stage.

A short while later, a pickup truck arrived loaded with parachutes and harness gear belonging to Acree and Hunter. The two prisoners were thrown in the cab of the truck and then forced onto the floor of the truck. Getting comfortable was impossible due to the injuries the two sustained during the ejection, the tight quarters, and having their hands secured behind their backs. The truck sped off into the desert. After a ten-minute ride, the truck came to a halt. Acree and Hunter were taken out of the truck and into a small underground bunker. Once inside the bunker, the two were thrown to the ground and handcuffed in a manner that broke every rule of civility. The cuffs were so tight that Acree's hands grew numb and eventually swelled. The two prisoners were then thrown back into the truck to continue their journey towards Iraq's capital city and military headquarters, Baghdad. After an estimated twenty-minute ride, they arrived at another underground bunker. This bunker appeared to be a lower level headquarters of some type. They were asked whether they were thirsty or injured. Acree accepted water once he saw that Hunter had done so before him.

Then the beatings began. Fists, clubs, kicks and slaps were now to be the response when they did not answer questions correctly. An interrogator started asking questions: "Where are you from?", "What base do you fly from?" and so on. At one point, they were told that if they did not answer these questions, they would be shot. After being told this, Acree said that if they were going to shoot him, they should at least allow him to pray first. They did not shoot Acree, but they continued kicking, slapping, and beating him.[9] Eventually, the two prisoners were taken back outside and put back into the vehicle. Had Acree not been familiar with the Islamic culture, this situation might have turned out dramatically different. By Acree asking to pray, it is possible that those guarding him gained a modicum of respect for his apparent religious devotion. Acree and Hunter were again moved.

After the same routine in the movement, this one only twenty minutes or so, they arrived at another bunker—still in occupied Kuwait. More beatings in what appeared to be just a showing off of their prisoners—the two were hit from all directions—so much so that they did not know when or from where they were going to be struck. Many times, the strikes were preceded by insults and questions about why the Americans were bombing and killing the Iraqi people. At one point, the two prisoners were questioned by an Iraqi officer who spoke very good English but with an obvious British accent. Again, the two were put into vehicles and moved further away from friendly lines—getting ever closer to Iraq's capital city.

In a vehicle once more, Acree and Hunter were surrounded by guards. This time, however, the seven or eight-hour trip was broken up by sporadic beatings. The vehicles passed through military checkpoints, and at some points drove through crowds of angry citizens yelling and chanting. They yelled accusations like "You kill our children!"[10] After more beatings, and suffering continued agony from his injured neck, the two prisoners finally reached the outskirts of Baghdad. They were taken to a cave-like holding area where they were held for the night with several other prisoners, one of whom was an Italian. Acree spent that night "slumped on the damp stone floor." He later said that his "neck was numb, except for intermittent electrical shock pains."[11]

That same evening, he was given food by an Iraqi: bread, water and later some corn gruel. Acree "would have savored the meal if [he had] known it would have to last [him] several days."[12] He was later allowed to use the bathroom, but the beatings and interrogations continued. He was continually asked questions like "Who is this man flying the airplane with you? He is too old to be on this mission . . . What is your rank? . . . Where did you take off from? . . . How many days of ordnance and fuel have you stockpiled at your base? . . . Where is the command center for your squadron? . . . Tell us about Marine ground forces . . . Tell us the type and location of all Marine aircraft."[13]

One of the harder tasks facing Acree was gauging how much and what information to tell his interrogators—yet not appear as if he was attempting to mislead them. In other wars, prisoners learned that it was senseless to die for useless information, so in some cases it was useful to give the enemy just enough information to make the beatings stop. Once the information was extracted, the prisoner would then recompose and re-stiffen his resistance, making them beat him harder for this same information the next time. There is a downside to this strategy, however. Interrogators often ask the same questions for hours, days, and sometimes months later, and if the same answer was not repeated, the prisoner would be caught in a lie.[14]

Therefore, the prisoner, who was already being starved and suffering from dehydration, sleep deprivation, and in many cases severe injuries would still have to remember the lies he told his captors. Acree later recalled, "Tell lies, but don't forget them."[15] This was extremely hard for him, given his physical state and lack of sleep. The interrogations became harsher. Acree was often placed in a chair, handcuffed, and blindfolded, so the brutality he experienced seemed unending. Minutes turned into hours. During an interview following the war, Acree said: "Of the 17 POWs, the array of torture is pretty wide, but for me it was starvation, numerous violent beatings frequently and interrogation, which included a fractured skull, nerve damage, things like that . . ."[16]

Without realizing it at the time, Acree and many other prisoners learned how to apply what was taught in the service SERE schools—a technique known as "bouncing back". When Acree was being beaten, he would often hope for his body's natural reaction of passing out when the pain became too great. When he regained consciousness, he would realize his small victories since each time the enemy tried to extract information and failed, he won. In any event, he vowed to make the Iraqi interrogators work harder for every piece of information they obtained, always remembering above all else that he would not give up information that would place other Marines in greater danger by giving information on their war plans.

Acree was continually asked about the coming invasion by the Marines. The Iraqis were so confident that this would happen that Hussein stationed several crack Iraqi divisions to protect Kuwaiti beaches. At one point, Acree was coerced into providing a video statement; which he did in the end, but the world saw the videos for what they were—evidence of torture and attempts to exploit these prisoners. Acree made the videos, knowing that if the videos were broadcasted to the world, this would serve as a proof of life for Acree and thereby make it harder for the Iraqis to kill him.

So far, what Acree and Hunter suffered was comparable to the initial treatment of prisoners in other wars. When initially captured, although they received medical aid and water, their treatment by those moving them was sometimes harsh—since many of these personnel had little training in prisoner handling. An additional factor that made their treatment harsh was the cultural context and timing of their shoot-down. Iraq was ruled by a dictator. This dictator's leadership style was harsh in order to keep his underlings in line and obedient. This was carried forth to their behavior towards prisoners. In addition to the training and culture of those who captured Acree and Hunter, many of these personnel had just been bombed by coalition air forces, so their emotions were high. Lastly, in the Middle East, being lenient or kind is a sign of weakness—and as far as the Iraqis were concerned, there would be no compassion. They were fighting for survival.

Once they arrived in Baghdad, the POWs were provided with limited medical care. Acree's medical care included the removing shrapnel from his body, as well as administering some medication to reduce the pain of his neck injuries. His meals, when received, were typically twice-a-day bowls of gruel, sometimes with rice and cabbage. After being at the Baghdad location for a day or two, Acree received yellow pajama-like clothing to wear instead of his soiled undergarments, flight clothes, and socks. Weak from the interrogations and torture, Acree slowly put on his new prison garb.

The minutes faded into hours and finally days when, on January 27, 1991, Acree heard voices from an adjoining cell. The voices were clearly American, talking about F-16 (aircraft) and various flying terms that would be used by Air Force pilots.[17] Acree thought this must have been be an American, or at least a western pilot. As time went on, the prisoners learned that the Iraqi guards were often within earshot during daylight hours, but during hours of darkness, the prisoners could often whisper with much less chance of being caught communicating. Although we now know that the ground war during DESERT STORM was fairly short, it must be remembered that Acree and Hunter had no idea how long they would be prisoners of the Iraqis. These men did not know if they would remain POWs for days, weeks, years, or even longer. Vietnam was America's last major conflict, and these two heard stories about the long captivities endured during that war. Therefore, communications with other prisoners was critical.

Acree learned that there was a nearby Air Force pilot named Jeffery Tice, as well as a British pilot whom he first knew only as John, but whom he later found out from Tice was named John Peters. The next day, Acree was allowed out into a courtyard to get some "fresh air," but shortly after going outside, he was approached by Iraqis holding clipboards and asking for personal information—his home address, his parents' address, his children's names, and so on. They insisted that the International Red Cross required this information. This was in all likelihood a ploy by Iraqi intelligence to get information from Acree and others when they let their guard down, in this case by pretending that they were international aid workers of some sort. This is a common tactic that has been seen in many of America's past wars. Sometimes captors claim to be International Red Cross workers and, on other occasions, they claimed to be members of the international press corps. In most of these cases, however, these were captors' ploys to get the prisoners to relax and then provide information they would have otherwise withheld.

Three days later, on January 30, 1991, Acree was provided woolen socks and tennis shoes. These helped reduce some of the pain in his swollen and painfully cold and injured feet. This day also offered a few more tidbits of optimism. Along with a meal that day, he received an unexpected treat—a tangerine. Moreover, when the next day's evening meal arrived, he received another tangerine. The vitamins gave him jolts of energy and provided a real boost to his spirits.

Later in the evening of January 31st, Acree was again handcuffed and told to prepare for movement. Shuffling outside his cell, the prisoners were put on a bus, and after about an hour's ride they arrived at their new home. After shuffling down hallways and up a stairwell, Acree was again in the presence of professional interrogators. He was immediately slammed into the wall. This place was cold—and although he did not know it at the time, he would spend the next 23 days in this place, which was called the Baghdad Biltmore Prison.[18]

On February 1st, Acree received a morning meal of rice, which he hoped would stave off his hunger until the evening meal—but the meal never came. By February 4th, his hunger pains were almost as unbearable as the cold. Although he received an extra blanket, his six-foot-three frame was not covered if he chose to stretch out—so he sat curled up most of the time, to protect him from the penetrating cold. Just as prisoners did in the war in Southeast Asia, Acree learned to adapt to the solitary confinement, cold, pain, and constant fears of continued interrogations and torture. As time went on, the Iraqis conducting roll call became a daily routine. Acree learned to say his name very loudly, communicating to others that he was present. In this same manner, he learned of a few other prisoners: Zaun, Eberly, and Andrews.

As in Vietnam, the prisoners needed to know who else was detained with them so that if they were released, they could tell American officials who else was being held. Acree was not alone in his misery, nor was he alone in his attempts to resist all interrogations and exploitation by the enemy. The POW cell was Acree's battle zone; like those American POWs that came before him, Acree's most potent weapon was his mind—his ability to think and bounce back following interrogations and torture. In Acree's case, this weapon was honed to a razor's edge.

During the period from the 1st through about the 10th of February, the prisoners received broth, and sometimes potatoes or fruit. Then, on February 12, the Iraqis resumed their questioning, and strategic targeting was the topic. Again, Acree claimed that he was just a pilot of an observation aircraft who simply reported what he saw. The Iraqis were concerned about which targets would be struck next. The questioning now turned from the operational level to questions of a more strategic nature. The Iraqis accused Acree of being an Israeli spy—and, of course, he denied this accusation. Yet he continued to receive the bare amount of food required to maintain any semblance of health—one meal a day. The Iraqis continued to question him about the beach landings by the Marines. In reality, the plans were changed—the amphibious landing was then a strategic level deception operation—but Acree did not know this.

Starting on February 23rd, explosions near the Baghdad Biltmore Prison grew noticeably worse as coalition forces bombed key communications and intelligence nodes in the Iraqi government. One of the locations being targeted was the "Regional Headquarters, Iraqi Intelligence Service"[19] and, as time went on the F-117 strikes got much closer. Acree often feared being killed by coalition air strikes, but took some measure of satisfaction in knowing that Saddam Hussein's war machine was being destroyed. On this same evening, 2000-pound bombs hit so close to their location that only the grace of God kept them from being killed. Two of five F-117 aircraft that been assigned to strike this building were on the mark, while the other three were diverted to other targets.[20] The building was damaged so badly that the prisoners had to be moved for fear of them escaping.

As in previous moves between holding locations, their movement was under harsh conditions. This time, however, the guards seemed to be as fearful for their own lives as much as they were of the prisoners escaping. Acree's door was pried open with a crowbar and sledgehammer and he was whisked away, unable to bring his cherished wool blankets. Again, he and the other prisoners were handcuffed, and this time they were thrown onto a bus for their next movement. By about 02:00 in the morning on February 24, 1991, the prisoners arrived at their new holding facility—a civilian jail named Abu Ghuraib. As the bus stopped so its prisoners could disembark, blankets that were been used to blind and disorient the prisoners were lifted off their heads. Although Abu Ghuraib was designed to hold prisoners by the thousands, it was not prepared to hold these new arrivals, so many were put in the same cells—and, of course, told to "no speak" by their Iraqi captors.

Once they were together, Acree, Hunter, and the other prisoners were able to compare the stories they previously told their interrogators. This drastically changed the playing field for future interrogations. Previously, the prisoners were unaware of what others told the guards, so it was easier to catch prisoners in lies—or in some cases, to play prisoners against each other by comparing notes on what they told interrogators. Now, the prisoners did not have to be needlessly beaten for information they knew the guards already possessed. This, however, was a fine balancing act. The prisoners would not simply give up information without coercion, yet they also knew they did not have to risk life and limb for information the Iraqis already knew.

Similarly, the prisoners were able to catch up on the war's progress from others who had not been held captive as long. Some were disappointed to know that the ground war did not progress as quickly as some might have liked. Likewise, the prisoners, now sitting together, talked about the war's progress, and the ability to interact with other Americans helped their morale soar. Eventually, the prisoners were able to bore small holes in the walls to communicate with fellow prisoners, many of whose fate was unknown and were then confirmed. As in the Vietnam War, the prisoners were able to use a code known as the TAP Code to covertly communicate with fellow prisoners (as previously described in the Vietnam War chapter).

As time went on and the 27th turned to the 28th of February, word started to spread of a ground offensive by coalition forces.

At this point, Iraqi forces began their massive retreat from Kuwait. American-armored and tracked units conducted a massive western swing north into western Iraq, and then swung east towards Kuwait, thereby blocking the retreat of many of the Iraqi units. Many thousands of Iraqi soldiers were killed along the highways leading back to Baghdad, later dubbed the highways of death.

Early the next morning, the guards previously seen in the Biltmore and believed dead reappeared and started taking roll call of the prisoners. Later that same day, food showed up that truly surprised the prisoners, including bread, cheese, tomatoes, lettuce, boiled eggs, and dates. Moreover, that night one of the prisoners found a toilet. Later that evening, a guard even went by the prisoners and asked "Do you need anything?"[21] On March 4 or 5, 1991, the cell doors opened and the prisoners were told to get their belongings. After a twenty or thirty-minute drive, the prisoners arrived at what was described as a halfway house. They were provided with clean POW uniforms and shaved. Later, Acree was told that he was on his way to freedom but he felt no joy, unsure whether or not this was a trick.[22] He walked through a door and was sprayed with cheap cologne.

On March 5, 1991, the prisoners boarded a white and blue bus headed for a hotel in a different part of Baghdad. The curtains on the bus were drawn, and the prisoners were placed two to a seat. On the way to the hotel, Acree looked around and saw others he knew, among them Army 1st Lieutenant Rhonda Cornum; a flight nurse shot down while she was on a rescue mission. Once at the hotel, ICRC representatives came on the bus and told the prisoners that they were now under the control of the International Red Cross and they would be going home. Still the apprehension was noticeable, since the prisoners did not know whether this was an elaborate ruse. Once in the hotel, they were divided up by nationality; Saudi, Kuwaiti, Italian, British, and American. After being allowed to eat at a buffet set up for them, the prisoners all retired to their rooms—many electing to stay in the rooms of fellow prisoners. Acree and Hunter shared a room that night. They showered, and for the first night in many weeks, were able to lay in a bed with a modicum of comfort.[23]

The next morning the prisoners were filed out of the hotel and onto awaiting buses for the trip to the Baghdad airport. As they drove towards the airport, they saw the remains of several important Iraqi government buildings, several Iraqi military headquarters, and the Iraqi phone exchange. Coalition aircraft and their bombs proved devastating to these once formidable structures. Once at the airport, two large civilian airliners landed and taxied over to two of the few remaining structures not destroyed in the war. The Iraqi prisoners of war got off the planes and, as they passed Iraqi troops milling about, looked upon their fellow Iraqis who were prisoners with contempt. When the plane took off, it was not long before Acree and the others spotted landmarks that they recognized. They soon landed in Riyadh, Saudi Arabia. The prisoners disembarked in rank order, meeting General Schwarzkopf at the bottom of the stairs and then forming a small receiving line after walking over a red carpet that was laid out for the returning prisoners of war.

Once off the plane, the reintegration plan took the returnees to an awaiting C-141 Starlifter. The aircraft was configured for med-evac purposes, allowing the former POWs to receive initial medical screenings prior to the next destination on their journey: Bahrain. Acree and his shadow, or escort, were directed towards the waiting plane which was bare on the inside walls except for an American flag.[24] Once on the airplane, Acree was offered a Marine Officers' uniform. Acree stripped, discarding his POW garb—in front of everyone on the plane, female crewmembers included. One thing many people do not realize is that once people have been prisoners of war, they are accustomed to captivity environments that did not afford them any privacy. The returnees were provided food and given initial medical assessments before landing in Bahrain at 19:00 that evening.[25]

After deplaning, the prisoners attended speeches given by dignitaries to welcome them back. They then boarded a bus destined for the United States Navy hospital ship, the *USS Mercy*. The returnees were escorted onboard and assigned doctors who would perform their physicals and additional testing. As Acree's doctor performed his cursory exam, the patient attempted to crack a joke. This, in turn, triggered a flood of emotions in the returnee, who never expected to survive captivity. Acree put his face in his hands and sobbed—a normal response for a newly released POW. Following his medical exam, Acree was given a cell phone to call his wife, Cindy. He walked up to the ship's main deck, and while looking over the vast ocean, called his wife. Again, he was flooded with emotions. After a short conversation, Acree returned below deck to shower and rid his body of lice. The next morning, Acree received a series of intelligence debriefings that reviewed his experiences from the moment of his capture to his return to American control.[26]

The POW's schedule on the *Mercy* was hectic. On March 7th, a busload of Marines from VMO-2 arrived, eager to see their Commanding Officer. After medical checks, cleaning up and resting - Acree and the other POWs were prepared to fly home. Once the returnees landed in the United States, the plan was for them to spend a short amount of time with their families and then check into the National Naval medical center in Bethesda for continued medical assessment. To assist in this reintegration process, all returnees were assigned shadows, now called battle buddies.

Although not a formal part of the reintegration process, shadows were necessary part of because they helped the returnees in matters requiring personal discretion and provided an in-depth understanding of military processes. During this time, Acree's shadow was Joel Lees, the squadron's flight surgeon. Lee Hunter also had a first-rate shadow, John Gamboa, who is now a retired Lieutenant Colonel. Acree wrote: "There was a shadow there, wherever we went those two guys were with us . . . . they simplified and expedited . . . from the moment we landed in Riyadh until he was released" at the conclusion of reintegration in the United States.[27] While this reintegration process was ongoing, the POWs' wives in the states were being prepared for their loved ones' return.

The POWs' wives were assigned military escorts and were taken to the POWs' entry points into the United States—Washington, DC. In the case of Cindy Acree, she was flown in a military plane from California to Washington, DC, rather than on a commercial flight with its inevitable delays. She knew that a military flight would ensure that she would be on the tarmac to meet her husband when he arrived. Personalized service on the plane and at the hotel made her feel special and helped her to relax. That night, however, not everything was so positive. Cindy thought some of the initial comments by the military officers in anticipation of their husbands' arrival were patronizing and even worrisome. Spouses were told that after speeches and a short reception, they would only briefly see their returning loved ones before they were whisked off.

When the returning POWs landed, tall military officers wearing covers blocked the views of Cindy and other family members. The spouses were forced to jockey for positions offering a good line of sight which would allow them see their loved ones exit the plane. Before they could be reunited with their relatives, the returnees were thrust in front of the press and senior military officials and then seated in one long row to listen to speeches. The British POWs from DESERT STORM enjoyed private reunions, which in the case of the Americans, "would have been welcomed."[28]

After doctors completed their preliminary assessments, the POWs were allowed to spend some time with their spouses, but not until the following day. After speeches to the wives that evening, Cindy approached and convinced the leadership giving these presentations that the POWs' healing would also depend on spending time with their spouses and loved ones. Military and medical officers adjusted their schedules to allow the former POWs alone time with their loved ones.

The Marriott chain offered hotel suites in the Washington, DC area free of charge to the returnees and their loved ones. The former POWs were also provided with free 24-hour room service. This room service was beneficial to the former POWs since their intestinal systems could not yet handle food in great amounts but needed to eat much more frequently to regain weight lost in captivity. Having free room service encouraged the former POWs to order frequent meals without concern for cost, which helped to normalize their bodies at a rate their systems could more easily handle, and to eat at odd hours.

On their first night at the hotel, Acree took a relaxing shower and then stood in front of the bathroom mirror to brush his teeth.

In the mirror, he noticed his wife staring in horror at his emaciated, bruised, and scarred body. Since Acree possessed a sense of humor and wanted to calm his wife's fears, Acree turned his head toward Cindy and said, "What, you don't like body by Baghdad and rebuild by the Navy?" Like other great men before them, these DESERT STORM prisoners learned to cope with bad situations, making the best out of whatever they had.

During the next four days, the former POWs spent time with their spouses, interspersed with batteries of Intelligence debriefings and hours of medical checks, including blood tests and MRIs. During their time in the hospital, the media became another new factor the POWs were forced to deal with. Initially, members of the press were cordoned off from the returnees, but enjoyed unfettered access to the former POWs and their spouses once they left the hospital or hotel.[29] Acree and his wife Cindy have mixed memories of the Navy's DESERT STORM reintegration program and, although there were some things she and Cliff would have changed, their overall memories remain very positive.

Although the reintegration process went well for Acree and many of the others from DESERT STORM, invasive and insensitive questions from both press and onlookers were sometimes hard to take. When Cliff and Cindy were guests or speakers at charity events, Acree "still compartmentalized many of the horrors of captivity." Moreover, when he talked to audiences, "he would talk about the build-up to the war and how he was shot down and then skip over his captivity by saying only that he was not treated very well. Then he would quickly skip to the present . . . He still held close his wartime experiences . . . Some non-military audiences had no idea of what prisoners went through. They would ask the most invasive questions at the most inappropriate times," such as when one reporter asked Acree, as he lifted a fork to his mouth, "'What was the worst torture you got at the hands of the Iraqis?"[30]

Acree is now retired from active-duty military service. Cliff and Cindy currently live and work in southern California, still supporting the military.

WILLIAM (BILL) ANDREWS

Air Force Captain William (Bill) Andrews, an F-16 pilot, member of the 10th Tactical Fighter Squadron and was a part of the air armada for operation DESERT STORM. The 10th Tactical Fighter Squadron joined other squadrons from Shaw AFB, South Carolina, home of Central Command's Air Force component headquarters. Andrews, originally from Waterloo, NY, was shot down on February 27, 1991 over occupied Kuwait by an Iraqi surface-to-air missile, and was released on March 6, 1991 when the American and allied POWs were freed at the end of the Gulf War. Andrews, a 1980 graduate of the U.S. Air Force Academy, flew other aircraft, but was later trained to fly the F-16 Fighting Falcon.

As Peter Grier tells it, once on the ground and with capture imminent, the "*Iraqis crept forward with AK-47s raised and motioned at Andrews to rise. He motioned that he couldn't. They were cautious and moved in slowly. When they were about 30 feet away, Andrews saw in the distance a puff of smoke and a white missile trail. An Iraqi air defense unit was firing at an F-16 circling overhead. Andrews knew the F-16 was his wingman trying to save him. It was Feb. 27, 1991. Ten minutes earlier, Andrews had been flying back to base, then was hit by an Iraqi surface-to-air missile.*

His airplane exploded in flames, and he was pinned against the canopy by negative Gs. He had a second to grab the ejection lever, knowing he was dead if he missed."[31] But how did this capture occur, and why was it almost ironic that Andrews was show down and captured?

Two days earlier, on February 25, 1991, there was an eight-man Special Forces A-team in real trouble deep within Iraq. This team was on a covert mission to observe and report Iraqi activities when they were compromised by an Iraqi child. At the moment they were compromised, some of the members of this Special Forces team had the option of shooting the child, but would never have done so given American the propensity to protect innocents, especially children. In this case, the child was retrieving a soccer ball and spotted members of the team under their camouflage netting. Soon after the child ran away, Iraqi military arrived. At this point, the A-team, under the command of Chief Warrant Officer—2 Richard Balwanz, found itself in a running gun battle with Iraqi forces who very quickly outnumbered this Special Forces team.

The team was unable to use the communications equipment they desired for talking to their higher headquarters, and ended up using an older Vietnam-era survival radio, a PRC-90. Using this radio, the team's communicator called over a frequency only used for distressed or isolated persons such as downed aviators. In this case, those answering the team's call for help were a flight of Air Force F-16s—among them Capt. Bill Andrews. At the end of the day, this Special Forces team was saved by the Air Force's ability to put bombs exactly where and when they were needed. Andrews later said, "we were going to do what ever it took to make sure those guys got back OK and felt a lot of responsibility on our shoulders . . . We were highly motivated to help those guys get out alive."[32] An Air Force rescue helicopter later came in and rescued this beleaguered team. Andrews later recalled:

> *" . . . A couple of hours later, after the sun went down, we were able to sneak in a helicopter behind the lines and pluck all eight of them out. They all got out safe. That mission gave me pause to reflect on, 'Well, I know for sure I killed a lot of the enemy. How do I feel about it?' I felt pretty damned good because I knew that it was them or us. It was our guys or the Iraqi soldiers that were fighting them and that sort of resolved for me any moral ambiguity over this mission and the fact that we were killing the enemy. It was sort of a watershed in my attitude towards the war and the enemy because pilots have the ability—usually the luxury—to consider the job that they're doing and think about things in terms of targets instead of terms of people. If you're knocking out a bunker or building or hangar or airplane, that's one thing. When you know you're attacking people it's a little bit different and everybody has to morally resolve in their minds if it's O.K. to do that because it goes against the Commandments."*[33]

As it turned out, Andrews did not have much time to dwell on this Special Forces team's rescue. There were plenty of missions to fly during DESERT STORM, most of them dangerous operations deep within occupied Kuwait or Iraqi territory. And in Andrew's case, two days later he would be one of the last Americans to be taken prisoner of war in DESERT STORM. On February 27, 1991, Andrews was in his F-16 supporting American military operations. While flying near Iraqi Republican Guard units, his aircraft was shot down. Once on the ground, it did not take long for the Iraqis to see and then start moving towards Andrews. There were still others overhead who wished to help the downed American aviator, including fellow F-16 pilots. It did not turn out positively for Andrews, however. Once he reached the Iraqi desert floor, Andrews laid vulnerable in the sand, his leg a mess and his F-16 destroyed. He did not want another US pilot to join him. "I'm thinking, 'I'm in a world of hurt, I don't want any company, I've got to do something,'' Andrews recalled in a later interview.

With the Iraqi guns trained on him, Andrews grabbed his radio. "It took maybe two seconds for Andrews to pull his hands down, grab his survival radio, and yell, 'Break right, flare, flare, flare!' The F-16 overhead broke right. Flares came tumbling out. 'I was stupid right; I was crazy,' said Andrews. These guys had guns trained on me from 30 feet away. But I just knew I had to do something. The Iraqi soldiers pulled their triggers and ran. Bullets hit all around Andrews. He threw the radio down—he thinks that he said, 'They're attacking me!' as he did so—and surrendered again. The soldiers swept up to and around him, still shooting. They shot everything: his radio, his helmet, his survival kit, and raft."[34]

Andrews risked his life to prevent other Americans from becoming prisoners of war. These Iraqis were not happy to see this American—whom they believed killed their fellow citizens. Like thousands others taken prisoner prior to this, Andrews had some very important decisions to make—and in a matter of seconds. He had to choose whether or not to fight, whether or not to run, and, even once he was restrained, whether he would act defiant, compliant, or somewhere in between.

Andrews was immediately disarmed and his flight ensemble was taken from him. The Iraqi vehicle transporting Andrews came under coalition fire, but Andrews and his captors were lucky. The vehicle they were driving stalled just before American munitions from F-16s exploded in its path. Only the vehicle's bad maintenance and stalled engine saved their lives. "Having survived a cluster bomb attack by a fellow airman, Andrews got dragged into an Iraqi Republican Guard bunker . . . The Iraqis gave him some food, splinted his leg with bamboo, and they all went to sleep. In the middle of the night, Andrews awoke to hear Iraqis running around like crazy and yelling. They dragged Andrews out and set him next to their vehicle as they packed. But they were clearly tired of hauling him around—Andrews weighed about 200 pounds, and the individual Iraqis weighed about 130. They appeared to figure the pilot was no threat to them, so they quit watching . . . . So he crawled away. Andrews hid underneath a piece of canvas in the now-empty bunker. He heard a lot of yelling. Eventually the Iraqis drove off . . . . He escaped. 'And then I thought, "OK, genius, you've got a broken leg in the middle of the desert. What are you going to do now?"', he recounted."[35]

Andrews hid under trash left behind by the Iraqis, believing his that best opportunity to rejoin American forces would be to find a hiding spot and remain undetected until American units advanced over his position. Unfortunately for Andrews, his plan did not work out the way he hoped. The Iraqis came back the next day—looking either for deserters or perhaps for him. In any case, he was recaptured and then taken to an Iraqi hospital for medical care. Andrews was then put on a bus for transportation to Baghdad. As per normal handling procedures, Andrews was blindfolded and instructed by the guards not to speak. "Andrews heard someone mutter, from behind him in the bus, 'Airborne'. He later discovered he was seated in front of Sgt. Troy Dunlap, a Pathfinder from the 101st Airborne Division. Dunlap was on a helicopter as part of a search and rescue team diverted to try and find Andrews when he was shot down. Two others from the helicopter also were on the bus, one of them 1stLt. Rhonda Cornum,[36] an Army flight surgeon."[37]

After arriving in Baghdad, the prisoners were given medical treatment. Following medical treatment, their initial questioning and interrogations began. When questioned about his unit, mission, and aircraft, Andrews refused to tell the Iraqis anything. At this point, Andrews crossed the line with his interrogators. Andrews challenged the interrogators' authority, saying that he would tell them nothing. For this Andrews paid a heavy price. Andrews later said they "beat the crap out of me".[38] For the next several days, Andrews was sometimes questioned or interrogated, but always restrained and never knowing when the war would end. The war ended slightly less than a week later—but this is an awful long time when suffering from combat wounds, enduring beatings and interrogations, and being denied sleep, adequate water, or pain medication for wounds sustained in combat.

Minutes turned to hours and days seemed like months. The war finally ended, and Andrews was among those flown back to Riyadh, Saudi Arabia and taken onboard the *U.S.S. Mercy*, which served as the US Central Command Phase I Reintegration site. In an interview after the war, Andrews recalled

"I think the date was March 6, 1991. I was repatriated back through the international committee of the Red Cross, who flew us out of Baghdad on one of their planes. It was a charter plane from Balair and had a big red cross on its tail. They took us to Riyadh, where I saluted General Schwarzkopf and then went to the U.S.S. Mercy, the hospital ship where they patched us back together. There was quite an outpouring of love and concern. The American medical folks took care of everything. It was interesting because when you're in a situation where you're just surrounded by hostile bad guys. I had a broken leg and I was hopping down the hall on one leg. Then I got on the U.S.S. Mercy and man, there was no way. I couldn't do anything for myself. They wouldn't let me. They were just great. They are great Americans."[39]

Key among the personnel running the repatriation operation for Andrews and other returning POWs was the Repatriation Team Chief, Colonel Thomas M. McNish (USAF Medical Corps/Flight Surgeon), a former F-105 pilot and former Vietnam War POW (1966-1973).[40] Like many other Americans before him, then-Captain Bill Andrews did his duty as a military officer and a leader. Andrews is now part of an elite breed of Americans that have given more than their fullest measure—all while serving honorably. Andrews and the other POWs from DESERT STORM lived up to the oft-quoted phrase about their duty as POWS, "Return with Honor". Still, Andrews found the fact that others died while coming to his aid "a hard thing to come to grips with . . . while talking to survivors with that crash [meaning the Blackhawk that attempted his rescue]."[41]

Following their return to full duty status, both Acree and Andrews were offered once a year in-depth medical tests and physicals through the Mitchell Center for Returning POWs.[42] As for long-term medical care, Andrews did not immediately take advantage of the Mitchell Center's offerings for the initial five years following his time as a POW.[43] Although years removed from the Vietnam War and the POWs produced as a result of that conflict, the POWs of DESERT SHIELD and DESERT STORM are heroes as well. Andrews, too, gave the full measure of dedication and support to our country in its hour of need.

Andrews retired from the US Air Force as a Colonel and currently lives and works in the Washington, DC area.

Chapter 8

Post Cold War / Asymmetric Prisoners, Detainees, And Hostages

The Cold War lasted from 1947 until 1989. During that time the west, led by the United States stood toe against the east, led by the former Union of Soviet Socialist Republic (or USSR) in a struggle for global dominance. On some occasions, American surveillance aircraft were shot down as they peered into the Soviet Union or her satellite countries. In part this was demonstrated by the shoot down of an American U-2 spy plane while over Russia in 1960 (many of these personnel are listed in Appendix A, MIAs from the Cold War). Likewise, an American U-2 spy plane was shot down as it over flew Cuba getting imagery of the Cuba's military build up immediately preceding the stand-off with the Russians in what is now known as the Cuban Missile Crisis. Although tensions were high in these and other events, calmer heads eventually prevailed and global nuclear war was averted. All was not well between the two superpowers, however.

Due to the U.S. sensitive reconnaissance flights over and along the periphery of the Soviet Union, the US Air Force started preparing its aircrew that flew these sensitive missions through early SERE or survival training. This training prepared the aircrews for detention by the Soviet Union's military apparatus. This training was closely aligned with what occurred in Korea; preparing the men for long term isolation, intelligence exploitation, and of course prolonged detention until political settlements and arrangements for prisoner returns could be made. In addition to the already mentioned standoff between the two super powers, the United States also became engaged with third country powers that were supported by the Soviet Union.

Examples of this proxy war with Soviet client states included the 1961 military disaster known as the Bay of Pigs when the CIA convinced President John F. Kennedy that the final plans for the attack on Cuba by Cuban expatriates should be approved. When this plan was launched, the plan unraveled almost from the onset. The Cuban expatriates were shot or captured and jailed following the decision by President Kennedy that US aircraft would not bomb or strafe Cuban targets at the precise time they were needed. President Kennedy learned two things during the first two years of his presidency. First, he believed the military simply wanted war, and secondly, due to nuclear weapons retained by both sides in this political and military stand-off, neither side could afford to start launching nuclear weapons. The world's survival rested in the balance.

As the war in Southeast Asia ended, the United States still held the belief that our main foe would be large conventional forces on the plains of Europe, as the theory held that the Russians would roll across with their waves of artillery and armored units to conquer Europe and defeat NATO. Due to this very conventional mindset; ignoring that the war in Southeast Asia contained aspects of counterinsurgency and unconventional warfare, the Department of Defense continued to teach its military personnel, primarily pilots and special operations personnel, how to survive in captivity environments reminiscent of the POW compounds of past wars. Then, starting in the late sixties and picking up in the early seventies, the world experienced terrorism.

Terrorism is the use of violence, or the threat of violence to gain notoriety because with world wide recognition of a cause and willingness to commit these acts often saw support in the forms of money and weapons. A prime example of this was the 1972 Olympic Games attacks in which eleven Israeli athletes and one West German police officer were killed when members of the Black September terrorist group took hostages and were preparing to fly away with hostages when the helicopters they were in were blown up by hand grenades.

Other high profile terrorist events included the 1981 kidnapping of American Army General Dozier by members of the Italian Red Brigade in Italy. This event ended when the hostage takers' location was discovered and General Dozier was rescued. Similarly, in South America, Europe, the Middle East, and Asia—terrorist groups popped up. Some terrorist organizations espoused goals that were religious in nature; other groups aligned their groups' goals with socialism or righting a perceived political wrong in a given country.

Throughout the seventies and eighties, and even into the nineties, the United States military's SERE schools continued training a predominance of its DOD clients with Cold War era information. But still, aside from limited numbers of Americans taken hostage such as the CIA Station Chief William Buckley kidnapped in March of 1984, the bombing carried out against the U.S. Embassy annex northeast of Beirut, and the 1985 high jacking of TWA flight 847 in Beirut, Lebanon where a US navy diver was killed, Americans heard of such terrorism—but it was not yet on their door steps—so terrorism remained a tertiary concern behind the economy and their everyday lives. During this timeframe, select American personnel received education[1] into these terrorists' identities, their tactics, weapons, and ideologies.

In 1978 and 1979, two events occurred that shook the United States. One was the Soviet invasion of Afghanistan in 1978 while the other was the 1979 storming and taking of 52 Americans hostage in the US Embassy, Tehran, Iran. On December 24, 1978, Soviet Spetznaz[2] parachuted into key airports and junctures in Afghanistan. The Soviets previously installed a puppet government in Afghanistan, and during the period 1977-1978, the Soviets became increasingly concerned about the motives of that installed government who, much to the chagrin of their Soviet masters increased their contact with other Muslim nations in the region. Moreover, the Soviets became increasingly concerned about the United States' activities in the region. Aside from the Afghan resistance fighters, there was also an Islamist feature to this Soviet invasion. This feature came to be known as Al Qaeda. The Al Qaeda came to the Afghan resistance elements' aid due to an international call for assistance in the Muslim world—since one of their Muslim nations was occupied by infidels, in this case the Soviets. Although the Soviets were eventually defeated in Afghanistan—for many of the same reasons the United States was defeated in Vietnam—using a primarily conventional force to fight an insurgency—Osama bin Laden's Al Qaeda joined thousands of other Muslims in this call to arms and went to Afghanistan to be part of this jihad or holy war to help eject the Soviet invaders. The United States also answered this call to arms against the Soviet invasion by supplying man-portable surface to air missiles known as Stinger missiles to the Afghan freedom fighters. In the end, these

American supplied man-portable surface to air missiles helped turn the tide in the war against the Soviet occupying forces.

By the spring of 1989, the Soviets were defeated and left Afghanistan. Shortly thereafter, the Soviet Union's economy collapsed. The Soviet Union was no more. Almost immediately, nationalist feelings that remained bottled up since the end of World War II reemerged as one former Soviet bloc nation after the other experienced civil wars where nationalists fought the former communist installed regimes. The Soviet's pull-out, combined with the lack of Islamists in places of power within Afghanistan left a power vacuum.

The Taliban defeated the former Soviet Union and enjoyed international fame for defeating a superpower. Aside from the power in Afghanistan, the Taliban joined forces with Osama bin Laden's fighters known as Al Qaeda. Al Qaeda operates as a global network comprising of both a multinational, stateless army and a radical Sunni Muslim movement calling for global Jihad.

The second event occurred was the November 4, 1979 take-over of the American embassy in Tehran, Iran. Radical Islamists took over the embassy, taking 62 Americans hostage. After releasing 10 females and minority hostages, Iran then held the remaining 52 hostages for 444 days (a listing of these detainees is contained in Appendix C). A rescue attempt occurred in the deserts of Iran shortly before then President Jimmy Carter left office. The rescue mission was a failure but the hostages were finally released moments before President-elect Ronald Reagan took office in 1981.

The environment experienced by those held in Iran was not POW compounds of past wars and for the most part did not amount to the violence know to have occurred in the Hanoi Hilton during the war in Southeast Asia. The Americans were introduced to a new viral brand of Islam—one that uses extreme interpretations of the Qur'an. Once released from Iran, the 52 Americans held eventually moved on with their lives but the United States would have issues with the Iranians again.

In April 2001, some months before the attacks on the twin towers in New York City and the Pentagon in Washington, DC, the United States became involved in an incident of a different nature altogether. In April 2001, a US naval intelligence aircraft, a Naval P-3 Orion aircraft complete with a full crew collided with a Chinese fighter aircraft over the Pacific Ocean. Following this mid-air collision, the fighter pilot was killed and the P-3 Orion was forced to make an emergency landing on the Republic of China's Hainan Island. The aircrew was detained about for two weeks, the aircraft a little longer but the United States eventually got the aircrew and aircraft back. This incident occurred at a time while the United States was not at war with China, nor did war result from this peacetime incident.

Many in the United States did not see the Taliban as a credible threat—even if they'd heard of them, much less Al Qaeda. Some Americans may recall the US embassies and consulates being blown up by Al Qaeda operatives in Yemen, a bombing at the World Trade Center in 1993, as well as the 2000 attack on the USS Cole, a warship attacked while berthed in the Yemeni port of Aden. Still, most viewed these attacks as limited attacks. The United States' wake up call did not occur until September 11, 2001 when the World Trade Center towers were brought down by two American aircraft taken over by Al Qaeda terrorists. The Pentagon—the United States' Department of Defense headquarters was attacked by a similar US aircraft taken hostage, and the third aircraft crashed in a Pennsylvania field when the Americans onboard that aircraft fought and refused to allow their aircraft to kill more innocent Americans.

With these attacks on American soil, the United States was at war. Not one declared by the United States—but a war nevertheless. President George W. Bush soon declared on national television that the United States knew who the perpetrators of these horrendous acts were and that they would be pursued, captured, and brought to justice. Within days of the attacks on the World Trade Center towers and Pentagon, America deployed special operations forces to the region. The United States Army's Special Forces personnel deployed to Afghanistan pursuing the Al Qaeda as well as aiding the Northern Alliance in toppling the Taliban and restoring what the United States viewed as a more stable and democratically elected government. In addition to US Army Special Forces, Army Rangers, and conventional army units, the United States also employed other more specialized units to capture, and if required kill those responsible.

At this same time, President George W. Bush was closely monitoring another country's activities which would ultimately haunt his presidency. In early 2003, US forces were being staged in Kuwait for what would be known as Operation IRAQI FREEDOM. In March 2003, US forces comprised of coalition, US Army, and US Marine ground and air forces attacked northwest through the Tigris River Valley towards Baghdad. In a very short time, the US forces noted the Iraqi military forces were not conducting defenses in depth as expected but conducting delaying actions as the coalition forces advanced. As this was occurring, US forces started noting unconventional attacks on their military forces; convoys were attacked with people taken prisoner of war—or so we thought.

With this turn of events, the Iraqis seemingly turned a military defense into what, at first the US thought was a civil war, but later realized the US stepped into another insurgency. In this case, foreign fighters came into Iraq from countries throughout the Middle East. Disturbingly, one of the origins of the foreign fighters appears to have been Osama bin Laden's home country, Saudi Arabia.[4] Numerous incidences of such unconventional attacks by former Iraqi military personnel turned insurgents, as well as fighters coming in from elsewhere in the Middle East started being a common occurrence on the evening news. A US Army convoy was attacked in Baghdad in which numerous Americans were taken hostage, including Jessica Lynch.[5] On September 24, 2004; more evidence of hostage takers grizzly tactics surfaced as a TV video was aired showing the terrorists cutting off the head of their American hostage.[6]

Later, the world watched as a few Americans were detained by Iranian naval forces for straying over national borders along the Al Arab Waterway. Still later, the British government saw several of its marines and sailors also detained by Iranian naval forces when they also, according to the Iranians, strayed across their international border.

Americans had three different environments they could be held in; all within the confines of Iraq and Iran. First, they could become a prisoner of war—held captive by the Iraqi military. Second, as seen in China, or at that time in Iraq, the personnel on the ground had a real concern of being taken into Iran and being the subject of a governmental detention. Finally, they had to worry about being taken a hostage by these seemingly disparate groups of insurgents or terrorists on the battlefield—commonly called hostage taking events.

Each of these types of detention offered their own complexities. However, the concerns extend past the uniformed members of the Department of Defense. What about all the contractors on the battlefield? There were thousands of these contractors on the battlefield they faced the same types of detentions as their military counterparts. How should these defense contract personnel act, whether in uniform or civilians, in each of these detention scenarios? Who was taken and how were they treated?

WARTIME DETENTION ENVIRONMENT

Starting with the American Civil War and up through and including the First Gulf War (Operations DESERT SHIELD and DESERT STORM), the main environments experienced by American POWs were conventional POW camps or compounds such as those found in Korea, Germany, Andersonville, Georgia, or even Baghdad in First Gulf War. As a review, the in such a conventional wartime environment, the POW normally experiences several phases. These phases are initial capture, movement (to a detention area or camp), the detention phase (where the interrogation and long term captivity normally takes place), and finally the last phase—release or escape. The reader will recall that during World War II, less in Korea but much more so in Vietnam and the First Gulf War, the prisoners understood the rules with regard to their actions before the enemy. These rules dictated actions by the captives as well as the captors.

For example, in WWII, the Germans fairly well abided by the Geneva Conventions (1919) and the Americans abided by *Part Two, Rules of Land Warfare, Basic Field Manual, Volume VII, Military Law.*[7] Korea was different, in that the Americans were by the most part untrained in how to act in such environment, as well as how to resist exploitation by their Communist captors. In these settings, the prisoners understood they were in a war, the enemy was the North Koreans (or Germans, North Vietnamese, or Japanese, etc.).

Prior to taking off for missions, the men (and women in the case of the First Gulf War), knew they could become POWs. Although many of these personnel likely had the age old thoughts "it will never happen to me", most at least entertained the thought and understood this to be a reality during times of war. Moreover, since the war in Southeast Asia, it has been understood that if taken POW, the POW camp was nothing more than an extension of the battlefield and that no one handed the POW a discharge due to the fact of them being a prisoner.

As such, some POWs in American history have attempted escapes. In a few such cases these escape attempts succeeded: Christopher Hawkins during the American Revolution in escaping his British captors; Stanley Hawkins escaped from his German captors in Europe during WWII; Nick Rowe escaped his captors while traveling to his execution location in during the war in Southeast Asia. In other places and other times, this responsibility of escaping from a known enemy blurred.

GOVERNMENTAL DETENTION: ROBERT LEVINSON

Robert Levinson is a retired FBI agent, who on March 8, 2007 went missing during his trip to Kish Island—an island that serves as a getaway for wealthy Iranians. Kish Island is just off the Iranian coast west of the Straights of Hormuz. Rumors circulated that Levinson worked for the US government when he turned up missing from the Kish Island hotel. "The State Department has consistently denied Levinson was working for the U.S. government and has unsuccessfully pressed Tehran for information about his whereabouts." Secretary of State Hillary Clinton has been involved in this case; pressuring the Iranian government for information on the missing American.[8]

According to a news article, during "December 2007, Levinson's wife and other family members traveled to Iran and met with officials. Christine Levinson has said the Iranian government was polite and guaranteed her family's security on their trip but provided no details regarding her husband's whereabouts. A year later, she flew to the United Nations to ask questions about her husband. Iranian President Mahmoud Ahmadinejad declined to meet her. Robert Levinson retired from the agency in 1997 and was not involved in intelligence matters with the bureau, officials have said. Levinson later became a principal at the consulting firm Business Integrity International."[9]

With the little amount of verifiable information available on this case; speculation and frustration seem to be the overarching feelings. Levinson's family, residing in Florida have not given up hope of their father and husband being returned.

GOVERNMENTAL DETENTION: HALEH ESFANDIARI

As was seen in the American EP-3 Orion aircraft being detained in China; war is not a necessary condition for people to be held against their will. In this case, the victim was an Iranian-American scholar and academic, as well as the Director of the Middle East

Programs at the Woodrow Wilson International Center for Scholars in Washington, DC. Mrs. Haleh Esfandiari was held by the Iranian Intelligence Services in Iran's famous Evin Prison in Tehran, Iran. In total, Esfandiari was held from May 8th to August 21st which amounted to more than 110 days, with much of that time in solitary confinement.

Esfandiari was originally raised in Tehran but later moved, married, and worked in Washington, DC. Esfandiari's mother typically visited Haleh (in the United States) a couple of times a year but her mother's health curtailed that luxury. On this occasion, Esfandiari visited her mother and was traveling from her mother's residence in Tehran to the airport to return to the United States. In route to the airport, she was robbed—and among the items taken was a critical item in Iran—her passport. Over the next several days, Esfandiari made several trips to the Iranian Ministry of Foreign Affairs where she needed to go for the issuance of a new passport. From the Foreign Affairs office, Esfandiari was given a letter which she was assured would assist her in securing her passport. The next day, she went to the Passport Office and after following the proper rules and waits, she was told that even after two more letters being issued; her wait would be at least two weeks. Esfandiari expected to spend Christmas with her husband and family in Washington, DC but those hopes were soon dashed.[10]

Esfandiari received a phone call which instructed her to go to the Intelligence Ministry and see a man named Mr. Ja'fari. Esfandiari went to a residence in an older residential section of Tehran. After identifying herself to the young soldier manning the door's entrance, Esfandiari was allowed entry, was seated and shortly summoned to see Mr. Ja'fari. Once at the table, Ja'fari wanted her to again tell them about the robbery. He asked for all the details. Later he produced paper and instructed Esfandiari to write down what occurred—signing each page after completing it. Slowly, the questioning started moving into other areas. Soon Esfandiari was asked questions about her social security withholdings in the United States, about her grandchildren, about the people that worked with her at the Wilson Center, and her salaries. For several weeks, the mornings started with more of the same questions, more writing statements, and of course more inconsequential questioning—or so Esfandiari at first believed.[11]

Then, Ja'fari started in with more questioning which progressed slowly but soon the reasons for this questioning became apparent. After gaining information about Esfandiari and her family, Ja'fari then started detailed questioning of Esfandiari's place of employment—the Wilson Center. When talking about the Wilson Center, Ja'fari questioned her about the leadership, who visited this organization—but specifically mentioning the Department of Defense and the Central Intelligence Agency. Ja'fari then asked about her husband, whether or not he was a Jew, and whether or not she ever traveled to Israel? And during these several weeks, the questions were non-stop, many times Esfandiari being interrupted and Ja'fari going on to other items that seemed to interest him. When discussing the Wilson Center, Ja'fari seemed to focus in on Lee Hamilton and his relationship with Esfandiari. Although she told Ja'fari that Mr. Hamilton was several levels above her and that she didn't know him personally, Ja'fari seemed intent on Esfandiari's professional relationship with Mr. Hamilton and his alleged complacency in the affairs of the CIA and the Middle East—Iran in particular. Then slowly, Ja'fari allowed his true interests to emerge.

"Because the OSI had funded some of my [Wilson Center's] programs on Iran, it followed that the Wilson Center was part of a conspiracy to bring about a velvet revolution-a 'soft overthrow', as Ja'fari sometimes put it . . ."[12] From this point forward, the road got rocky very quickly for Esfandiari. First she had several appointments and court dates with various Iranian officials. What Esfandiari did not realize was that when she re-entered Iran, she was walking into a political firestorm. "It was fueled by long-standing animosity between Tehran and Washington, an ineffective and ultimately harmful program of democracy promotion that contributed to my detention and that of many others . . ."[13]

The political winds in Iran reeked of great divisions of trust between Washington and Tehran due to past relations starting with the 1978 Iranian Revolution in which the current leaders took part. Finally, her curtain fell and she was ordered before the magistrate to defend herself concerning crimes against the Iranian state. Esfandiari was accused of "endangering national security". Then, to her surprise, a prison truck came and took her to the infamous Evin Prison in Tehran, Iran. Once in Evin, she was taken to Ward 209. Following this, the guards and prison staff worked closely with the Intelligence Ministry and soon a document was signed ordering her in detention for three months to prevent her escape from the country.[14]

"Ward 209 was reserved for political prisoners and run by the Intelligence Ministry." This was her home for the foreseeable future. At home, however, political maneuvering continued to try and secure her release. From the very first day of her confinement, Esfandiari decided that she had to avoid giving into despair and feeling sorry for herself. She instituted a physical training regimen to maintain muscle tone. Aside from her physical activity, Esfandiari vowed to herself not to show weakness to the guards or interrogators.[15] In addition to her moral stance, she also avoided thinking about her family—a topic that will pull most any detainee down. Her daily schedule consisted of:

— Six a.m. Up and doing morning walk followed by a shower, changing clothes and breakfast.

— After lunch: Continue with her physical activity; aerobics and Pilates.

— At Six p.m. Shower and change. Sometimes read in the evenings.[16]

In the beginning, Esfandiari was in strict solitary confinement but eventually she was allowed contact with another American locked up in Evin Prison, Kian Tajbakhsh. Esfandiari's only other contact was through potted plants in the walking area of the prison and her only contact with living creatures came in the form of a white butterfly she saw one day. Eventually, after several months of being locked up, Esfandiari was notified that the Iranian government showed leniency and allowed her to go home.

CIVILIAN HOSTAGES: THE SRS CREW

Hostage detentions differ greatly from normal wartime POW scenarios. As the reader saw with the 2001 EP-3 incident in China, the lines definitely blurred with regard to the environment;

the United States was not at war with China and yet China held American personnel against their will. The members on this EP-3 Orion aircraft were all American servicemen. The question arises of what happens when those being held against their will are civilians? And to further blur these lines; what happens if this detention is a quasi government, say in the middle of a civil war or insurgency?

Such is the case involving three American citizens held in the jungles of Colombia for over five years by FARC guerillas. The FARC or Revolutionary Armed Forces of Colombia is at war with the government of Colombia. Some call the FARC a guerilla organization engaged in a civil war while others call the FARC a narco-terrorist or just plain terrorist group. The FARC is a Marxist-Leninist revolutionary guerrilla organization based in Colombia who started as a socialist movement in the 1950s and now uses drug money from the cocaine coming out of Colombia as a way to fund their operations.

The case of the SRS (**S**outhern Command **R**econnaissance **S**ystem) hostage scenario is unique because it makes us truly makes us think about how the United States government acts when our citizens are held against their will, but as we will see those held captive were (and are not) always military personnel. In this case the three surviving hostages were all US contractor personnel; some of whom had a military background. Marc Gonsalves is "a former member of the United States Air Force who civilian military contractor for four years before the crash." Another of the crew, Keith Stansell "is a former Marine. Finally, Tom Howes "has been a pilot working in the United States and South America for thirty-seven years."[17]

On February 13, 2003 this SRS aircraft was flying over Colombia when their Grand Caravan developed engine trouble and crashed into the Colombian jungle. The aircraft was loaded with electronic gear but on that fateful day developed engine trouble—an especially big deal when in a single engine aircraft while they "descended from twelve thousand feet over the rigged Cordilleria Oriental Mountains, south of [the capital of Colombia] Bogotá."[18] The crew looked for a possible clearing to land their dead airplane.

There were no good options at this point, since the two pilots, Tommy Janis and Tom Howes could not get the crippled aircraft over the mountains and back to an airfield where they originally planned on getting refueled. The crew sent a distress call—a MAYDAY call to their controlling headquarters, JIATF-S (**J**oint **I**ntera**g**ency **T**ask **F**orce-**S**outh). In this MAYDAY call, they included the crewmembers names (Howes, Janis, Gonsalves, Stansell, and Cruz [a Colombian military member]) to ensure their headquarters understood they were fixing to become isolated in a very hostile area of Colombia.

Once on the ground, the five were almost immediately surrounded by fifty or sixty well armed FARC guerillas. This particular group was led by a woman "named Sonia."[19] Among the five crew members, three lived through the five years of imprisonment in jungle camps. The five members of the SRS crew were segregated into groups of three and two, respectively. The group of three (Gonsalves, Howes, and Stansell) were stripped and searched—being told that that if the FARC discovered micro-chips embedded in their skin, they'd be killed. Following this search for micro-chips, the three were allowed to keep just their clothes; we tied up and marched into the Colombian jungle. The group of two (Janis and the Colombian, Sgt Cruz) were killed at the onset. Throughout their captivity the three surviving crewmembers were guarded but their freedoms within the jungle camps varied.

While in the jungles, the SRS crewmembers' living conditions were very much like the FARC guerillas with the exception of being restrained at night. When they moved from one camp to another, they moved at break-neck speeds, the FARC avoiding Colombian military patrols. The FARC were ruthless; these three Americans were a small part of the total number of prisoners held by the FARC guerillas. Others included a female Colombian politician, police officers, and Colombian military personnel—all being held against their will. They were allowed to take baths, were eventually given tooth brushes and other basic necessities since, as they eventually learned, these three Americans were a prize catch by the FARC.

One of the harder things the SRS crew dealt with was the steep terrain and jungle marches (movement from camp to camp). These moves were not for pleasure but the FARC's attempts to stay one step ahead of the Colombian military who they knew were always searching for them. In the words of one of the three SRS, Keith: "Every breath was like someone had clamped a bench vise down on my chest and was cranking it tighter and tighter. The pain was tolerable, but I couldn't deal with the thought of marching up and down the mountain slopes, each breath more arduous than the last. In the end, it didn't matter what I could deal with. They simply pushed us onto our feet and we began to march through the shadows of the jungle."[20]

Throughout the five years that followed, the three Americans endured the chilly nights, constant wet, jungle diseases prevalent in this area, and as many other prisoners in the past—boredom. The three made a chess board and spent countless hours playing chess, improving (and in some cases learning) Spanish, as well as the occasional treat of being able to listen to Colombian radio. In the end, on July 2, 2008, a ruse by the Colombian military resulted in the freeing of these three SRS crewmembers. After their rescue, the three were flown to the designated reintegration located in a military hospital in Texas. After a successful reintegration, re-joining with their families and many memories, the three SRS were free. For the United States government, this would not be the last time that civilians would be held against their will.

CIVILIAN HOSTAGE: ROY HALLUMS

In another case, this time in war-torn Iraq in 2004, a civilian contracting officer named Roy Hallums[21] was taken hostage with the intent of gaining a ransom payment to secure his release. This event started at a time in Iraq when those taking hostages could have been former Iraqi military personnel, criminal groups, foreign fighters, or in some cases combinations of the aforementioned. For example, it is possible that criminal groups took hostages, and then for purely monetary gain, sold the hostages to others—sometimes foreign fighters such as Al Qaeda[22] or associated groups.

Hallums worked as a US contractor for a Saudi Arabian based firm that worked contracts for the re-building of Iraq. In this case, Hallums was at an evening dinner party in the fall of 2004 when the host announced the food wasn't quite done so Hallums decided he'd go to his office next door to check e-mails until dinner was done. After using the walkways between the host's house and his office, Hallums was at work when AK-47 armed Iraqis suddenly burst in and took Hallums hostage. This event was, at least partially made possible by one of the guards working at Hallum's firm who betrayed them. With Hallums, five others were taken hostage that day; three Iraqis, Hallums, and two other civilians—a Nepalese and Filipino citizen. When the building was assaulted, Hallums and the others were immediately flex-cuffed with their hands behind their backs and black hoods placed over their heads so they could not see where they were being taken.[23]

Hallums was told that if he talked, tried to escape or didn't follow their instructions to the letter, he'd be killed. Although Hallums retired from the US Navy as a Commander—while on active duty, he was a conventional line officer as opposed to being a Navy SEAL. Hallums still knew that the initial minutes of a kidnapping event were critical—for the kidnappers as well as the victim. Hallums knew the kidnappers were under stress and that their lives were at risk if others knew of their existence or what they did. In this instance, Hallums decided that it was better to be a live hostage instead of trying to be a hero and have a shoot out with these men. Hallums was placed in a Toyota sedan and moved a short distance away. Upon arriving at the first detention area, Hallums was taken to the third story of a building, and while remaining flex cuffed, stayed there for the night.

Hallum's family was notified of his being missing—not from Saudi Arabia but from Iraq. Hallums' children and former wife were notified by the US State Department with follow-up visits by Special Agents from the Federal Bureau of Investigation. As one would expect, news like this is life altering and unimaginably hard to take, especially in Hallums' case. Since Hallums did not want his family to worry about him, his family was not told when he transferred from his company's operating base in Saudi Arabia to Iraq.[24]

Hallums was taken to several locations throughout his captivity. In all cases, Hallums was flex-cuffed and hooded which prevented him from knowing exactly where he was at. The locations varied in type; on a few occasions, Hallums was held in mosques and in other occasions held in homes. Hallums maintained his situational awareness sufficiently so that he knew what time it was by the mosque callers—Islam officials calling other Muslims to prayers through the use of loud speakers.

Hallums' movements between detention locations varied in length and type vehicles used. On some occasions, small sedan cars were used while on other occasions larger Suburban type vehicles were used. Hallums was fed; every third day or so in the beginning, and then later a little more frequent, unless the tactical conditions prevented it. On some occasions, the captors modified their feeding plan due to coalition operations occurring in the area of the safe house being used to house Hallums.[25]

Hallums was video taped on a few occasions. For these tapings, Hallums was instructed to memorize the contents of the poorly written messages and then recite the dialogue when in front of the camera for the hostage-takers' proof of life video. Hallums was forced to practice reciting the dialogue for his captors several times before the live recording. Although Hallums was fed and given water, Hallums lost weight and was beaten several times by his captors. The final location Hallums was held was under an occupied house outside of Baghdad.

All this time, Dan O'Shea and the Hostage Working Group were working to secure information about Hallums and the others hostages taken during this same timeframe. Roy Hallums was not forgotten. Meanwhile, Hallums was placed beneath a house, and in fact was the dirt basement of a family having several small children. Throughout the many months at this house, Hallums recalled many occasions of discerning that his captors were watching American cartoons (dubbed in Arabic), the woman of the house cooking, as well as the pitter-patter of tiny feet running about the house.[26]

Time went on in their cellar below the house. On occasion, Hallums heard helicopter activity. When coalition operations were expected, his captors left sufficient food and drink for several days. Likewise, the captors cemented up the entrance to their cellar as to hide the true location of these hostages since they knew American Special Forces searched for captive Americans. After 331 days as a hostage, Hallums heard American helicopters; this time however they were very close and seemed to be landing in the immediate proximity of the house they were being held in. After some initial searching, the Special Forces soldiers located Hallums and the Iraqi national held with him. Hallums was given an American flag by one of his rescuers and was then taken to receive medical treatment, intelligence debriefings, and eventually to Germany and finally to his home in Tennessee.[27]

WHAT DOES ALL THIS MEAN?

At this point, the reader has been exposed to American military held as POWs, Americans held during non-wartime as detainees by foreign governments, civilians held hostage (Roy Hallums) and in the case of Haleh Esfandiari, an American citizen detained by a foreign power. The first question that the reader might then ask is what training is done for the military? Although specifics of the materials and techniques taught at the services' SERE school is classified, the Secretary of Defense issued guidance on what could be said to the press regarding DOD SERE schools.[28]

In part what follows highlights the guidance authorized to be released for the public with regards to the United States SERE schools:

> *"The Department of Defense operates Code of Conduct/ Survival, Evasion, Resistance and Escape (SERE) schools at several locations throughout the United States. These schools are designed to replicate realistic conditions which military members might face in the event they are isolated in enemy or hostile territory. (para) Four areas are taught to assist the military member with the knowledge base needed to combat enemy actions. (para) Training conditions at these schools are designed to be as realistic as possible to simulate conditions should a service member be in enemy territory or enemy hands. Readiness and training are extremely important to the protection and safety of U.S. Forces and these schools provide that for our personnel (Unquote)"*[29]

This then begs the question, who attends this training? In part: *"In general, aviators and members of special operations forces go through this training. Each service has a SERE school tailored toward specific mission related requirements."*[30] Now the question, where are these schools located? *"They are located at Fairchild AFB, Spokane, WA (Air Force), Ft Bragg, NC (Army), NAS Brunswick, ME (Navy/Marines), NAS North Island, San Diego, CA (Navy/ Marines)"*[31] Finally, who oversees the DOD SERE Program? *"The*

Joint Personnel Recovery Agency [whose headquarters is located] *in Ft. Belvoir, VA monitors and oversees all DOD SERE school programs."*[32]

One issue that should come to mind then is who exactly is supposed to receive this Code of Conduct / SERE training? According to Department of Defense Regulation 1300.21 (Code of Conduct (CoC) Training and Education) dated Jan 2001, the Combatant Commanders in each of the geographic areas of responsibility, e.g., Middle East—Central Command; Central and South America—SOUTHERN Command, etc. are responsible for identifying the CoC / SERE training requirements for the personnel entering into their theaters. In part, the

> *"Commanders of the Combatant Commands shall:*
>
> *Designate the level of training (i.e., Level A, B, or C) personnel operating in the command's area of operation must have prior to deployment to theater, and communicate these requirements to the respective Services. CoC training needs should be identified for wartime requirements as well as for areas considered high risk due to terrorist activities and areas with the likely potential for detention of members of the Armed Forces by foreign governments for the purpose of exploitation. The Commanders of the Combatant Commands must determine who is considered high-riskof—capture and exploitation for the purpose of CoC training. During war and operations other than war, personnel operating beyond the forward line of troops (e.g. all aviators, Special Operations Forces, long-range*

reconnaissance patrol members) are clearly in more danger than others of becoming prisoners of war. Combat forces generally require higher-level CoC training than support forces. As such, the commands must identify their requirements precisely, and they and the Services must train them to the applicable level."[33]

The aforementioned instruction provides guidance to Department of Defense members of the various services and Combatant Commands but what about civilians on the battlefield? For that we can see Department of Defense Instruction 3020.41 (Contractor Personnel Authorized to Accompany the U.S. Armed Forces) dated October 2005. In part, this document speaks to civilians and planning for their participation on the battlefield in very precise language instructing these same Combatant Commanders to:

"4.2 Implement this Instruction in operations plans (OPLANs) and operations orders (OPORDs) and coordinate any proposed contractor logistic support arrangements that may affect the OPLAN/OPORD with the affected geographic Combatant Commands. Contingency plans shall be developed to ensure continuation of services if a defense contractor is unable to perform according to DoD Directive 1100.4 and DoD Instruction 3020.37 (references (d) and (e)).

4.3. Ensure contracts clearly and accurately specify the terms and conditions under which the contractor is to perform, describe the specific support relationship between the contractor and the Department of Defense, and contain standardized clauses to ensure efficient deployment, visibility, protection, authorized levels of health service and other support, sustainment, and redeployment of contingency contractor personnel. The contract shall also specify the appropriate flow-down of these provisions and clauses to subcontracts. Generally, defense contractors are responsible for providing for their own logistical support and logistical support for their employees. Logistical support shall be provided by the Department of Defense only when the commander or the contracting officer determines provision of such support is needed to ensure continuation of essential contractor services and adequate support cannot be obtained by the contractor from other sources.

4.4. Develop a security plan for protection of contingency contractor personnel in locations where there is not sufficient or legitimate civil authority and the commander decides it is in the interests of the Government to provide security because the contractor cannot obtain effective security services, such services are unavailable at a reasonable cost, or threat conditions necessitate security through military means. The contracting officer shall include the level of protection to be provided to contingency contractor personnel in the contract. In appropriate cases, the geographic Combatant Commander may provide security through military means, commensurate with the level of security provided DoD civilians . . ."[34]

At the end of the day, what does this mean to our brave men and women serving all around the globe, be they in uniform, contractors, or US government civilians? It means that on the modern battlefield—whether in Afghanistan, Iraq, the Horn of Africa, or Libya, we should be proud of what they are doing as an all volunteer force. Furthermore, that the government as a whole is doing more than it ever has before to prepare our personnel for captivity environments, and further that a mechanism is place to locate and then return these personnel to their families.

Since the days of George Washington and the battles at Concord, our government has been getting better at assisting those serving in our nations' defense. It is these serving our nation that asks so little yet give so much. Whether the United States participates in counterinsurgencies, conventional wars, have our citizens detained by hostile powers, or have our people taken hostage; we must continue to prepare them for this eventuality.

Chapter 9

An Analysis Of The Captivity Environment

Within the preceding chapters, the reader has been exposed to POW experiences throughout America's history. Although this book has primarily focused on American prisoners of war, the issues detailed here are regularly dealt with by any prisoners of war, hostages, or detainees, regardless of nationality or historical period. That being said, it is helpful to be able to amass the information learned in a compact way so the reader can get the "so what" of several hundred years of POWs' experiences.

Like many things in life, complex issues absorbed in small chunks are easier to digest and more easily recalled; sometimes called chunking. It is thus helpful to remember an acronym which amasses many of the lessons the United States, as well as individuals held captive, will want to remember. This acronym is **HEALTH.** The letters stand for **H**ealth, **E**nvironment, **A**rchive, **L**eadership, **T**raining, and **H**umor.

An explanation of **HEALTH** will be followed by summaries of the effects of captivity on POWs (and their families) upon repatriation and reintegration. This information was gleaned from two primary reports and compiled through several interviews and much research.

The first report was written post-Vietnam[1] and the second one was written with respect to the POWs from DESERT STORM[2] in 1991. But first, **HEALTH**.

Although it might seem like a simple issue, health in a captivity environment consists of much more than just taking vitamins or feeling well. A POW's health is the product of a lifelong endeavor, since a prisoner is in his or her best physical condition when initially captured, barring injuries. It is this physical condition that allows for the possibility of evasion—since the prisoner is often able to run farther or faster than those pursuing him.

Likewise, good health is also the product of proper immunizations, sufficient amounts of sleep, and a diet providing the proper nutrients. Moreover, health is more than a physiological state of the body. It also includes the psychological well-being of the captive, which is fostered by a healthy lifestyle and other factors such as outlook on life, military service, comradeship, a belief in a higher being, family life, and a sense of belonging.

Health should also be considered throughout the ups and downs of captivity, good and bad. In the case of former POW Bill Andrews from DESERT STORM, some observations are offered here as things that helped him through his captivity experiences with the Iraqis. In part:

> *"I can't recall laughing about much or things striking me as being humorous at the time . . . the overall experience was an emotional roller coaster. You had some very high-highs and very low-lows . . . . So, for example, if I fared an interrogation well and I figured I didn't give them anything and it wasn't that bad then it was easy to be*

> *an emotional high after that . . . I remember thinking milk this for all its worth . . . enjoy the moment . . . . because there's going to be a crash later . . . . despair at some point . . . so I sort of felt some elation and some dejection at the lows . . . . remember faith and hope for something better . . . and where there is life there is hope* [3]

Health alone, however, does not guarantee survival; the captive must also understand his or her **ENVIRONMENT**. The word "environment" can apply to a myriad of factors, but in the case of POWs, weather, enemy, and terrain are the specific terms that apply. The U.S. Department of Defense as well as the individual must make allowances for these factors. The weather in a particular area must be understood, since it can have disastrous effects on the survivor, hostages, recovery forces, and even the intelligence community's sensors if not understood and taken into account when planning. As the reader saw in the Korean War chapter, Robert Maclean was already adept at living in cold-weather environments, as well as having the proper clothing. Likewise, prior to deploying to Southeast Asia, jungle training was often undertaken to acquaint those personnel with this new and often alien environment. Mary Anderson's work on DESERT STORM POWs described how many of the seventeen former POWs interviewed discussed how their cultural awareness supported their resistance postures by educating them on the Arab mindset and customs.[4]

In later wars, such as the war in Southeast Asia and Operation DESERT STORM, personnel deploying into such environments are issued necessary gear to guard against climatic factors such as cold and rain. This gear included cold-weather (or hot-weather) attire as well as survival kits adapted for use in those specific areas. Likewise, potential evaders in desert environments must understand the effects of weather phenomena, and perhaps pack scarves and sand goggles as part of their field gear prior to deploying. The same can be said of cold weather, rain, snow, or wildlife factors such as mosquitoes. Aside from the weather, our personnel must also take into account the enemy.

The enemy plays a role in the evader's actions and is only ignored at the evader's peril. First, the individual must understand the potential enemy, their tactics[5], and how they might affect the evader's (or POW's) actions. As was seen in the war in Korea, a great percentage of our fighting men had no idea of the exploitation techniques or tactics used by their captors, and were thus unprepared to counter North Korean or Chinese. Likewise, the evader must know whether the enemy has the ability to see at night or uses dogs to track them. The potential escapee must have a place to go to get this information prior to being committed to combat operations. As was seen by the actions of Bill Wilson during his one-week evasion in North Vietnam, such information on evasion and enemy tactics is invaluable.

That brings U.S. to the survivor's unit staff personnel. Staff members must understand the enemy that their personnel will face in combat and ensure that the personnel in their unit are aware of this information, as well as how to counter the enemy's tactics. For example, if the enemy uses certain interrogation techniques or tactics for pursuing evaders, without prior knowledge of this, the potential evaders or captives are defenseless. Currently, this information may be gained from the services' SERE schools as well as other briefs prior to deploying into theaters of war. In addition to the services'

SERE schools, the US Air Force trains selected enlisted personnel to train others in SERE techniques. These personnel go through a rigorous selection and training process to become the DOD's premier experts on survival, evasion, resistance and escape.

At the small-unit level, the recovery or rescue forces must understand the enemy's use of defensive measures if they are to overcome these when recovering Americans. Planners must account for enemy defenses and properly prepare for operational maneuvers that avoid enemy air defenses, enemy radars, or enemy intelligence collection efforts. Only by staying undetected, or in a position where the enemy can do nothing about our actions, can we hope to be successful in recovery operations. But, the enemy and weather are only part of the environment; we must also understand the terrain we are to operate in.

Terrain affects enemy forces, the evader, and even recovery and intelligence sensors. The potential captives must understand the terrain so that they can properly plan for their evasion operations—or escape operations if they are already captives, fully taking into account the cover and concealment[6] that the terrain might offer. These operations often take place in the enemy's backyard, so more often than not, the enemy will be familiar with the terrain, knowing all the crevices and valleys the evaders may try to hide in, as well as the routes American rescue forces might use in attempts to recover their isolated forces.

Aside from possible hiding locations, potential evaders must also understand the terrain so that the proper evasion routes can be planned. Terrain favorable for foot movement might not support wheeled or tracked vehicles. Finally, American recovery forces, for all the same reasons previously mentioned, must also understand the terrain. In short, American forces at all levels must fully appreciate the terrain and its effects on the evaders, recovery forces, intelligence sensors, and the enemy. They must also understand that wars are often fought in locations where others have already been. Therefore, we must retain information from past wars or operations which brings us to the question of storing data: **ARCHIVE**.

As the reader has seen thus far, planners, evaders, and captives must all understand the enemy, the terrain, the weather, and other factors such as health and their effects on current operations. If the United States fails capture data from past wars, including former POWs' experiences, mistakes previously made will no doubt be repeated—sometimes at a very high cost. For example, OPERATION HOME COMING, conducted in the early spring of 1973, successfully repatriated and reintegrated many hundreds of Americans who were held captive in Southeast Asia.

If we were to compare the reintegration operations carried out for Operation DESERT STORM in 1991 to those carried out for OPERATION HOME COMING in 1973, we would see that the former was not executed with the same level of precision and training. Our nation's collective memory seemed to have been short. America had to relearn many of these lessons; we rewrote many of the rescue and reintegration procedures, and finally, because people moved on to other assignments, new reintegration personnel needed to be trained. Likewise, as we moved forward to the early days of OPERATION IRAQI FREEDOM when members of the 507th Maintenance Company were brought home, some of the mistakes from DESERT STORM were repeated because, again, our collective memory was lost.

At the tactical level, if a pilot applied certain operational techniques when missiles were fired at him—and they worked—or if an evader successfully used a given technique to signal aircraft, or even if a truck driver used a weapon in a new and helpful way when his convoy was ambushed, if no one captured these lessons learned, others might pay a very heavy price the next time similar situations occurred. To fix this problem, the Department of Defense developed and then issued policy guidelines and instituted a set of processes for the collection, analysis, and resolution of issues, formally called the Joint Lessons Learned Program.

The [former] U.S. Joint Forces Command's website stated that the program, run by the Joint Center for Operational Analysis, "collects, analyzes and disseminates lessons learned and best practices across the full spectrum of military operations in order to integrate recommendations and improve the joint force's warfighting capability."[7] The program's requirements are listed in Chairman of the Joint Chief of Staff Instruction 3150.25A. In part, this instruction states: "The JLLP applies to both the training and operational environments of the Armed Forces of the United States."[8] What this then means is that commanders at all levels place data on lessons learned into the proper databases. It is the hope of the Joint Center for Operational Analysis that lessons can be learned just once; in effect, most of the preparation should occur by learning from others' mistakes.

One of the United States Joint Forces Command's subordinate commands, the Joint Personnel Recovery Agency, participates in this Joint Lessons Learned Program, collecting and cataloging information from past recovery operations or captivity experiences (of service members and others) so that mistakes are not repeated. Moreover, when appropriate, this information is transferred to the services' SERE schools, so that those most in need of this information can receive it. In other cases, after being analyzed, it might be discovered that the problem is the result of a training shortfall. In these cases, the proper service schools are contacted with recommendations on how to correct those shortfalls. But for this training program to work, leadership is required.

LEADERSHIP is a word often spoken, but is truly put to the test under the horrid conditions suffered by POWs. Before discussing specific examples of leadership—good or bad—an understanding of our military views leadership is helpful. Leadership can be seen from two perspectives: officer and noncommissioned (or enlisted) roles, authorities, and responsibilities.

First, officers' authorities and responsibilities are vested in United States law, and our officers swear an oath of allegiance to the President of the United States (formerly called the oath of office). In short,

> *"I, _____, do solemnly swear (or affirm) that I will support and defend the Constitution of the United States against all enemies, foreign and domestic; that I will bear true faith and allegiance to the same; and that I will obey the orders of the President of the United States and the orders of the officers appointed over me, according to regulations and the Uniform Code of Military Justice. So help me God." (Title 10, U.S. Code; Act of 5 May 1960 replacing the wording first adopted in 1789, with amendment effective 5 October 1962).*[9]

Our enlisted personnel swear an allegiance when they agree to their terms of enlistment (commonly called "signing up for another hitch"). The enlisted oath is seen here:

> *"I,____________, do solemnly swear (or affirm) that I will support and defend the Constitution of the United States against all enemies, foreign and domestic; that I will bear true faith and allegiance to the same; and that I will obey the orders of the President of the United States and the orders of the officers appointed over me, according to regulations and the Uniform Code of Military Justice. So help me God. I swear (or affirm) that I am fully aware and fully understand the conditions under which I am enlisting . . ."*[10]

These two statements are at the core of how American prisoners, officers and enlisted, should comport themselves while in the military, and when combined with the Code of Conduct, in captivity environments. As was seen in the Civil War chapter, some American prisoners of war conducted mob actions to take belongings from fellow prisoners when they were most vulnerable—such as in the Civil War's Andersonville prison compound. Likewise, during the war in Southeast Asia, there were examples of American prisoners accepting early release without specific authorization from the American Senior Ranking Officer, or in a few cases, American POWs spying on and reporting fellow prisoners' actions to gain favorable treatment by the North Vietnamese.[11] More recently, in operations in Iraq involving the 507th Maintenance Company, American military officers formally trained to resist interrogation assisted and advised other less knowledgeable POWs on how to conduct themselves while being held prisoner.

Why is this discussion important? Enlisted personnel are expected to obey the orders of the officers appointed above them—as stated in their oath of enlistment. Enlisted personnel do not command troops; they are often put in leadership positions, but command responsibilities remain with the officers. Officers, on the other hand, are expected to lead, and this is heart of the matter. Officers are assigned command positions like Commanding General, Commanding Officer, Executive Officer, Operations Officer, Platoon Commander, and many other titles. Even when assigned mundane duties such as running military dining facilities or maintenance facilities, it is these officers who are charged with all that occurs—or fails to occur—and that is what separates them from enlisted personnel. In short, the real and undeniable difference between officers and enlisted is that all officers are in positions of leadership. Senior enlisted personnel such as Sergeants Major (or equivalents) occasionally hold senior staff positions—but in most cases, they perform duties as the Commanders' senior enlisted advisors. This is important to understand because, as was seen in the Hanoi Hilton, the American POWs' chain of command and the communications their officers established is what made the U.S. prisoners' efforts in this war successful. This was a wholly different situation than existed in Korea or in the American Civil War.

All this is not meant to take anything away from our military's enlisted personnel; who have performed admirably in the past, continue to do so in the present, and will also prevail in the future. All-volunteer forces do work, but only as long as we continue to have the best and brightest lead our nation's military. A large part of leadership is character and integrity, but training is also required.

Personnel Recovery **TRAINING** can broken down into two different areas: military training and training for the military's medical / psychological care providers. Military training encompasses three basic groups of people: the commanders and staff that must plan the recoveries, the rescue forces that must execute these recoveries, and, of course, the potential isolated members. When considering these three groups that collectively make up a system, it can easily be understood that all three facets of this triad must be trained at equal levels in order to be most effective. We will start with the commanders and staff.

The commanders and staff of the various joint task forces distributed throughout the globe must have a planning methodology that allows them all to plan in a like manner. Said a different way,

> *The Joint Operations Planning and Execution System (JOPES) is the Department of Defense's (DoD's) principal means for translating national security policy decisions into military plans and operations. JOPES Functional Managers grant permissions, restrict access to operation plans on the database, and perform periodic reviews of user IDs and the content of the JOPES database to ensure outdated plans and accounts are removed when no longer required.*[12]

We now understand that the commanders and staff of our military have a common planning system, as seen in JOPES. The next logical question is understanding how the recovery forces are trained?

The leadership of the armed services (Army, Air Force, Navy, the Marine Corps), as well as the U.S. Special Operations Command, are responsible for the recruiting, training, and equipping their forces that will be required by the various geographic combatant commanders. Later, when these troops are part of joint task forces around the globe, the various geographic combatant commanders, such as the U.S. Central Command (in the Middle East), U.S. Southern Command (in Central and South America), and so on are then responsible for organizing their forces into coherent fighting units. At this point, we theoretically have trained staff that can plan using similar systems, such as JOPES, and the rescue forces are recruited and trained to a standard, but whom do they rescue?

As has already been discussed, the individuals deemed high-risk attend the various service SERE schools.[13] The aforementioned services are responsible for providing properly trained personnel to the various geographic commands. Two issues then remain when considering military training. Do these personnel get the proper training, and how is this triad of capabilities employed by the various geographic combatant commanders?

Today's SERE schools are no different than any other organization. Based on funding, they are assigned (or hire) a given number of instructors and staff. This funding also controls how large the classroom facilities are, how many classrooms are built, and how much land is dedicated to this training. Like everything else in life, the services must balance the use of limited resources against an ever-increasing list of requirements. What this most often means is that the commander makes judgment calls as to where and how the limited funding is allocated based upon their units' (or services') assigned missions. The commanders also have to weigh the money spent on SERE training against all the other requirements his unit faces in the short amount of time prior to deployments. This "other" training might include instruction in new weapons systems, new vehicles, airplane parts, or even survival radio use. What this often means is that not all desired training will be conducted, due to a lack of funding or time.

Earlier, leadership and the decisions that those in command must make were discussed. In America's current wars in Iraq and Afghanistan, commanders are allotted a given number of days and specific amount of money to complete this training. Given the political sensitivity to prisoners on television, following Arab news networks like Al-Jazeera broadcasting Americans being publicly executed, this training has received much more funding than in past years. Still, commanders at all levels must make the hard decisions of who to train in certain skills, who gets what equipment, and who goes to the SERE schools.

At the end of the day, these military officers are making the best decisions possible with regards to the best use of money, space, time, and personnel to accomplish their assigned missions—survival and evasion being part of that. But how are these rescue or recovery forces and capabilities employed by the geographic combatant commanders?

The geographic combatant commanders (GCCs) establish rescue centers—most often near the geographic command's headquarters. These GCC level rescue centers facilitate joint recovery planning and assist the separate components or joint task forces and coordinate recovery planning when more than one component's recovery forces are required. These rescue centers are most often led by commissioned officers, and are manned jointly by the military services' officers, enlisted, government civilian, and contractor personnel. The Joint Personnel Recovery Agency (JPRA) trains these staff members in multiple locations, but predominantly at JPRA's PR Training and Education Center in Fredericksburg, Virginia. The students attending these courses receive training in planning as well as command and control functions common to GCC (or subordinate element) rescue centers. So far, we have discussed several aspects of training. But what happens when returnees require medical or psychological care following their reintegration or recovery?

Sometimes it is helpful to remember where we have been in order to see more clearly where we need to go. Following the Revolutionary War, once released, the prisoners simply went back home and got medical care wherever and whenever they could. And, given the standards of medical care in the eighteenth century, there was much less understanding of psychological issues; post-captivity care was inadequate at best. Following the Civil War, John Northrop was released from the prisoner transports in Maryland and spent time in the hospital recovering. Medical care was getting better.

Although this was not discussed in the previous pages, on some occasions medical care from the Veterans' Administration, based on the training of their medical and administrative professionals, seemed insensitive to the needs of these very special patients. In one such case, a B-17 crewmember, Virgil Gordon from Watkinsville, Georgia, was part of the 570th Bombardment Squadron, 390th Bombardment Group when his B-17 Flying Fortress was shot down over Germany on September 9, 1944. Along with the remainder of the crippled aircraft's crew, young Gordon jumped out of this doomed airplane. Although his parachute deployed normally, Gordon landed on a building and broke his ankle. He later recalled:

> *"I couldn't figure out where I was," Gordon recalled. "I thought I was in France." Gordon bailed out of the plane and landed on the roof of a house, suffering a broken left ankle and a gash to the back of his head. Despite the leg injury, he had to climb down a ladder from the roof of the house and into the custody of the Germans. A German woman helped Gordon, whose leg was later set with sticks and cloth. "I said, 'Lady, where am I?' "Gordon remembered asking the woman. "You're in Germany," she replied, to which he responded, "Oh, God, Germany." Gordon remained a POW until he and about 2,000 other soldiers were liberated on April 26, 1945—a day Gordon calls "one of the greatest days of my life."*[14]

A German doctor provided aid to Gordon, and then he was shipped off to a POW compound where he stayed until the spring of the next year. That spring, Gordon was one of thousands of POWs who were forcibly marched towards Berlin to stay ahead of the advancing Russians. Eventually, Gordon and the other POWs were repatriated and, after a successful Air Force career, he retired in Georgia. Decades later, his troubles with the Veterans' Administration began.

Following his retirement from the Air Force, Gordon's wife Sara kept after him to petition the government for the Purple Heart medal she felt he deserved due to his actions in World War II. When Gordon finally approached the Veterans Administration (VA) in Georgia, they confirmed that he was a former POW, but said that in order for him to claim a combat-related injury, which would qualify him for the Purple Heart medal, he would have to provide the name of the doctor who treated his ankle in wartime Germany.

As one might guess, providing such information is not an easy task for events that occurred several years ago, much less several decades in the past and in a war ravaged country. At this point, it was doubtful that the doctor in question was even alive. Gordon was already 82 years old, and the doctor would have been much older. According to U.S. government records, Gordon was housed in "Stalag Luft 3 Sagan-Silesia Bavaria (Moved to Nuremberg-Langwasser) 49-11."[15]

Finally, after petitioning Georgia legislators for several years, Gordon was awarded his Purple Heart Medal for actions received as the direct result of combat. This is important because the care and sensitivity with which our military veterans are treated speaks to who we are as a nation; it displays our national character. Does that mean that our government will never make mistakes? Absolutely not. It does remind us that we owe the veterans the very best medical care and follow-up we can provide. There is good news, however. Things have changed over the years—for the better. Virgil Gordon was awarded his well-deserved Purple Heart Medal, and the VA has improved its treatment of servicemen.

A separate facility for our former POWs was created. The Robert E. Mitchell Center for Returning POWs in Pensacola, Florida was built to provide care for and research long-term medical needs of former POWs.[16] The Mitchell Center provides the returning POWs with annual complete physicals and screenings free of charge. The Mitchell Center then uses this information as part of its long-term medical study on the effects of captivity. Likewise, the armed services train their healthcare providers in the care of combat-related medical conditions like the commonly mentioned post-traumatic stress disorder (PTSD). In addition to the medical community's training in these combat-related conditions, selected clinical psychologists receive specialized training in working with returning POWs, detainees, and hostages. These specially trained psychologists are called SERE Psychologists and are stationed throughout the Department of Defense, in the United States and at overseas locations. These SERE Psychologists are divided into two categories: SERE-Oriented and SERE-Certified Psychologists.

SERE-Oriented Psychologists receive academic training from the Joint Personnel Recovery Agency's Human Factor's section. The SERE-Certified Psychologists receive this same academic training to receive the coveted "SERE-Certified" from JPRA, these psychologists also attend a DOD-approved Level C (High Risk) SERE Course, including a Resistance Training Laboratory portion. Attending these sessions (sometimes called "RTLs") allows these professionals to truly understand the pressures and issues commonly dealt with by those in captivity environments.[17]

In the end, readers will hopefully understand that many more military and medical professionals receive training to assist these returning heroes than was the case two decades ago. As compared to ten or twenty years ago, the military services, as well as the United States government, have improved its services by leaps and bounds—all of which increase the likelihood of our returnees receiving the highest level of medical care. Another factor in surviving captivity environments is humor.

HUMOR. There are skills held by those held against their will that can be quantifiably shown to increase the detainee's chance of survival, escape, and possible return to friendly control. These items include survival kits, emergency signaling devices, and even escape tools. These are often measurable in such a way that potential evaders can be trained to make their correct use more likely. Conversely, there are other attributes, like a sense of humor, that are not always quantifiable but can nevertheless increase a detainee's chances of survival by maintaining a positive mental outlook.

Sometimes this is done through jokes with fellow detainees; at other times such humor is directed at the detaining powers, most often the guards. Aside from the psychological benefits of humor as a stress reliever, humor in detention scenarios often provides the detainee with an edge over his captors by way of a small and not insignificant moral victory.[18] Several examples follow—some of which were mentioned in the previous chapters, while other examples of POW-related humor will be new to the reader.

RIDDING NORTH KOREA OF FLIES

Although already recounted during a previous chapter, the following bears re-telling as to provide the reader a full comprehension of the importance of humor during captivity. During the Korean War, the senior Chinese leadership told the POW camp leadership that China was going to get rid of all flies and that their nation's effort would start with the POW camps. Although ridiculous as it might sound, the prisoners quickly pitched into this ridding China of flies. For their efforts, the prisoners were offered a Chinese cigarette for every two hundred flies the prisoners caught. This idea soon caught on like wildfire; not because the prisoners wanted to help the Chinese in their fly ridding exercise, but this gave the prisoners something to do—and for those that smoked—a chance to get a cigarette or two while they were at it. As far as the POWs were concerned, this was a win-win situation.

Soon prisoners were catching flies by the hundreds. Industrious prisoners made fly traps that amazed the Chinese. The Chinese were astounded by how many hundreds of flies the prisoners were catching and turning in. Soon the Chinese raised the ante and started weighing the flies since individually counting this number of flies soon proved to be unrealistic. The Chinese then started cheating the POWs; adjusting the scales in their favor. Again, ingenious prisoners, not to be outdone by their captors used discarded tooth paste tubes. The prisoners cut their aluminum tooth paste tubes into small slivers and inserted these small strips of metal into the flies' bodies—greatly adding to these flies' overall weight. Soon the flies being turned in by the prisoners weighed more than anyone else's flies and their captors could not figure out why? The Chinese never figured out how the American caught such heavy flies.[19] This was not the last war where humor was used by the prisoners.

MY DOG IS LOST

In one of the Korean War POW camps—Camp Five, Army SGT Chikami decided he'd annoy the guards. One night, the guards peered in at Chikami and realized he wasn't sleeping. They came in and said "you sleep" He replied that he could not sleep. The guard asked Chikami why he could not sleep and reiterated that the "camp regulations required him to sleep". Chikami replied that he lost his dog. The guard said, "you don't have a dog" and Chikami replied NO, "its gone." This went on for a few more minutes when the guard again said, you don't have a dog". Chikami said "the Turks gave me a dog." The guard finally heard enough and got his Sergeant of the Guard and told him of Chikami's insolence. Chikami repeated the same story, the Chinese Sergeant, who spoke a little English, said "OK, let's call a spade—a spade". Chikami then said, "Oh you want to play cards?" At this point, the guards put Chikami in several days solitary confinement.[20] Solitary was a small price to pay for a story that was likely told thousands of times following his release from solitary—increasing the prisoners' morale.

COVERT BINOCULARS

In 1989, a U.S. citizen, Kurt Muse, was arrested by Panamanian strongman Manuel Antonio Noriega's security forces. Muse was held in the infamous Modelo Prison in Panama. Muse was accused of working for the Central Intelligence Agency, and was on numerous occasions beaten and threatened with death if he did not cooperate. Finally, in late 1989, Muse was rescued in Operation Acid Gambit, a hostage rescue operation carried out by U.S. Special Operations Forces.

In the nine months prior to his rescue, Muse was detained, beaten, and tortured but never lost his sense of humor. In one specific incident, he realized that two Panamanian military personnel were watching him in his prison cell from an adjacent building across the courtyard, using binoculars. Muse, not to be outdone and finally getting tired of this, retrieved two cardboard inserts from rolls of toilet paper. Holding these two toilet paper rolls parallel to his face, he appeared as if he also possessed binoculars and was looking back at these personnel. The Panamanians became obviously infuriated that he possessed binoculars, and on several occasions came running into Muse's cell to search for them in vain.[21] Although an annoyance for the Panamanians (who never found the "binoculars"), this was a psychological victory for Muse.

BODY BY BAGHDAD

Following his return from Iraq and now in a hotel room with his wife, Marine LtCol. and former DESERT STORM POW Clifford Acree was standing in front of the mirror in the bathroom brushing his teeth and otherwise taking care of personal hygiene needs when he happened to notice his wife staring at his emaciated and obviously scarred body in horror. Having a sense of humor and wanting to calm his wife's fears and emotions, Acree looked over at Cindy and said "What, you don't like body by Baghdad and rebuild by the Navy?" Like other great men before him, these prisoners of war learned to cope with bad situations—making the best out of what ever they had.

HE FLEW THE COOP

During the last 3-4 months of the Vietnam War, the POWs were allowed much more freedom; moving amongst the rooms in their holding areas, physical activities, and just being with fellow Americans. In such an environment, the POWs received more food, and invariably had to use the bathroom more often. Humor was seen in this setting as re-told by one former Vietnam POW.

> *"After I [Vietnam POW, Bill Wilson] went to the Zoo and it was about 2-3 weeks before release, we were eating 'dinner' one night and one of the guys went to take a crap*

or something. The guard came in and asked "where's Joe". One of the POWs replied with a climbing motion and pointed to the wall. The guard's jaw almost hit the floor. His reaction was so extreme that we started laughing where upon the guard realized he had been 'had". The next day, he was no where to be seen and when another guard was asked where he was, the reply was that he was in the hospital with an ulcer."[22]

Up to this point, the reader has been exposed to the experiences of a few of the thousands of Americans who became prisoners of war, governmental detainees, or hostages. In most of these cases, these brave Americans conducted themselves with the honor and fidelity reflecting the highest of American virtues. But, the reader might also ask: "What is a good summary, then, of the effects of the varied conditions and circumstances a POW might face?"

CAPTIVITY'S EFFECTS ON THE POW

While research-based analysis is often useful for complex issues, the reader must understand the limitations of applying extrapolated data more broadly. It is important to remember that each captivity environment is unique in terms of the training and experiences of the participants prior to being held captive, the captors' attitudes and training, lengths and conditions of captivity, and the captives', spouses, and greater publics' attitudes towards the war, not to mention the training and attitudes of the guards and detaining powers. Moreover, this data is typically gathered at a time when some of the emotions of the events discussed may be raw, so reports may not be entirely objective due to the freshness of events in the minds of the POWs and their spouses. Therefore, the information that follows may prove useful but the reader will have to understand these findings are generalized and each isolating event must be judged based on the facts and circumstances surrounding that case.

VIETNAM WAR'S EFFECTS ON POWs

The war in Southeast Asia, commonly called the Vietnam War, was one of the longest and most controversial wars in our nation's history. That being said, it was recognized very shortly after this war's conclusion that a detailed study of American POWs' experiences was warranted. Such a study was undertaken to fully understand not just the physical, psychological, and social adjustments following the POWs' return, but also the impacts these events had upon the families, during and after their loved ones' incarcerations. Prior to OPERATION HOME COMING, the Army, Navy, and the Marine Corps set up a research effort to gather this data in a meaningful way with the hope that future POWs could learn from these Americans' experiences.

The men used for this study were unique in several ways, which is one of the main reasons the author has urged caution when trying to apply these same findings to other POW events or periods of history. First, these prisoners' numbers were very small in comparison to earlier wars such as in Korea or World War II, where the POWs numbered in the thousands. The Vietnam POWs were predominantly officers with college educations (and often advanced degrees) and were trained as part of a professional officer corps, unlike in some of America's earlier wars. Lastly, the length of captivity was greater in some cases, such as with Everett Alvarez who was a POW for eight and a half years. That is not to say that this data is useless—far from it. There are many common factors and many different possible takeaways.

As far as the conditions in the various POW locations in Southeast Asia, these also varied greatly, as did their impact on the POWs. The conditions in southern jungle camps were harsh in terms of the actual environmental factors: the disease, the temperatures, the quantity and quality of the food, and in most cases, with very little torture. The greatest enemy for prisoners like Nick Rowe, Daniel Pitzer, and others held in the jungle camps was the harsh environment. Conversely, in the north—the Hanoi Hilton and other fixed locations—the physical environment was brutal. Although the POWs were detained in fixed buildings, they had no heat and inadequate clothing and bedding, and were kept on a diet which, when combined with the torture, made for a very challenging environment for survival. Although the statistics are from a small group, it was observed that the POWs in the northern locations faced a better chance of survival when compared to those held in the jungle camps. This is not to say the northern camps were pleasure trips by any means.

Virtually all POWs in the northern camps were held in solitary for the first periods of their captivity; forty percent of these northern prisoners spent six months in solitary confinement, twenty percent of these POWs spent six months in solitary, and four POWs spent over four years in solitary confinement.[23] Moreover, the northern camps' POWs were the subject of harsh interrogation and exploitation attempts in the form of letters, tapes, and filmed propaganda statements. This is, of course, in addition to the brutal and life-threatening "Vietnamese rope trick" torture methods used to get confessions by all who underwent this horrendous ordeal. As already stated, those held in the south rarely underwent such torture or interrogations—their enemy was the environment.

No matter which area the POWs were held in—north or south Vietnam, they possessed two weapons that were crucial to the survival of these POWs; military leadership and chain of command within the POWs ranks, and the POWs' covert communications. Although the North Vietnamese knew the Americans were communicating, due to the very ingenious methods used and perseverance of the men, this communication lifeline was never stopped. That being said, there were three main causes of stress for these POWs (and may be applied to most POW events): 1) the stresses and uncertainty of initial capture, 2) physical torture, and 3) social isolation. Of these three, the one with the longest-lasting effects on the POWs was isolation. As E. J. Hunter's study "*The Vietnam POW Veteran: Immediate and Long Term Effects of Captivity*" tells us:

> *"At the time of their release from captivity, those men who had been subjected to prolonged periods of solitary confinement were more likely to show lower suggestibility, higher superego development, and higher need for achievement." Moreover, the POWs held in solitary confinement for longer periods appeared older than their chronological ages would suggest. 24 When the Vietnam POWs returned home, many of the wives commented on how little the personalities of their husbands had changed. As in normal military deployments, many of the POWs' wives had assumed household chores and responsibilities*

> *their husbands previously did. Thus, upon the return of their husbands (former POWs), a very large part of their reintegration adjustments dealt with readjusting family routines to once again include the fathers. Similarly, POW families that had solid marriages tended to fare better than those POWs who had questionable marriage foundations, or where one or both of the spouses were young and not yet accustomed to the normal stresses of deployed life, much less their loved ones being held captive or, in some cases, not knowing anything about their spouses' fate for years. These POWs described their returns as cyclical in nature starting with "psychological shock and numbing, followed by a period of several days or weeks of hyper alertness and intense interest in even the most trivial details of the prison environment and his captors. Then ensued a period of weeks, months, or even years of depression, which finally culminated in a conscious decision to survive . . ."*[25]

Of particular note is the celebration that surrounded the return of returning Vietnam POWs as compared to the low-key or sometimes humiliating repatriations of returning servicemen who fought in Vietnam, some of whom were thrown tomatoes at in our nation's airports. This circumstance often manifested itself in guilt felt by the returning POWs since they were receiving medals and acclaim while their counterparts, who also did their jobs and were often wounded, were treated very poorly. This sentiment was communicated to the author by most of the former Vietnam era POWs interviewed for this book. The reader must remember that at this point, the environment and its impacts on the POWs spoken of earlier includes not just the captivity environment but also the political environment following release.

OTHER CAPTIVE EXPERIENCES

A second study, written by Navy Captain Mary Anderson of the Navy's Medical Corps, also speaks of POWs, but in this case of cultural experiences from the War of 1812 through DESERT STORM (in the First Gulf War). Moreover, Anderson's research reflects a different focus, looking at cultural aspects as well as training that POWs received prior to becoming captives. Nevertheless, this information is useful in assessing long-term effects on POWs since varying levels of cultural awareness held by captives can have definite effects on how the prisoner comports himself while captive, therefore potentially having profound effects on the POWs' long-term chances for survival and resumption of a normal life once released.

In the War of 1812, the French and American prisoners especially "did not adapt well enough to the harsh conditions to undertake commercial ventures as a sideline to imprisonment."[26] The information in Anderson's work provides one view of the circumstances surrounding this captivity environment, but without knowing the training, backgrounds, ages, health, etc. of those held captive, it does not seem wise to pass judgment on what the Americans might have done better. Suffice it to say, however, that if the Americans survived the ordeal, they were successful—the rare exception being the few Americans who collaborated with the enemy.

World War II, on the other hand, was entirely different in terms of cultural differences and the captivity environment. Having read

Chapter 4 (World War II), the reader understands that the Asian and Germanic cultures are worlds apart and has seen this manifested in varying treatment of the POWs. In World War II, the differences in European and Asian culture greatly effected the POWs' ability to thrive and, in many cases, simply to survive. We saw the Japanese military's sadistic treatment of their prisoners when they did not instantly obey commands—commands given in a language the prisoners did not understand but quickly realized they must adapt to very quickly or perish.

Conversely, the German guards and POW camp personnel often spoke rudimentary English. The Americans' limited knowledge of Japanese culture cannot be blamed on a lack of training, given the short time the United States had to react following the surprise attacks on Pearl Harbor on December 7, 1941. The Americans in these environments did what Americans have nearly always done: they adapted to the circumstances that were forced upon them. Culturally speaking, however, former American POWs of the Japanese often spoke of lingering hatred against the Japanese—not just the guards and military, but all Japanese.[27]

When considering the Korean War POWs' captivities, it is easy to understand that the culture of this Asian country was different from those experienced by the POWs held by the Chinese and North Koreans. Earlier chapters have noted the cultural divide between Americans and Chinese, as shown by the humor concerning the soldier's missing dog and axioms about playing cards. Moreover, this same level of cultural ignorance also manifested itself in cruel punishment by the Chinese when American POWs did not comprehend their commands or instructions.

Cultural differences were seen in much the same fashion in the war in Southeast Asia. In many cases, the Americans clearly understood what the North Vietnamese wanted them to do, such as in the Hanoi Hilton. The same was not necessarily true for personnel who had the misfortune of being taken prisoner in Laos. The language spoken and the manner in which these peoples lived were often alien to the Americans held in that country. One such case was that of Dieter Dengler, the Navy flyer shot down in Laos and escaped after many months of being held prisoner. In this case, following Dengler's escape, it was only his previous preparation and cultural awareness that allowed him to survive in the jungle prior to being recovered by American forces.[28]

Once he has completed the required medical checks and debriefings, the former POW can proceed to take back control of his own life. Will he then grant interviews, write a book, give speeches for civic groups or schools, or—if able—complete his military career?

This is where the concept of the "American Soul" comes in, as discussed in the initial pages of this book. By now, the reader has been exposed to numerous examples of Americans performing extraordinary acts of survival, defiance, and the exercise of sheer will to live. It is in the Americans discussed in these pages, some named but many unnamed, that provide us with an image of the "American Soul." These Americans possess the greatness that comes out in the worst of times and displays the very best that America stands for.

Bill Andrews, a former DESERT STORM POW described how, while going through the Air Force Academy, he was lectured and mentored by many fine officers—a half dozen or so—who were themselves former POWs. The reverence with which this officer spoke of the POWs who mentored him at the Air Force Academy and the humility of his own heroism while a POW reflects all of what America stands for.[29]

It has been this author's great privilege to peer into America's greatness through the exploits of many great men and women who were POWs, hostages, or governmental detainees. Further and finally, it is the author's hope that the reader has also been humbled by such greatness and might communicate the exploits between these pages to others, so that the commitment and service of so many is not forgotten but revered for generations to come. This has indeed been a look into America's Soul.

God Bless the United States of America and the men and women who continue to sacrifice so that we can live free.

Appendix A

DPMO Cold War Report—Sorted By Name

"Thirty-nine U.S. military aircraft and one civilian aircraft were either shot down by communist forces or crashed on the periphery of communist countries while flying operational missions during the Cold War (1946-1991). This table summarizes the 14 operational missions whose crews were either wholly or partially unaccounted for when DPMO was created in 1993."

For greater detail on each incident, go to the incident description pages (following the below summary). For brevity's sake, some data has been removed, e.g, city/state of residence, service number, rank/paygrade, and rate (military occupational specialty).[1]

Loss Date	Aircraft Type	Location	Aircrew	Returned or Recovered Alive	Remains Recovered	Missing
8 Apr 50	PB4Y2	Baltic Sea	10	0	0	10
6 Nov 51	P2V	Sea of Japan	10	0	0	10
13 Jun 52	RB-29	Sea of Japan	12	0	0	12
7 Oct 52	RB-29	Pacific Ocean	8	0	1	7
29 Nov 52	Civilian	Peoples Republic of China	4	2	1	1
18 Jan 53	P2V	Formosa Straits	13	7	0	6
29 Jul 53	RB-50	Sea of Japan	17	1	2	14
17 Apr 55	RB-47	Bering Sea	3	0	0	3
22 Aug 56	P4M	East China Sea	16	0	4	12
10 Sep 56	RB-50	Sea of Japan	16	0	0	16
2 Sep 58	C-130	Armenia	17	0	17	0
1 Jul 60	RB-47	Barents Sea	6	2	1	3
14 Dec 65	RB-57	Black Sea	2	0	0	2
15 Apr 69	EC-121	Sea of Japan	31	0	2	29
		Totals	165	12	28	125

Name	Service	Incident Date	Aircraft	Status	DOD	Repat. Date
ANGELL, DC	Navy	1/18/53	P2V	MM	9/15/55	
ARROWOOD, PD	Air Force	9/10/56	RB50	MM	9/10/56	
BAGGETT, RS	Navy	11/6/51	P2V	MM	11/7/52	
BALDERMAN, LF	Navy	4/15/69	EC121	MM	5/2/69	
BALLENGER, DANIEL J	Navy	1/18/53	P2V	RR	1/18/53	
BARBER, DONALD W	Navy	8/22/56	P4M	MM	8/31/57	
BEAHM, RONALD A	Navy	1/18/53	P2V	MM	9/15/55	
BECKER, ROSCO G	Air Force	6/13/52	RB29	MM	11/14/55	
BECKMAN, FRANK L	Navy	4/8/50	PB4Y-2	MM	4/9/51	
BEISTY, JOHN EDWARD	Air Force	9/10/56	RB50	MM	9/10/56	
BERG, EDDIE R	Air Force	6/13/52	RB29	MM	11/14/55	
BEYER, FRANK E	Air Force	7/29/53	RB50	MM	11/14/55	
BLIZZARD, WILLIAM A	Air Force	6/13/52	RB29	MM	11/14/55	
BONURA, LEON FRANK	Air Force	6/13/52	RB29	MM	11/14/55	
BOURASSA, JOSEPH JAY	Navy	4/8/50	PB4Y-2	MM	4/9/51	
BOURG, ARCHIE T	Air Force	9/2/58	C130	NR	9/2-24/58	
BROCK, PAUL E	Air Force	10/7/52	RB29	MM	11/15/55	
BROOKS, ROBERT N	Air Force	4/17/55	RB47E	MM	4/17/56	
BROWN, CECIL H	Navy	31/18/53	P2V	RR	1/18/53	
BROWN, FRANCIS L	Air Force	7/29/53	RB50	BR		
BURGESS, TOMMY L	Navy	4/8/50	PB4Y-2	MM	4/9/51	
BUSCH, SAMUEL N	Air Force	6/13/52	RB29	MM	11/14/55	
BYARS, CLIFFORD R	Navy	/18/53	P2V	MM	9/15/55	
CARON, WE	Navy	8/22/56	P4M	MM	8/31/57	
CHARTIER, STEPHEN C	Navy	4/15/69	EC121	MM	5/2/69	
COLGAN, SAMUEL A	Air Force	10/7/52	RB29	MM	11/15/55	

COLGIN, BERNIE J	Navy	4/15/69	EC121	MM	5/2/69	
CONNORS, BALLARD F	Navy	4/15/69	EC121	MM	5/2/69	
CURTIS, JACK ALBERT	Navy	8/22/56	P4M	NR	8/25/56	9/4/56
CZYZ, EDMUND J	Air Force	7/29/53	RB50	MM	11/14/55	
DANENS, JOE H	Navy	4/8/50	PB4Y-2	MM	4/9/51	
DAVIS, BOBBY RAY	Air Force	9/10/56	RB50	MM	9/10/56	
DEANE, JAMES B	Navy	8/22/56	P4M	MM	8/31/57	
DISBROW, LORIN C	Air Force	9/10/56	RB50	MM	9/10/56	
DOWNEY, JOHN T	Civilian	11/29/52	ACFT	RR	3/12/73	
DUCHARME, GARY RAY	Navy	4/15/69	EC121	MM	5/2/69	
DUNCAN, PAUL E	Air Force	9/2/58	C130	NR	9/2/58	9/2/98
DUNHAM, JOHN R	Air Force	10/7/52	RB29	NR	11/15/55	8/1/95
DZEMA, JOHN	Navy	4/15/69	EC121	MM	5/2/69	
ELLIS, WILLIAM H	Air Force	9/10/56	RB50	MM	9/10/56	
ENGLISH, EUGENE M	Air Force	10/7/52	RB29	MM	11/15/55	
FAIR, WAYNE J	Air Force	9/10/56	RB50	MM	9/10/56	
FECTEAU, RICHARD	Civilian	11/29/52	ACFT	RR	12/13/71	
FEES, RODGER A	Air Force	9/10/56	RB50	MM	9/10/56	
FERGUSON, JAMES E	Air Force	9/2/58	C130	NR	9/2/58	9/2/98
FETTE, JOHN H	Navy	4/8/50	PB4Y-2	MM	4/9/51	
FIELDS, JOEL H	Air Force	9/2/58	C130	NR	9/2/58	9/2/98
FLOOD, FRANCIS A	Navy	8/22/56	P4M	MM	8/31/57	
FOSTER, PAUL R	Navy	11/6/51	P2V	MM	11/7/52	
FRENCH, ROBERT L	Navy	1/18/53	P2V	RR	1/18/53	
GABREE, DONALD W	Air Force	7/29/53	RB50	MM	11/14/55	
GLEASON, DENNIS B	Navy	4/15/69	EC121	MM	5/2/69	
GOFORTH, OSCAR L	Air Force	7/1/60	RB47	MM	7/1/60	
GOULET, ROLAND E	Air Force	7/29/53	RB50	MM	11/14/55	
GRAHAM, GENE K	Navy	4/15/69	EC121	MM	5/2/69	

GREINER, LAVERNE A	Navy	4/15/69	EC121	MM	5/2/69	
HASKINS, WILLIAM F	Navy	8/22/56	P4M	NR	8/25/56	9/4/56
HILL, DONALD G	Air Force	7/29/53	RB50	MM	11/14/55	
HIRSCH, JOHN ARTHUR	Air Force	10/7/52	RB29	MM	11/15/55	
HODGSON, JUDD C	Navy	11/6/51	P2V	MM	11/7/52	
HOMER, WILLIAM R	Air Force	6/13/52	RB29	MM	11/14/55	
HORRIGAN, DENNIS J	Navy	4/15/69	EC121	MM	5/2/69	
HUMBERT, WILLIAM M	Navy	8/22/56	P4M	MM	8/31/57	
HUTCHINSON, MILTON	Navy	8/22/56	P4M	MM	8/31/57	
JERUSS, EDWARD J	Air Force	9/2/58	C130	NR	9/2/58	9/24/58
JOHNSON, RAYMOND D	Air Force	9/10/56	RB50	MM	9/10/56	
JURIC, PAUL G	Navy	11/6/51	P2V	MM	11/7/52	
KAMPS, HAROLD T	Air Force	9/2/58	C130	NR	9/2/58	9/2/98
KEITH, JAMES G	Air Force	7/29/53	RB50	MM	6/21/54	
KENDRICK, FRED G	Air Force	10/7/52	RB29	MM	11/15/55	
KINCAID, RICHARD H	Navy	4/15/69	EC121	MM	5/2/69	
KOBAYASHI, RICHARD	Air Force	9/10/56	RB50	MM	9/10/56	
LACKEY, LESTER L	Air Force	12/14/65	RB57	MM	6/4/66	
LIVELY, JACK	Navy	11/6/51	P2V	MM	11/7/52	
LOUNSBURY, HAROLD E	Navy	8/22/56	P4M	MM	8/31/57	
LUDENA, ROY	Navy	1/18/53	P2V	RR	1/18/53	
LYNCH, HUGH M	Marine	Corps	4/15/69	EC121	MM	5/2/69
MACDONALD, WL	Navy	1/18/53	P2V	RR	1/18/52	
MADEIROS, GERALD H	Air Force	9/2/58	C130	NR	9/2/58	9/24/58
MAGGIACOMO, GC Air Force	9/2/58	C130	NR	9/2/58	9/2/98	
MANKINS, CLEMENT O	Air Force	9/2/58	C130	NR	9/2/58	9/2/98
MATTIN, ALBERT P	Navy	8/22/56	P4M	BR	8/25/56	8/30/56

MAXWELL, HARRY S	Air Force	9/10/56	RB50	MM	9/10/56	
MCCLURE, WILLIAM F	Navy	1/18/53	P2V	MM	9/15/55	
MCDONNELL, ROBERT J	Air Force	6/13/52	RB29	MM	11/14/55	
MCKONE, JOHN R	Air Force	7/1/60	RB47	RR	1/25/61	
MCLAUGHLIN, W	Air Force	9/10/56	RB50	MM	9/10/56	
MCNAMARA, MH	Navy	4/15/69	EC121	MM	5/2/69	
MCNEIL, TIMOTHY H	Navy	4/15/69	EC121	MM	5/2/69	
MELLO, ARTHUR L	Air Force	9/2/58	C130	NR	9/2/58	9/2/98
MESSINGER, CARL E	Navy	8/22/56	P4M	MM	8/31/57	
MEYER, WILLIAM S	Navy	11/6/51	P2V	MM	11/7/52	
MILLER, JOHN A	Navy	4/15/69	EC121	MM	5/2/69	
MONSERRAT, MW	Air Force	6/13/52	RB29	MM	11/14/55	
MOORE, DAVID L	Air Force	6/13/52	RB29	MM	11/14/55	
MOORE, ROBERT H	Air Force	9/2/58	C130	NR	9/2/58	9/2/98
MORLEY, PAUL A.	Navy	1/18/53	P2V	MM	9/15/55	
NEAIL, FRANK E	Air Force	10/7/52	RB29	MM	11/15/55	
NEIGHBORS, LACIE C	Air Force	4/17/55	RB47E	MM	4/17/56	
O'KELLEY, STANLEY K.	Air Force	7/29/53	RB50	BR		
OLMSTEAD, FREEMAN B	Air Force	7/1/60	RB47	RR	1/25/61	
OSHINSKIE, ROBERT J	Air Force	9/2/58	C130	NR	9/2/58	9/2/98
OVERSTREET, JAMES H	Navy	4/15/69	EC121	MM	5/2/69	
PALM, WILLARD G	Air Force	7/1/60	RB47	NR	7/1/60	7/25/60
PERROTTET, PETER P	Navy	4/15/69	EC121	MM	5/2/69	
PETROCHILOS, GEORGE	Air Force	9/2/58	C130	NR	9/2/58	9/2/98
PHILLIPS, DEAN B	Air Force	7/1/60	RB47	MM	7/1/60	
PILLSBURY, DANNY H	Air Force	6/13/52	RB29	MM	11/14/55	
PONSFORD, JAMES W	Navy	8/22/56	P4M	BR	8/25/56	8/30/56

POSA, EUGENE E	Air Force	7/1/60	RB47	MM	7/1/60	
POTTS, JOHN H	Navy	4/15/69	EC121	MM	5/2/69	
POWELL, WALLACE W	Navy	8/22/56	P4M	MM	8/31/57	
PRICE, LAROY	Air Force	9/2/58	C130	NR	9/2/58	9/2/98
PRINDLE, RICHARD THO	Navy	4/15/69	EC121	MM	5/2/69	
PROUHET, CLEMENT R	Navy	1/18/53	P2V	RR	1/18/53	
PURCELL, EDWARD J	Navy	4/8/50	PB4Y-2	MM	4/9/51	
RADLEIN, EARL W	Air Force	7/29/53	RB50	MM	11/14/55	
RAGLIN, ERWIN D	Navy	11/6/51	P2V	MM	11/7/52	
RAHANIOTES, PETER J	Air Force	9/10/56	RB50	MM	9/10/56	
RANDALL, FREDRICK AR	Navy	4/15/69	EC121	MM	5/2/69	
REYNOLDS, ROBERT D	Navy	4/8/50	PB4Y-2	MM	4/9/51	
RIBAR, JOSEPH R	Navy	4/15/69	EC-121	BR	4/15/69	4/17/69
RINNIER, JOSEPH NORR	Navy	4/8/50	PB4Y-2	MM	4/9/51	
ROACH, JAMES EROY	Navy	4/15/69	EC121	MM	5/2/69	
ROCHE, JOHN E	Air Force	7/29/53	RB50	RR	7/30/53	
ROSENFELD, SAMUEL	Navy	11/6/51	P2V	MM	11/7/52	
RUSSELL, CHARLES J	Air Force	7/29/53	RB50	MM	11/14/55	
SANDERSON, WARREN J	Air Force	7/29/53	RB50	MM	11/14/55	
SCHWARTZ, NORMAN	Civilian	11/29/52	ACFT	BB	11/29/52	
SCULLEY, JAMES A	Air Force	6/13/52	RB29	MM	11/14/55	
SEESCHAF, HOWARD W	Navy	4/8/50	PB4Y-2	MM	4/9/51	
SERVICE, SAMUEL D	Air Force	6/13/52	RB29	MM	11/14/55	
SHIPP, THOMAS G	Air Force	10/7/52	RB29	MM	11/5/55	
SIMPSON, JOHN E	Air Force	9/2/58	C130	NR	9/2/58	9/24/58
SINGER, JOHN H	Navy	4/15/69	EC121	MM	5/2/69	
SLOAN, LEO J	Air Force	9/10/56	RB50	MM	9/10/56	

SMITH, DONALD ALLEN	Navy	11/6/51	P2V	MM	11/7/52	
SMITH, LLOYD	Navy	1/18/53	P2V	MM	9/15/55	
SMITH, RICHARD E	Navy	4/15/69	EC121	MM	5/2/69	
SNODDY, ROBERT	Civilian	11/29/52	ACFT	BB	11/29/52	
SPRINKLE, DONALD	Navy	8/22/56	P4M	MM	8/31/57	
STALNAKER, ROBERT E	Air Force	7/29/53	RB50	MM	11/14/55	
STRYKOWSKY, L	Navy	8/22/56	P4M	MM	8/31/57	
SUNDBY, PHILIP D	Navy	4/15/69	EC121	MM	5/2/69	
SWEENEY, RICHARD E	Navy	4/15/69	EC-121	BR	4/15/69	4/17/69
SWIESTRA, RUDY J	Air Force	9/2/58	C130	NR	9/2/58	9/24/58
SWINEHART, PAUL W	Air Force	9/10/56	RB50	MM	9/10/56	
SYKORA, ROBERT J	Navy	4/15/69	EC121	MM	5/2/69	
TAYLOR, PAT P	Air Force	9/10/56	RB50	MM	9/10/56	
TAYLOR, ROBERT F	Navy	4/15/69	EC121	MM	5/2/69	
TEJEDA, FRANCISCO J	Air Force	7/29/53	RB50	MM	11/14/55	
TESMER, STEPHEN J	Navy	4/15/69	EC121	MM	5/2/69	
THOMAS, JACK W	Navy	4/8/50	PB4Y-2	MM	4/9/51	
TRIAS, THEODORUS J	Air Force	9/10/56	RB50	MM	9/10/56	
VARNEY, VEARL V	Navy	1/18/53	P2V	RR	1/18/53	
VILLAREAL, RM	Air Force	9/2/58	C130	NR	9/2/58	9/24/58
WARD, JOHN C	Air Force	7/29/53	RB50	MM	11/14/55	
WATKINS, RICHARD E	Air Force	4/17/55	RB47E	MM	4/17/56	
WIGERT, RALPH A	Navy	11/6/51	P2V	MM	11/7/52	
WIGGINS, LLOYD C	Air Force	7/29/53	RB50	MM	11/14/55	
WILKERSON, NL	Navy	4/15/69	EC121	MM	5/2/69	
WILLIS, DAVID MONROE	Navy	4/15/69	EC121	MM	5/2/69	
WOODS, JAMES E	Air Force	7/29/53	RB50	MM	11/14/55	
YATES, ROBERT A	Air Force	12/14/65	RB57	MM	6/4/66	
YOUNG, LLOYD L.	Navy	8/22/56	P4M	MM	8/31/57	

Total Personnel: 165

Status: MM = unaccounted for

RR = rescued or returned alive

BR = body recovered by friendly forces

NR = remains returned as a result of negotiations

Appendix B

Defense Prisoner of War/Missing Personnel Office

US Prisoners of War who returned alive from the Vietnam War

(Sorted by Name, DPMO doc dated 9/1/2011)[1.]

Last Name	First Name	Rank	Service	Country Of Loss	Date Loss	Date Return	Months Held
ABBOTT	JOSEPH S JR	O3	Air Force	NVN	Apr 30, 1967	Feb 18, 1973	71
ABBOTT	ROBERT ARCHIE	O2	Air Force	NVN	Apr 30, 1967	Mar 04, 1973	71
ABBOTT	WILFRED KESSE	O3	Air Force	NVN	Sep 05, 1966	Mar 04, 1973	79
ACOSTA	HECTOR MICHAEL	O2	Air Force	NVN	Dec 09, 1972	Mar 29, 1973	4
ADKINS	CLODEON		Civilian	SVN	Jan 31, 1968	Mar 05, 1973	62
AGNEW	ALFRED HOWARD	O4	Navy	NVN	Dec 28, 1972	Mar 29, 1973	3
AGOSTO-SANTOS	JOSE	E3	Marines	SVN	May 12, 1967	Jan 23, 1968	9
ALBERT	KEITH ALEXANDER	E4	Army	SVN	May 21, 1970	Feb 12, 1973	33
ALCORN	WENDELL REED	O2	Navy	NVN	Dec 22, 1965	Feb 12, 1973	87
ALEXANDER	FERNANDO	O4	Air Force	NVN	Dec 19, 1972	Mar 29, 1973	3
ALLWINE	DAVID FRANKLIN	E5	Army	SVN	Mar 04, 1971	Mar 27, 1973	25
ALPERS	JOHN HARDESTY JR	O3	Air Force	NVN	Oct 05, 1972	Mar 29, 1973	6
ALVAREZ	EVERETT, Jr.	O2	Navy	NVN	Aug 05, 1964	Feb 12, 1973	104
ANDERSON	GARETH LAVERNE	O2	Navy	NVN	May 19, 1967	Mar 04, 1973	71

ANDERSON	JOHN THOMAS	E7	Army	SVN	Feb 05, 1968	Mar 05, 1973	62
ANDERSON	JOHN WESLEY	O3	Air Force	NVN	Dec 27, 1972	Feb 12, 1973	2
ANDREWS	ANTHONY CHARLES	O3	Air Force	NVN	Oct 17, 1967	Mar 14, 1973	66
ANGUS	WILLIAM KERR	O3	Marines	NVN	Jun 11, 1972	Mar 28, 1973	10
ANSHUS	RICHARD CAMERON	O2	Army	SVN	Mar 08, 1971	Mar 27, 1973	25
ANSON	ROBERT		Civilian	Cambodia	Aug 03, 1970	Aug 23, 1970	1
ANTON	FRANCIS GENE	W2	Army	SVN	Jan 05, 1968	Mar 16, 1973	63
ANZALDUA	JOSE JESUS JR	E4	Marines	SVN	Jan 23, 1970	Mar 27, 1973	39
ARCHER	BRUCE RAYMOND	O3	Marines	SVN	Mar 28, 1968	Mar 16, 1973	60
ARCURI	WILLIAM YOUL	O2	Air Force	NVN	Dec 20, 1972	Feb 12, 1973	2
ASTORGA	JOSE MANUEL	E4	Army	SVN	Apr 02, 1972	Mar 05, 1973	11
AUSTIN	WILLIAM RENWICK	O3	Air Force	NVN	Oct 07, 1967	Mar 14, 1973	66
AYRES	TIMOTHY ROBERT	O3	Air Force	NVN	May 03, 1972	Mar 28, 1973	11
BAGLEY	BOBBY RAY	O4	Air Force	NVN	Sep 16, 1967	Mar 14, 1973	67
BAILEY	JAMES WILLIAM	O2	Navy	NVN	Jun 28, 1967	Feb 18, 1973	69
BAILEY	LAWRENCE ROBERT	O4	Army	Laos	Mar 23, 1961	Aug 15, 1962	17
BAIRD	BILL ALLEN	E4	Army	SVN	May 06, 1968	Mar 05, 1973	59
BAKER	DAVID EARLE	O3	Air Force	Cambodia	Jun 27, 1972	Feb 12, 1973	8
BAKER	ELMO CLINNARD	O4	Air Force	NVN	Aug 23, 1967	Mar 14, 1973	68
BALDOCK	FREDERICK CHARLES	O2	Navy	NVN	Mar 17, 1966	Feb 12, 1973	84
BALLARD	ARTHUR T JR	O3	Air Force	NVN	Sep 26, 1966	Mar 04, 1973	78
BALLENGER	ORVILLE ROGER	E5	Army	Laos	Apr 22, 1961	Aug 15, 1962	16
BARBAY	LAWRENCE	O3	Air Force	NVN	Jul 20, 1966	Mar 04, 1973	81
BARNETT	ROBERT WARREN	O4	Air Force	NVN	Oct 03, 1967	Mar 14, 1973	66
BARRETT	THOMAS JOSEPH	O2	Air Force	NVN	Oct 05, 1965	Feb 12, 1973	90
BARROWS	HENRY CHARLES	O3	Air Force	NVN	Dec 19, 1972	Mar 29, 1973	3
BATES	RICHARD LYMAN	O2	Air Force	NVN	Oct 05, 1972	Mar 29, 1973	6
BAUGH	WILLIAM JOSEPH	O3	Air Force	NVN	Jan 21, 1967	Mar 04, 1973	74
BEAN	JAMES ELLIS	O6	Air Force	NVN	Jan 03, 1968	Mar 14, 1973	63
BEAN	WILLIAM RAYMOND JR	O3	Air Force	NVN	May 23, 1972	Mar 28, 1973	10
BEDINGER	HENRY JAMES	O2	Navy	Laos	Nov 22, 1969	Mar 28, 1973	41
BEEKMAN	WILLIAM DAVID	O3	Air Force	NVN	Jun 24, 1972	Mar 28, 1973	9
BEELER	CARROLL ROBERT	O3	Navy	NVN	May 24, 1972	Mar 28, 1973	10
BEENS	LYNN RICHARD	O3	Air Force	NVN	Dec 21, 1972	Mar 29, 1973	3
BELL	JAMES FRANKLIN	O4	Navy	NVN	Oct 16, 1965	Feb 12, 1973	89
BENGE	MICHAEL		Civilian	SVN	Jan 28, 1968	Mar 05, 1973	62
BERG	KILE DAG	O3	Air Force	NVN	Jul 27, 1965	Feb 12, 1973	92
BERGER	JAMES ROBERT	O3	Air Force	NVN	Dec 02, 1966	Feb 18, 1973	76
BERNASCONI	LOUIS HENRY	O5	Air Force	NVN	Dec 22, 1972	Mar 29, 1973	3
BISS	ROBERT IRVING	O3	Air Force	NVN	Nov 11, 1966	Mar 04, 1973	77

BLACK	ARTHUR NEIL	E2	Air Force	NVN	Sep 20, 1965	Feb 12, 1973	90
BLACK	COLE	O4	Navy	NVN	Jun 21, 1966	Feb 12, 1973	81
BLACK	JON DAVID	O3	Air Force	NVN	Oct 27, 1967	Feb 16, 1968	4
BLEVINS	JOHN CHARLES	O3	Air Force	NVN	Sep 09, 1966	Mar 04, 1973	79
BLISS	RONALD GLENN	O2	Air Force	NVN	Sep 04, 1966	Mar 04, 1973	79
BOLSTAD	RICHARD EUGENE	O3	Air Force	NVN	Nov 06, 1965	Feb 12, 1973	89
BOMAR	JACK WILLIAMSON	O4	Air Force	NVN	Feb 04, 1967	Mar 04, 1973	74
BORLING	JOHN LORIN	O2	Air Force	NVN	Jun 01, 1966	Feb 12, 1973	82
BOYD	CHARLES GRAHAM	O3	Air Force	NVN	Apr 22, 1966	Feb 12, 1973	83
BOYER	TERRY LEE	O2	Air Force	NVN	Dec 17, 1967	Mar 14, 1973	64
BRACE	ERNEST C		Civilian	Laos	May 21, 1965	Mar 28, 1973	96
BRADY	ALLEN COLBY	O5	Navy	NVN	Jan 19, 1967	Mar 04, 1973	75
BRANCH	MICHAEL PATRICK	E4	Army	SVN	May 06, 1968	Mar 16, 1973	59
BRANDE	HARVEY G	E7	Army	SVN	Feb 07, 1968	Mar 16, 1973	62
BRAZELTON	MICHAEL LEE	O2	Air Force	NVN	Aug 07, 1966	Mar 04, 1973	80
BRECKNER	WILLIAM J JR	O5	Air Force	NVN	Jul 30, 1972	Mar 29, 1973	8
BRENNEMAN	RICHARD CHARLES	O2	Air Force	NVN	Nov 08, 1967	Mar 14, 1973	65
BRIDGER	BARRY BURTON	O3	Air Force	NVN	Jan 23, 1967	Mar 04, 1973	74
BRIGHAM	JAMES W	E4	Army	SVN	Sep 13, 1968	Jan 01, 1969	4
BRODAK	JOHN WARREN	O3	Air Force	NVN	Aug 14, 1966	Mar 04, 1973	80
BROOKENS	NORMAN J		Civilian	SVN	Feb 04, 1968	Feb 12, 1973	61
BROWN	CHARLES A JR	O3	Air Force	NVN	Dec 19, 1972	Mar 29, 1973	3
BROWN	PAUL GORDON	O2	Marines	NVN	Jul 25, 1968	Mar 14, 1973	56
BROWNING	RALPH THOMAS	O2	Air Force	NVN	Jul 08, 1966	Feb 12, 1973	80
BRUDNO	EDWARD ALAN	O2	Air Force	NVN	Oct 18, 1965	Feb 12, 1973	89
BRUNHAVER	RICHARD MARVIN	O2	Navy	NVN	Aug 24, 1965	Feb 12, 1973	91
BRUNSON	CECIL H	O2	Air Force	NVN	Oct 12, 1972	Mar 29, 1973	6
BRUNSTROM	ALAN LESLIE	O4	Air Force	NVN	Apr 22, 1966	Feb 12, 1973	83
BUCHANAN	HUBERT ELLIOT	O2	Air Force	NVN	Sep 16, 1966	Mar 04, 1973	79
BUDD	LEONARD R JR	E3	Marines	SVN	Aug 21, 1967	Mar 05, 1973	67
BURER	ARTHUR WILLIAM	O3	Air Force	NVN	Mar 21, 1966	Feb 12, 1973	84
BURGESS	RICHARD GORDON	E4	Marines	SVN	Sep 25, 1966	Mar 05, 1973	78
BURNS	DONALD RAY	O4	Air Force	NVN	Dec 02, 1966	Mar 04, 1973	76
BURNS	JOHN DOUGLASS	O4	Navy	NVN	Oct 04, 1966	Mar 04, 1973	78
BURNS	MICHAEL THOMAS	O2	Air Force	NVN	Jul 05, 1968	Mar 14, 1973	57
BURROUGHS	WILLIAM DAVID	O4	Air Force	NVN	Jul 31, 1966	Mar 04, 1973	80
BUTCHER	JACK M	O2	Air Force	Laos	Mar 24, 1971	Mar 28, 1973	25
BUTLER	PHILLIP NEAL	O3	Navy	NVN	Apr 20, 1965	Feb 12, 1973	95
BUTLER	WILLIAM WALLACE	O3	Air Force	NVN	Nov 20, 1967	Mar 14, 1973	65
BYRNE	RONALD EDWARD JR	O4	Air Force	NVN	Aug 29, 1965	Feb 12, 1973	91

BYRNS	WILLIAM G	O3	Air Force	NVN	May 23, 1972	Mar 28, 1973	10
CALLAGHAN	PETER A	O2	Air Force	NVN	Jun 21, 1972	Mar 28, 1973	9
CAMEROTA	PETER P	O3	Air Force	NVN	Dec 22, 1972	Mar 29, 1973	3
CAMPBELL	BURTON WAYNE	O2	Air Force	NVN	Jul 01, 1966	Feb 12, 1973	81
CAREY	DAVID JAY	O2	Navy	NVN	Aug 31, 1967	Mar 14, 1973	67
CARLSON	ALBERT E	O4	Army	SVN	Apr 07, 1972	Feb 12, 1973	10
CARPENTER	ALLEN RUSSELL	O3	Navy	NVN	Nov 01, 1966	Mar 04, 1973	77
CARPENTER	JOE V	O3	Air Force	NVN	Feb 15, 1968	Aug 02, 1968	6
CARRIGAN	LARRY EDWARD	O3	Air Force	NVN	Aug 23, 1967	Mar 14, 1973	68
CASSELL	HARLEY M	E4	Army	Cambodia	Jul 17, 1968	Dec 19, 1968	5
CAVAIANI	JON R	E5	Army	SVN	Jun 05, 1971	Mar 27, 1973	22
CERAK	JOHN P	O3	Air Force	NVN	Jun 27, 1972	Mar 28, 1973	9
CERTAIN	ROBERT G	O3	Air Force	NVN	Dec 18, 1972	Mar 29, 1973	3
CHAMBERS	CARL DENNIS	O2	Air Force	NVN	Aug 07, 1967	Mar 14, 1973	68
CHAPMAN	HARLAN PAGE	O3	Marines	NVN	Nov 05, 1965	Feb 12, 1973	89
CHARLES	NORRIS ALPHONZO	O2	Navy	NVN	Dec 30, 1971	Sep 25, 1972	9
CHAUNCEY	ARVIN RAY	O4	Navy	NVN	May 31, 1967	Mar 04, 1973	70
CHENEY	KEVIN J	O3	Air Force	NVN	Jul 01, 1972	Mar 28, 1973	9
CHENOWETH	ROBERT PRESTON	E5	Army	SVN	Feb 08, 1968	Mar 16, 1973	62
CHERRY	FRED VANN	O4	Air Force	NVN	Oct 22, 1965	Feb 12, 1973	89
CHESLEY	LARRY JAMES	O2	Air Force	NVN	Apr 16, 1966	Feb 12, 1973	83
CHEVALIER	JOHN R	E3	Army	Cambodia	Jul 17, 1968	Dec 19, 1968	5
CHIRICHIGNO	LUIS GENARDO	O3	Army	SVN	Nov 02, 1969	Mar 27, 1973	41
CHRISTIAN	MICHAEL DURHAM	O2	Navy	NVN	Apr 24, 1967	Mar 04, 1973	71
CIUS	FRANK E	E3	Marines	Laos	Jun 03, 1967	Mar 05, 1973	70
CLARK	JOHN WALTER	O3	Air Force	NVN	Mar 12, 1967	Feb 18, 1973	72
CLEMENTS	JAMES ARLEN	O4	Air Force	NVN	Oct 09, 1967	Mar 14, 1973	66
CLOWER	CLAUDE DOUGLAS	O4	Navy	NVN	Nov 19, 1967	Mar 14, 1973	65
COFFEE	GERALD LEONARD	O3	Navy	NVN	Feb 03, 1966	Feb 12, 1973	86
COKER	GEORGE THOMAS	O2	Navy	NVN	Aug 27, 1966	Mar 04, 1973	79
COLLINS	JAMES QUINCY	O3	Air Force	NVN	Sep 02, 1965	Feb 12, 1973	91
COLLINS	THOMAS EDWARD III	O3	Air Force	NVN	Oct 18, 1965	Feb 12, 1973	89
CONDON	JAMES C	O4	Air Force	NVN	Dec 28, 1972	Mar 29, 1973	3
CONLEE	WILLIAM W	O5	Air Force	NVN	Dec 22, 1972	Mar 29, 1973	3
COOK	JAMES R	E6	Air Force	NVN	Dec 26, 1972	Feb 12, 1973	2
COPELAND	HC	O4	Air Force	NVN	Jul 17, 1967	Mar 14, 1973	69
CORDIER	KENNETH WILLIAM	O3	Air Force	NVN	Dec 02, 1966	Mar 04, 1973	76
CORMIER	ARTHUR	E5	Air Force	NVN	Nov 06, 1965	Feb 12, 1973	89
COSKEY	KENNETH LEON	O5	Navy	NVN	Sep 06, 1968	Mar 14, 1973	55
CRAFTS	CHARLES	E2	Army	SVN	Dec 29, 1964	Feb 07, 1967	26

CRANER	ROBERT ROGER	O4	Air Force	NVN	Dec 20, 1967	Mar 14, 1973	64
CRAYTON	RENDER	O4	Navy	NVN	Feb 07, 1966	Feb 12, 1973	85
CRECCA	JOSEPH	O2	Air Force	NVN	Nov 22, 1966	Feb 18, 1973	76
CRONIN	MICHAEL PAUL	O2	Navy	NVN	Jan 13, 1967	Mar 04, 1973	75
CROW	FREDERICK AUSTIN	O5	Air Force	NVN	Mar 26, 1967	Mar 04, 1973	72
CROWE	WINFRED D	E7	Army	Cambodia	Jul 17, 1968	Dec 19, 1968	5
CROWSON	FREDERICK H	E4	Army	Cambodia	May 02, 1970	Feb 12, 1973	34
CRUMPLER	CARL BOYETTE	O5	Air Force	NVN	Jul 05, 1968	Mar 14, 1973	57
CURTIS	THOMAS JERRY	O3	Air Force	NVN	Sep 20, 1965	Feb 12, 1973	90
CUSIMANO	SAMUEL B	O3	Air Force	NVN	Dec 28, 1972	Mar 29, 1973	3
CUTTER	JAMES D	O3	Air Force	NVN	Feb 17, 1972	Mar 28, 1973	14
DAIGLE	GLENN HENRI	O2	Navy	NVN	Dec 22, 1965	Feb 12, 1973	87
ALY	JAMES ALEXANDER JR	E3	Army	SVN	Jan 09, 1968	Mar 16, 1973	63
DANIELS	VERLYNE WAYNE	O5	Navy	NVN	Oct 26, 1967	Mar 14, 1973	66
DAUGHERTY	LENARD EDWARD	E4	Army	SVN	May 11, 1969	Mar 27, 1973	47
DAUGHTREY	ROBERT NORLAN	O3	Air Force	NVN	Aug 02, 1965	Feb 12, 1973	92
DAVES	GARY LAWRENCE		Civilian	SVN	Feb 01, 1968	Mar 27, 1973	63
DAVIES	JOHN OWEN	O2	Air Force	NVN	Feb 04, 1967	Feb 18, 1973	74
DAVIS	EDWARD ANTHONY	O2	Navy	NVN	Aug 26, 1965	Feb 12, 1973	91
DAVIS	THOMAS JAMES	E5	Army	SVN	Mar 11, 1968	Mar 16, 1973	61
DAWSON	DONALD		Civilian	SVN	Apr 01, 1965	Aug 24, 1965	5
DAY	GEORGE EVERETTE	O4	Air Force	NVN	Aug 26, 1967	Mar 14, 1973	68
DEERING	JOHN ARTHUR	E4	Marines	SVN	Feb 05, 1968	Mar 05, 1973	62
DELUCA	ANTHONY J	E3	Navy	Cambodia	Feb 05, 1970	Feb 28, 1970	1
DENTON	JEREMIAH ANDREW	O5	Navy	NVN	Jul 18, 1965	Feb 12, 1973	92
DESPIEGLER	GALE A	O4	Air Force	NVN	Apr 15, 1972	Mar 28, 1973	12
DIBERNARDO	JAMES VINCENT	O2	Marines	SVN	Feb 05, 1968	Mar 05, 1973	62
DINGEE	DAVID B	O3	Air Force	NVN	Jun 27, 1972	Mar 28, 1973	9
DONALD	MYRON LEE	O2	Air Force	NVN	Feb 23, 1968	Mar 14, 1973	62
DOREMUS	ROBERT BARTSCH	O4	Navy	NVN	Aug 24, 1965	Feb 12, 1973	91
DOSS	DALE WALTER	O4	Navy	NVN	Mar 17, 1968	Mar 14, 1973	61
DOUGHTY	DANIEL JAMES	O3	Air Force	NVN	Apr 02, 1966	Feb 12, 1973	84
DRABIC	PETER E	E3	Army	SVN	Sep 24, 1968	Mar 16, 1973	54
DRAMESI	JOHN ARTHUR	O3	Air Force	NVN	Apr 02, 1967	Mar 04, 1973	72
DRISCOLL	JERRY DONALD	O2	Air Force	NVN	Apr 24, 1966	Feb 12, 1973	83
DRUMMOND	DAVID I.	O3	Air Force	NVN	Dec 22, 1972	Mar 29, 1973	3
DUART	DAVID HENRY	O3	Air Force	NVN	Feb 18, 1967	Mar 04, 1973	74
DUDMAN	RICHARD		Civilian	Cambodia	May 07, 1970	Jun 15, 1970	1
DUNN	JOHN GALBREATH	O3	Army	SVN	Mar 18, 1968	Feb 12, 1973	60
DUNN	JOHN HOWARD	O4	Marines	NVN	Dec 07, 1965	Feb 12, 1973	87

DUTTON	RICHARD ALLEN	O4	Air Force	NVN	Nov 05, 1967	Mar 14, 1973	65
EASTMAN	LEONARD CORBETT	O3	Navy	NVN	Jun 21, 1966	Feb 12, 1973	81
ELANDER	WILLIAM J JR	O4	Air Force	NVN	Jul 05, 1972	Mar 29, 1973	9
ELBERT	FRED	E3	Marines	SVN	Aug 16, 1968	Mar 16, 1973	56
ELIAS	EDWARD K	O4	Air Force	NVN	Apr 20, 1972	Sep 25, 1972	5
ELLIOTT	ARTICE W	O4	Army	SVN	Apr 26, 1970	Mar 27, 1973	36
ELLIS	JEFFREY THOMAS	O3	Air Force	NVN	Dec 17, 1967	Mar 14, 1973	64
ELLIS	LEON FRANCIS	O3	Air Force	NVN	Nov 07, 1967	Mar 14, 1973	65
ELM	HOMER L		Civilian	SVN	Oct 06, 1973	Dec 19, 1973	2
ENSCH	JOHN C	O3	Navy	NVN	Aug 25, 1972	Mar 29, 1973	7
ESTES	EDWARD DALE	O4	Navy	NVN	Jan 03, 1968	Mar 14, 1973	63
ETTMUELLER	HARRY L	E5	Army	SVN	Feb 05, 1968	Mar 05, 1973	62
EVERETT	DAVID A	O2	Navy	NVN	Aug 27, 1972	Mar 29, 1973	7
EVERSON	DAVID	O4	Air Force	NVN	Mar 10, 1967	Mar 04, 1973	73
FANT	ROBERT ST CLAIR	O3	Navy	NVN	Jul 25, 1968	Mar 14, 1973	56
FELLOWES	JOHN HEAPHY	O4	Navy	NVN	Aug 27, 1966	Mar 04, 1973	79
FER	JOHN	O3	Air Force	NVN	Feb 04, 1967	Mar 04, 1973	74
FINLAY	JOHN STEWART	O5	Air Force	NVN	Apr 28, 1968	Mar 14, 1973	59
FISHER	JOHN B	E5	Army	SVN	Feb 12, 1969	Mar 11, 1969	1
FISHER	KENNETH	O3	Air Force	NVN	Nov 07, 1967	Mar 14, 1973	65
FLEENOR	KENNETH RAYMOND	O4	Air Force	NVN	Dec 17, 1967	Mar 14, 1973	64
FLESHER	HUBERT KELLY	O4	Air Force	NVN	Dec 02, 1966	Feb 18, 1973	76
FLOM	FREDRIC R	O2	Air Force	NVN	Aug 08, 1966	Mar 04, 1973	80
FLORA	CARROLL E	E6	Army	SVN	Jul 21, 1967	Mar 05, 1973	68
FLYNN	JOHN PETER	O6	Air Force	NVN	Oct 27, 1967	Mar 14, 1973	66
FLYNN	ROBERT J	O3	Navy	China	Aug 21, 1967	Mar 15, 1973	68
FORBY	WILLIS ELLIS	O3	Air Force	NVN	Sep 20, 1965	Feb 12, 1973	90
FORD	DAVID EDWARD	O3	Air Force	NVN	Nov 19, 1967	Mar 14, 1973	65
FOWLER	HENRY POPE	O2	Air Force	NVN	Mar 26, 1967	Feb 18, 1973	72
FRANCIS	RICHARD L	O3	Air Force	NVN	Jun 27, 1972	Mar 28, 1973	9
FRANK	MARTIN S	E5	Army	SVN	Jul 12, 1967	Mar 05, 1973	69
FRANKE	FRED AUGUSTUS	O5	Navy	NVN	Aug 24, 1965	Feb 12, 1973	91
FRASER	KENNETH J	O3	Air Force	NVN	Feb 17, 1972	Mar 28, 1973	14
FRIESE	LAWRENCE VICTOR	O3	Marines	NVN	Feb 24, 1968	Mar 14, 1973	62
FRISHMANN	ROBERT F	O2	Navy	NVN	Oct 24, 1967	Aug 05, 1969	22
FRITZ	JOHN J		Civilian	SVN	Feb 08, 1969	Feb 12, 1973	49
FRYETT	GEORGE F	E4	Army	SVN	Dec 24, 1961	Jun 24, 1962	6
FULLER	ROBERT BYRON	O5	Navy	NVN	Jul 14, 1967	Mar 04, 1973	69
FULTON	RICHARD J	O2	Air Force	NVN	Jun 13, 1972	Mar 28, 1973	10
GADDIS	NORMAN CARL	O6	Air Force	NVN	May 12, 1967	Mar 04, 1973	71
GAITHER	RALPH ELLIS	O1	Navy	NVN	Oct 17, 1965	Feb 12, 1973	89
GALANTI	PAUL EDWARD	O3	Navy	NVN	Jun 17, 1966	Feb 12, 1973	81

GALATI	RALPH W	O2	Air Force	NVN	Feb 16, 1972	Mar 28, 1973	14
GARTLEY	MARKHAM LIGON	O2	Navy	NVN	Aug 17, 1968	Sep 25, 1972	50
GAUNTT	WILLIAM A	O3	Air Force	SVN	Aug 13, 1972	Mar 27, 1973	8
GAY	ARLO N		Civilian	SVN	Apr 30, 1975	Sep 21, 1976	17
GELONECK	TERRY M	O3	Air Force	NVN	Dec 20, 1972	Feb 12, 1973	2
GERNDT	GERALD LEE	O2	Air Force	NVN	Aug 23, 1967	Mar 14, 1973	68
GIDEON	WILLARD SELLECK	O4	Air Force	NVN	Aug 07, 1966	Mar 04, 1973	80
GILLESPIE	CHARLES R	O5	Navy	NVN	Oct 24, 1967	Mar 14, 1973	66
GIROUX	PETER J	O3	Air Force	NVN	Dec 22, 1972	Feb 12, 1973	2
GLENN	DANNY ELLOY	O2	Navy	NVN	Dec 21, 1966	Mar 04, 1973	76
GLENN	THOMAS PAUL	E3	Navy	Cambodia	Feb 05, 1970	Feb 28, 1970	1
GOODERMOTE	WAYNE KEITH	O2	Navy	NVN	Aug 13, 1967	Mar 14, 1973	68
GOSTAS	THEODORE W	O3	Army	SVN	Feb 01, 1968	Mar 16, 1973	62
GOTNER	NOBERT A	O4	Air Force	Laos	Feb 03, 1971	Mar 28, 1973	26
GOUGH	JAMES W	E7	Air Force	NVN	Dec 28, 1972	Mar 29, 1973	3
GOUIN	DONAT JOSEPH	E7	Army	SVN	Feb 05, 1968	Mar 05, 1973	62
GRANGER	PAUL L	O2	Air Force	NVN	Dec 20, 1972	Mar 29, 1973	3
GRANT	DAVID B	O3	Air Force	NVN	Jun 24, 1972	Mar 28, 1973	9
GRAY	DAVID FLETCHER	O2	Air Force	NVN	Jan 23, 1967	Mar 04, 1973	74
GREENE	CHARLES E	O3	Air Force	NVN	Mar 11, 1967	Mar 04, 1973	73
GREGORY	KENNETH R	E6	Army	SVN	Aug 25, 1968	May 26, 1969	9
GRIGSBY	DONALD E	E4	Army	Cambodia	Jul 17, 1968	Dec 19, 1968	5
GROOM	GEORGE EDWARD	E5	Army	SVN	Apr 08, 1962	May 01, 1962	1
GRUTERS	GUY DENNIS	O3	Air Force	NVN	Dec 20, 1967	Mar 14, 1973	64
GUARINO	LAWRENCE NICHOLAS	O4	Air Force	NVN	Jun 14, 1965	Feb 12, 1973	93
GUENTHER	LYNN	O3	Air Force	NVN	Dec 26, 1971	Feb 12, 1973	14
GUGGENBERGER	GARY JOHN	E4	Army	SVN	Jan 14, 1969	Feb 12, 1973	50
GURNSEY	EARL F	E4	Army	SVN	Nov 27, 1968	Jan 06, 1969	1
GUTTERSON	LAIRD	O4	Air Force	NVN	Feb 23, 1968	Mar 14, 1973	62
GUY	THEODORE WILSON	O5	Air Force	Laos	Mar 22, 1968	Mar 16, 1973	61
HAINES	COLLINS HENRY	O4	Navy	NVN	Jun 05, 1967	Mar 04, 1973	70
HALL	GEORGE ROBERT	O3	Air Force	NVN	Sep 27, 1965	Feb 12, 1973	90
HALL	KEITH NORMAN	O3	Air Force	NVN	Jan 10, 1968	Mar 14, 1973	63
HALL	THOMAS RENWICK	O2	Navy	NVN	Jun 10, 1967	Mar 04, 1973	70
HALYBURTON	PORTER ALEX	O2	Navy	NVN	Oct 17, 1965	Feb 12, 1973	89
HANSON	GREGG O	O2	Air Force	NVN	Jun 13, 1972	Mar 28, 1973	10
HANTON	THOMAS J	O3	Air Force	NVN	Jun 27, 1972	Mar 28, 1973	9
HARDMAN	WILLIAM MORGAN	O4	Navy	NVN	Aug 21, 1967	Mar 14, 1973	68
HARDY	WILLIAM H	O3	Army	SVN	Jun 29, 1967	Feb 12, 1973	69
HARKER	DAVID NORTHRUP	E3	Army	SVN	Jan 08, 1968	Mar 05, 1973	63
HARRIS	CARLYLE SMITH	O3	Air Force	NVN	Apr 04, 1965	Feb 12, 1973	96

HARRIS	JESSIE B	E3	Army	SVN	Jun 08, 1969	Oct 20, 1969	4
HATCHER	DAVID BURNETT	O3	Air Force	NVN	May 30, 1966	Feb 12, 1973	82
HAWLEY	EDWIN A JR	O3	Air Force	NVN	Feb 17, 1972	Feb 12, 1973	12
HEEREN	JEROME D	O3	Air Force	NVN	Sep 11, 1972	Mar 29, 1973	7
HEFEL	DANIEL	E4	Army	SVN	Feb 05, 1970	Mar 27, 1973	38
HEGDAHL	DOUGLAS B	E2	Navy	NVN	Apr 06, 1967	Aug 05, 1969	28
HEILIG	JOHN	O3	Navy	NVN	May 05, 1966	Feb 12, 1973	83
HEILIGER	DONALD LESTER	O3	Air Force	NVN	May 15, 1967	Feb 18, 1973	70
HELLE	ROBERT R	E3	Marines	SVN	Apr 24, 1968	Mar 16, 1973	60
HENDERSON	ALEXANDER		Civilian	SVN	Jan 31, 1968	Mar 16, 1973	62
HENDERSON	WILLIAM J	O2	Air Force	SVN	Apr 03, 1972	Mar 27, 1973	12
HENRY	LEE EDWARD	E5	Army	Cambodia	Jul 17, 1968	Dec 19, 1968	5
HENRY	NATHAN BARNEY	E4	Army	SVN	Jul 12, 1967	Mar 05, 1973	69
HERLIK	QUERIN E	O4	Army	SVN	Feb 12, 1969	Mar 11, 1969	1
HESS	JAY CRIDDLE	O3	Air Force	NVN	Aug 24, 1967	Mar 14, 1973	68
HESTAND	JAMES HARDY	W1	Army	Cambodia	Mar 17, 1971	Feb 12, 1973	23
HICKERSON	JAMES MARTIN	O4	Navy	NVN	Dec 22, 1967	Mar 14, 1973	64
HIGDON	KENNETH H	O3	Navy	NVN	Dec 21, 1972	Feb 12, 1973	2
HILDEBRAND	LELAND	O4	Air Force	NVN	Dec 18, 1971	Mar 28, 1973	16
HILL	HOWARD JOHN	O2	Air Force	NVN	Dec 16, 1967	Mar 14, 1973	64
HINCKLEY	ROBERT BRUCE	O3	Air Force	NVN	Jan 18, 1968	Mar 14, 1973	63
HITESHEW	JAMES EDWARD	O4	Air Force	NVN	Mar 11, 1967	Mar 04, 1973	73
HIVNER	JAMES OTIS	O3	Air Force	NVN	Oct 05, 1965	Feb 12, 1973	90
HOFFMAN	DAVID WESLEY	O4	Navy	NVN	Dec 30, 1971	Mar 28, 1973	15
HOFFSON	ARTHUR THOMAS	O2	Air Force	NVN	Aug 17, 1968	Mar 14, 1973	56
HORINEK	RAMON ANTON	O4	Air Force	NVN	Oct 25, 1967	Mar 14, 1973	66
HORIO	THOMAS TERUO	E4	Army	SVN	May 11, 1969	Mar 27, 1973	47
HUBBARD	EDWARD LEE	O2	Air Force	NVN	Jul 20, 1966	Mar 04, 1973	81
HUDSON	ROBERT M	O2	Air Force	NVN	Dec 26, 1972	Mar 29, 1973	3
HUGHES	JAMES LINDBERG	O5	Air Force	NVN	May 05, 1967	Mar 04, 1973	71
HUGHEY	KENNETH RAYMOND	O4	Air Force	NVN	Jul 06, 1967	Mar 04, 1973	69
HUNSUCKER	JAMES	E4	Navy	Cambodia	Feb 05, 1970	Feb 28, 1970	1
HUTTON	JAMES LEO	O4	Navy	NVN	Oct 16, 1965	Feb 12, 1973	89
HYATT	LEO GREGORY	O4	Navy	NVN	Aug 13, 1967	Mar 14, 1973	68
INGVALSON	ROGER DEAN	O4	Air Force	NVN	May 28, 1968	Mar 14, 1973	58
JACKSON	CHARLES A	O3	Air Force	NVN	Jun 24, 1972	Feb 12, 1973	8
JACKSON	JAMES E	E7	Army	SVN	Jul 05, 1966	Nov 11, 1967	16
JACQUEZ	JUAN L	E4	Army	SVN	May 11, 1969	Mar 27, 1973	47
JAMES	CHARLIE NEGUS	O5	Navy	NVN	May 18, 1968	Mar 14, 1973	59
JAMES	GOBEL DALE	O4	Air Force	NVN	Jul 15, 1968	Mar 14, 1973	57
JAYROE	JULIUS SKINNER	O3	Air Force	NVN	Jan 19, 1967	Mar 04, 1973	75
JEFCOAT	CARL H	O4	Air Force	NVN	Dec 27, 1972	Mar 29, 1973	3

JENKINS	HARRY TARLETON	O5	Navy	NVN	Nov 13, 1965	Feb 12, 1973	88
JENSEN	JAY ROGER	O3	Air Force	NVN	Feb 18, 1967	Feb 18, 1973	73
JOHNSON	BOBBY LOUIS	E4	Army	SVN	Aug 25, 1968	Feb 12, 1973	54
JOHNSON	EDWARD ROBERT	E8	Army	SVN	Jul 21, 1964	Nov 11, 1967	40
JOHNSON	HAROLD E	O3	Air Force	NVN	Apr 30, 1967	Mar 04, 1973	71
JOHNSON	KENNETH	O4	Air Force	NVN	Dec 18, 1971	Mar 14, 1973	15
JOHNSON	RICHARD E	O4	Air Force	NVN	Dec 18, 1972	Mar 29, 1973	3
JOHNSON	SAMUEL ROBERT	O4	Air Force	NVN	Apr 16, 1966	Feb 12, 1973	83
JOHNSON	SANDRA		Civilian	SVN	Feb 05, 1968	Mar 31, 1968	2
JONES	DIANE		Civilian	SVN	Jan 22, 1974	Feb 03, 1974	0
JONES	MURPHY NEAL	O3	Air Force	NVN	Jun 29, 1966	Feb 12, 1973	81
JONES	ROBERT CAMPBELL	O2	Air Force	NVN	Jan 18, 1968	Mar 14, 1973	63
JONES	THOMAS N	E4	Army	SVN	Aug 25, 1968	Jan 01, 1969	4
KARI	PAUL ANTHONY	O3	Air Force	NVN	Jun 20, 1965	Feb 12, 1973	93
KASLER	JAMES HELMS	O4	Air Force	NVN	Aug 08, 1966	Mar 04, 1973	80
KAVANAUGH	ABEL L	E4	Marines	SVN	Apr 24, 1968	Mar 16, 1973	60
KAY	EMMET JAMES		Civilian	Laos	May 07, 1973	Sep 18, 1974	17
KEESEE	BOBBY JOE		Civilian	NVN	Sep 18, 1970	Mar 14, 1973	30
KEIRN	RICHARD PAUL	O3	Air Force	NVN	Jul 24, 1965	Feb 12, 1973	92
KERNAN	JOSEPH EUGENE	O2	Navy	NVN	May 07, 1972	Mar 28, 1973	11
KERNS	GAIL M	E5	Army	SVN	Mar 27, 1969	Mar 05, 1973	48
KERR	MICHAEL SCOTT	O2	Air Force	NVN	Jan 16, 1967	Mar 04, 1973	75
KEY	WILSON DENVER	O3	Navy	NVN	Nov 17, 1967	Mar 14, 1973	65
KIENTZLER	PHILLIP A	O4	Navy	SVN	Jan 27, 1973	Mar 27, 1973	2
KIRK	THOMAS HENRY	O5	Air Force	NVN	Oct 28, 1967	Mar 14, 1973	65
KITTINGER	JOSEPH W JR	O5	Air Force	NVN	May 11, 1972	Mar 28, 1973	11
KJOME	MICHAEL H		Civilian	SVN	Jan 31, 1968	Feb 12, 1973	61
KLOMANN	THOMAS J	O3	Air Force	NVN	Dec 20, 1972	Feb 12, 1973	2
KNUTSON	RODNEY ALLEN	O2	Navy	NVN	Oct 17, 1965	Feb 12, 1973	89
KOBASHIGAWA	TOM Y	E5	Army	SVN	Feb 05, 1970	Mar 27, 1973	38
KOPFMAN	THEODORE FRANK	O4	Navy	NVN	Jun 15, 1966	Feb 12, 1973	81
KOSH	GERALD E		Civilian	SVN	Jan 19, 1974	Jan 31, 1974	0
KRAMER	GALAND DWIGHT	O2	Air Force	NVN	Jan 19, 1967	Feb 12, 1973	74
KRAMER	TERRY L	E5	Army	Cambodia	Jul 17, 1968	Dec 19, 1968	5
KRAUSE	ARTHUR E		Civilian	SVN	Jun 08, 1963	Nov 18, 1963	5
KROBOTH	ALAN J	O2	Marines	SVN	Jul 07, 1972	Mar 27, 1973	9
KULA	JAMES D	O3	Air Force	NVN	Jul 29, 1972	Mar 29, 1973	8
KUSHNER	FLOYD HAROLD	O3	Army	SVN	Nov 30, 1967	Mar 16, 1973	64
LABEAU	MICHAEL H	O3	Air Force	NVN	Dec 26, 1972	Mar 29, 1973	3
LAMAR	JAMES LASLEY	O5	Air Force	NVN	May 06, 1966	Feb 12, 1973	82
LANE	MICHAEL CHRISTOPHER	O2	Air Force	NVN	Dec 02, 1966	Feb 18, 1973	76

LARSON	GORDON ALBERT	O5	Air Force	NVN	May 05, 1967	Mar 04, 1973	71
LASITER	CARL WILLIAM	O3	Air Force	NVN	Feb 05, 1968	Mar 14, 1973	62
LATELLA	GEORGE F.	O2	Air Force	NVN	Oct 06, 1972	Mar 29, 1973	6
LATENDRESSE	THOMAS B	O3	Navy	NVN	May 27, 1972	Mar 28, 1973	10
LATHAM	JAMES D	O3	Air Force	NVN	Oct 05, 1972	Mar 29, 1973	6
LAWRENCE	WILLIAM PORTER	O5	Navy	NVN	Jun 28, 1967	Mar 04, 1973	69
LEBERT	RONALD MERL	O2	Air Force	NVN	Jan 14, 1968	Mar 14, 1973	63
LEBLANC	LOUIS E JR	E7	Air Force	NVN	Dec 22, 1972	Mar 29, 1973	3
LEHNEN	GARY ROBERT	E4	Navy	Cambodia	Feb 05, 1970	Feb 28, 1970	1
LEHRMAN	RONALD JOHN	E4	Army	Cambodia	May 20, 1968	Jun 10, 1968	1
LENGYEL	LAUREN ROBERT	O3	Air Force	NVN	Aug 09, 1967	Mar 14, 1973	68
LENKER	MICHAEL ROBERT	E4	Army	SVN	Feb 08, 1968	Mar 16, 1973	62
LEONARD	EDWARD W	O3	Air Force	Laos	May 31, 1968	Mar 28, 1973	59
LEOPOLD	STEPHEN RYDER	O2	Army	SVN	May 09, 1968	Mar 05, 1973	59
LERSETH	ROGER G	O3	Navy	NVN	Sep 06, 1972	Feb 12, 1973	5
LESESNE	HENRY D	O4	Navy	NVN	Jul 11, 1972	Mar 29, 1973	9
LEWIS	EARL GARDNER	O2	Navy	NVN	Oct 24, 1967	Mar 14, 1973	66
LEWIS	FRANK D	O3	Air Force	NVN	Dec 28, 1972	Mar 29, 1973	3
LEWIS	JAMES F		Civilian	SVN	Apr 16, 1975	Oct 30, 1975	7
LEWIS	KEITH H	O3	Air Force	NVN	Oct 05, 1972	Mar 29, 1973	6
LEWIS	ROBERT	E4	Army	SVN	Jan 05, 1968	Mar 05, 1973	63
LIGON	VERNON PEYTON	O5	Air Force	NVN	Nov 19, 1967	Mar 14, 1973	65
LILLY	WARREN E	O3	Air Force	NVN	Nov 06, 1965	Feb 12, 1973	89
LOCKHART	HAYDEN JAMES	O3	Air Force	NVN	Mar 02, 1965	Feb 12, 1973	97
LOGAN	DONALD K	O2	Air Force	NVN	Jul 05, 1972	Mar 29, 1973	9
LOLLAR	JAMES L	E5	Air Force	NVN	Dec 21, 1972	Mar 29, 1973	3
LONG	JULIUS WOLLEN JR	E4	Army	SVN	May 12, 1968	Mar 16, 1973	59
LONG	STEPHEN G	O2	Air Force	Laos	Feb 28, 1969	Mar 28, 1973	50
LOW	JAMES FREDERICK	O4	Air Force	NVN	Dec 16, 1967	Aug 02, 1968	8
LUNA	JOSE DAVID	O3	Air Force	NVN	Mar 10, 1967	Mar 04, 1973	73
LURIE	ALAN PIERCE	O3	Air Force	NVN	Jun 13, 1966	Feb 12, 1973	81
MACPHAIL	DON A	E3	Army	SVN	Feb 08, 1969	Mar 16, 1973	50
MADDEN	ROY JR	E5	Air Force	NVN	Dec 20, 1972	Feb 12, 1973	2
MADISON	THOMAS MARK	O4	Air Force	NVN	Apr 19, 1967	Mar 04, 1973	72
MAKOWSKI	LOUIS FRANK	O4	Air Force	NVN	Oct 06, 1966	Mar 04, 1973	78
MALO	ISAAKO F	E3	Army	SVN	Apr 24, 1971	Mar 27, 1973	23
MANHARD	PHILLIP W		Civilian	SVN	Jan 31, 1968	Mar 16, 1973	62
MARSHALL	MARION A	O3	Air Force	NVN	Jul 03, 1972	Mar 29, 1973	9
MARTIN	EDWARD HOLMES	O4	Navy	NVN	Jul 09, 1967	Mar 04, 1973	69
MARTINI	MICHAEL R	O2	Air Force	NVN	Dec 20, 1972	Mar 29, 1973	3
MARVEL	JERRY WENDELL	O4	Marines	NVN	Feb 24, 1968	Mar 14, 1973	62
MASLOWSKI	DANIEL F	W1	Army	Cambodia	May 02, 1970	Feb 12, 1973	34
MASTERSON	FREDERICK J	O3	Navy	NVN	Jul 11, 1972	Mar 29, 1973	9

MASTIN	RONALD LAMBERT	O2	Air Force	NVN	Jan 16, 1967	Mar 04, 1973	75
MATAGULAY	ROQUE S	E7	Army	SVN	Jul 23, 1962	Dec 24, 1962	5
MATHENY	DAVID P	O1	Navy	NVN	Oct 05, 1967	Feb 16, 1968	4
MATSUI	MELVIN K	O3	Air Force	NVN	Jul 29, 1972	Mar 29, 1973	8
MATTIX	SAM		Civilian	Laos	Oct 27, 1972	Mar 28, 1973	5
MAYALL	WILLIAM T	O2	Air Force	NVN	Dec 22, 1972	Mar 29, 1973	3
MAYHEW	WILLIAM JOHN	O3	Navy	NVN	Aug 17, 1968	Mar 14, 1973	56
MCCAIN	JOHN SIDNEY	O4	Navy	NVN	Oct 26, 1967	Mar 14, 1973	66
MCCLURE	CLAUDE D	E6	Army	SVN	Nov 24, 1963	Nov 28, 1965	25
MCCOMBS	PHILLIP A		Civilian	SVN	Apr 30, 1974	May 22, 1974	1
MCCUISTION	MICHAEL K	O3	Air Force	NVN	May 08, 1967	Mar 04, 1973	71
MCCULLOUGH	RALPH W	W4	Army	Cambodia	Jul 17, 1968	Dec 19, 1968	5
MCDANIEL	EUGENE BAKER	O4	Navy	NVN	May 19, 1967	Mar 04, 1973	71
MCDANIEL	NORMAN ALEXANDER	O3	Air Force	NVN	Jul 20, 1966	Feb 12, 1973	80
MCDOW	RICHARD H	O2	Air Force	NVN	Jun 27, 1972	Mar 28, 1973	9
MCGRATH	JOHN MICHAEL	O3	Navy	NVN	Jun 30, 1967	Mar 04, 1973	69
MCKAMEY	JOHN BRYAN	O3	Navy	NVN	Jun 02, 1965	Feb 12, 1973	94
MCKNIGHT	GEORGE GRIGSBY	O3	Air Force	NVN	Nov 06, 1965	Feb 12, 1973	89
MCMANUS	KEVIN JOSEPH	O2	Air Force	NVN	Jun 14, 1967	Feb 18, 1973	69
MCMILLAN	ISIAH	E4	Army	SVN	Mar 11, 1968	Mar 16, 1973	61
MCMORROW	JOHN P	E3	Navy	Laos	May 15, 1961	Aug 17, 1962	15
MCMURRAY	CORDINE	E5	Army	SVN	Jul 12, 1967	Mar 05, 1973	69
MCMURRAY	FREDERICK C	O3	Air Force	NVN	Sep 12, 1972	Mar 29, 1973	7
MCMURRY	WILLIAM G	E4	Army	SVN	Feb 07, 1968	Mar 16, 1973	62
MCNISH	THOMAS MITCHELL	O2	Air Force	NVN	Sep 04, 1966	Mar 04, 1973	79
MCSWAIN	GEORGE PALMER	O1	Navy	NVN	Jul 28, 1966	Mar 04, 1973	80
MEANS	WILLIAM HARLEY	O3	Air Force	NVN	Jul 20, 1966	Feb 12, 1973	80
MECHENBIER	EDWARD JOHN	O2	Air Force	NVN	Jun 14, 1967	Feb 18, 1973	69
MECLEARY	READ BLAINE	O2	Navy	NVN	May 26, 1967	Mar 04, 1973	70
MEHL	JAMES PATRICK	O5	Navy	NVN	May 30, 1967	Mar 04, 1973	70
MEHRER	GUSTAV ALOIS	E2	Army	SVN	Dec 25, 1968	Mar 16, 1973	51
MERRITT	RAYMOND JAMES	O4	Air Force	NVN	Sep 16, 1965	Feb 12, 1973	90
METZGER	WILLIAM JOHN	O2	Navy	NVN	May 19, 1967	Mar 04, 1973	71
MEYER	ALTON BENNO	O3	Air Force	NVN	Apr 26, 1967	Mar 04, 1973	71
MEYER	LEWIS E		Civilian	SVN	Feb 01, 1968	Mar 27, 1973	63
MILLER	CAROLYN PAINE		Civilian	SVN	Mar 12, 1975	Oct 30, 1975	8
MILLER	EDISON WAINRIGHT	O5	Marines	NVN	Oct 13, 1967	Feb 12, 1973	65
MILLER	EDWIN FRANK	O2	Navy	NVN	May 22, 1968	Mar 14, 1973	59
MILLER	JOHN DANIEL		Civilian	SVN	Mar 12, 1975	Oct 30, 1975	8
MILLER	LUANNE		Civilian	SVN	Mar 12, 1975	Oct 30, 1975	8
MILLER	ROGER ALAN	W1	Army	SVN	Apr 15, 1970	Mar 05, 1973	35
MILLIGAN	JOSEPH EDWARD	O2	Air Force	NVN	May 20, 1967	Feb 18, 1973	70
MITCHELL	BETTY JANET		Civilian	SVN	Mar 12, 1975	Oct 30, 1975	8
MOBLEY	JOSEPH SCOTT	O2	Navy	NVN	Jun 24, 1968	Mar 14, 1973	57
MOE	THOMAS NELSON	O2	Air Force	NVN	Jan 16, 1968	Mar 14, 1973	63
MOLINARE	ALBERT R	O3	Navy	NVN	Apr 27, 1972	Mar 28, 1973	11
MONAHAN	ROBERT W		Civilian	SVN	May 27, 1966	Jan 01, 1967	7

MONLUX	HAROLD DELOSS	O2	Air Force	NVN	Nov 11, 1966	Mar 04, 1973	77
MONTAGUE	PAUL JOSEPH	O3	Marines	SVN	Mar 28, 1968	Mar 16, 1973	60
MOORE	DENNIS ANTHONY	O3	Navy	NVN	Oct 27, 1965	Feb 12, 1973	89
MOORE	ERNEST MILVIN	O5	Navy	NVN	Mar 11, 1967	Mar 04, 1973	73
MOREAU	RON		Civilian	SVN	May 03, 1973	May 14, 1973	0
MORGAN	GARY L	E5	Air Force	NVN	Dec 22, 1972	Mar 29, 1973	3
MORGAN	HERSCHEL SCOTT	O3	Air Force	NVN	Apr 03, 1965	Feb 12, 1973	96
MORROW	MICHAEL		Civilian	Cambodia	May 07, 1970	Jun 15, 1970	1
MOTT	DAVID P	O3	Air Force	SVN	May 19, 1972	Mar 27, 1973	10
MULLEN	RICHARD DEAN	O4	Navy	NVN	Jan 06, 1967	Mar 04, 1973	75
MULLIGAN	JAMES ALFRED	O5	Navy	NVN	Mar 20, 1966	Feb 12, 1973	84
MURPHY	JOHN S. JR	O3	Air Force	SVN	Jun 08, 1972	Mar 27, 1973	10
MYERS	ARMAND JESSE	O3	Air Force	NVN	Jun 01, 1966	Feb 12, 1973	82
MYERS	GLENN LEO	O2	Air Force	NVN	Aug 09, 1967	Mar 14, 1973	68
NAGAHIRO	JAMES Y	O5	Air Force	NVN	Dec 21, 1972	Mar 29, 1973	3
NAKAGAWA	GORDON R	O5	Navy	NVN	Dec 21, 1972	Mar 29, 1973	3
NASMYTH	JOHN HERBERT	O2	Air Force	NVN	Sep 04, 1966	Feb 18, 1973	79
NAUGHTON	ROBERT JOHN	O3	Navy	NVN	May 18, 1967	Mar 04, 1973	71
NECO-QUINONES	FELIX V	E3	Army	SVN	Jul 16, 1968	Feb 12, 1973	56
NELSON	MARJORIE		Civilian	SVN	Feb 05, 1968	Mar 31, 1968	2
NEUENS	MARTIN JAMES	O2	Air Force	NVN	Aug 12, 1966	Mar 04, 1973	80
NEWCOMB	WALLACE GRANT	O3	Air Force	NVN	Aug 03, 1967	Mar 14, 1973	68
NEWELL	STANLEY ARTHUR	E4	Army	SVN	Jul 12, 1967	Mar 05, 1973	69
NEWINGHAM	JAMES A		Civilian	SVN	Feb 08, 1969	Feb 12, 1973	49
NICHOLS	AUBREY ALLEN	O3	Navy	NVN	May 19, 1972	Mar 28, 1973	10
NIX	COWAN GLENN	O3	Air Force	NVN	Oct 01, 1966	Mar 04, 1973	78
NORRINGTON	GILES RODERICK	O3	Navy	NVN	May 05, 1968	Mar 14, 1973	59
NORRIS	THOMAS ELMER	O3	Air Force	NVN	Aug 12, 1967	Mar 14, 1973	68
NORTH	KENNETH WALTER	O3	Air Force	NVN	Aug 01, 1966	Mar 04, 1973	80
NOWICKI	JAMES ERNEST	W1	Army	SVN	Nov 02, 1969	Mar 27, 1973	41
OCONNOR	MICHAEL FRANCIS	W2	Army	SVN	Feb 04, 1968	Mar 05, 1973	62
ODELL	DONALD EUGENE	O4	Air Force	NVN	Oct 17, 1967	Mar 14, 1973	66
OLSEN	ROBERT F		Civilian	SVN	Feb 01, 1968	Mar 27, 1973	63
ONEIL	JAMES W	O5	Air Force	NVN	Sep 29, 1972	Mar 29, 1973	6
ORTIZ-RIVERA	LUIS A	E3	Army	SVN	Dec 27, 1966	Jan 23, 1968	13
OSBORNE	DALE HARRISON	O4	Navy	NVN	Sep 23, 1968	Feb 12, 1973	53
OSBURN	LAIRD P	W4	Army	SVN	Feb 12, 1969	Mar 11, 1969	1
OVERLY	NORRIS M	O4	Air Force	NVN	Sep 11, 1967	Feb 16, 1968	5
PADGETT	JAMES P	O4	Air Force	NVN	May 11, 1972	Mar 28, 1973	11
PAGE	RUSSELL J		Civilian	SVN	Jan 31, 1968	Mar 16, 1973	62
PAIGE	GORDON CURTIS	O4	Navy	NVN	Jul 22, 1972	Mar 29, 1973	8
PARROTT	THOMAS VANCE	O3	Air Force	NVN	Aug 12, 1967	Mar 14, 1973	68
PARSELS	JOHN WILLIAM	O3	Army	SVN	Feb 05, 1970	Mar 27, 1973	38
PEEL	ROBERT D	O3	Air Force	NVN	May 31, 1965	Feb 12, 1973	94
PENN	MICHAEL GENE JR	O2	Navy	NVN	Aug 06, 1972	Mar 29, 1973	8
PERKINS	GLENDON WILLIAM	O3	Air Force	NVN	Jul 20, 1966	Feb 12, 1973	80
PERRICONE	RICHARD ROBERT	E4	Army	SVN	Jul 12, 1967	Mar 05, 1973	69
PETERSON	DOUGLAS BRIAN	O3	Air Force	NVN	Sep 10, 1966	Mar 04, 1973	79

PETERSON	MICHAEL T	W1	Army	SVN	Nov 02, 1969	Dec 10, 1969	1
PFISTER	JAMES F JR	E3	Army	SVN	Jan 05, 1968	Mar 05, 1973	63
PHILLIPS	LILLIAN MARGUERI		Civilian	SVN	Mar 12, 1975	Oct 30, 1975	8
PHILLIPS	RICHARD LEE		Civilian	SVN	Mar 12, 1975	Oct 30, 1975	8
PIRIE	JAMES GLENN	O4	Navy	NVN	Jun 22, 1967	Feb 18, 1973	69
PITCHFORD	JOHN JOSEPH	O3	Air Force	NVN	Dec 20, 1965	Feb 12, 1973	87
PITZER	DANIEL L	E8	Army	SVN	Oct 29, 1963	Nov 11, 1967	49
PLUMB	JOSEPH CHARLES	O2	Navy	NVN	May 19, 1967	Feb 18, 1973	70
POLFER	CLARENCE	O5	Navy	NVN	May 07, 1972	Mar 28, 1973	11
POLLACK	MELVIN	O2	Air Force	NVN	Jul 06, 1967	Mar 04, 1973	69
POLLARD	BEN M	O3	Air Force	NVN	May 15, 1967	Mar 04, 1973	71
POND	ELIZABETH		Civilian	Cambodia	May 07, 1970	Jun 15, 1970	1
PRATHER	PHILLIP DEAN	W1	Army	SVN	Mar 08, 1971	Mar 27, 1973	25
PRICE	DONALD E	E4	Army	Cambodia	Jul 17, 1968	Dec 19, 1968	5
PRICE	LARRY D	O2	Air Force	NVN	Jul 30, 1972	Mar 29, 1973	8
PROFILET	LEO TWYMAN	O5	Navy	NVN	Aug 21, 1967	Mar 14, 1973	68
PRYOR	ROBERT J	E5	Army	SVN	Feb 12, 1969	Mar 11, 1969	1
PURCELL	BENJAMIN H	O5	Army	SVN	Feb 08, 1968	Mar 27, 1973	62
PURCELL	ROBERT BALDWIN	O3	Air Force	NVN	Jul 27, 1965	Feb 12, 1973	92
PURRINGTON	FREDERICK RAYM	O2	Navy	NVN	Oct 20, 1966	Feb 18, 1973	77
PYLE	DARREL EDWIN	O2	Air Force	NVN	Jun 13, 1966	Feb 12, 1973	81
PYLE	THOMAS SHAW	O3	Air Force	NVN	Aug 07, 1966	Mar 04, 1973	80
QUINN	FRANCIS	E7	Army	SVN	Apr 08, 1962	May 01, 1962	1
QUINN-JUDGE	SOPHIE		Civilian	SVN	Jan 22, 1974	Feb 03, 1974	0
RAEBEL	DALE V	O4	Navy	NVN	Aug 17, 1972	Mar 29, 1973	7
RAMSEY	DOUGLAS		Civilian	SVN	Jan 17, 1966	Feb 12, 1973	86
RANDALL	ROBERT I	O3	Navy	NVN	Jul 11, 1972	Mar 29, 1973	9
RANDER	DONALD J	E6	Army	SVN	Feb 01, 1968	Mar 27, 1973	63
RATZLAFF	BRIAN M	O3	Air Force	NVN	Sep 11, 1972	Mar 29, 1973	7
RATZLAFF	RICHARD RAYMOND	O3	Navy	NVN	Mar 20, 1966	Feb 12, 1973	84
RAY	JAMES EDWIN	O2	Air Force	NVN	May 08, 1966	Feb 12, 1973	82
RAY	JOHNNIE L	O3	Army	SVN	Apr 08, 1972	Feb 12, 1973	10
RAYFORD	KING DAVID JR	E3	Army	SVN	Jul 02, 1967	Mar 16, 1973	69
REEDER	WILLIAM S	O3	Army	SVN	May 09, 1972	Mar 27, 1973	11
REHMANN	DAVID GEORGE	O2	Navy	NVN	Dec 02, 1966	Feb 12, 1973	75
REICH	WILLIAM J	O2	Air Force	NVN	May 11, 1972	Mar 28, 1973	11
REYNOLDS	JON ANZUENA	O3	Air Force	NVN	Nov 28, 1965	Feb 12, 1973	88
RIATE	ALFONSO RAY	E4	Marines	SVN	Apr 26, 1967	Mar 16, 1973	72
RICE	CHARLES DONALD	O2	Navy	NVN	Oct 26, 1967	Mar 14, 1973	66
RIDGEWAY	RONALD LEWIS	E3	Marines	SVN	Feb 25, 1968	Mar 16, 1973	62
RIESS	CHARLES F	O3	Air Force	Laos	Dec 24, 1972	Mar 28, 1973	3
RINGSDORF	HERBERT BENJAMI	O2	Air Force	NVN	Nov 11, 1966	Feb 18, 1973	76
RISNER	ROBINSON	O5	Air Force	NVN	Sep 16, 1965	Feb 12, 1973	90
RIVERS	WENDELL BURKE	O6	Navy	NVN	Sep 10, 1965	Feb 12, 1973	90
ROBINSON	PAUL K	O4	Air Force	NVN	Jul 01, 1972	Mar 28, 1973	9
ROBINSON	WILLIAM ANDREW	E5	Air Force	NVN	Sep 20, 1965	Feb 12, 1973	90
RODRIQUEZ	FERDINAND A	E2	Army	SVN	Apr 14, 1968	Feb 12, 1973	59
ROLLINS	DAVID JOHN	O3	Navy	NVN	May 14, 1967	Mar 04, 1973	71

ROLLINS	JAMES U		Civilian	SVN	Feb 05, 1968	Feb 12, 1973	61
ROSE	GEORGE A	O3	Air Force	NVN	Jun 21, 1972	Mar 28, 1973	9
ROSE	JOSEPH	W2	Army	SVN	Feb 08, 1968	Mar 05, 1973	62
RUDLOFF	STEPHEN A	O3	Navy	NVN	May 10, 1972	Mar 28, 1973	11
RUHLING	MARK JOHN	O3	Air Force	NVN	Nov 23, 1968	Mar 14, 1973	52
RUMBLE	WESLEY L	O2	Air Force	NVN	Apr 28, 1968	Aug 05, 1969	15
RUNYAN	ALBERT EDWARD	O4	Air Force	NVN	Apr 29, 1966	Feb 12, 1973	83
RUSHTON	THOMAS		Civilian	SVN	Feb 01, 1968	Mar 27, 1973	63
RUSSELL	KAY	O4	Navy	NVN	May 19, 1967	Mar 04, 1973	71
RUTLEDGE	HOWARD ELMER	O5	Navy	NVN	Nov 28, 1965	Feb 12, 1973	88
SANDVICK	ROBERT JAMES	O3	Air Force	NVN	Aug 07, 1966	Mar 04, 1973	80
SAWHILL	ROBERT RALSTON	O4	Air Force	NVN	Aug 23, 1967	Mar 14, 1973	68
SCALES	THOMAS R		Civilian	SVN	May 27, 1966	Jan 01, 1967	7
SCARBOROUGH	JAY ROSS		Civilian	SVN	Mar 12, 1975	Oct 30, 1975	8
SCHIERMAN	WESLEY DUANE	O3	Air Force	NVN	Aug 28, 1965	Feb 12, 1973	91
SCHOEFFEL	PETER VANRUYTER	O4	Navy	NVN	Oct 04, 1967	Mar 14, 1973	66
SCHRUMP	RAYMOND CECIL	O4	Army	SVN	May 23, 1968	Feb 12, 1973	58
SCHULZ	PAUL HENRY	O4	Navy	NVN	Nov 16, 1967	Mar 14, 1973	65
SCHWEITZER	ROBERT JAMES	O5	Navy	NVN	Jan 05, 1968	Mar 14, 1973	63
SCHWERTFEGER	WILLIAM R	O3	Air Force	NVN	Feb 16, 1972	Mar 28, 1973	14
SEEBER	BRUCE G	O3	Air Force	NVN	Oct 05, 1965	Feb 12, 1973	90
SEEK	BRIAN J	O2	Air Force	NVN	Jul 05, 1972	Mar 29, 1973	9
SEHORN	JAMES ELDON	O3	Air Force	NVN	Dec 14, 1967	Mar 14, 1973	64
SEXTON	JOHN C	E4	Army	SVN	Aug 12, 1969	Oct 08, 1971	26
SHANAHAN	JOSEPH FRANCIS	O3	Air Force	NVN	Aug 15, 1968	Mar 14, 1973	56
SHANKEL	WILLIAM LEONARD	O2	Navy	NVN	Dec 23, 1965	Feb 12, 1973	87
SHATTUCK	LEWIS WILEY	O3	Air Force	NVN	Jul 11, 1966	Feb 12, 1973	80
SHEPARD	VERNON C	E5	Army	SVN	Nov 02, 1969	Dec 10, 1969	1
SHINGAKI	TAMOTSU	O4	Air Force	NVN	Aug 19, 1972	Mar 29, 1973	7
SHIVELY	JAMES RICHARD	O2	Air Force	NVN	May 05, 1967	Feb 18, 1973	71
SHORE	EDWARD R JR	O3	Army	Laos	May 15, 1961	Aug 15, 1962	15
SHUMAKER	ROBERT HARPER	O4	Navy	NVN	Feb 11, 1965	Feb 12, 1973	97
SHUMAN	EDWIN ARTHUR	O4	Navy	NVN	Mar 17, 1968	Mar 14, 1973	61
SIENICKI	THEODORE S	O2	Air Force	NVN	May 03, 1972	Mar 28, 1973	11
SIGLER	GARY RICHARD	O2	Air Force	NVN	Apr 29, 1967	Mar 04, 1973	71
SIMA	THOMAS WILLIAM	O3	Air Force	NVN	Oct 15, 1965	Feb 12, 1973	89
SIMMONS	WILLIE E		Civilian	Laos	Aug 16, 1975	Oct 01, 1975	2
SIMMS	HAROLD D	E5	Army	Cambodia	Jul 17, 1968	Dec 19, 1968	5
SIMONET	KENNETH ADRIAN	O4	Air Force	NVN	Jan 18, 1968	Mar 14, 1973	63
SIMPSON	RICHARD T	O3	Air Force	NVN	Dec 18, 1972	Mar 29, 1973	3
SINGLETON	JERRY ALLEN	O2	Air Force	NVN	Nov 06, 1965	Feb 12, 1973	89
SMITH	BRADLEY EDSEL	O2	Navy	NVN	Mar 25, 1966	Feb 12, 1973	84
SMITH	DEWEY LEE	O4	Air Force	NVN	Jun 02, 1967	Mar 04, 1973	70
SMITH	DONALD GLENN	E3	Army	SVN	May 13, 1968	Jan 01, 1969	8
SMITH	GEORGE EDWARD	E6	Army	SVN	Nov 24, 1963	Nov 28, 1965	25
SMITH	MARK A	O3	Army	SVN	Apr 07, 1972	Feb 12, 1973	10
SMITH	PHILIP E	O3	Air Force	China	Sep 20, 1965	Mar 15, 1973	91
SMITH	RICHARD EUGENE	O4	Air Force	NVN	Oct 25, 1967	Mar 14, 1973	66

SMITH	WAYNE OGDEN	O2	Air Force	NVN	Jan 18, 1968	Mar 14, 1973	63
SOOTER	DAVID WILLIAM	W1	Army	SVN	Feb 17, 1967	Mar 05, 1973	74
SOUDER	JAMES BURTON	O4	Navy	NVN	Apr 27, 1972	Mar 28, 1973	11
SOUTHWICK	CHARLES EVERETT	O4	Navy	NVN	May 14, 1967	Mar 04, 1973	71
SPARKS	JOHN G	E3	Army	SVN	Apr 24, 1968	Mar 16, 1973	60
SPAULDING	RICHARD		Civilian	SVN	Jan 31, 1968	Mar 16, 1973	62
SPENCER	LARRY HOWARD	O2	Navy	NVN	Feb 18, 1966	Feb 12, 1973	85
SPENCER	WILLIAM A	O3	Air Force	NVN	Jul 05, 1972	Mar 29, 1973	9
SPONEYBARGER	ROBERT D	O3	Air Force	NVN	Dec 22, 1972	Mar 29, 1973	3
SPOON	DONALD RAY	O2	Air Force	NVN	Jan 21, 1967	Mar 04, 1973	74
SPRAGENS	JOHN		Civilian	SVN	Apr 30, 1974	May 22, 1974	1
SPRINGMAN	RICHARD	E4	Army	Cambodia	May 25, 1970	Feb 12, 1973	33
STACKHOUSE	CHARLES DAVID	O3	Navy	NVN	Apr 25, 1967	Mar 04, 1973	71
STAFFORD	HUGH ALLEN	O4	Navy	NVN	Aug 31, 1967	Mar 14, 1973	67
STARK	LAWRENCE J		Civilian	SVN	Feb 01, 1968	Mar 05, 1973	62
STARK	WILLIAM ROBERT	O4	Navy	NVN	May 19, 1967	Mar 04, 1973	71
STAVAST	JOHN EDWARD	O4	Air Force	NVN	Sep 17, 1967	Mar 14, 1973	67
STERLING	THOMAS JAMES	O4	Air Force	NVN	Apr 19, 1967	Mar 04, 1973	72
STIER	THEODORE GERHARD	O2	Navy	NVN	Nov 19, 1967	Mar 14, 1973	65
STIRM	ROBERT LEWIS	O4	Air Force	NVN	Oct 27, 1967	Mar 14, 1973	66
STISCHER	WALTER MORRIS	O4	Air Force	Laos	Apr 13, 1968	Mar 28, 1973	60
STOCKDALE	JAMES BOND	O5	Navy	NVN	Sep 09, 1965	Feb 12, 1973	90
STOCKMAN	HERVEY STUDDIE	O5	Air Force	NVN	Jun 11, 1967	Mar 04, 1973	70
STOREY	THOMAS GORDON	O3	Air Force	NVN	Jan 16, 1967	Mar 04, 1973	75
STRATTON	RICHARD ALLEN	O4	Navy	NVN	Jan 05, 1967	Mar 04, 1973	75
STRICKLAND	JAMES H	E3	Army	SVN	Jan 08, 1968	Nov 05, 1969	22
STRUHARIK	PAUL ALLEN		Civilian	SVN	Mar 10, 1975	Oct 30, 1975	8
STUTZ	LEROY WILLIAM	O2	Air Force	NVN	Dec 02, 1966	Mar 04, 1973	76
SULLIVAN	DWIGHT EVERETT	O4	Air Force	NVN	Oct 17, 1967	Mar 14, 1973	66
SULLIVAN	TIMOTHY BERNARD	O2	Navy	NVN	Nov 16, 1967	Mar 14, 1973	65
SUMPTER	THOMAS WRENNE	O4	Air Force	NVN	Jan 14, 1968	Mar 14, 1973	63
SWEENEY	JON M	E3	Marines	SVN	Feb 19, 1969	Aug 17, 1970	18
SWINDLE	ORSON GEORGE 111	O3	Marines	NVN	Nov 11, 1966	Mar 04, 1973	77
TABB	ROBERT ERNEST	E6	Army	SVN	Apr 12, 1970	Mar 27, 1973	36
TALLEY	BERNARD LEO	O2	Air Force	NVN	Sep 10, 1966	Mar 04, 1973	79
TALLEY	WILLIAM H	O4	Air Force	NVN	May 11, 1972	Mar 28, 1973	11
TANGEMAN	RICHARD GEORGE	O3	Navy	NVN	May 05, 1968	Mar 14, 1973	59
TANNER	CHARLES NELS	O4	Navy	NVN	Oct 09, 1966	Mar 04, 1973	78
TELLIER	DENNIS A	E3	Marines	SVN	Jun 19, 1969	Mar 27, 1973	46
TEMPERLEY	RUSSELL EDWIN	O3	Air Force	NVN	Oct 27, 1967	Mar 14, 1973	66
TERRELL	IRBY DAVID	O4	Air Force	NVN	Jan 14, 1968	Mar 14, 1973	63
TERRY	ROSS RANDLE	O3	Navy	NVN	Oct 09, 1966	Mar 04, 1973	78
TESTER	JERRY ALBERT	E3	Army	Cambodia	May 20, 1968	Jun 10, 1968	1
THOMAS	WILLIAM E	W2	Marines	SVN	May 19, 1972	Mar 27, 1973	10
THOMPSON	DENNIS L	E6	Army	SVN	Feb 07, 1968	Mar 05, 1973	62
THOMPSON	FLOYD JAMES	O3	Army	SVN	Mar 26, 1964	Mar 16, 1973	109
THOMPSON	FRED N	O4	Air Force	NVN	Mar 20, 1968	Aug 02, 1968	5

THORNTON	GARY LYNN	O1	Navy	NVN	Feb 20, 1967	Mar 04, 1973	73
THORSNESS	LEO KEITH	O4	Air Force	NVN	Apr 30, 1967	Mar 04, 1973	71
TINSLEY	COY R	E3	Army	SVN	Mar 09, 1969	Nov 05, 1969	8
TOMES	JACK HARVEY	O3	Air Force	NVN	Jul 07, 1966	Feb 12, 1973	80
TORKELSON	LOREN H	O2	Air Force	NVN	Apr 29, 1967	Mar 04, 1973	71
TRAUTMAN	KONRAD WIGAND	O3	Air Force	NVN	Oct 05, 1967	Mar 14, 1973	66
TRIEBEL	THEODORE W	O4	Navy	NVN	Aug 27, 1972	Mar 29, 1973	7
TRIMBLE	JACK R	O2	Air Force	NVN	Dec 27, 1972	Mar 29, 1973	3
TSCHUDY	WILLIAM MICHAEL	O2	Navy	NVN	Jul 18, 1965	Feb 12, 1973	92
TYLER	CHARLES ROBERT	O4	Air Force	NVN	Aug 23, 1967	Mar 14, 1973	68
UTECHT	RICHARD W		Civilian	SVN	Feb 04, 1968	Feb 12, 1973	61
UYEYAMA	TERRY JUN	O3	Air Force	NVN	May 18, 1968	Mar 14, 1973	59
VANLOAN	JACK LEE	O4	Air Force	NVN	May 20, 1967	Mar 04, 1973	71
VAUGHAN	SAMUEL R	O2	Air Force	NVN	Dec 18, 1971	Mar 28, 1973	16
VAVROCH	DUANE P	O2	Air Force	NVN	Dec 26, 1972	Mar 29, 1973	3
VENANZI	GERALD SANTO	O2	Air Force	NVN	Sep 17, 1967	Mar 14, 1973	67
VISSOTZKY	RAYMOND WALTON	O4	Air Force	NVN	Nov 19, 1967	Mar 14, 1973	65
VOGEL	RICHARD DALE	O4	Air Force	NVN	May 22, 1967	Mar 04, 1973	70
VOHDEN	RAYMOND ARTHUR	O4	Navy	NVN	Apr 03, 1965	Feb 12, 1973	96
WADDELL	DEWEY WAYNE	O4	Air Force	NVN	Jul 05, 1967	Mar 04, 1973	69
WAGGONER	ROBERT FROST	O3	Air Force	NVN	Sep 12, 1966	Mar 04, 1973	79
WALDHAUS	RICHARD G		Civilian	SVN	Aug 04, 1971	Feb 12, 1973	19
WALKER	HUBERT C	O3	Air Force	NVN	Jan 14, 1968	Mar 14, 1973	63
WALKER	MICHAEL JAMES	E4	Navy	Cambodia	Feb 05, 1970	Feb 28, 1970	1
WALLINGFORD	KENNETH	E8	Army	SVN	Apr 07, 1972	Feb 12, 1973	10
WALSH	JAMES P	O3	Marines	SVN	Sep 26, 1972	Feb 12, 1973	5
WALTMAN	DONALD G	O3	Air Force	NVN	Sep 19, 1966	Mar 04, 1973	79
WANAT	GEORGE K JR	O3	Army	SVN	Apr 08, 1972	Feb 12, 1973	10
WARD	BRIAN H	O2	Air Force	NVN	Dec 27, 1972	Mar 29, 1973	3
WARNER	JAMES HOIE	O2	Marines	NVN	Oct 13, 1967	Mar 14, 1973	66
WATKINS	WILLIE A	E4	Army	SVN	Jan 09, 1968	Nov 05, 1969	22
WEAVER	EUGENE		Civilian	SVN	Jan 31, 1968	Mar 16, 1973	62
WEBB	RONALD JOHN	O3	Air Force	NVN	Jun 11, 1967	Mar 04, 1973	70
WELLS	KENNETH	O2	Air Force	NVN	Dec 18, 1971	Mar 28, 1973	16
WELLS	NORMAN LOUROSS	O3	Air Force	NVN	Aug 29, 1966	Mar 04, 1973	79
WENDELL	JOHN HENRY	O3	Air Force	NVN	Aug 07, 1966	Mar 04, 1973	80
WHEAT	DAVID ROBERT	O2	Navy	NVN	Oct 17, 1965	Feb 12, 1973	89
WHITE	ROBERT THOMAS	O3	Army	SVN	Nov 15, 1969	Apr 01, 1973	41
WIDEMAN	ROBERT EARL	O2	Navy	NVN	May 06, 1967	Mar 04, 1973	71
WIELAND	CARL T	O3	Navy	NVN	Dec 20, 1972	Mar 29, 1973	3
WILBER	WALTER EUGENE	O5	Navy	NVN	Jun 16, 1968	Feb 12, 1973	57
WILLIAMS	JAMES W	O3	Air Force	NVN	May 20, 1972	Mar 28, 1973	10
WILLIAMS	LEWIS IRVNG	O2	Navy	NVN	Apr 24, 1967	Mar 04, 1973	71
WILLIS	CHARLES E		Civilian	SVN	Jan 31, 1968	Mar 27, 1973	63
WILMOTH	FLOYD A	E7	Army	Cambodia	Jul 17, 1968	Dec 19, 1968	5
WILSON	GLENN HUBERT	O3	Air Force	NVN	Aug 07, 1967	Mar 14, 1973	68
WILSON	HAL K	O3	Air Force	NVN	Dec 19, 1972	Mar 29, 1973	3
WILSON	WILLIAM W	O2	Air Force	NVN	Dec 22, 1972	Mar 29, 1973	3

WINN	DAVID WILLIAM	O6	Air Force	NVN	Aug 09, 1968	Mar 14, 1973	56
WOLFKILL	GRANT		Civilian	Laos	May 15, 1961	Aug 15, 1962	15
WOMACK	SAMMIE NORMAN	E5	Army	SVN	Oct 08, 1966	Feb 07, 1967	4
WOODS	BRIAN DUNSTAN	O4	Navy	NVN	Sep 18, 1968	Feb 12, 1973	54
WOODS	ROBERT DEANE	O3	Navy	NVN	Oct 12, 1966	Mar 04, 1973	78
WRITER	LAWRENCE DANIEL	O3	Air Force	NVN	Feb 15, 1968	Mar 14, 1973	62
YOUNG	JAMES FAULDS	O4	Air Force	NVN	Jul 06, 1966	Feb 12, 1973	80
YOUNG	JOHN ARTHUR	E4	Army	SVN	Jan 31, 1968	Mar 16, 1973	62
YOUNG	MYRON A	O3	Air Force	NVN	Oct 12, 1972	Mar 29, 1973	6
YUILL	JOHN H	O5	Air Force	NVN	Dec 22, 1972	Mar 29, 1973	3
ZIEGLER	ROY ESPER II	W1	Army	SVN	Feb 08, 1968	Mar 05, 1973	62
ZUBERBUHLER	RUDOLPH U	O3	Air Force	NVN	Sep 12, 1972	Mar 29, 1973	7
ZUHOSKI	CHARLES PETER	O2	Navy	NVN	Jul 31, 1967	Mar 14, 1973	68
ZUPP	KLAUS H	E4	Army	Cambodia	Jul 17, 1968	Dec 19, 1968	5

Appendix C

The Iranian Hostages

Sixty-six Americans were taken captive when Iranian militants seized the U.S. Embassy in Tehran on November 4, 1979, including three who were at the Iranian Foreign Ministry. Six more Americans escaped. Of the 66 who were taken hostage, 13 were released on November 19 and 20, 1979; one was released on July 11, 1980, and the remaining 52 were released on January 20, 1981. Ages in this list are at the time of release.[1.]

The 52 hostages:

1. Thomas L. Ahern, Jr., 48, McLean, VA. Narcotics control officer.
2. Clair Cortland Barnes, 35, Falls Church, VA. Communications specialist.
3. William E. Belk, 44, West Columbia, SC. Communications and records officer.
4. Robert O. Blucker, 54, North Little Rock, AR. Economics officer specializing in oil.
5. Donald J. Cooke, 26, Memphis, TN. Vice consul.
6. William J. Daugherty, 33, Tulsa, OK. Third secretary of U.S. mission.

7. Lt. Cmdr. Robert Englemann, 34, Hurst, TX. Naval attaché.
8. Sgt. William Gallegos, 22, Pueblo, CO. Marine guard.
9. Bruce W. German, 44, Rockville, MD. Budget officer.
10. Duane L. Gillette, 24, Columbia, PA. Navy communications and intelligence specialist.
11. Alan B. Golancinksi, 30, Silver Spring, MD. Security officer.
12. John E. Graves, 53, Reston, VA. Public affairs officer.
13. Joseph M. Hall, 32, Elyria, OH. Military attaché with warrant officer rank.
14. Sgt. Kevin J. Hermening, 21, Oak Creek, WI. Marine guard.
15. Sgt. 1st Class Donald R. Hohman, 38, Frankfurt, West Germany. Army medic.
16. Col. Leland J. Holland, 53, Laurel, MD. Military attaché.
17. Michael Howland, 34, Alexandria, VA. Security aide, one of three held in Iranian Foreign Ministry.
18. Charles A. Jones, Jr., 40, Communications specialist and teletype operator. Only African-American hostage not released in November 1979.
19. Malcolm Kalp, 42, Fairfax, VA. Position unknown.
20. Moorhead C. Kennedy Jr., 50, Washington, DC. Economic and commercial officer.

21. William F. Keough, Jr., 50, Brookline, MA. Superintendent of American School in Islamabad, Pakistan, visiting Tehran at time of embassy seizure.
22. Cpl. Steven W. Kirtley, 22, Little Rock, AR. Marine guard.
23. Kathryn L. Koob, 42, Fairfax, VA. Embassy cultural officer; one of two women hostages.
24. Frederick Lee Kupke, 34, Francesville, IN. Communications officer and electronics specialist.
25. L. Bruce Laingen, 58, Bethesda, MD. Chargé d'affaires. One of three held in Iranian Foreign Ministry.
26. Steven Lauterbach, 29, North Dayton, OH. Administrative officer.
27. Gary E. Lee, 37, Falls Church, VA. Administrative officer.
28. Sgt. Paul Edward Lewis, 23, Homer, IL. Marine guard.
29. John W. Limbert, Jr., 37, Washington, DC. Political officer.
30. Sgt. James M. Lopez, 22, Globe, AZ. Marine guard.
31. Sgt. John D. McKeel, Jr., 27, Balch Springs, TX. Marine guard.
32. Michael J. Metrinko, 34, Olyphant, PA. Political officer.
33. Jerry J. Miele, 42, Mt. Pleasant, PA. Communications officer.
34. Staff Sgt. Michael E. Moeller, 31, Quantico, VA. Head of Marine guard unit.

35. Bert C. Moore, 45, Mount Vernon, OH. Counselor for administration.
36. Richard H. Morefield, 51, San Diego, CA. U.S. Consul General in Tehran.
37. Capt. Paul M. Needham, Jr., 30, Bellevue, NE. Air Force logistics staff officer.
38. Robert C. Ode, 65, Sun City, AZ. Retired Foreign Service officer on temporary duty in Tehran.
39. Sgt. Gregory A. Persinger, 23, Seaford, DE. Marine guard.
40. Jerry Plotkin, 45, Sherman Oaks, CA. Private businessman visiting Tehran.
41. MSgt. Regis Ragan, 38, Johnstown, PA. Army noncom, assigned to defense attaché's officer.
42. Lt. Col. David M. Roeder, 41, Alexandria, VA. Deputy Air Force attaché.
43. Barry M. Rosen, 36, Brooklyn, NY. Press attaché.
44. William B. Royer, Jr., 49, Houston, TX. Assistant director of Iran-American Society.
45. Col. Thomas E. Schaefer, 50, Tacoma, WA. Air Force attaché.
46. Col. Charles W. Scott, 48, Stone Mountain, GA. Army officer, military attaché.
47. Cmdr. Donald A. Sharer, 40, Chesapeake, VA. Naval air attaché.
48. Sgt. Rodney V. (Rocky) Sickmann, 22, Krakow, MO. Marine Guard.

49. Staff Sgt. Joseph Subic, Jr., 23, Redford Township, MI. Military policeman (Army) on defense attaché's staff.
50. Elizabeth Ann Swift, 40, Washington, DC. Chief of embassy's political section; one of two women hostages.
51. Victor L. Tomseth, 39, Springfield, OR. Senior political officer; one of three held in Iranian Foreign Ministry.
52. Phillip R. Ward, 40, Culpeper, VA. Administrative officer.

One hostage was freed July 11, 1980, because of an illness later diagnosed as multiple sclerosis:

Richard I. Queen, 28, New York, NY. Vice consul.

Six American diplomats avoided capture when the embassy was seized. For three months they were sheltered at the Canadian and Swedish embassies in Tehran. On Jan. 28, 1980, they fled Iran using Canadian passports:

1. Robert Anders, 34, Port Charlotte, FL. Consular officer.
2. Mark J. Lijek, 29, Falls Church, VA. Consular officer.
3. Cora A. Lijek, 25, Falls Church, VA. Consular assistant.

4. Henry L. Schatz, 31, Coeur d'Alene, ID. Agriculture attaché.
5. Joseph D. Stafford, 29, Crossville, TN. Consular officer.
6. Kathleen F. Stafford, 28, Crossville, TN. Consular assistant.

Thirteen women and African-Americans among the Americans who were seized at the embassy were released on November 19 and 20, 1979:

1. Kathy Gross, 22, Cambridge Springs, PA. Secretary.
2. Sgt. James Hughes, 30, Langley Air Force Base, VA. Air Force administrative manager.
3. Lillian Johnson, 32, Elmont, NY. Secretary.
4. Sgt. Ladell Maples, 23, Earle, AR. Marine guard.
5. Elizabeth Montagne, 42, Calumet City, IL. Secretary.
6. Sgt. William Quarles, 23, Washington, DC. Marine guard.
7. Lloyd Rollins, 40, Alexandria, VA. Administrative officer.
8. Capt. Neal (Terry) Robinson, 30, Houston, TX. Administrative officer.
9. Terri Tedford, 24, South San Francisco, CA. Secretary.
10. Sgt. Joseph Vincent, 42, New Orleans, LA. Air Force administrative manager.
11. Sgt. David Walker, 25, Prairie View, TX. Marine guard.
12. Joan Walsh, 33, Ogden, UT. Secretary.
13. Cpl. Wesley Williams, 24, Albany, NY. Marine guard.

Eight U.S. servicemen from the all-volunteer Joint Special Operations Group were killed in the Great Salt Desert near Tabas, Iran, on April 25, 1980, in the aborted attempt to rescue the American hostages:

1. Capt. Richard L. Bakke, 34, Long Beach, CA. Air Force.
2. Sgt. John D. Harvey, 21, Roanoke, VA. Marine Corps.
3. Cpl. George N. Holmes, Jr., 22, Pine Bluff, AR. Marine Corps.
4. Staff Sgt. Dewey L. Johnson, 32, Jacksonville, NC. Marine Corps.
5. Capt. Harold L. Lewis, 35, Mansfield, CT. Air Force.
6. Tech. Sgt. Joel C. Mayo, 34, Bonifay, FL. Air Force.
7. Capt. Lynn D. McIntosh, 33, Valdosta, GA. Air Force.
8. Capt. Charles T. McMillan II, 28, Corrytown, TN. Air Force.

Appendix D

Desert Storm Captives Unaccounted-For*

Information Courtesy Of DPMO[1.]

Name	Vehicle	Date	Status	Release
Speicher, M.S.	F-18	17 Jan 91	KIA*	2 July 2010
Zaun, J.N.	A-6	17 Jan 91	Released	3 Mar 91
Wetzel, R			Released	3 Mar 91
Holland, D.R.	F-15	17 Jan 91	KIA-BR	
Koritz, T.F.			KIA-BR	
Costen, W.T.	A-6	18 Jan 91	KIA-BR	
Turner, C.J.			KIA-BR	
Acree, C.	OV-10	18 Jan 91	Released	6 Mar 91
Hunter, G.			Released	6 Mar 91
Eberly, D.W.	F-15	19 Jan 91	Released	6 Mar 91
Griffith, T.E.			Released	3 Mar 91
Roberts, H.M.	F-16	19 Jan 91	Released	6 Mar 91
Tice, J.S.	F-16	19 Jan 91	Released	6 Mar 91
Slade, L.R.	F-14	21 Jan 91	Released	3 Mar 91
Berryman, M.C.	AV-8	28 Jan 91	Released	6 Mar 91
Nealy, M.	Truck	30 Jan 91	Released	3 Mar 91
Lockett, D.			Released	3 Mar 91
Weaver, P.J.	AC-130	31 Jan 91	KIA-BR	
Walters, D.L.			KIA-BR	
Galvan, A.			KIA-BR	
Grimm, W.D.			KIA-BR	
Bland, T.C.			KIA-BR	
Buege, P.G.			KIA-BR	
May, J.B.			KIA-BR	
Hodges, R.K.			KIA-BR	

Schmauss, J.J.			KIA-BR	
Oelschlager, J.			KIA-BR	
Kanuha, D.V.			KIA-BR	
Blessinger, J.			KIA-BR	
Harrison, T.R.			KIA-BR	
Clark, B.M.			KIA-BR	
Cooke, B.T.	A-6	2 Feb 91	KIA-BNR	
Connor, P.K.			KIA-BR	
Storr, R.D.	A-10	2 Feb 91	Released	6 Mar 91
Dwyer, R.J.	F-18	5 Feb 91	KIA-BNR	
Sanborn, R.A.C.	AV-8 9	Feb 91	Released	6 Mar 91
Sweet, R.J.	A-10	15 Feb 91	Released	6 Mar 91
Phillis, S.R.	A-10			
Fox, J.D.	OA-10	19 Feb 91	Released	6 Mar 91
Wilbourn, J.N.	AV-8 23	Feb 91	KIA-BR	
Small, J.J.	OV-10 25	Feb 91	Released	6 Mar 91
Spellacy, D.M.			KIA-BR	
Underwood, R.	AV-8 27	Feb 91	KIA-BR	
Andrews, W.F.	F-16 27	Feb 91	Released	6 Mar 91
Cornum, R.S.	UH-60 27	Feb 91	Released	6 Mar 91
Dunlap, T.A.			Released	6 Mar 91
Stamaris, D.J.			Released	6 Mar 91

Notes:

KIA-BR = Killed in Action, Body Recovered.

KIA-BNR = Killed in Action, Body not Recovered.

* Capt. Speicher's remains were recovered in July 2010, and he was finally laid to rest in Jacksonville, FL.

NOTES

CHAPTER 1

INTRODUCTION TO POWS

1. In the American Civil War, prisoners taken in the Middle Atlantic States were often transported by train to such infamous prisons such as Andersonville, Georgia. In the case of Confederate forces captures by Union forces, the treks north often ended in such locations such as Rock Island, Illinois. In either case, Confederate or Union, the prisoners were often subjected to a month or more in the movement phase.
2. In current terms, reintegration is the psychological, medical, and debriefing process former POWs are taken through to assist them in processing the events that occurred to them while in captivity. The older term "repatriation" is now used to describe the return of a body to its country of origin. According to Joint Publication 3-50 (Personnel Recovery): "The goal of the reintegration task is to gather critical information from recovered isolated personnel and conduct the plethora of processes inherent in their reintegration, while protecting their health and welfare. This allows them to return to duty as expeditiously as possible, physically and emotionally fit. All isolated personnel should be entered into the reintegration process immediately following

recovery. The reintegration task may be as simple as a SERE debriefing, or as involved as the complete three-phase reintegration process that terminates in the US, depending on the recovered person's situation (health, length, type of isolation, etc.)." For more information on reintegration, see Chapter I, page 8 of this joint publication, which is available online at http://www.fas.org/irp/doddir/dod/jp3_50.pdf.

3. The Chairman of the Joint Chief of Staff Instruction (CJCSI) 3270.01A dated 1 July 2003 provides that the DOD "provides guidance to DOD components concerning implementation of personnel recovery (PR) policy established" and further applies to "the Joint Staff, Services, combatant commands, and Defense agencies, otherwise referred to as DOD components." In addition to this classified Chairman's instruction (Unclassified upon removal of Enclosure B—Classified Responsibilities for Personnel Recovery), there are a host of other regulations and laws, including the Missing Persons Act, which all serve to direct the United States Government, its interagency partners, and others that might become involved in the preparation, planning, and execution of survival, evasion, escape, recovery, or reintegration operations across the spectrum of warfare. The leading authority on POW issues, the United States Government's Defense Prisoner of War/Missing Personnel Office, stated: "The number one priority of our government is 'live recovery.' American service personnel are deployed globally, resulting in our need to bring our men and women home alive anytime, anywhere." Source: http://www.dtic.mil/dpmo/personnel_recovery/overview.htm

4. The Department of Defense has several SERE (or survival, evasion, resistance, and escape) schools where selected personnel can attend this specialized training. Among these are the Air Force's school at Fairchild Air Force base (see http://www.fairchild.af.mil/library/factsheets/factsheet.asp?id=3771) and the Army's SERE school (for an article, see http://www.soc.mil/swcs/swmag/Archives/00sum.PDF).
5. Brian M. Linn, *The Philippine War, 1899-1902.* (Lawrence, KS: University Press of Kansas, 2000.) 9.

Chapter 2

POWs During The American Revolution

1. Alan R. Millet and Peter Maslowski, *For the Common Defense: A Military History of the United States of America* (The Free Press: New York, NY), 49.

2. Alan R. Millet and Peter Maslowski, *For the Common Defense: A Military History of the United States of America* (The Free Press: New York, NY), 38-49.

3. John Marshall. *The Life of George Washington, Commander in Chief of the American Forces During the War Which established the Independence of His Country, Vol II (The Citizen's Guild of Washington's Boyhood Home, Fredericksburg, VA* (Publisher Unknown: Location Unknown, 1926), 37. Copy accessed online at http://www.ponury.com.pl/The_Life_of_George_Washington_Vol_2_of_5-7275-1.html on 24 Apr 2010.

4. One of the better published works on Revolutionary War prison conditions is *American Prisoners of the Revolution* by Danske Dandridge. This work, originally published in

hardcover, is now available on the Gutenberg website as well.

5. Danske Dandridge, *American Prisoners of the Revolution* (Gutenberg Ebook: online collection), 2-12.

6. Danske Dandridge, *American Prisoners of the Revolution* (Gutenberg Ebook: online collection), 12.

7. Like many other enlistees, these soldiers only signed up for a year's duty.

8. Danske Dandridge, *American Prisoners of the Revolution* (Gutenberg Ebook: online collection), 14.

9. John Marshall. *The Life of George Washington, Commander in Chief of the American Forces During the War Which Established the Independence of His Country, Vol II (The Citizen's Guild of Washington's Boyhood Home, Fredericksburg, VA* (Publisher Unknown: Location Unknown, 1926), 37. Copy accessed online at http://www.ponury.com.pl/The_Life_of_George_Washington_Vol_2_of_5-7275-1.html on 24 Apr 2010.

10. Danske Dandridge, *American Prisoners of the Revolution* (Gutenberg Ebook: online collection), 15-16.

11. Danske Dandridge, *American Prisoners of the Revolution* (Gutenberg EBook: online collection), 17.

12. Danske Dandridge, *American Prisoners of the Revolution* (Gutenberg EBook: online collection), 17. Additionally, other sources also reflected a similar number (see p. 24 (Jonathan Gillett)).

13. Danske Dandridge, *American Prisoners of the Revolution* (Gutenberg EBook: online collection), 17.

14. Danske Dandridge, *American Prisoners of the Revolution* (Gutenberg EBook: online collection), 17.

15. Danske Dandridge, *American Prisoners of the Revolution* (Gutenberg EBook: online collection), 18.

16. Danske Dandridge, *American Prisoners of the Revolution* (Gutenberg EBook: online collection), 18.

17. Danske Dandridge, *American Prisoners of the Revolution* (Gutenberg EBook: online collection), 18.

18. Danske Dandridge, *American Prisoners of the Revolution* (Gutenberg EBook: online collection), 25.

19. Danske Dandridge, *American Prisoners of the Revolution* (Gutenberg EBook: online collection), 137.

20. Danske Dandridge, *American Prisoners of the Revolution* (Gutenberg EBook: online collection), 115-118.

21. Danske Dandridge. *American Prisoners of the Revolution* (Gutenberg EBook: online collection), 117-118.

22. Christopher Hawkins. *The Adventures of Christopher Hawkins* (Privately Printed: New York, NY, 1864). The version referenced was an electronic version available through Google books online.

23. Christopher Hawkins. *The Adventures of Christopher Hawkins* (Privately Printed: New York, NY, 1864), 23.

24. Cat—o-nine tails are whips, typically with nine separate pieces of cord and knots on the ends of the device. When struck with the cat-o-nine tails, the pain was intense since the ends of the "cats' tails" normally had knots that would cut into the skin of its victims.

25. Christopher Hawkins. *The Adventures of Christopher Hawkins* (Privately Printed: New York, NY, 1864), 29.

26. For prisoners of war, the food consumed can often mean the difference between illnesses and long-term health concerns that, more so than in everyday life, can spell the difference between life or death in a captivity environment. Vitamin deficiencies, iron deficiencies, and other related dietary abnormalities are common for prisoners of war since nations at war often struggle to keep their military forces properly fed in battle. In some cases, as will be discussed with the

Japanese in World War II, such dietary deficiencies are intentionally implemented to starve the prisoners.

27. Christopher Hawkins. *The Adventures of Christopher Hawkins* (Privately Printed: New York, NY, 1864), 42.

28. Christopher Hawkins. *The Adventures of Christopher Hawkins* (Privately Printed: New York, NY, 1864), 45.

29. Christopher Hawkins. *The Adventures of Christopher Hawkins* (Privately Printed: New York, NY, 1864), 48.

30. Christopher Hawkins. *The Adventures of Christopher Hawkins* (Privately Printed: New York, NY, 1864), 43-44.

31. Christopher Hawkins. *The Adventures of Christopher Hawkins* (Privately Printed: New York, NY, 1864), 50-56.

32. Christopher Hawkins. *The Adventures of Christopher Hawkins* (Privately Printed: New York, NY, 1864), 59.

33. Christopher Hawkins. *The Adventures of Christopher Hawkins* (Privately Printed: New York, NY, 1864), 66.

34. Christopher Hawkins. *The Adventures of Christopher Hawkins* (Privately Printed: New York, NY, 1864), 69.

35. Christopher Hawkins. *The Adventures of Christopher Hawkins* (Privately Printed: New York, NY, 1864), 69-72.

36. Christopher Hawkins. *The Adventures of Christopher Hawkins* (Privately Printed: New York, NY, 1864), 77.

37. One of the concerns Hawkins, and any other escapees from the prison ships, faced was the effects of the cold water. Foremost among the effects of the cold water was hypothermia, followed by immersion foot—sometimes called trench foot. Hypothermia is a condition whereby the body's core temperature reaches dangerously low levels, often to the point where those affected lose touch with reality and their decision-making abilities are seriously impaired. Trench foot, on the other hand, is a condition where the feet are exposed to cool temperatures, in addition to being wet. Trench foot is not typically life-threatening. On rare occasion, such as with prolonged exposure to water, trench foot could get to the point where extensive medical care or amputations could be required if not properly treated.

38. "Hessian troops were not mercenaries in the modern sense of military professionals who voluntarily hire out their own services for money. As in most armies of the 18th century, the men were mainly conscripts, debtors, or the victims of impressment; some were also petty criminals. Pay was low; some soldiers received nothing but their daily food. The officer corps usually consisted of career officers who had served in earlier European wars. The revenues paid for the men's service went back to the German royalty. Nevertheless, some Hessian units were respected for their discipline and excellent military skills. Hessians comprised approximately

one-quarter of the forces fielded by the British in the American Revolution. They included jäger, hussars, three artillery companies, and four battalions of grenadiers. Most of the infantry were chasseurs (sharpshooters), musketeers, and fusiliers. They were armed mainly with smoothbore muskets, while the Hessian artillery used three-pounder cannon. Initially the average regiment was made up of 500 to 600 men. Later in the war, the regiments had only 300 to 400 men." Quoted from: http://en.wikipedia.org/wiki/Hessian_%28soldiers%29

39. Although Hawkins and the other prisoners had not received any escape training, their technique of moving during the hours of darkness and resting during daylight hours was and remains a technique taught in many modern-day survival schools. Likewise, the many times Hawkins made decisions to move or perish due to the bone-chilling rain also remains a planning factor in evasion movement techniques. On page 92 of his diary-turned-book, Hawkins made a very specific comment about moving in the rain or perishing due to the cold and wet conditions he endured.

40. As in modern survival schools and courses, evaders are taught to eat foods they might not ordinarily consider savory or tasteful. In many cases, some of which will be touched upon in other periods of history, prisoners' reluctance to eat such foods has hastened their demise.

41. On this occasion, it appears as if the female providing assistance asked Hawkins to lay clothes across the clothes line so that she could say, with an element of truth, that someone must have taken the clothing she had on her clothes line without her seeing who took it. This provides the woman plausibility for her story because, although she might believe she knew who took the clothes, she did not witness the taking.

42. Modern evasion techniques, such as those contained in the US Air Force's survival manual, AFR 64-4, depict evaders moving along uninhabited areas and trying to stay away from inhabited areas such as paths, roads, or other areas where people might gather or traverse. For an online copy, see: http://www.survivalprimer.com/NWSS/AirForceSurvial_NBC_WMD.pdf

43. Christopher Hawkins. *The Adventures of Christopher Hawkins* (Privately Printed: New York, NY, 1864), 112.

44. John Marshall. *The Life of George Washington, Commander in Chief of the American Forces During the War Which established the Independence of His Country, Vol II (The Citizen's Guild of Washington's Boyhood Home, Fredericksburg, VA* (Publisher Unknown: Location Unknown, 1926), 52. Copy accessed online at http://www.ponury.com.pl/The_Life_of_George_Washington_Vol_2_of_5-7275-1.html on 24 Apr 2010.

45. Danske Dandridge, *American Prisoners of the Revolution* (Gutenberg EBook: online collection), 121.

46. John Marshall. *The Life of George Washington, Commander in Chief of the American Forces During the War Which established the Independence of His Country, Vol II (The Citizen's Guild of Washington's Boyhood Home, Fredericksburg, VA* (Publisher Unknown: Location Unknown, 1926), 267. Copy accessed online at http://www.ponury.com.pl/The_Life_of_George_Washington_Vol_2_of_5-7275-1.html on 24 Apr 2010.

47. John Marshall. *The Life of George Washington, Commander in Chief of the American Forces During the War Which established the Independence of His Country, Vol II (The Citizen's Guild of Washington's Boyhood Home, Fredericksburg, VA* (Publisher Unknown: Location Unknown, 1926), 267. Copy accessed online at http://www.ponury.com.pl/The_Life_of_George_Washington_Vol_2_of_5-7275-1.html on 24 Apr 2010.

48. Danske Dandridge, *American Prisoners of the Revolution* (Gutenberg EBook: online collection), 112-113.

49. Danske Dandridge, *American Prisoners of the Revolution* (Gutenberg EBook: online collection), 113.

50. Danske Dandridge, *American Prisoners of the Revolution* (Gutenberg EBook: online collection), 114.

51. In the spring of 1775, American prisoners had been taken during the siege of Boston and, in fact, some of the first correspondence on POWs in a belligerent nation was passed. In short, during this siege, prisoners were taken by both sides. As a result, General Washington sent a letter to General Gage about the treatment of American prisoners of war. General Gage sent back correspondence reflecting his belief that those taken prisoner by his British forces were not prisoners at all, rather, they were rebels thus not deserving of humane treatment. For more on this exchange concerning prisoners, see: John Marshall's *The Life of George Washington, Commander in Chief of the American Forces During the War Which established the Independence of His Country, Vol II.* Reprint: Filiquarian Publishing, LLC / Qontro: Lexington, KY, pp. 46-47.

52. Danske Dandridge, *American Prisoners of the Revolution* (Gutenberg EBook: online collection), 115.

53. Danske Dandridge, *American Prisoners of the Revolution* (Gutenberg EBook: online collection), 121.

54. Rastatter, Paul J. *'Rebel' Prisoners Detained in North America.* Accessed on 3 Jan 2009 at http://www.earlyamerica.com/review/2002_summer_fall/pows.htm.

Chapter 3

Civil War POWs

1. Official US Senate records extracted on 19 Jan 2011: http://www.senate.gov/artandhistory/history/minute/The_Caning_of_Senator_Charles_Sumner.htm
2. John W. Northrop. *Chronicles From the Diary of a War Prisoner in Andersonville and other Military Prisons of the South in 1864* (Reprint: Published and copyrighted by the Author, Wichita, KS., 1904), 27.
3. John W. Northrop. *Chronicles From the Diary of a War Prisoner in Andersonville and other Military Prisons of the South in 1864* (Reprint: Published and copyrighted by the Author, Wichita, KS., 1904), 28.
4. John W. Northrop. *Chronicles From the Diary of a War Prisoner in Andersonville and other Military Prisons of the South in 1864* (Reprint: Published and copyrighted by the Author, Wichita, KS., 1904), 31.
5. John W. Northrop. *Chronicles From the Diary of a War Prisoner in Andersonville and other Military Prisons of the South in 1864* (Reprint: Published and copyrighted by the Author, Wichita, KS., 1904), 49.
6. A similar sight was recalled by a fellow Union soldier imprisoned at Andersonville. Sgt. Warren Lee Goss's

story has been told in Michael Martinez's seminal work, *Life and Death in Civil War Prisons: A Story of Hardship, Horror—and Extraordinary Courage.*

7. John W. Northrop. *Chronicles From the Diary of a War Prisoner in Andersonville and other Military Prisons of the South in 1864* (Reprint: Published and copyrighted by the Author, Wichita, KS., 1904), 60.
8. John W. Northrop. *Chronicles From the Diary of a War Prisoner in Andersonville and other Military Prisons of the South in 1864* (Reprint: Published and copyrighted by the Author, Wichita, KS., 1904), 61.
9. John W. Northrop. *Chronicles From the Diary of a War Prisoner in Andersonville and other Military Prisons of the South in 1864* (Reprint: Published and copyrighted by the Author, Wichita, KS., 1904), 69.
10. John W. Northrop. *Chronicles From the Diary of a War Prisoner in Andersonville and other Military Prisons of the South in 1864* (Reprint: Published and copyrighted by the Author, Wichita, KS., 1904), 88.
11. John W. Northrop. *Chronicles From the Diary of a War Prisoner in Andersonville and other Military Prisons of the South in 1864* (Reprint: Published and copyrighted by the Author, Wichita, KS., 1904), 122.
12. John W. Northrop. *Chronicles From the Diary of a War Prisoner in Andersonville and other Military Prisons of the South in 1864* (Reprint: Published and copyrighted by the Author, Wichita, KS., 1904), 125.
13. Unknown to the prisoners, the move of the prisoners in September was due to the Confederacy keeping prisoners

from being freed by advancing Union forces, such as in the siege and fall of Atlanta, Georgia.

14. Martinez, J, Michael. *Life and Death in Civil War Prisons: A Story of Hardship, Horror and Extraordinary Courage* (Rutledge Hill Press: Nashville, TN 2004), 1-4.
15. Martinez, J, Michael. *Life and Death in Civil War Prisons: A Story of Hardship, Horror and Extraordinary Courage* (Rutledge Hill Press: Nashville, TN 2004), 29.
16. Martinez, J, Michael. *Life and Death in Civil War Prisons: A Story of Hardship, Horror and Extraordinary Courage* (Rutledge Hill Press: Nashville, TN 2004), 31-35.
17. Martinez, J, Michael. *Life and Death in Civil War Prisons: A Story of Hardship, Horror and Extraordinary Courage* (Rutledge Hill Press: Nashville, TN 2004), 78-79.
18. Martinez, J, Michael. *Life and Death in Civil War Prisons: A Story of Hardship, Horror and Extraordinary Courage* (Rutledge Hill Press: Nashville, TN 2004), 79-81.
19. Martinez, J, Michael. *Life and Death in Civil War Prisons: A Story of Hardship, Horror and Extraordinary Courage* (Rutledge Hill Press: Nashville, TN 2004), 84-85.
20. Martinez, J, Michael. *Life and Death in Civil War Prisons: A Story of Hardship, Horror and Extraordinary Courage* (Rutledge Hill Press: Nashville, TN 2004), 86-87.
21. Martinez, J, Michael. *Life and Death in Civil War Prisons: A Story of Hardship, Horror and Extraordinary Courage* (Rutledge Hill Press: Nashville, TN 2004), 101-103.
22. Although this tale, or others like it could not be fully confirmed, the basic events are likely to have occurred as shown by piecemeal prison records. Martinez, J, Michael.

Life and Death in Civil War Prisons: A Story of Hardship, Horror and Extraordinary Courage (Rutledge Hill Press: Nashville, TN 2004), 100-104.

23. Martinez, J, Michael. *Life and Death in Civil War Prisons: A Story of Hardship, Horror and Extraordinary Courage* (Rutledge Hill Press: Nashville, TN 2004), 130.
24. Martinez, J, Michael. *Life and Death in Civil War Prisons: A Story of Hardship, Horror and Extraordinary Courage* (Rutledge Hill Press: Nashville, TN 2004), 134.
25. Martinez, J, Michael. *Life and Death in Civil War Prisons: A Story of Hardship, Horror and Extraordinary Courage* (Rutledge Hill Press: Nashville, TN 2004), 140-141.
26. Martinez, J, Michael. *Life and Death in Civil War Prisons: A Story of Hardship, Horror and Extraordinary Courage* (Rutledge Hill Press: Nashville, TN 2004), 142-145.
27. Martinez, J, Michael. *Life and Death in Civil War Prisons: A Story of Hardship, Horror and Extraordinary Courage* (Rutledge Hill Press: Nashville, TN 2004), 182-183.
28. Martinez, J, Michael. *Life and Death in Civil War Prisons: A Story of Hardship, Horror and Extraordinary Courage* (Rutledge Hill Press: Nashville, TN 2004), 184.
29. Many sources existed for the Dix-Hill Cartel. The one cited here, and used for its great clarity, is Benjamin Gregory Cloyd's doctoral dissertation "Civil War Prisons in American History" (Dissertation Submitted to the Graduate Faculty of the Louisiana State University and Agricultural and Mechanical College in partial fulfillment of the requirements for the degree of Doctor of Philosophy, August 2005).

30. Cloyd, Benjamin Gregory. Doctoral dissertation "*Civil War Prisons in American History*" (Dissertation Submitted to the Graduate Faculty of the Louisiana State University and Agricultural and Mechanical College in partial fulfillment of the requirements for the degree of Doctor of Philosophy, August 2005), pp 1-22.

Chapter 4

World War II POWs

1. Iris Chang, *The Rape of Nanking: The Forgotten Holocaust of World War II* (New York, NY: Penguin Books), 1997. Chang's seminal work clearly illustrates the cruelty of the WWII Japanese military.
2. A war plan known as ORANGE was developed to stem what many in Washington, DC saw as very likely Japanese aggression and expansion in the region. Developed as the result of early pioneers into the Japanese interests, Marine Corps and naval Officers developed the strategy of island hopping as a means to get back lost islands; a term that eventually came to fruition in 1942 through 1945 as the Japanese were ejected by their Pacific bases—inch by inch, one island at the time. For an excellent resource on the planning for this eventuality, see Russell F. Weigley's *The American Way of War: A Military History of the United States Military Strategy and Policy* (Bloomington, Indiana: Indiana University Press, 1973), pages 269-311.
3. In his excellent book detailing experienced suffered while prisoners of the Japanese (*Prisoners of the Japanese: POWs of World War II in the Pacific:* New York, NY: Quill Press, 1994), Gavan Daws tells the story of these two contract

personnel as well as hundreds of other Marines, soldiers, and prisoners of war in the Pacific. A key book for understanding the Japanese military's treatment of POWs in this theater of war, many of this book's POWs' wartime recollections are borrowed from Daws' account.

4. Gavan Daws. *Prisoners of the Japanese: POWs of World War II in the Pacific* (New York, NY: Quill Press, 1995), 39.
5. Gavan Daws. *Prisoners of the Japanese: POWs of World War II in the Pacific* (New York, NY: Quill Press, 1995), 38-43.
6. Gavan Daws. *Prisoners of the Japanese: POWs of World War II in the Pacific* (New York, NY: Quill Press, 1995), 43-46.
7. Gavan Daws. *Prisoners of the Japanese: POWs of World War II in the Pacific* (New York, NY: Quill Press, 1995), 47.
8. Gavan Daws. *Prisoners of the Japanese: POWs of World War II in the Pacific* (New York, NY: Quill Press, 1995), 49.
9. Iris Chang. *The Rape of Nanking: The Forgotten Holocaust of World War II* (New York, NY: Penguin Books, 1997), 94-95.
10. Iris Chang. *The Rape of Nanking: The Forgotten Holocaust of World War II* (New York, NY: Penguin Books, 1997), picture insets pp 146-147. These pages also show many of the atrocities conducted by the Japanese in their rape of Nanking.

11. Gavan Daws. *Prisoners of the Japanese: POWs of World War II in the Pacific* (New York, NY: Quill Press, 1995), 111.
12. Gavan Daws. *Prisoners of the Japanese: POWs of World War II in the Pacific* (New York, NY: Quill Press, 1995), 131.
13. Gavan Daws. *Prisoners of the Japanese: POWs of World War II in the Pacific* (New York, NY: Quill Press, 1995), 140-148.
14. Gavan Daws. *Prisoners of the Japanese: POWs of World War II in the Pacific* (New York, NY: Quill Press, 1995), 275.
15. Gavan Daws. *Prisoners of the Japanese: POWs of World War II in the Pacific* (New York, NY: Quill Press, 1995), 300-305.
16. Gavan Daws. *Prisoners of the Japanese: POWs of World War II in the Pacific* (New York, NY: Quill Press, 1995), 303-332.
17. Gavan Daws. *Prisoners of the Japanese: POWs of World War II in the Pacific* (New York, NY: Quill Press, 1995), 340-341.
18. Gavan Daws. *Prisoners of the Japanese: POWs of World War II in the Pacific* (New York, NY: Quill Press, 1995), 342-345.
19. Gavan Daws. *Prisoners of the Japanese: POWs of World War II in the Pacific* (New York, NY: Quill Press, 1995), 343-345.
20. A copy of this work is issued as ISBN: 1-880875-28-4 but can also be retrieved at: http://74.6.238.254/search/

srpcache?ei=UTF-8&p=Researching+ Japanese+War+Crimes+Records&fr=yfp-t—892&u=http://cc.bingj.com/cache.aspx?q= Researching+ Japanese+War+Crimes+Records&d=4976849367597164&mkt=en-US&setlang=en-US&w=e4d03ef7,2671c554&icp=1&.intl=us&sig=T2Yvqj.nn6PVDUOaNmh9Jg—

21. Drea, Edward (and others). *Researching Japanese Wartime Records: Introductory Essays* (Washington, DC: Nazi War Crimes and Japanese Imperial Government Records Nazi War Crimes and Japanese Imperial Government Records Interagency Working Group Interagency Working Group), 6-7.
22. Drea, Edward (and others). *Researching Japanese Wartime Records: Introductory Essays* (Washington, DC: Nazi War Crimes and Japanese Imperial Government Records Nazi War Crimes and Japanese Imperial Government Records Interagency Working Group Interagency Working Group). See pages 1-2 of Chapter 2—*Documentary Evidence and Studies of Japanese War Crimes: An Interim Assessment*.
23. This story is retold using portions of Julie M. Phend and Stanley Edwards', Jr. *D-Day and Beyond: A True Story of Escape and POW Survival* (Shippensburg, PA: Burd Street Press), 2004.
24. This story is retold using portions of George Watt's *The Comet Connection: Escape from Hitler's Europe* (Lexington, KY: University Press of Kentucky), 1990.
25. Phend, Julie M. and Edwards, Stanley, Jr. *D-Day and Beyond: A True Story of Escape and POW Survival* (Shippensburg, PA: Burd Street Press, 2004), 1-34.

26. Phend, Julie M. and Edwards, Stanley, Jr. *D-Day and Beyond: A True Story of Escape and POW Survival* (Shippensburg, PA: Burd Street Press, 2004), 32-34.
27. Phend, Julie M. and Edwards, Stanley, Jr. *D-Day and Beyond: A True Story of Escape and POW Survival* (Shippensburg, PA: Burd Street Press, 2004), 40-47.
28. Phend, Julie M. and Edwards, Stanley, Jr. *D-Day and Beyond: A True Story of Escape and POW Survival* (Shippensburg, PA: Burd Street Press, 2004), 50-53.
29. Phend, Julie M. and Edwards, Stanley, Jr. *D-Day and Beyond: A True Story of Escape and POW Survival* (Shippensburg, PA: Burd Street Press, 2004), 60-69.
30. Phend, Julie M. and Edwards, Stanley, Jr. *D-Day and Beyond: A True Story of Escape and POW Survival* (Shippensburg, PA: Burd Street Press, 2004), 70-99.
31. Watt, George. *The Comet Connection: Escape from Hitler's Europe* (Lexington, KY: University Press of Kentucky, 1990), 21-26.
32. Watt, George. *The Comet Connection: Escape from Hitler's Europe* (Lexington, KY: University Press of Kentucky, 1990), 27.
33. Watt, George. *The Comet Connection: Escape from Hitler's Europe* (Lexington, KY: University Press of Kentucky, 1990), 39.
34. Watt, George. *The Comet Connection: Escape from Hitler's Europe* (Lexington, KY: University Press of Kentucky, 1990), 82.
35. Four books detailing these escape networks are Leo Heap's *The Evaders: The Story of the Most Amazing Escape of World*

War II (New York, NY: William Morrow and Company), 1976; George Watt's *The Comet Connection: Escape from Hitler's Europe* (Lexington, KY: University Press of Kentucky), 1990; Julie M. Phend and Stanley Edwards, Jr.'s *D-Day and Beyond: A True Story of Escape and POW Survival* (Shippensburg, PA: Burd Street Press), 2004; and finally, Frank Diggs' *Americans Behind the Barbed Wire: A Gripping World War II Memoir* (New York, NY: Simon & Schuster), 2000. Examples from these four books will be cited throughout the remainder of the chapter.

36. Drea, Edward (and others). *Researching Japanese Wartime Records: Introductory Essays* (Washington, DC: Nazi War Crimes and Japanese Imperial Government Records Nazi War Crimes and Japanese Imperial Government Records Interagency Working Group Interagency Working Group), 39.
37. Brunner, Joseph. *American Involvement in the Nuremberg War Crimes Trial Process*. Accessed online at: http://www.umich.edu/~historyj/pages_folder/articles/ American_Involvement_in_the_Nuremberg_War_Crimes_Trial_Process.pdf. Accessed on 17 Aug 2011.

CHAPTER 5

KOREAN WAR POWs

1. A copy of this Executive Order may be retrieved from.
2. Lewis H. Carlson's timeless work, *Remembered Prisoners of a Forgotten War: An Oral History of Korean War POWs* (New York, NY: St. Martins Griffin, 2002) will be used. Carlson's work is one of the top-shelf works on the war almost forgotten; worse yet, the POWs themselves have been forgotten.
3. Carlson, Lewis H. *Remembered Prisoners of a Forgotten War: An Oral History of Korean War POWs* (New York, NY: St. Martins Griffin, 2002), 23-25.
4. Carlson, Lewis H. *Remembered Prisoners of a Forgotten War: An Oral History of Korean War POWs* (New York, NY: St. Martins Griffin, 2002), 26.
5. Carlson, Lewis H. *Remembered Prisoners of a Forgotten War: An Oral History of Korean War POWs* (New York, NY: St. Martins Griffin, 2002), 25-26.
6. Carlson, Lewis H. *Remembered Prisoners of a Forgotten War: An Oral History of Korean War POWs* (New York, NY: St. Martins Griffin, 2002), 27.

7. Carlson, Lewis H. *Remembered Prisoners of a Forgotten War: An Oral History of Korean War POWs* (New York, NY: St. Martins Griffin, 2002), 27.
8. Carlson, Lewis H. *Remembered Prisoners of a Forgotten War: An Oral History of Korean War POWs* (New York, NY: St. Martins Griffin, 2002), 28.
9. Carlson, Lewis H. *Remembered Prisoners of a Forgotten War: An Oral History of Korean War POWs* (New York, NY: St. Martins Griffin, 2002), 28.
10. Carlson, Lewis H. *Remembered Prisoners of a Forgotten War: An Oral History of Korean War POWs* (New York, NY: St. Martins Griffin, 2002), 29.
11. Carlson, Lewis H. *Remembered Prisoners of a Forgotten War: An Oral History of Korean War POWs* (New York, NY: St. Martins Griffin, 2002), 32.
12. Carlson, Lewis H. *Remembered Prisoners of a Forgotten War: An Oral History of Korean War POWs* (New York, NY: St. Martins Griffin, 2002), 32.
13. Carlson, Lewis H. *Remembered Prisoners of a Forgotten War: An Oral History of Korean War POWs* (New York, NY: St. Martins Griffin, 2002), 33.
14. Carlson, Lewis H. *Remembered Prisoners of a Forgotten War: An Oral History of Korean War POWs* (New York, NY: St. Martins Griffin, 2002), 34-35.
15. Carlson, Lewis H. *Remembered Prisoners of a Forgotten War: An Oral History of Korean War POWs* (New York, NY: St. Martins Griffin, 2002), 35.

16. Carlson, Lewis H. *Remembered Prisoners of a Forgotten War: An Oral History of Korean War POWs* (New York, NY: St. Martins Griffin, 2002), 36.
17. Carlson, Lewis H. *Remembered Prisoners of a Forgotten War: An Oral History of Korean War POWs* (New York, NY: St. Martins Griffin, 2002), 37-38.
18. Carlson, Lewis H. *Remembered Prisoners of a Forgotten War: An Oral History of Korean War POWs* (New York, NY: St. Martins Griffin, 2002), 38.
19. United States Government. *Field Manual 34-52: Intelligence Interrogation* (Washington, DC: Government Printing Office, 1987), Appendix H, page H-0. In total, this field manual cites twenty different approach techniques; some variations of others, e.g., fear up/fear down, and most of the approaches can be used in combination with each other, depending on the weaknesses or vulnerabilities displayed by the prisoners. The 1987 as well as the later 1992 version were both cleared for public release, distribution unlimited. Later versions of this same field manual may also be found, but newer versions do not contain the Interrogator Approaches cited here.
20. United States Government. *Field Manual 34-52: Intelligence Interrogation* (Washington, DC: Government Printing Office, 1987), Appendix H, page H-0.
21. Carlson, Lewis H. *Remembered Prisoners of a Forgotten War: An Oral History of Korean War POWs* (New York, NY: St. Martins Griffin, 2002), 39-42.
22. Carlson, Lewis H. *Remembered Prisoners of a Forgotten War: An Oral History of Korean War POWs* (New York, NY: St. Martins Griffin, 2002), 44.

23. Carlson, Lewis H. *Remembered Prisoners of a Forgotten War: An Oral History of Korean War POWs* (New York, NY: St. Martins Griffin, 2002), 45-46.
24. Carlson, Lewis H. *Remembered Prisoners of a Forgotten War: An Oral History of Korean War POWs* (New York, NY: St. Martins Griffin, 2002), 47-48.
25. L.E. Hinkle, Jr. and H.G. Wolff wrote an article in the Bulletin for New York Academy of Medicine (*The Methods of Interrogation and Indoctrination Used by the Communist Police State*, Sept 1957, 33:9). Although this article contains information on by Russian and client states, a wealth of information about Chinese programs is also included.
26. Hinkle, Jr. L.E. and Wolff, H.G. *The Methods of Interrogation and Indoctrination Used by the Communist Police State* (New York, New York: The Bulletin for New York Academy of Medicine, 33:9, 1957), 601. The chart developed by the authors was used in parts; not all the periods of time displayed in the original were used.
27. Hinkle, Jr. L.E. and Wolff, H.G. *The Methods of Interrogation and Indoctrination Used by the Communist Police State* (New York, New York: The Bulletin for New York Academy of Medicine, 33:9, 1957), 603.
28. Hinkle, Jr. L.E. and Wolff, H.G. *The Methods of Interrogation and Indoctrination Used by the Communist Police State* (New York, New York: The Bulletin for New York Academy of Medicine, 33:9, 1957), 606-607.
29. U.S. Government. *Department of the Army Pamphlet 27-100-10, Military Law Review article: Barbed Wire*

Command: The Legal Nature of the Command Responsibilities of the Senior Prisoner in a Prisoner of War Camp written by Lieutenant Colonel Donald L. Manes, Jr. (Washington, DC: Government Printing Office, 1960), 3.

Chapter 6

Southeast Asia POWs

1. William J. Dukier, *Ho Chi Minh: A Life* (New York: Hyperion Press, 2000), 4.
2. Wray R. Johnson. *Vietnam and American Doctrine for Small Wars* (Bangkok, Thailand: White Lotus Press, 2001), 51.
3. U.S. Department of State. *Foreign Relations of the United States: Vietnam 1962* (Washington DC: GPO, 2002), 48-50.
4. United States Government. *Project CHECO Southeast Asia Report: Evasion and Escape, SEA 1964-1971* (Honolulu, HI: Pacific Air Forces), 1972. "Declassified IAW E.O. 12958 by the Air Force Declassification Office and Approved for Public Release." Accessed at http://handle.dtic.mil/100.2/ADA486749.
5. United States Government. *Project CHECO Southeast Asia Report: Joint Personnel Recovery in Southeast Asia* (Honolulu, HI: Pacific Air Forces), 1976. "Declassified IAW E.O. 12958 by the Air Force Declassification Office and Approved for Public Release." Accessed at.
6. Earl H. Tilford. The United States Air Force: Search and Rescue in Southeast1961-1975 Asia (Washington, DC: Office of Air Force History), 1992. Accessed on 24 May 2011 at:.

7. Everett Alvarez, Jr. Interview with the author conducted in Silver Springs, MD on 9 May 2011.
8. Everett Alvarez, Jr. and Anthony S. Pitch. *Chained Eagle: The True Heroic Story of Eight-and-one-half Years as a POW By the First American Shot Down Over North Vietnam* (New York, NY: Donald I. Fine, Inc, 1989), 20-24.
9. Everett Alvarez, Jr. and Anthony S. Pitch. *Chained Eagle: The True Heroic Story of Eight-and-one-half Years as a POW By the First American Shot Down Over North Vietnam* (New York, NY: Donald I. Fine, Inc, 1989), 25.
10. Everett Alvarez, Jr. and Anthony S. Pitch. *Chained Eagle: The True Heroic Story of Eight-and-one-half Years as a POW By the First American Shot Down Over North Vietnam* (New York, NY: Donald I. Fine, Inc, 1989), 26.
11. Everett Alvarez, Jr. and Anthony S. Pitch. *Chained Eagle: The True Heroic Story of Eight-and-one-half Years as a POW By the First American Shot Down Over North Vietnam* (New York, NY: Donald I. Fine, Inc, 1989), 27-30.
12. John G. Hubbell. *P.O.W.: A Definitive History of the American Prisoner of War Experience in Vietnam* (Lincoln, NE: iUniverse.com, Inc., 2000), 7-9.
13. John G. Hubbell. *P.O.W.: A Definitive History of the American Prisoner of War Experience in Vietnam* (Lincoln, NE: iUniverse.com, Inc., 2000), 45.
14. John G. Hubbell. *P.O.W.: A Definitive History of the American Prisoner of War Experience in Vietnam* (Lincoln, NE: iUniverse.com, Inc., 2000), 65-95.

15. John G. Hubbell. *P.O.W.: A Definitive History of the American Prisoner of War Experience in Vietnam* (Lincoln, NE: iUniverse.com, Inc., 2000), 220-226.
16. John G. Hubbell. *P.O.W.: A Definitive History of the American Prisoner of War Experience in Vietnam* (Lincoln, NE: iUniverse.com, Inc., 2000), 228-229.
17. Everett Alvarez, Jr. and Anthony S. Pitch. *Chained Eagle: The True Heroic Story of Eight-and-one-half Years as a POW By the First American Shot Down Over North Vietnam* (New York, NY: Donald I. Fine, Inc, 1989), 160-161.
18. Everett Alvarez, Jr. and Anthony S. Pitch. *Chained Eagle: The True Heroic Story of Eight-and-one-half Years as a POW By the First American Shot Down Over North Vietnam* (New York, NY: Donald I. Fine, Inc, 1989), 162-163.
19. Everett Alvarez, Jr. Interview with the author conducted in Silver Springs, MD on 9 May 2011.
20. Everett Alvarez, Jr. and Anthony S. Pitch. *Chained Eagle: The True Heroic Story of Eight-and-one-half Years as a POW By the First American Shot Down Over North Vietnam* (New York, NY: Donald I. Fine, Inc, 1989), 188-189.
21. Everett Alvarez, Jr. Interview with the author conducted in Silver Springs, MD on 9 May 2011.
22. Everett Alvarez, Jr. and Anthony S. Pitch. *Chained Eagle: The True Heroic Story of Eight-and-one-half Years as a POW By the First American Shot Down Over North Vietnam* (New York, NY: Donald I. Fine, Inc, 1989), 190-191.
23. Everett Alvarez, Jr. Interview with the author conducted in Silver Springs, MD on 9 May 2011.

24. Everett Alvarez, Jr. and Anthony S. Pitch. *Chained Eagle: The True Heroic Story of Eight-and-one-half Years as a POW By the First American Shot Down Over North Vietnam* (New York, NY: Donald I. Fine, Inc, 1989), 191-195.
25. Everett Alvarez, Jr. and Anthony S. Pitch. *Chained Eagle: The True Heroic Story of Eight-and-one-half Years as a POW By the First American Shot Down Over North Vietnam* (New York, NY: Donald I. Fine, Inc, 1989), 196.
26. Everett Alvarez, Jr. and Anthony S. Pitch. *Chained Eagle: The True Heroic Story of Eight-and-one-half Years as a POW By the First American Shot Down Over North Vietnam* (New York, NY: Donald I. Fine, Inc, 1989), 196.
27. Everett Alvarez, Jr. and Anthony S. Pitch. *Chained Eagle: The True Heroic Story of Eight-and-one-half Years as a POW By the First American Shot Down Over North Vietnam* (New York, NY: Donald I. Fine, Inc, 1989), 219-221.
28. Everett Alvarez, Jr. Interview with the author conducted in Silver Springs, MD on 9 May 2011.
29. Everett Alvarez, Jr. Interview with the author conducted in Silver Springs, MD on 9 May 2011.
30. Everett Alvarez, Jr. and Anthony S. Pitch. *Chained Eagle: The True Heroic Story of Eight-and-one-half Years as a POW By the First American Shot Down Over North Vietnam* (New York, NY: Donald I. Fine, Inc, 1989), 235-241.
31. Everett Alvarez, Jr. Interview with the author conducted in Silver Springs, MD on 9 May 2011
32. Everett Alvarez, Jr. Interview with the author conducted in Silver Springs, MD on 9 May 2011.

33. The Hanoi Hilton consisted of several smaller buildings and holding areas. These other cells or areas included Camp Unity, Little Vegas, Heartbreak Hotel, the Stockyard, and New Guy Village.
34. Everett Alvarez, Jr. Interview with the author conducted in Silver Springs, MD on 9 May 2011.
35. Cherry, Fred V. Personal Interview with the author in Silver Springs, MD. 9 Apr 2011.
36. Cherry, Fred V. Personal Interview with the author in Silver Springs, MD. 9 Apr 2011.
37. Cherry, Fred V. Personal Interview with the author in Silver Springs, MD. 9 Apr 2011.
38. "In 1941, the 2,900 acres of land about four miles north of Malden, Missouri, consisted of a few houses, barns, trees and lots of cotton fields. In late 1941, as the United States entered the war against Japan and Germany, the need for fighter pilots grew, as did the need for additional training facilities. The War Department purchased the property north of Malden and in the fall of 1942 construction began on Malden Army Airfield, the new installation of the Eastern Flying Training Command." Source: http://www.maaps.net/history.html. Accessed on 9 Apr 2011.
39. "Webb Air Force Base, previously named Big Spring Air Force Base, was a United States Air Force facility of the Air Training Command (ATC) that operated from 1951 to 1977 in west Texas within the current city limits of Big Spring. It was a major training facility, and by 1969 almost 9,000 pilots had been trained at Webb. The last wing was the 78th Flying Training Wing (78 FTW)." (Minor editing for

content). Source: http://en.wikipedia.org/wiki/Webb_Air_Force_Base. Accessed on 9 Apr 2011.

40. Cherry, Fred V. Personal Interview with the author in Silver Springs, MD. 9 Apr 2011.
41. See online source: http://en.wikipedia.org/wiki/F-84_Thunderjet. Accessed 12 May 2011.
42. Cherry, Fred V. Personal Interview with the author in Silver Springs, MD. 9 Apr 2011.
43. Cherry, Fred V. Personal Interview with the author in Silver Springs, MD. 9 Apr 2011.
44. Cherry, Fred V. Personal Interview with the author in Silver Springs, MD. 9 Apr 2011.
45. Cherry had had previous combat tours in the Korean War but had also done a tour of duty in Vietnam, flying out of Thailand (1964-1965).
46. Cherry, Fred V. Personal Interview with the author in Silver Springs, MD. 9 Apr 2011.
47. "Mark 81 Snakeye fitted with a Mark 14 TRD (Tail Retarding Device) to increase the bomb's drag after release. The bomb's increased air-time, coupled with its (relatively) forgiving safe drop envelope, allowed for very low-level bombing runs at slower speed. Used commonly in the close air support (CAS) role in Vietnam (prior to wider availability of GBU precision ordnance). Nicknamed "snake", as in the typical Vietnam CAS loadout of "snake and nape" (250-lb. Mk-81 Snakeye bombs and 500-lb. M-47 napalm canisters)." Ref: http://en.wikipedia.org/wiki/Mark_81_bomb Accessed on 10 Apr 2011.

48. Cluster munitions, cluster bombs or sub-munitions are air-dropped or ground-launched explosive weapons that eject smaller munitions: a cluster of bomblets. The most common types are designed to kill enemy personnel and destroy vehicles." Source: http://en.wikipedia.org/wiki/Cluster_bomb Accessed on 10 Apr 2011.
49. Cherry, Fred V. Personal Interview with the author in Silver Springs, MD. 9 Apr 2011.
50. Cherry, Fred V. Personal Interview with the author in Silver Springs, MD. 9 Apr 2011.
51. Cherry, Fred V. Personal Interview with the author in Silver Springs, MD. 9 Apr 2011.
52. Cherry, Fred V. Personal Interview with the author in Silver Springs, MD. 9 Apr 2011.
53. During this period, some American POWs got themselves released early through unauthorized deals with the VC—typically by signing papers agreeing that the war was wrong, that they were war criminals, and the like. In some cases, these POWs, known to the rest of the POWs as progressives, snitched or performed actions that went against the Code of Conduct, and in some cases, were in violation of the Uniformed Code of Military Justice.
54. "Uncle Tom is a derogatory term for a member of a low-status group who is overly subservient with authority, or a black person who behaves in a subservient manner to white people." Source: http://en.wikipedia.org/wiki/Uncle_tom. Accessed on 10 Apr 2011. Although not used as much in current times, this term was common in the South prior to the mid-seventies.

55. Cherry, Fred V. Personal Interview with the author in Silver Springs, MD. 9 Apr 2011.
56. Cherry, Fred V. Personal Interview with the author in Silver Springs, MD. 11 Apr 2011.
57. James N. Rowe. *The True Story of a Vietnam POW, James N. Rowe: Five Years to Freedom* (New York, NY: Ballantine Books, 1971), 3-21.
58. James N. Rowe. *The True Story of a Vietnam POW, James N. Rowe: Five Years to Freedom* (New York, NY: Ballantine Books, 1971), 80-82.
59. James N. Rowe. *The True Story of a Vietnam POW, James N. Rowe: Five Years to Freedom* (New York, NY: Ballantine Books, 1971), 82-87.
60. James N. Rowe. *The True Story of a Vietnam POW, James N. Rowe: Five Years to Freedom* (New York, NY: Ballantine Books, 1971), 90-130.
61. James N. Rowe. The *The True Story of a Vietnam POW, James N. Rowe: Five Years to Freedom* (New York, NY: Ballantine Books, 1971), 112.
62. James N. Rowe. *The True Story of a Vietnam POW, James N. Rowe: Five Years to Freedom* (New York, NY: Ballantine Books, 1971), 113.
63. James N. Rowe. *The True Story of a Vietnam POW, James N. Rowe: Five Years to Freedom* (New York, NY: Ballantine Books, 1971), 119.
64. James N. Rowe. *The True Story of a Vietnam POW, James N. Rowe: Five Years to Freedom* (New York, NY: Ballantine Books, 1971), 405.

65. Retrieved from the POW Network's online site: http://www.pownetwork. org/bios/h/h135.htm. Accessed on 16 April 2011.
66. Stuart I. Rochester and Frederick Kiley. *Honor Bound: American Prisoners of War in Southeast Asia, 1961-1973* (Annapolis, MD: Naval Institute Press, 1999), 347.
67. The three referenced POWs were released on February 16, 1968 when three Americans, against the orders of the SRO and other officers, accepted their early release from captivity. See page 366 of *Honor Bound: American Prisoners of War in Southeast Asia, 1961-1973* (Annapolis, MD: Naval Institute Press, 1999). There were 12 POWs who accepted early release during the war in Southeast Asia; only one POW was authorized by the SRO to take such a release—US Navy Douglas Hegdahl. Hegdahl had remembered the names of over two hundred POWs, some of which had not been yet confirmed as live POWs.
68. Stuart I. Rochester and Frederick Kiley. *Honor Bound: American Prisoners of War in Southeast Asia, 1961-1973* (Annapolis, MD: Naval Institute Press, 1999), 278.
69. Tom Hanton. Phone interview with the author on 11 May 2011.
70. Tom Hanton. Phone interview with the author on 11 May 2011.
71. Karst is defined as "An area of irregular limestone in which erosion has produced fissures, sinkholes, underground streams, and caverns." Accessed at : http://www. answers. com/topic/karst#ixzz1M5jAbzv2 on 11 May 2011.

72. Tom Hanton. Phone interview with the author on 11 May 2011.
73. Tom Hanton. Phone interview with the author on 11 May 2011.
74. Clark Air Force Base in the Philippines stepped up its jungle survival school in 1965 due to the heightening of the air war in Vietnam. For more on this, see page 14 of the *CHECO Report: Evasion and Escape, SEA 1964-1971* (Honolulu, HI: Pacific Air Forces), 1972. "Declassified IAW E.O. 12958 by the Air Force Declassification Office and Approved for Public Release." and was accessed at http://handle.dtic.mil/100.2 /ADA486749.
75. Tom Hanton. Phone interview with the author on 11 May 2011.
76. Tom Hanton. Phone interview with the author on 11 May 2011.
77. Bill Wilson. Phone conversation with the author on 22 May 2011.
78. Bill Wilson. Personal correspondence with the author dated 19 May 2011.
79. Bill Wilson. Personal correspondence with the author dated 22 May 2011. Call signs are assigned to aircraft as a part of each air tasking order, which assigns aircraft their missions, contains refueling information, and who will be controlling them on their way to (or from) their target area. In this case, the F111-A they were flying was code named Jackal 33. To designate which crewmembers they are on the radio, the aircrew members each assume this call sign with a letter following the call sign indicating their position. In this case,

Sponeybarger was the pilot; Jackal 33A, his weapons system operator; and Wilson was assigned Jackal 33B. If there had been two more people on this aircraft, their call signs would have been Jackal 33C and Jackal 33D.

80. Bill Wilson. Personal correspondence with the author dated 19 May 2011.
81. Bill Wilson. Personal correspondence with the author dated 19 May 2011.
82. Bill Wilson. Personal correspondence with the author dated 19 May 2011.
83. Bill Wilson. Personal correspondence with the author dated 19 May 2011.
84. Bill Wilson. Phone conversation with the author on 22 May 2011. Wilson communicated to the author that later safety personnel were investigating the cause of this mishap. The aircraft was not shot down—some believe one of the bombs dropped from this aircraft detonated prematurely after being released from the airplane.
85. Bill Wilson. Interview with the author on 21 May 2011.
86. Bill Wilson. Interview with the author on 21 May 2011.
87. Bill Wilson. Personal correspondence received by the author dated 22 May 2011. This portion of the story used with permission from Bill Wilson.
88. Bill Wilson. Personal correspondence received by the author dated 22 May 2011.
89. Bill Wilson. Personal correspondence received by the author dated 22 May 2011.

90. See http://www.associatedcontent.com/article/484209/christmas_movies_ of_1972.html. Accessed on 24 May 2011.
91. SANDY is a call sign assigned to aircraft or pilots specially trained in controlling the airspace and directing the actions of evaders on the ground. At this time, Wilson's SANDY aircraft were A-7 jets; however, earlier in the war in Southeast Asia; SANDY aircraft were A-1 Skyraiders, a single engine propeller-powered airplane designed just after World War II. Evaders are especially fortunate when they talk to SANDY aircraft, because it is these same aircraft that will vector the rescue helicopters into the evaders' location to pick them up, as well as provide suppressive fires if enemy forces are too close to the survivor.
92. Bill Wilson. Personal correspondence received by the author dated 22 May 2011.
93. Linebacker was a series of operations in late 1972 designed to convince the North Vietnamese to come to agree to a negotiated peace settlement at the Paris Peace Accords. During follow-up operations known as Linebacker II, occurring between December 18 and 24, and again resuming on December 26 through 29, US aircraft continued their operations in North Vietnam. Although US military bombing was centered on military targets on the outskirts of Hanoi, the international press claimed that the US had killed an inordinate number of civilians in the ruthless campaign they claimed was reminiscent of the World War II raids on the industrial center in Central Germany called the Ruhr.

94. Bill Wilson. Personal correspondence received by the author dated 22 May 2011.
95. Bill Wilson. Personal correspondence received by the author dated 22 May 2011. This portion of the story used with permission from Mr. Bill Wilson. Some very minor editing for clarification.
96. Bill Wilson. Interview with the author on 21 May 2011.
97. Bill Wilson. Interview with the author on 21 May 2011.
98. Jim and Sybil Stockdale. *In Love and War* (Annapolis, MD: Naval Institute Press), (Revised, 1990).
99. Jim and Sybil Stockdale. *In Love and War* (Annapolis, MD: Naval Institute Press), (Revised, 1990), 295-300.
100. Jim and Sybil Stockdale. *In Love and War* (Annapolis, MD: Naval Institute Press), (Revised, 1990), 296-297.
101. Jim and Sybil Stockdale. *In Love and War* (Annapolis, MD: Naval Institute Press), (Revised, 1990), 301.
102. International Committee of the Red Cross. The Geneva Conventions of August 12 1949 (Reprint). (Geneva Switzerland: International Committee of the Red Cross, 1983), 4. The version cited is a 1983 reprint of the 1949 document.
103. International Committee of the Red Cross. The Geneva Conventions of August 12 1949 (Reprint). (Geneva Switzerland: International Committee of the Red Cross, 1983), 76-88.
104. The International Committee for the Red Cross's site (at http://www.icrc.org/ihl.nsf /NORM/3092893761F8 178BC1256402003F9940?OpenDocument) contains these exceptions. Moreover, the North Vietnamese (the Democratic

Republic of Vietnam) declared that the American POWs were war criminals since no formal war had been declared.

105. While the Hanoi Hilton is spoken of as a single unit, there are actually smaller buildings and areas within it. These sub-parts of Hanoi Hilton include: Camp Unity, Little Vegas, Heartbreak Hotel, Stock Yard, and New Guy Village. The names are not romantic as some might imply. For example, Heartbreak Hotel is a small compound with seven separate rooms—exclusively used for torture and interrogations.

Chapter 7

First Gulf War POWs (Desert Shield / Desert Storm)

1. United States Government. *National Security Directive 45: US Policy in Response to the Iraqi Invasion of Kuwait* (Washington, DC: The White House, 1990.) The referenced copy is a declassified copy accessed on 4 Feb 2011 at http://www.gwu.edu/ ~nsarchiv/ NSAEBB/NSAEBB39/ document2.pdf
2. One such SERE course was the U.S. Army Special Forces SERE School at Ft. Bragg, NC. This course, just over two weeks in length, consisted of academic classroom training, field training (where the students learned and practiced field craft), a field evasion exercise, and a resistance training exercise. The author attended this course in the spring of 1986 while the Intelligence Chief of the 2nd Reconnaissance Battalion, 2nd Marine Division, in Camp Lejeune, North Carolina.
3. Speicher's remains were located and recovered during July 2010 during a sensitive site exploitation, near where it was believed he first was declared missing in 1991.

4. This information was extracted form the Defense Prisoner of War Missing Personnel Office (DPMO) "Desert Storm Captives/Unaccounted—for" document accessed at: http://www.dtic.mil/dpmo/gulf_war/documents/IRAQI05B.pdf on 4 Feb 2011.
5. Cynthia Acree and Col Cliff Acree, USMC (Ret). *The Gulf Between Us: A Story of Love and Survival in Desert Storm* (Washington, DC: Brassey's Inc, 2001), 2.
6. Cynthia Acree and Col Cliff Acree, USMC (Ret). *The Gulf Between Us: A Story of Love and Survival in Desert Storm* (Washington, DC: Brassey's Inc, 2001), 3.
7. Cynthia Acree and Col Cliff Acree, USMC (Ret). *The Gulf Between Us: A Story of Love and Survival in Desert Storm* (Washington, DC: Brassey's, Inc, 2001), 8-11.
8. Cynthia Acree and Col Cliff Acree, USMC (Ret). *The Gulf Between Us: A Story of Love and Survival in Desert Storm* (Washington, DC: Brassey's, Inc, 2001), 19.
9. Cynthia Acree and Col Cliff Acree, USMC (Ret). *The Gulf Between Us: A Story of Love and Survival in Desert Storm* (Washington, DC: Brassey's, Inc, 2001), 60-63.
10. Cynthia Acree and Col Cliff Acree, USMC (Ret). *The Gulf Between Us: A Story of Love and Survival in Desert Storm* (Washington, DC: Brassey's, Inc, 2001), 74-75.
11. Cynthia Acree and Col Cliff Acree, USMC (Ret). *The Gulf Between Us: A Story of Love and Survival in Desert Storm* (Washington, DC: Brassey's, Inc, 2001), 75.
12. Cynthia Acree and Col Cliff Acree, USMC (Ret). *The Gulf Between Us: A Story of Love and Survival in Desert Storm* (Washington, DC: Brassey's, Inc, 2001), 75

13. Cynthia Acree and Col Cliff Acree, USMC (Ret). *The Gulf Between Us: A Story of Love and Survival in Desert Storm* (Washington, DC: Brassey's, Inc, 2001), 79-83.
14. Interrogations are done with planning and forethought. Professional interrogators will study their captives' military records, family lives, military histories, and often their equipment—in this case, the OV-10 Bronco aircraft. Likewise, interrogators will read transcripts or notes from previous interrogations, noting responses to previous lines of questioning. This allows them to confirm, from previous questioning, what the prisoners have recounted—and in many cases, permits the interrogator to judge the accuracy of the information given, since they know that under duress and adverse conditions, prisoners will try to deceive them.
15. Cynthia Acree and Col Cliff Acree, USMC (Ret). *The Gulf Between Us: A Story of Love and Survival in Desert Storm* (Washington, DC: Brassey's, Inc, 2001), 84.
16. Anderson Cooper 360° Interview "Al Qaeda Still Intent on Attack U.S. Mainland; Interview with Col. Clifford Acree, a tortured Desert Storm POW." Aired February 16, 2005. Transcripts accessed by author on 4 Feb 2011 at http:// transcripts.cnn. Com /TRANSCRIPTS/0502/16/acd.01. html
17. Cynthia Acree and Col Cliff Acree, USMC (Ret). *The Gulf Between Us: A Story of Love and Survival in Desert Storm* (Washington, DC: Brassey's, Inc, 2001), 127.
18. Cynthia Acree and Col Cliff Acree, USMC (Ret). *The Gulf Between Us: A Story of Love and Survival in Desert Storm* (Washington, DC: Brassey's, Inc, 2001), 147-149.

19. Cynthia Acree and Col Cliff Acree, USMC (Ret). *The Gulf Between Us: A Story of Love and Survival in Desert Storm* (Washington, DC: Brassey's, Inc, 2001), 181.
20. Cynthia Acree and Col Cliff Acree, USMC (Ret). *The Gulf Between Us: A Story of Love and Survival in Desert Storm* (Washington, DC: Brassey's, Inc, 2001), 196-197.
21. Cynthia Acree and Col Cliff Acree, USMC (Ret). *The Gulf Between Us: A Story of Love and Survival in Desert Storm* (Washington, DC: Brassey's, Inc, 2001), 210-213.
22. This was the exact same sentiment and caution expressed by the POWs reintegrated from North Vietnam during the period February-April 1973 during OPERATION HOME COMING. Many of the prisoners released in 1973 refused to smile or show emotion until they were onboard the US aircraft that carried them to freedom.
23. Cynthia Acree and Col Cliff Acree, USMC (Ret). *The Gulf Between Us: A Story of Love and Survival in Desert Storm* (Washington, DC: Brassey's, Inc, 2001), 220-223.
24. Cynthia Acree and Col Cliff Acree, USMC (Ret). Personal interview with the author. 24 Apr 2011. The use of shadow or escort officers during DESERT STORM greatly contributed to the overall success of the program. Such escorts assisted the returning POWs with small tasks, which in turn allowed the returnees to focus on the reintegration process and their families.
25. Cynthia Acree and Col Cliff Acree, USMC (Ret). *The Gulf Between Us: A Story of Love and Survival in Desert Storm* (Washington, DC: Brassey's, Inc, 2001), 227-229.

26. Cynthia Acree and Col Cliff Acree, USMC (Ret). Personal interview with the author. 24 Apr 2011.
27. Cynthia Acree and Col Cliff Acree, USMC (Ret). Personal interview with the author. 24 Apr 2011.
28. Cynthia Acree and Col Cliff Acree, USMC (Ret). Personal interview with the author. 24 Apr 2011. This comment was made by Cindy during our interview.
29. Cynthia Acree and Col Cliff Acree, USMC (Ret). Personal interview with the author. 24 Apr 2011.
30. Cynthia Acree and Col Cliff Acree, USMC (Ret). Personal interview with the author. 24 Apr 2011. This comment was made by Cindy during our interview.
31. Peter Grier. *Call From the Desert* (*Air Force Magazine*: Feb 2011). Accessed on 27 April 2011. The complete article is available at: http://www.airforce-magazine.com/MagazineArchive /Pages/ 2011/ February%20 2011/0211desert.aspx. Peter Grier is a Washington, DC-based editor for the *Christian Science Monitor* and a longtime defense correspondent and contributor to *Air Force Magazine*.
32. William (Bill) Andrews. Interview with the author at National Defense University (Washington, DC) on 1 June 2011.
33. Phillip Cadet Wilkinson. Interview with Col Bill Andrews on 15 March 2008 while at the National Defense University (page 9). This interview may be accessed at http://www.vmi.edu/ archives.aspx?id=22241.
34. Peter Grier. *Call From the Desert* (Air Force Magazine: Feb 2011). Accessed on 27 April 2011. The complete article is available at: http://www.airforce-magazine.

com/MagazineArchive /Pages/ 2011/ February%20 2011/0211desert.aspx.

35. Peter Grier. *Call From the Desert* (Air Force Magazine: Feb 2011). Accessed on 27 April 2011. The complete article is available at: http://www.airforce-magazine.com/MagazineArchive /Pages/ 2011/ February%20 2011/0211desert.aspx.
36. Rhonda Cornum later wrote a book about her experiences as a Gulf War POW, *She Went to War* (New York, NY: Ballantine Books, 1992). Today Cornum is still on active duty in the US Army, currently a Brigadier General in the US Army serving in the Washington, DC area.
37. Peter Grier. *Call From the Desert* (*Air Force Magazine*: Feb 2011). Accessed on 27 April 2011. The complete article is available at: http://www.airforce-magazine.com/MagazineArchive /Pages/ 2011/ February%20 2011/0211desert.aspx.
38. Peter Grier. *Call From the Desert* (*Air Force Magazine*: Feb 2011). Accessed on 27 April 2011. The complete article is available at: http://www.airforce-magazine.com/MagazineArchive /Pages/ 2011/ February%20 2011/0211desert.aspx.
39. Phillip Cadet Wilkerson. Interview with Colonel Bill Andrews on 15 March 2008 while at the National Defense University (pages 12-13). This interview may be accessed at http://www.vmi.edu/ archives.aspx?id=22241.
40. William (Bill) Andrews. Interview with the author at National Defense University (Washington, DC) on 1 June 2011.

41. William (Bill) Andrews. Interview with the author at National Defense University (Washington, DC) on 1 June 2011.
42. For more information on this site's activities, see their home page at: http://www.med.navy.mil/sites/navmedmpte/nomi/rpow/Pages/default.aspx. Accessed on 24 April 2011.
43. William (Bill) Andrews. Interview with the author at National Defense University (Washington, DC) on 1 June 2011.

Chapter 8

Post Cold War Asymmetric Prisoners, Detainees, And Hostages

1. One such school is the U.S. Air Force Special Air Warfare School's Dynamic of International Terrorism Course taught at Hulbert Field Florida (see: http://www.afsoc.af.mil/usafsos/). Another such course is the U.S. Army's Individual Terrorism Awareness Course as taught by the John F. Kennedy Special Warfare Center at Fort Bragg, NC. The author attended these courses during the mid-eighties and one in 1991. One was a mobile training team in Camp Lejeune, North Carolina (1984), the others were held in various DOD facilities in the United States.
2. Soviet Special Forces, are called Spetznaz and are similar in training and capabilities to U.S. Special Forces. These personnel received the best of the Soviets' equipment, training and, perhaps most importantly, the money to train in manners that supported the often Top Secret missions they were sent on.
3. See http://armylive.dodlive.mil/index.php/2010/09/operation-new-dawn/.

4. See http://www.nytimes.com/2007/11/22/world/middleeast/22fighters.html
5. See http://www.army.mil/features/507thMaintCmpy/ for a short as well as full-length unclassified description of this event.
6. See http://www.cbsnews.com/stories/2004/09/21/iraq/main644707.shtml
7. United States Government. *Part Two, Rules of Land Warfare, Basic Field Manual, Volume VII, Military Law* (Washington, DC: United States Government Printing Office), 1934.
8. A CNN article provides the basics on this long and frustrating case. See: http://articles.cnn.com/2011-03-04/politics/robert.levinson_1_levinson-family-christine-levinson-dawud-salahuddin?_s=PM:POLITICS. Accessed on 24 April 2011.
9. A CNN article provides the basics on this long and frustrating case.See: http://articles.cnn.com/2011-03-04/politics/robert.levinson_1_levinson-family-christine-levinson-dawud-salahuddin?_s=PM:POLITICS. Accessed on 24 April 2011. The reader can also see the following links: First, the main Bob Levinson website can be found at http://www.helpboblevinson.com/. In addition to this site, many new and good articles exist that provide more insight into our government's attempts at securing more information: http://results.myway.com/redirect.jhtml?searchfor=robert+levinson+AND+iran&cb=YH&ptnrS=YH&qid=b6b49a5c78e6c38d2bc50de10cd42125&action=pick&ss=&pn=1&st=bar&si=&pg=GGmain&ord=6&redirect=mPWsrdz9heamc8iHEhldEdx5UcB0SKKr18k%2BERefX2xUqOe%2BhZXaSOWq48MRVTMw5OyoOZPbnKY2Tqyg%

2FLRVCXAIQdETkiLtTu09UYEKoFk5k3K9KDdN7yzBuDhm2zOKwmPZPD7RKtj0KNJD2wT%2FxlN0IeryhQY%2BRWBOKlfXn3O%2B6pGObXJf1JJwpz%2F88EK3&tpr=&ct=AR;One article speaks to Levinson being held in an Iranian jail which some believe to be Evin Prison, known for holding political prisoners. See: http://www.telegraph.co.uk/news/worldnews/wikileaks/8299292/WikiLeaks-Vanished-FBI-officer-Robert-Levinson-held-by-Iranian-Revolutionary-Guards.html.

10. Haleh Esfandiari. *My Prison, My Home* (New York, NY: Harper Collins, 2009), 1-14.
11. Haleh Esfandiari. *My Prison, My Home* (New York, NY: Harper Collins, 2009), 10-53.
12. Haleh Esfandiari. *My Prison, My Home* (New York, NY: Harper Collins, 2009), 65.
13. Haleh Esfandiari. *My Prison, My Home* (New York, NY: Harper Collins, 2009), 121.
14. Haleh Esfandiari. *My Prison, My Home* (New York, NY: Harper Collins, 2009), 132.
15. Haleh Esfandiari. *My Prison, My Home* (New York, NY: Harper Collins, 2009), 155-157.
16. Haleh Esfandiari. *My Prison, My Home* (New York, NY: Harper Collins, 2009), 158.
17. Marc Gonsalves, Keith Stansell, and Tom Howes. *Out of Captivity: Surviving the 1967 Days in the Colombian Jungle* (New York, NY: Harper Collins Publishers, 2009), back sleeve.

18. Marc Gonsalves, Keith Stansell, and Tom Howes. *Out of Captivity: Surviving the 1967 Days in the Colombian Jungle* (New York, NY: Harper Collins Publishers, 2009), xv.
19. Marc Gonsalves, Keith Stansell, and Tom Howes. *Out of Captivity: Surviving the 1967 Days in the Colombian Jungle* (New York, NY: Harper Collins Publishers, 2009), 16-17.
20. Marc Gonsalves, Keith Stansell, and Tom Howes. *Out of Captivity: Surviving the 1967 Days in the Colombian Jungle* (New York, NY: Harper Collins Publishers, 2009), 30.
21. Roy Hallums' story is told through references to his post-captivity book: Roy Hallums. *Buried Alive: The True Story of Kidnapping, Captivity, and a Dramatic Rescue* (Nashville, TN: Thomas Nelson Publishing, 2009).
22. One such example was the very graphic murder of an American hostage, Nicholas Berg, who was beheaded by Al Qaeda in Iraq (known as AQI). In this case, the death of Mr. Berg was blamed on the Americans' treatment of prisoners held by coalition forces at Abu Ghraib Prison near Baghdad. This video and report can be seen at: http://www.foxnews.com/story/0,2933,119615,00.html. Accessed on 23 April 2011.
23. Roy Hallums. *Buried Alive: The True Story of Kidnapping, Captivity, and a Dramatic Rescue* (Nashville, TN: Thomas Nelson Publishing, 2009), 1-12.
24. Roy Hallums. *Buried Alive: The True Story of Kidnapping, Captivity, and a Dramatic Rescue* (Nashville, TN: Thomas Nelson Publishing, 2009), 13-24.

25. Roy Hallums. *Buried Alive: The True Story of Kidnapping, Captivity, and a Dramatic Rescue* (Nashville, TN: Thomas Nelson Publishing, 2009), 25-173.
26. Roy Hallums. *Buried Alive: The True Story of Kidnapping, Captivity, and a Dramatic Rescue* (Nashville, TN: Thomas Nelson Publishing, 2009), 193. On the occasion of the negotiated release of one of those held with Hallums, the Filipino was immediately asked, "What happened to Roy?" This was several months into the hostage event and was the first confirmation that Roy was still alive.
27. Roy Hallums. *Buried Alive: The True Story of Kidnapping, Captivity, and a Dramatic Rescue* (Nashville, TN: Thomas Nelson Publishing, 2009), 201-244.
28. United States Government. Secretary of Defense, Washington DC "Public Affairs Guidance (PAG) for DOD Support to the Code of Conduct/Survival, Evasion, Resistance, and Escape (SERE) Training Schools" (Washington, DC: Pentagon), 2002. Issued as an official message with a date-time group of "R 282300Z May 02".
29. United States Government. Secretary of Defense, Washington DC "Public Affairs Guidance (PAG) for DOD Support to the Code of Conduct/Survival, Evasion, Resistance, and Escape (SERE) Training Schools" (Washington, DC: Pentagon), 2002. Issued as an official message with a date-time group of "R 282300Z May 02". Paragraph 4.
30. United States Government. Secretary of Defense, Washington DC "Public Affairs Guidance (PAG) for DOD Support to the Code of Conduct/Survival, Evasion, Resistance, and Escape (SERE) Training Schools" (Washington, DC: Pentagon),

2002. Issued as an official message with a date-time group of "R 282300Z May 02". Paragraph 5.A. 2.

31. United States Government. Secretary of Defense, Washington DC "Public Affairs Guidance (PAG) for DOD Support to the Code of Conduct/Survival, Evasion, Resistance, and Escape (SERE) Training Schools" (Washington, DC: Pentagon), 2002. Issued as an official message with a date-time group of "R 282300Z May 02". Paragraph 5.A.4.
32. United States Government. Secretary of Defense, Washington DC "Public Affairs Guidance (PAG) for DOD Support to the Code of Conduct/Survival, Evasion, Resistance, and Escape (SERE) Training Schools" (Washington, DC: Pentagon), 2002. Issued as an official message with a date-time group of "R 282300Z May 02". Paragraph 5.A.9.
33. United States Government. *Department of Defense Instruction 1300.21 (Code of Conduct (CoC) Training and Education*) (Washington, DC: Government Printing Office, 2001), page 3. This document was downloaded from the World Wide Web at http://www.dtic.mil/whs/directives/corres/pdf/130021p.pdf. Accessed on 23 April 2011. See specifically paragraph 4.4.
34. United States Government. *Department of Defense Instruction 3020.41 (Contractor Personnel Authorized to Accompany the U.S. Armed Forces)* (Washington, DC: Government Printing Office, 2001), page 3. This document was downloaded from the World Wide Web at http://www.dtic.mil/whs/directives/corres/pdf/302041p.pdf. Accessed on 23 April 2011. See specifically paragraphs 4.2, 4.3 and 4.4.

Chapter 9

An Analysis Of The Captivity Environment

1. E. J. Hunter. The *Vietnam POW Veteran: Immediate and Long Term Effects of Captivity* (San Diego, CA: Naval Health Research Center), 1977.
2. Mary A. Anderson (CAPT, Medical Corps, USN). *Captivity and Culture: Insights from the Desert Storm Prisoner of War Experience* (Newport, RI: Naval War College), 1996.
3. Andrews, William (Bill). Interview with the author at National Defense University (Washington, DC) on 1 June 2011. These comments were passed on to Bill Andrews from a former Vietnam POW, Gene Smith.
4. Mary A. Anderson (CAPT, Medical Corps, USN). *Captivity and Culture: Insights from the Desert Storm Prisoner of War Experience* (Newport, RI: Naval War College), 1996.
5. United States Government. *Field Manual 34-3, Intelligence Analysis* (Washington, DC: GPO), 1990.
6. In military terminology, cover is protection from enemy fire while concealment is protection from enemy observation.

7. Found on the Joint Center for Operational Analysis at: http://www.jfcom.mil/ about/fac_jcoa.htm. Accessed on 19 May 2011.
8. Chairman's Instruction 3150.25A, accessed at http://www.dtic.mil/doctrine/jel/cjcsd /cjcsi/3150_25a.pdf on 19 May 2011.
9. Taken from http://www.history.army.mil/html/faq/oaths.html. Accessed on 14 May 2011.
10. Taken from http://www.cnrc.navy.mil/DEP/oath.htm. Accessed on 14 May 2011.
11. This misconduct before the enemy was relayed to the author by several former POWs from the war in Southeast Asia. Likewise, Stuart Rochester's *Honor Bound* (pages 202, 210, 249-250, 274, 276, 378, 440, 478, 563, and 568) contain information of misconduct or collaboration with the enemy. Although the reasons vary according to exact circumstances, it is believed that a major reason personnel were not court martialed upon their return to the United States was the prevalent thought that America needed to get this war behind us.
12. Extracted from US Joint Forces Command information page located at: http://www.jfcom.mil/ about/fact_jopesfm.htm Accessed on 15 May 2011.
13. One such school is the U.S. Air Force Special Air Warfare School's Dynamic of International Terrorism Course taught at Hulbert Field, Florida (see: http://www.afsoc.af.mil/usafsos/). Another such course is the U.S. Army's Individual Terrorism Awareness Course taught by the John F. Kennedy Special Warfare Center at Fort Bragg, NC. The author attended some of these courses during the mid-eighties,

and one in 1991. One was a mobile training team in Camp Lejeune, North Carolina (1984); the others were in various DOD facilities in the United States.

14. Extracts from a hometown news article about the awarding of the Purple Heart Medal to the aging Gordon. "Vet given medal decades after service: Barrow man receives purple heart in surprise ceremony" Source: http://onlineathens.com/stories/041306/ news_20060413047.shtml. Accessed on 17 May 2011.
15. Virgil Gordon, then a Sergeant in the Army Air Corps (Service Number 34445447) whose POW period is recorded at: http://aad.archives.gov/aad/display-partial-records.jsp?f=645&mtch=1&q=virgil+gordon& cat= WR26&dt=466&tf=F&bc=sl
16. The Mitchell Center for Returning POWs is found at: http://www.med.navy.mil/sites /navmedmpte /nomi/rpow/Pages/default.aspx. Accessed on 18 May 2011.
17. Several online resources discuss these specially selected and trained personnel—some in a positive light, others in a more negative view. These sources include: 1) "Welcome from the Jungle Psychological Perspectives on Reintegration" found at: http://www.shadowspear.com/vb/threads/welcome-from-the-jungle-psychological-perspectives-on-reintegration.3734/ (accessed on 18 May 2011); 2) An article citing a former JPRA SERE Psychologist, "SERE Psychologist Dissented" found at http://washingtonindependent.com/972/sere-psychologist-dissented (accessed on 18 May 2011); 3) Headquarters, US Marine Corps criteria for debriefings—part of which

discusses using JPRA SERE Psychologists—found at: http://hqinet001.hqmc.usmc.mil/ pp&o/POE/ POE-301/Documents/JPRA%20EAI%20-%20Handling %20Guidance% 20for%20Recovered,%20Returned,%20 and%20Rep.doc (accessed on 18 May 2011); 4) US Army Womack Medical Center discusses medical qualifications for SERE Psychologists at: http://www.wamc.amedd. army.mil/dme/GME/res/ dbh/coprp/Pages /elig.aspx (accessed on 18 May 2011); 5) FedBizOps.Gov displays a US Special Operations Command a job posting for SERE Psychologists at https://www.fbo.gov/ index?s=opportunit y&mode=form&id= 11d448e2812107525ed 50b40b0d02 db1&tab =core&_cview=1 (accessed on 18 May 2011).

18. In addition to the specific examples cited during the various wars, E. J. Hunter also makes reference to this in his publication, *The Vietnam POW Veteran: Immediate and Long Term Effects of Captivity* (San Diego, CA: Naval Health Research Center, 1977), 193.
19. Carlson, Lewis H. *Remembered Prisoners of a Forgotten War: An Oral History of Korean War POWs* (New York, NY: St. Martins Griffin, 2002), 44.
20. Carlson, Lewis H. *Remembered Prisoners of a Forgotten War: An Oral History of Korean War POWs* (New York, NY: St. Martins Griffin, 2002), 44.
21. Aside from this story having been communicated to the author several times during the period 2009 to the present, a book detailing Muse's detention is also available. See: Kurt Muse and John Gilstrap, *Six Minutes to Freedom* (Citadel Press, 2006). The ISBN is 0-8065-2723-4. Kurt Muse is a

small business owner in the Washington, DC area and now conducts motivational talks for varied audiences.

22. Bill Wilson. Personal correspondence with the author on 20 May 2011.
23. E. J. Hunter. *The Vietnam POW Veteran: Immediate and Long Term Effects of Captivity* (San Diego, CA: Naval Health Research Center, 1977), 192.
24. E. J. Hunter. *The Vietnam POW Veteran: Immediate and Long Term Effects of Captivity* (San Diego, CA: Naval Health Research Center, 1977), 194.
25. E. J. Hunter. *The Vietnam POW Veteran: Immediate and Long Term Effects of Captivity* (San Diego, CA: Naval Health Research Center, 1977), 195-196.
26. Mary A. Anderson (CAPT, Medical Corps, USN). *Captivity and Culture: Insights from the Desert Storm Prisoner of War Experience* (Newport, RI: Naval War College, 1996), 3.
27. For more details on these lingering feelings against the Japanese, see Gavan Daws' excellent book—*Prisoners of the Japanese: POWs of World War II in the Pacific* (New York, NY: Quill Press, 1995),
28. For more on his captivity and escape, see Dieter Dengler's book, *My Escape from Laos* (New York, NY: Kensington Publishing), 1979.
29. Bill Andrews. Personal interview with the author on 1 June 2011.

Appendix A: Cold War MIAs

1. Source: http://www.dtic.mil/dpmo/cold_war/reports/. The information in the original source has been modified. For brevity's sake, the MIAs' cities and states of residence were removed from all entries.

Appendix B: Returned Vietnam POWs

1. Source: http://www.dtic.mil/dpmo/vietnam/reports/.

Appendix C: Iranian Embassy Hostages

1. Source: http://www.jimmycarterlibrary.gov/documents/ list_of_hostages.phtml.

Downloaded on 16 May 2011. The list included is the same as that of the original document in the Jimmy Carter Presidential Library. Some re-formatting has been done.

Appendix D: DESERT STORM POWs

1. Source: http://www.dtic.mil/dpmo/gulf_war/.

Bibliography*

Abbot, Allen O. Prison Life in the South: At Richmond, Macon, Savannah, Charleston, Columbia, Charlotte, Raleigh, Goldsboro, and Andersonville During the Years 1864 and 1865 (New York City, Harper), 1865.

Acker, William P. The POW and Limited War. Maxwell Air Force Base: Air University, 1970.

*Acree, Cynthia and Col Cliff Acree, USMC (Ret). The Gulf Between Us: A Story of Love and Survival in Desert Storm (Washington, DC: Brassey's, Inc.), 2001. **

*Acree, Cynthia and Col Cliff Acree, USMC (Ret). Personal phone interview with the author. 24 April 2011.**

Alexander, John K. Forton Prison During the American Revolution: A Case Study of British Prisoner of War Policy and the American Prisoner Response to that Policy. Essex Institute Historical Collections, 103 (October 1967).

Altner, Hanns G. The Diary of Captain Wiederhold and the Hessians: A Military Idyll of the Days of 1776. Historical Review of Berks County, 2 (January 1937).

*Alvarez, Everett Jr. and Pitch, Anthony S. Chained eagle: The True Heroic Story of Eight-and-one-half Years as a POW By the First American Shot Down Over North Vietnam (New York, NY: Donald I. Fine, Inc.), 1989.**

—. Sound: A POW's Weapon. US Naval Institute Proceedings 102 (Aug 1976): 91-93.

—. Interview with the author conducted in Silver Springs, MD on 9 May 2011. *

Allison, Don (ed.). Hell on Belle Isle: Diary of a Civil War POW (Bryan, OH: Faded Banner Publications), 1997.

Amerman, Richard H. Treatment of American Prisoners During the Revolution. Proceedings of the New Jersey Historical Society, New Ser., 78 (October 1960).

Andrews, William (Bill). Interview with the author at National Defense University (Washington, DC) on 1 June 2011.*

Anderson, Harold W. Code of Conduct: Too Hard or Too Soft? (Maxwell Air Force Base: Air University), 1972.

Anderson, Mary A. (CAPT, Medical Corps, USN). Captivity and Culture: insights From the Desert Storm Prisoner of War Experience (Newport, RI: Naval War College), 1996. *

Anderson, Olive. The Treatment of Prisoners of War in Britain During the American War of Independence. Bulletin of the Institute of Historical Research, 28 (May 1955).

Anton, Frank with Tommy Denton, Why Didn't You Get Me Out? (Arlington, TX: Summit Publishing Group), 1997.

Armstrong, Roger W. USA, the Hard Way: An Autobiography of a B-17 Crew Member (Orange County, CA: Quail House), 1991. *

Arthur, Anthony. Deliverance at Los Banos (New York, NY: St. Martins), 1985.

Asadi, Houshang. Letters to My Torturer: Love, Revolution, and Imprisonment in Iran (Oxford, UK: One World Publishing), 2010.

Baily, Lawrence R. Solitary Survivor: The First American POW in Southeast Asia (Washington, DC: Brassey's, Inc.), 1995.

Bard, Mitchell G. Forgotten Victims: The Abandonment of American in Hitler's Camps (Boulder, CO: Westview), 1994.

Bartleson, Frederick A. Letters from Libby Prison: Being the Authentic Letters Written While in Confederate Captivity in the Notorious Libby Prison at Richmond. Ed. Ed Margaret W. Peele (New York, NY: Greenwich), 1956

Becker, Laura L. Prisoners of War in the American Revolution: A Community Perspective. Military Affairs, 46 (December 1982).

Beitzell, Edwin W. Point Lookout Prison Camp for Confederates (Abell, MD: E.W. Beitzell), 1983.

Beroth, Janet. The Convention of Saratoga. Quarterly Journal of the New York State Historical Association, 8 (July 1927), pp. 257-280.

Biderman, Albert D. Effects of Communist Indoctrination Attempts: Some Comments Based on an Air Force Prisoner of War Study (Randolph Air Force Base: Air Research and Development Command), 1957.

Biggs, Chester K. Behind the Barbed Wire: Memoir of a World War II U.S. Marine Captured in North China in 1941 and Imprisoned by the Japanese Until 1945 (Jefferson, NC: McFarland), 1995.

Bird, Tom. American POWs of World War II: Forgotten Men Tell Their Stories (Westport, CT: Praeger), 1992.

Blakey, Scott. Prisoner at War: The Survival of Commander Richard A. Stratton (Garden City, NY: Anchor Press/Doubleday), 1978.

Boatner, Mark M. III. Encyclopedia of the American Revolution (New York City, NY: McKay, 1986.

Bolton, Charles K. The Private Soldier Under Washington (Port Washington, NY: Kennekat), 1964.

Boudinot, Elias. Journal or Historical Recollections of American Events During the Revolutionary War (Philadelphia, PA: Frederick Bourquin), 1894.

—. Colonel Elias Boudinot's Notes of Two Conferences Held by the American and British Commissioners to Settle a General Cartel for the Exchange of Prisoners of War, 1778. Pennsylvania Magazine of History and Biography, 24 (1900).

—. Colonel Elias Boudinot in New York City, February, 1778. Edited by Helen Jordan. Pennsylvania Magazine of History and Biography, 24 (1900).

Bowden, Mark. Black Hawk Down: A Story of Modern War (New York, NY: Atlantic Monthly Press), 1999.

Bowman, Martin H. Home by Christmas? The Story of US Airmen at War (Wellingbourough, Northhamptonshire: Stephen), 1987.

Bowie, Lucy Leigh. The Ancient Barracks at Fredericktown Where Hessian Prisoners Were Quartered During the Revolutionary War (Frederick, MD: Maryland State School for the Deaf), 1939.

—. German Prisoners in the American Revolution. Maryland Historical Magazine, 40 (September 1945).

Bowman, Larry G. Captive Americans: Prisoners during the American Revolution (Athens, OH: Ohio University Press), 1977.

—. The Pennsylvania Prisoner Exchange Conferences, 1778. Pennsylvania History, 45 (July 1978).

—. Military Parolees on Long Island, 1777-1782. Journal of Long Island History, 18 (Spring 1982).

Boyd, George A. Elias Boudinot: Patriot and Statesman, 1740-1821 (Princeton: Princeton University Press), 1952.

Boyd, John and Gary Garth. Tenko! Rangoon Jail: The Amazing Story of Sgt. John Boyd's Survival as a POW in a Notorious Japanese Prison Camp (Paducah, KY: Turner), 1996.

Brace, Ernest C., A Code to Keep: The True Story of America's Longest-Held Civilian Prisoner of War in Vietnam (New York: St. Martin's Press), 1988.

Breuer, William B. The Great Raid on Cabanatuan: Rescuing the Doomed Ghost of Bataan and Corregidor (New York, NY: Wiley), 1994.

Brown, Louis A. The Salisbury Prison: A Case Study of Confederate Military Prisons (Wilmington, NC: Broadfoot), 1992.

Brown, Wallace L. The Endless Hours: My Two and a Half Years as A Prisoner of the Chinese Communists (New York, NY: Norton), 1961.

Brunner, Joseph. American Involvement in the Nuremberg War Crimes Trial Process. Accessed online at: http://www.umich.edu/~historyj/pages_folder/articles/American_Involvement_in_the_Nuremberg_War_Crimes_Trial_Process.pdf. Accessed on 17 Aug 2011.

Bucher, CDR Loyd M. with Mark Rascovich, Bucher: my Story. USS Pueblo, North Korean Capture on Jan 23, 1968 (New York: Doubleday), 1970. Bumgarner, John R. Parade of the Dead: A U.S. Army Physician's Memoir of

Imprisonment by the Japanese, 1942-1945 (Jefferson, NC: McFarland), 1995.

Carey, Dave, The Ways We Choose: Lessons for Life from a P.O.W.'s Experience. (Portland, OR.: Arnica Publishing), 2005.

*Carlson, Lewis H. Remembered Prisoners of a Forgotten War: An Oral History of Korean War POWs (New York, NY: St. Martins Griffin), 2002. **

—. We Were Each Others Prisoners: An Oral History of World War II American and German Prisoners of War (New York, NY: Basic Books), 1997.

Carter, Alvin R. Brother to the Eagle The Civil War Journal of Sgt. Ambrose Armitage 8th Wisconsin Volunteer Infantry (Booklocker.com, Inc.), 2006.

Cave, Dorothy. Beyond Courage: One Regiment Against Japan, 1941-1945 (Las Cruces, NM: Yuca Tree), 1992.

Certain, Robert G. Unchained Eagle: From Prisoner of War to Prisoner of Christ (Palm Springs: ETC Publications), 2003.

Chandler, C. Sherrell, Maj USA. A HISTORICAL ANALYSIS OF UNITED STATES PRISONER OF WAR/ MISSING IN ACTION REPATRIATION AND REMAINS RECOVERY (Ft Leaven Worth, KS: US Army Command and General Staff), 1998.

*Chang, Iris. The Rape of Nanking: The Forgotten Holocaust of World War II (New York, NY: Penguin Books), 1997 **

*Cherry, Fred V. Personal Interview with the author in Silver Springs, MD. 9 Apr 2011. **

*Cherry, Fred V. Personal phone Interview with the author. 11 Apr 2011. **

Chesley, Larry. Seven Years in Hanoi; a POW tells his Story (Salt Lake City: Bookcraft), 1973.

Christ, C. Captured Americans: War Criminals or Prisoners of War?) Carlisle Barracks, PA: Army War College), 1972.

Clark, Jane, editor. The Convention Troops and the Perfidy of Sir William Howe. American Historical Review, 37 (July 1932).

Clarke, Marjorie (Nelson) Captive on the Ho Chi Minh Trail (Chicago: Moody Press), 1974.

Clinton, Susan, Everett Alvarez, Jr. A Hero For Our Times (Chicago: Children's Press), 1990.

Coan, Marion S. A Revolutionary Prison Diary: The Journal of Dr. Jonathon Haskins. New England Quarterly 17 (June 1944): 290-309

Coffee, Gerald. Beyond Survival: Building on the Hard Times—A POW's Inspiring Story (New York, NY: Putnam), 1990.

Coffin, Alexander. The American Captives at New York During the Revolutionary War. New York: 1865.

Cohen, Sheldon S. Thomas Wren: Ministering Angel of Forton Prison. Pennsylvania Magazine of History and Biography, 103 (July 1979).

Cook, Graeme. Break Out: Famous Military Escapes of the World Wars (New York, NY: Taplinger), 1974.

Coker, George T. Prisoners of War. U. S. Naval Institute Proceedings 100 (Oct 1974): 41-6.

Colebrook, Joan. Prisoners of War: Treatment of Prisoners in Vietnam, Korea, and Communist Countries. Commentary 57 (Jan 1974): 30-3.

Connor, Timothy. A Yankee Privateersman in Prison in England, 1777-1779. Edited by William Richard Cutter. New England Historical and Genealogical Register, 30 (1876).

Coram, Robert. American Patriot: The Life and Wars of Colonel Bud Day (New York, NY: Back Bay Books), 2007.

*Cornum, Rhonda. She Went to War: The Inspiring True Story of a Mother who Went to War (New York, NY: Ballantine Books), 1992. **

Corum, Robert, American Patriot—The Life and Wars of Colonel Bud Day (New York, NY: Little Brown & Co.), 2007.

Crawford, George G. When Surrender was not an Option (Salado, TX: Salado Press), 2001.

Dabney, William M. After Saratoga: The Story of the Convention Army (Albuquerque, NM: University of New Mexico Press), 1954.

Daley, James A., and Lee Bergman. A Hero's Welcome: the Conscience of Sergeant James Daley versus the United States Army (Indianapolis, MN: Bobbs-Merrill), 1975.

*Dandridge, Danske. American Prisoners of the Revolution (Guttenberg Ebook: online Collection; accessed Dev 2010). **

David, Heather. Operation Rescue (New York, NY: Pinnacle), 1975.

Davis, Vernon. The Long Road Home: U.S. Prisoner of War Policy and Planning in Southeast Asia (Washington, D.C.: Historical Office, Office of the Secretary of Defense), 2000.

*Daws, Gavan. Prisoners of the Japanese: POWs of World War II in the Pacific (New York, NY: Quill Press), 1994. **

Day, Clarence N. Hodio: Tales of an American POW (Merriville, IN: ICS), 1984.

Day, George A. Return With Honor (Mesa, AZ: Champlin Museum), 1989.

*Dengler, Dieter. My Escape from Laos (New York, NY: Kensington Publishing), 1979. **

*—. Escape From Laos (San Rafael, CA: Presidio Press), 1979. **

Denn, Robert J. Prison Narratives of the American Revolution. Ph.D. Dissertation, Michigan State University, 1980.

—. Captivity Narratives of the American Revolution. Journal of American Culture, 2 (Winter 1980).

Denney, Robert E. Civil War Prisons & Escapes: A Day by Day Chronicle (New York, NY: Sterling Publishing Co.), 1993.

Devereux, James P. The Story of Wake Island (New York, NY: Charter), 1947.

Diggs, Frank J. Americans Behind the Barbed Wire: A Gripping World War II Memoir (New York, NY: Simon & Schuster), 2000.

Dixon, Martha W. Divided Authority: The American Management of Prisoners in the Revolutionary War, 1775-1783. Ph.D. Dissertation, University of Utah, 1977.

Doyle, Robert C. A Prisoner's Duty: great escapes in U.S. Military History (Annapolis: Naval Institute Press), 1997.

—. Voices from Captivity (Lawrence, KS: University Press of Kansas), 1994.

Dramesi, John A. Code of Honor (New York: W. W. Norton), 1975.

*Drea, Edward (and others). Researching Japanese Wartime Records: Introductory Essays (Washington, DC: Nazi War Crimes and Japanese Imperial Government Records Nazi War Crimes and Japanese Imperial Government Records Interagency Working Group Interagency Working Group), 2006. **

Dring, Thomas. Recollections of the Jersey Prison-Ship. Edited by Albert G. Greene. Providence: H. H. Brown, 1829.

Dudman, Richard. Forty Days with the Enemy (New York: Liveright), 1971.

Duke, Florimond. Name, Rank, and Serial Number (New York, NY: Meredith) 1969.

*Dukier, William J. Ho Chi Minh: A Life (New York, NY: Hyperion), 2000. **

Einolf, Christopher J. The Fall and Rise of Torture: A Comparative and Historical Analysis. (Sociological Theory 25:2 June 2007: American Sociological Association. 1307 New York Avenue NW, Washington, DC 20005-4701).

*Esfandiari, Haleh. My Prison, My Hope: One Woman's Story of Captivity in Iran (New York, NY: Harper Collins Books), 2009. **

Fabel, Robin F. Self Help in Dartmoor: Black and White Prisoners in the War of 1812. Journal of the Early Republic 9 (Summer 1989): 165-90.

Falk, Stanly L. Bastaan: The March of Death (New York, NY: Berkeley), 1983.

Feinberg, Abraham L. Hanoi Diary (Dan Mills, Ontario: Alger), 1968.

Fields, Kenny Wayne. The Rescue of Streetcar 304 (Annapolis, MD: Naval Institute Press), 2008.

Filmore, Clyde. Prisoner of War (Quanah, TX: Nortex), 1973.

Fooks, Herbert C. Prisoners of War (Federalsburg, MD: The J. W. Stowell Printing Co.), 1924. *

Ford, Worthington C., editor. British and American Prisoners of War, 1778. Pennsylvania Magazine of History and Biography, 17 (1893).

Fordney, Chris "The Long Road to Andersonville" National Parks 72 (Sept 1998): 30-3.

Gaither, Ralph, as told to Steve Henry. With God in a POW Camp (Nashville, Broadman Press), 1973.

Gallagher, Patrick. Through Battle, Prison, and Disease: The Civil War Diaries of George Richardson Crosby. Vermont History Vol. 76, No. 1 (Winter/Spring 2008): 19-45. © 2008 by the Vermont Historical Society. ISSN: 0042-4161; on-line ISSN: 1544-3043

Gargus, John. The Son Tay Raid—American POWs in Vietnam Were Not Forgotten (College Station, Texas A&M University Press), 2007.

Garrett, Richard. P.O.W.: The Uncivil Face of War (England: David and Charles Publishers), 1981.

*Gonsalves, Marc, Keith Stansell, and Tom Howes. Out of Captivity: Surviving the 1967 Days in the Colombian Jungle (New York, NY: Harper Collins Publishers), 2009.**

Gordon, Michael R. and General Bernard E. Trainor. The General's War: The Inside Story of the Conflict in the Gulf (New York, NY: Little, Brown and Company), 1995.

*Gordon, Virgil. Interview with the author in Winder Georgia in 2005. **

*Goss, Warren Lee. The Soldiers Story of his Captivity at Andersonville, Belle Isle and other Rebel Prisons (Lee and Shepard Publishers: Boston, MA.) 1866. The copy referenced is a 2001 DSI digital re-issuance of this book.**

Gostas, Theodore, Prisoner (Western Publishing Co: Published by the author), no date.

Grant, Zalin. Survivors: Vietnam P.O.W.s tell their Stories (New York: W. W. Norton), 1975.

Gragg, Rod, Bobby Bagley, POW (Van Nuys, CA: Bible Voice), 1978.

Greene, Albert. Recollections of the Jersey Prison Ship from the Manuscript of Capt. Thomas Dring (New York, NY: Cornith), 1961.

Groom, Winston and Duncan Spencer. Conversations With the Enemy: the Story of PFC Robert Garwood (New York: G. P. Putnam's Sons), 1983.

Guarino, Evelyn with Carol Jose. Saved by Love—a True Story (Cape Canaveral: Blue Note Publications), 2000.

Guarino, Larry. A POW's Story: 2801 Days in Hanoi (New York, NY: Ivy Books), 1990.

Guenon, Wm. A. Jr., forword by Jon Reynolds. SECRET And DANGEROUS: Night of the Son Tay P.O.W. Raid (Ashland, MA, Wagon Wings Press), 2002.

Hall, Colonel George R. and Pat Hall with Bob Pittman. Commitment to Honor: A Prisoner of War Remembers Vietnam (Jackson, MS.: Franklin Printers), 2005.

*Hallums, Roy. Buried Alive: The True Story of Kidnapping, Captivity, and a Dramatic Rescue (Nashville, TN: Thomas Nelson Publishing), 2009. **

*Hawkins, Christopher. The Adventures of Christopher Hawkins (Privately Printed: New York, NY, 1864). The version referenced was an electronic version available through Google books online. **

*Heaps, Leo. The Evaders: The Story of the Most Amazing Escape of World War II (New York, NY: William Morrow and Company), 1976. **

Heslop, J. M. and Dell R. Van Orden. From the Shadows of Death (Salt Lake City: Deseret Book Co.), 1973.

Hess, Fredrick W. "A Post-Korea Look at the Geneva Convention". Military Review 35 (Nov 1955): 52-8.

Hinkle, Jr. L.E. and Wolff, H.G. The Methods of Interrogation and Indoctrination Used by the Communist Police State (New York, New York: The Bulletin for New York Academy of Medicine, 33:9), 1957.

*Hirsh, James S. Two Souls Indivisible—The Friendship That Saved Two POWs in Vietnam (New York: Houghton Mifflin Company), 2004. **

Hobson, Chirs. Vietnam Air Losses—United States Air Force, Navy and Marine Corps Fixed-Wing aircraft Losses in Southeast Asia 1961-1973 (England: Midland Publishing), 2001.

Holzer, Henry Mark and Erika. Aid and Comfort: Jane Fonda in North Vietnam (Jefferson, North Carolina, and London: McFarland & Company, Inc.), 2002.

Howes, Craig. Voices of the Vietnam POWs: Witnesses to Their fight (New York: Oxford), 1993.

Howren, Jamie and Taylor Baldwin. Open Doors: Various POWs 30 years Later (Dulles, VA: Potomac Books, Inc.), 2005.

Hubbard, Col. Edward L. Edited by Art Nicolet. Escape From the Box: the Wonder of Human Potential (West Chester, PA: Praxis, International), 1994.

*Hubbell, John G. P.O.W.: A Definitive History of the American Prisoner of War Experience in Vietnam (Lincoln, NE: iUniverse.com, Inc.), 2000. **

Hunter, Edna J. Families in Crisis: The Families of Prisoners of War. San Diego, CA: Naval Health Research Center, 1977.

*—. The Vietnam POW Veteran: Immediate and Long Term Effects of Captivity (San Diego, CA: Naval Health Research Center) 1977. **

—. "Treating the Military Captive's Family." The Military Family: Dynamics and Treatment. 167-196 Ed. Florence W. Kaslow and Richard I. Ridenour (New York City, NY: Guilford), 1984.

—. Wartime Stress: Family Adjustment to Loss. San Diego, CA: U.S. International, 1981.

International Committee of the Red Cross. The Geneva Conventions of August 12 1949 (Reprint). (Geneva Switzerland: International Committee of the Red Cross) 1983.

Ivy, Jack M. Camp Chase, Columbus, Ohio, 1861-1865: A Study of the Union's Treatment of Confederate Prisoners of War (Ft. Leavenworth, KS: Army Command and General Staff College), 1990.

Jensen, Jay R. Home with Honor: a POW tells how to Conquer Adversity Through Courage, Honor and Faith (Orcutt, CA: Publications of Worth), 1991. Original publication, "Six Years in Hell."

Johnson, Harold E. I Will Never Forget . . . an Analysis of the POW/MIA Episode in the War in Southeast Asia (Maxwell Air Force base: Air College), 1983.

Jensen-Stevensen, Monica and Wm. Stevensen, Kiss the Boys Goodbye, with material from Captain Eugene "Red" McDaniel, USN (Ret) (New York City, NY: Penguin Books), 1991.

Johnson, Sam and Jan Winebrenner. Captive Warrior: a Vietnam POW's Story (College Station, TX: Texas A & M University Press), 1992.

Johnson, Wray R. Vietnam and American Doctrine for Small Wars (Bangkok, Thailand: White Lotus Press), 2001.

Johnson, Shoshana. I'm Still Standing: From Captive U.S. Soldier to Free Citizen—My Journey Home (New York, NY: Simon & Shuster, Inc), 2010.

Joslyn, Mauriel P. Immortal Captives: The Story of 600 Confederate Officers and the United States Prisoner of War Policy (Gretna, LA: Pelican Publishing, Co.), 2008.

King, Charles (and others). The Photographic History of the Civil War, Vol II., Soldier Life and Secret Service Prisons and Hospitals (Secaucus, NY: Blue and Grey Press), 1987.

Kinkead, Eugene. Why They Collaborated (London, UK: Norton), 1960.

Lawrence, F. Lee and Robert W. Glover. Camp Ford C.S.A The Story of Union Prisoners in Texas (Austin, TX: Civil War Centennial Advisory Committee), 1964.

Lawrence, William P. and Rosario Rausa. Tennessee Patriot—The Naval Career of Vice Admiral William P. Lawrence, U.S. Navy (Annapolis: Naval Institute Press), 2006.

Lawrence, William P. POW: Al Santoli, Everything We Had (New York: Ballantine), 1981.

Lewis, George G., and John Mewha. History of Prisoner of War Utilization by the United States Army, 1776-1945. (Washington, DC: Department of the Army), 1955.

*Linn, Brian M. The Philippine War, 1899-1902 (University Press of Kansas: Lawrence, KS), 2000. * MacDonald, James A. The Problems of U.S. Marine Corps Prisoners of War in Korea (Washington, DC: History and Museums Division, Headquarters, U.S. Marine Corps), 1988.*

Marshall, John. The Life of George Washington, Commander in Chief of the American Forces During the War Which established the Independence of His Country, Vol II (The Citizen's Guild of Washington's Boyhood Home, Fredericksburg, VA (Publisher Unknown: Location Unknown, 1926), 37. Copy accessed online at http://www.ponury.com.pl/The_Life_of_George_Washington_Vol_2_of_5-7275 -1.html on 24 Apr 2010.

Marshall, John A. American Bastile: A History of the Illegal Arrests and Imprisonment of American Citizens During the Late Civil War (New York: Da Capo), 1970

*Martinez, J, Michael. Life and Death in Civil War Prisons: A Story of Hardship, Horror—and Extraordinary Courage (Rutledge Hill Press: Nashville, TN) 2004. **

McCain, John. Faith of my Fathers: A Family Memoir (New York, NY: Random House), 1999. McCain, John with Mark Salter. (Character Is Destiny: Inspiring Stories Every Young Person Should Know and Every Adult Should Remember). 2005.

McElroy, John. Andersonville: A Story of Military Prisons (Greenwich, CT: Fawcett), 1962.

McConnell, Malcolm, Into the Mouth of the Cat: The Story of Lance Sijan, Hero of Vietnam (Bridgewater, NJ: Replica Books), 1997. Originally pub: New York: W.W. Norton, 1985.

McDaniel, Eugene B. with James L. Johnson. Before Honor. Philadelphia: A.J. Holman Co., 1975. McDaniel, Eugene B., Scars and Stripes: the Red McDaniel Story. Published by friends of Red McDaniel (Philadelphia: A.J. Holman), 1975.

McDaniel, Dorthy Howard, After the Hero's Welcome: a POW wife's story of the battle against a new enemy (Chicago: Bonus Books), c1991.

McDaniel, Norman A. Yet Another Voice (New York City, NY: Leisure, Hawthorne Books), 1975. McGrath, John M. Prisoner of War: Six Years in Hanoi. Annapolis, MD: Naval Institute Press, 1975. Miller, Carolyn Paine, Captured: A Mother's True Story of Her Family's Imprisonment by the Viet Cong (Chappaqua, NY: Christian Herald Books, 1977.

Metzger, Charles H. The Prisoner in the American Revolution. Chicago: Loyola University Press, 1971.

*Millet, Alan R. and Maslowski, Peter. For the Common Defense: A Military History of the United States of America (New York City, NY: The Free Press), 1984. **

Moise, Edwin E. Historical Dictionary of the Vietnam War (Lanham, Maryland and London: The Scarecrow Press), 2001.

Murphy, Edward R. Jr. Second in Command: The Uncensored Account of the Capture of the Spy Ship Pueblo (New York, NY: Holt), 1971.

*Muse, Kurt and Gilstrap, John. Six Minutes to Freedom (Citadel Press), 2006. ISBN 0 -8065-2723-4. **

*Muse, Kurt. Personal Correspondence with the author. 18 May 2011. * Myers, Walter Dean. A Place Called Heartbreak: A Story of Vietnam (Juvenile Literature. Austin, TX: Raintree Steck-Vaughn), 1993.*

Nolan, Liam. Small Man of Nanataki: The True Story of a Japanese Who Risked His Life to Provide Comfort for His Enemies (New York, NY: Dutton), 1966.

*Northrop, John W. Chronicles From the Diary of a War Prisoner in Andersonville and other Military Prisons of the South in 1864 (Reprint: Published and copyrighted by the Author, Wichita, KS., 1904. **

O'Brien, William V. "The Rule of War in Small Wars" Annals of the American Academy of Political and Social Sciences 541 (Sept 1995): 36-46.

O'Grady, Scott M. Return With Honor (New York, NY: Harper Paperbacks), 1995.

Olds, J. H. "The Geneva Conventions" Marine Corps Gazette 55 (Feb 1971): 34-8.

Overton, Albert G., and J. W. W. Loose. An Unusual Discovery: Prisoner-of-War Barracks in Lancaster Used during the Revolutionary War. Lancaster County Historical Society Journal, 84 (Trinity 1980).

Parker, Unknown. Avalon Yale Law Review. Judgment: War Crimes and Crimes Against Humanity. Accessed at http://avalon.law.yale.edu/imt/judwarcr.asp on 19 March 2011.

*Phend, Julie M. and Edwards, Stanley, Jr. D-Day and Beyond: A True Story of Escape and POW Survival (Shippensburg, PA: Burd Street Press), 2004. **

Philpott, Tom. The Saga of Jim Thompson, America's Longest-Held Prisoner of War (New York, NY: Norton & Norton Co.), 2001.

Pierce, Donald R. The Effects of the Cessation of Escgange of Prisoners During the Civil War (Fort Leavenworth, KS: US Army General and Staff College), 1993.

Pitzer, Daniel L. Animal Called POW: My Four Years in a Vietcong Prison Look 33 (Feb 18, 1969): 46-51.

*Pitzer, Daniel L. Conversations with the author; Fort Bragg North Carolina (Apr 1986). * Prelinger, Catherine M. Benjamin Franklin and the American Prisoners of War in England During the American Revolution. William and Mary Quarterly, 3d Ser., 32 (April 1975).*

Purcell, Ben and Anne. Love and Duty (New York: St. Martin's Press, 1992. Random House, New York), 1973.

Rastatter, Paul J. 'Rebel' Prisoners Detained in North America. Accessed on 3 Jan 2009 at http://www.earlyamerica.com/review/2002_summer_fall/pows.htm.

Raymond, Matthew W. Medical Prisoners of War: The Realities of Practicing Medicine in Captivity (Brooks Air Force base, TX: School of Aerospace Medicine), 1996.

Riconda, Harry P. Prisoners of War in American Conflicts (Lanham, MD: Scarecrow Press), 2003.

Risner, General Robinson. The Passing of the Night: My Seven Years as a Prisoner of the North Vietnamese (New York, NY: Ballantine Books), 1973.

Rochester, Stuart I. and Kiley, Frederick. Honor Bound: American Prisoners of War in Southeast Asia, 1961-1973 (Annapolis, MD: Naval Institute Press), 1999.

*Rowe, James N. The True Story of a Vietnam POW, James N. Rowe: Five Years to Freedom (New York, NY: Ballantine Books), 1971. **

Sander, H. J. Analysis of the Korean War Prisoner of War Experience (Springfield, VA: Monroe Corporation), 1974.

Schemmer, Benjamin F. The Raid: The Son Tay Rescue Mission (New York, NY: Ballantine Books), 2002.

Speed, Richard B. Prisoners, Diplomats, and the Great War: A Study in the Diplomacy of Captivity (New York: Greenwoord), 1990.

Stearns, Amos E. The Civil War Diary of Amos E. Stearns, A Prisoner at Andersonville (Rutherford, NJ: Fairleigh-Dickinson UP), 1981.

*Steel, Jeffry A. An Analysis of United States Prisoner of War Missing in Action Accounting Operations and their Correlation to the Normalization of Relations Between The United States and the Socialist Republic Vietnam Thesis for Master's Degree as partial requirements for a Masters of Military Art and Science Degree (Fort Leaven Worth, KS: US Army Command and General Staff College), 2005. **

Stockdale, Jim and Sybil. In Love and War (Annapolis, MD: Naval Institute Press), (Revised) 1990.

Stockdale, Jim. Experiences as A POW in Vietnam Naval War College Review 26 (Jan—Feb 1974): 2-6.

*Swedberg, Claire. In Enemy Hands: Personal Accounts of Those Taken Prisoner in World War II (Mechanicsburg, PA: Stackpole Books), 1997. **

Tenney, Lester I. My Hitch in Hell: The Bataan Death March (Washington, DC: Brassey's), 2000.

The International Committee of the Red Cross. The Geneva Conventions of August 12 1949 (Geneva, Switzerland: ICRC), 1983 (Reprint).

Tilford, Earl H. The United States Air Force: Search and Rescue in Southeast1961-1975 Asia (Washington, DC: Office of Air Force History), 1992. Tolbert, William A. The Prisoners of War: Experiences and Survival (Maxwell Air Force Base: Air University) 1987.

Ullrich, Dieter C. ed. Civil War Diaries of Van Buren Oldham. Published online at http://www.utm.edu/departments/acadpro/library/departments/special_collections/E579.5%20Oldham/text/vboldham_1863.htm and http://www.utm.edu/ departments/ acadpro/ library/ departments/special_collections/E579.5 %20Oldham/ text/vboldham _1864.htm. Downloaded on: 12 Jan 2010.

*United States Congress (House) Committee on Un-American Activities. Investigation of Communist Propaganda Among Prisoners of War in Korea, Save our Sons Committee Hearings (Washington, DC: GPO), 1956. **

*United States Department of State. Foreign Relations of the United States: Vietnam 1962 (Washington DC: GPO), 2002. **

United States Government. Captivity: The Extreme Circumstance (Washington, DC: Naval Education and Training Professional Development and Technology Center), 2001.—. Chairman of the Joint Chief of Staff Instruction (CJCSI) 3270.01A Personnel Recovery in the Department of Defense (Washington, DC: Government Printing Office), 1 July 2003.

—. Project CHECO Southeast Asia Report: Search and Rescue Operations in SEA, 1 January 1971-31 March 1972 (U) (Honolulu, HI: Pacific Air Forces), 1974. "Declassified IAW E.O. 12958 by the Air Force Declassification Office and Approved for Public Release." and was accessed at http://handle.dtic. mil/100.2/ADA486518.

—. Project CHECO Southeast Asia Report: Project CHECO Southeast Asia. USAF Search and Rescue, July 1966—November 1967(Honolulu, HI: Pacific Air Forces), "Declassified IAW E.O. 12958 by the Air Force Declassification Office and Approved for Public Release." and was accessed at http://handle.dtic.mil/100.2 / ADA486481.

—. Project CHECO Southeast Asia Report: Search and Rescue Operations in SEA, 1 April 1972-30 June 1973 (Honolulu, HI: Pacific Air Forces), 1974. "Declassified IAW E.O. 12958 by the Air Force Declassification Office and Approved for Public Release." and was accessed at http://handle.dtic.mil/100.2/ADA486517. *

—. Project CHECO Southeast Asia Report: USAF Search and Rescue, November 1967—June 1969 (Honolulu, HI: Pacific Air Forces), 1969. "Declassified IAW E.O. 12958 by the Air Force Declassification Office and Approved for Public Release." and was accessed at http://handle.dtic.mil/100.2/ADA486480.

—. Project CHECO Southeast Asia Report: Evasion and Escape, SEA 1964-1971 (Honolulu, HI: Pacific Air Forces), 1972. "Declassified IAW E.O. 12958 by the Air Force Declassification Office and Approved for

Public Release." and was accessed at http://handle.dtic.mil/100.2/ADA486749.

—. *Project CHECO Southeast Asia Report: Joint Personnel Recovery in Southeast Asia (Honolulu, HI: Pacific Air Forces), 1976. "Declassified IAW E.O. 12958 by the Air Force Declassification Office and Approved for Public Release." and was accessed at http://handle.dtic.mil/100.2/ADA486919*

—. *Educing Information, Interrogation: Science and Art, Foundations for the Future—Intelligence Science Board, Phase I Report (Washington, DC: National Defense Intelligence College), 2006. **

—. *Extracts from Columbia Law Review on Prisoners of War (Fairchild AFB, WA: US Air Force Survival School), 1956.*

—. *Field Manual 21-76: Survival (Washington, DC: GPO), 1992. **

—. *Field Manual 21-76-1: SERE (Washington, DC: GPO), 1999. **

—. *Field Manual 27-10: The Law of Land Warfare (Washington, DC: Government Printing Office), 1956. **

—. *Field Manual 27-10: The Law of Land Warfare (Washington, DC: The War Department), 1940. **

—. *Field Manual 34-3, Intelligence Analysis (Washington, DC: GPO), 1990. **

—. *Air Force Regulation 64-4, Search and Rescue Survival Training (Washington, DC: Government Printing Office), 15 July 1985. **

—. *Department of the Army Pamphlet 27-100-10, Military Law Review article: Barbed Wire Command:*

The Legal Nature of the Command Responsibilities of the Senior Prisoner in a Prisoner of War Camp written by Lieutenant Colonel Donald L. Manes, Jr. (Washington, DC: Government Printing Office) 1960.

—. *Executive Order 10631 (Code of Conduct for Member of the Armed Forces of the United States) (Washington, DC: Government Printing Office), 1955. A copy of this Executive Order is available at: http://www.archives.gov/federal-register/codification/executive-order/10631.html.* *

—. *Field Manual 34-52: Intelligence Interrogation (Washington, DC: Government Printing Office), 1987.* *

—. *National Security Directive 45: US Policy in Response to the Iraqi Invasion of Kuwait (Washington, DC: The White House), 1990. The copy was a declassified copy accessed at George Washington University's national archives on 4 Feb 2011 at http://www.gwu.edu/~nsarchiv/NSAEBB/NSAEBB39 /document2.pdf* *

—. *Part Two, Rules of Land Warfare, Basic Field Manual, Volume VII, Military Law (United States Government Printing Office: Washington, DC), 1934.* *

—. *The U.S. Fighting Man's Code (Washington, DC: Office of the Armed Forces Information and Education, Department of Defense), 1955.* *

Van Dyk, Jere. Captive: My Time as a Prisoner of the Taliban (New York, NY: Times Books), 2010.

Van Dyke, John. Narrative of Confinement in the Jersey Prison Ship, by John Van Dyke, Captain in Lamb's Regiment, N.Y.S.A. Historical Magazine, 7 (May 1863).

Vo Nguyen Giap, *People's War, People's Army* (New York, 1962).

Warren, John N. Release from the Bull Pen: Andersonville, 1864 Atlantic Monthly 202 (Nov 1958): 130-136.

*Watt, George. The Comet Connection: Escape from Hitler's Europe (Lexington, KY: University Press of Kentucky), 1990. **

Whitcomb, Darrel D. The Rescue of Bat 21 (Annapolis, MD: Naval Institute Press), 1998.

White, Herbert H. British Prisoners of War in Hartford During the Revolution. Connecticut Historical Society Bulletin, 19 (July 1954).

Wilkerson, Phillip Cadet. Interview with Col Bill Andrews on 15 March 2008 while at the National Defense University. This interview may be accessed at http://www.vmi. edu/ archives.aspx?id=22241.

Willis, Morris R. and J. Robert Moskin. Turncoat: an American's 12 Years in Communist China (Englewood Cliff, NJ: Prentice-Hall), 1968.

Wilson, Bill. Personal correspondence received by the author dated 21 May 2011.

—. Interview with the author on 22 May 2011.

—. Personal correspondence received by the author dated 21 May 2011.

INDEX